Methodism and Society in Historical Perspective

METHODISM AND SOCIETY

Volume I

Methodism and Society in Historical Perspective

Richard M. Cameron

Edited by the Board of Social and Economic Relations
of The Methodist Church and Published by

Abingdon Press

NEW YORK • NASHVILLE

METHODISM AND SOCIETY IN HISTORICAL PERSPECTIVE

Copyright © 1961 by Abingdon Press

Library of Congress Catalog Card Number: 61-8407

SET UP, PRINTED, AND BOUND BY THE
PARTHENON   PRESS,   AT   NASHVILLE,
TENNESSEE, UNITED STATES OF AMERICA

Introduction

In the conclusion of his classical study of *The Social Teaching of the Christian Churches*, Ernst Troeltsch made the remark: "Faith is the source of energy in the struggle of life, but life still remains a battle which is continually renewed upon ever new fronts." If Troeltsch were alive today, he would find ample confirmation of this statement in the upheavals of the twentieth century. The arena of the social struggle has become global. Myriads of human beings in Asia, Africa, and Latin America have seen a glimpse of a better life and are rising to claim their share in the resources of the earth. Revolutions in expectation are breeding revolutions of the social order. Changes which once took centuries are now telescoped into decades. Modern science and technology are providing unprecedented opportunities for the enhancement of life or for totalitarian regimentation of human ants. The entire globe is an explosive "area of rapid social change" from which no country is exempt. In an interdependent world, the battle for freedom from hunger and misery, from diseases and illiteracy, from injustice and tyranny, from the threat of atomic annihilation, is everybody's concern and everybody's responsibility.

Does the Christian faith furnish a "source of energy" and a sense of urgency and direction in this new battle for the dignity and welfare, no longer of particular groups of underprivileged alone, but of every member of the human race? It must frankly be acknowledged that the churches, as often in the past, are disappointingly slow in their response to swiftly changing situations and weak and divided in their social witness. For many Christians, the world-transforming power of the gospel is reduced to the virtue of social respectability.

5

Yet, in the longer perspectives of history, it must also gratefully be recognized that this century has witnessed an almost miraculous upsurge of social concern in widening Christian circles. The labors of the pioneers of the American social gospel movement and related endeavors in Europe, though often decried by advocates of a theological and economic *status quo*, have not been without fruit. From an irritant, the movement has turned into a ferment. From an act of prophetic revolt, it has developed into an impressive range of official and unofficial program activities of the churches—largely reformist and educational, it is true, yet not insensitive to the urgings of the prophets to translate "social creeds" into bolder and more costly deeds.

Acceptance of social responsibility on the part of the churches, however variously conceived, has to such an extent become a part of American culture that it is easy to overlook its comparative novelty. A glance at the international scene furnishes an even more telling indication of the truly amazing growth of social awareness within the short span of a few decades. When the Methodist Episcopal Church and the Federal Council of the Churches of Christ in America in 1908 adopted the "Social Creed," such a step would have been unacceptable to most Protestant and Eastern Orthodox bodies on other continents. The first ecumenical world conference on Practical Christianity, held in Stockholm in 1925, was above all a stirring confession of the failure of the Christian churches to live up to their mission in society. But one needs to have only the slightest acquaintance with the program of the World Council of Churches, a generation later, to become aware of the extent to which the struggle for a responsible society has become a commonly accepted obligation. The huge project currently undertaken by the World Council on "The Common Christian Responsibility Toward Areas of Rapid Social Change" is a very instructive illustration of this change of mind.

The progressive leavening of the life of the denominations and the growth in sensitivity and professional expertness, which characterize the movement of social Christianity at home and abroad today, are doubtless in part a response to the pervasive pressures of history. But they also reflect profound changes in the Church's understanding of its own life and mission: A few of these changing emphases may be listed in summary fashion:

(1) There is a new emphasis on the Church—the people of God,

the body of Christ—as a corporate agent of social criticism and re-demption. Its primary impact on society does not reside in its social teachings and program activities. Its impact derives above all from its very existence in the world as a community of believers and from the redemptive radiance of their life in prayer and worship, in Christian self-discipline, and in care for the neighbor near and afar. (2) The gospel of salvation is the opposite of religious individualism; it is social because it is personal. Its concern is not with disembodied souls nor with material progress without soul, but with the wholeness of man-in-community. (3) The Christian social witness becomes relevant and effective in the myriads of decisions and actions of laymen and laywomen as they seek to live out their faith in the rough-and-tumble of everyday life. The Evanston Assembly of the World Council of Churches in 1954 offered a pointed formulation of this view: "The real battles of the faith today are being fought in factories, shops, offices, and farms, in political parties and government agencies, in countless homes, in the press, radio, and television, in the relationship of nations." (4) There is also a growing recognition that social proph-ecy, in order not to remain a pious but ineffectual gesture, must be instrumented by social and political realism and translated into stra-tegic planning. In the complexities of an increasingly organized and technicized society, the scattered efforts of individuals and small groups in immediate situations do not suffice. Christian efforts need to be co-ordinated in an all-inclusive strategy—a strategy which rests on an incisive diagnosis of national values and evils, which projects Christian imperatives into captivating and realizable goals, and which knows how to utilize the decision-making processes in an organized society.

The last point is worth stressing. Despite its flourishing busyness, the Christian social witness is caught up in a grave though mostly unavowed crisis. The root cause of the crisis lies, no doubt, in the fact that the "source of energy in the struggle of life" (to quote again Troeltsch's phrase) for many Christians has lost its transforming dynamism. But there is also a disturbing feeling that much of the Christian social witness is "beating the air"—not only because it is often hesitant and weak but because it has become uncertain of its target. Hampered by social and ethical myopia, Christian groups are slow to recognize that the battlefield of social responsibility has be-

7

come vastly expanded and more complex. A missionary strategist once remarked: "The devil never laughs so heartily as when he succeeds in luring devout Christians to concentrate their efforts on secondary fronts. For then he has the central front, unguarded, all to himself." Though some may take exception to the language, no one can deny the pertinency of this observation in a time when the configuration of the battle is undergoing such swift and extraordinary changes.

It is not without reason, therefore, that Christian leaders are paying increasing attention to broader questions of aims and goals and the attendant problems of long-range planning. What are the purposes of this nation? What are the purposes of the Christian Church in and beyond the nation? To be sure, there is a legitimate place for particular "causes" and "emphases." But, in the opinion of many, the present situation calls for an imaginative attempt to rethink larger priorities. To take an illustration, are those right who suggest that the overriding Christian social concerns in the years ahead should be world peace under law, a more equitable partnership in utilizing the abundant material and technological resources of the earth, and the population explosion?

It is in this world context that the project on *Methodism and Society* is set. Like other Christian bodies, Methodism is challenged to ponder the lessons of its heritage, to redefine its social motivations and ideals, to assess its present activities and resources, and to project adequate strategies for more vigorous advance. The MESTA [1] study is an exploratory contribution to this task. Although it is chiefly concerned with the interaction of Methodism and American society, its broad Protestant approach, it is hoped, will commend it to the attention of social-minded Christians in other denominations as well.

Following the invitation from the Board of Social and Economic Relations, the committee appointed by the Boston University School of Theology faculty prepared a prospectus which was approved by the Board in September 1957. The committee has worked as a team in the general planning and in the definition and constant review of scope and research procedures. While the designated authors have carried primary responsibility for the writing of the individual volumes, these also include, in varying degrees, contributions of other members.

[1] The term "MESTA," frequently used in these volumes, is an abbreviation of the original working title, "Methodist Social Thought and Action."

8

The preliminary survey of source materials indicated that such a study, to fulfill its purpose, would require a far greater amount of primary research than had been originally anticipated. Hence the committee carried out a series of specialized projects covering such sources as Annual Conference Journals and regional periodicals, files of boards and agencies of The Methodist Church, educational curriculum materials, and personal records. Limitations of time and resources have prevented more than a sampling of representative periods, regions, and types of data. The largest single project (designated MR [2]) was a nation-wide inquiry into the religious and social beliefs of Methodists. A full account of this particular inquiry is given in a mimeographed monograph by Herbert E. Stotts.

The findings of the whole project have been condensed in a series of four volumes appearing under the general title of *Methodism and Society*.

Volume I, *Methodism and Society in Historical Perspective*, traces the social history of Methodism up to 1908, when the adoption of the "Social Creed" by the Methodist Episcopal Church and subsequently by the Federal Council of Churches of Christ in America opened up a new period. Beginning with a consideration of British Methodism from John Wesley to 1850, it recounts the checkered history of Methodism's interaction with the American environment.

Volume II, *Methodism and Society in the Twentieth Century*, brings the story up to the present time, correlating the growth of social concerns with major developments in national life. In further parts, the volume examines the contributions of specific agencies and groups, both official and unofficial, and gives a topical presentation of Methodism's stand on major issues.

Volume III, *Methodism and Society in Theological Perspective*, pursues a twofold aim. After analyzing the social implications of John Wesley's thought, it discusses major trends and emphases in relating religious convictions and social conduct as they appear in twentieth-century Methodism in the United States. The constructive part suggests in broad outline a theology of society which is both rooted in the truths of the Christian faith and relevant to the contemporary social scene.

Volume IV, *Methodism and Society: Guidelines for Strategy*, relates the findings of the preceding studies to the insights of social science into the processes of decision-making and planning. Against this background it seeks to develop a framework of principles and considerations which may serve as guidelines for a realistic strategy of social education, leadership, and action.

Some of the general features, and limitations, of the project should be pointed out. As the reader of the volumes will notice, the study pays major attention to the institutional manifestations of Methodist social concern. Such an approach may tend to create the onesided impression that the social witness of Methodism is to be seen chiefly in its institutional activities and in deliberate efforts of clergy and lay professionals to promote social change. The committee was, of course, aware of the fact that the social radiation of a church is an expression of its total life as it interacts with the environing culture, and especially of the countless decisions of individual Christians in the run of everyday life. It has therefore sought to probe also these elusive realities at certain points—particularly through the inquiry into the actual religious beliefs and social attitudes of Methodists, referred to above as MR [2].

The fact is often overlooked that The Methodist Church as a denomination is not limited to America alone. It is world-wide in structure and polity, as evidenced by the composition of its top legislative and executive organs, the General Conference and the Council of Bishops. A study of the varied relations existing between Methodism and society around the globe would be of great benefit in fostering a deeper sense of fellowship and a mutual understanding of the widely differing conditions under which Methodists are called to bear their social witness. The present volumes, however, are focused on the religious and social scene of the United States, with some notable exceptions. Thus Volume I includes an account of the social history of British Methodism from Wesley to 1850. The narrative of twentieth-century developments in Volume II suggests the influence of international perspectives on General Conference resolutions and Board actions. The deliberative parts of Volumes III and IV possess, in the nature of the case, a transcultural reference.

The ecumenical aspirations and affiliations of Methodism pose a somewhat similar problem, especially with respect to Volumes III and IV. It would have been theoretically possible to attempt to define a distinctive Methodist theology of society and a corresponding social strategy. Both theological and pragmatic reasons led the committee to adopt a different course. Methodism is officially committed to the cause of Christian unity. Methodist pronouncements and attitudes today are more expressive of the common outlook of social-minded Protestantism than of a separate tradition. Moreover, in the realm of strategy and action, it would clearly be self-defeating to seek to do in isolation what can be accomplished more effectively by a pooling of resources. Guided by such considerations, the committee has deliberately chosen to place its discussion of Methodist social responsibility in the broader framework of co-operative Christianity. Especially in the constructive parts, emphases of the Methodist heritage have been freely combined with the experiences and insights of the ecumenical community. It is hoped that this approach not only will be recognized as congenial to Methodism, but also will enhance the contribution of the project to a common task.

As previously indicated, the research phase of the project has been a co-operative venture of high order. It has benefited from the assistance of hundreds of correspondents, collaborators, and advisers across the country—denominational and interdenominational executives, liaison persons with the boards of The Methodist Church, ministers and laymen engaged in social work, academic scholars, social researchers, theological students, and so forth. Altogether over six thousand persons participated in the inquiry on "The Beliefs of Methodists." Drafts of the manuscripts were reviewed by members of the subcommittee of the Board of Social and Economic Relations as well as by outside experts.

Substantial reviews of the manuscript of the present volume on *Methodism and Society in Historical Perspective* were contributed by Douglas R. Chandler, Robert Michaelsen, Frederick A. Norwood, Robert T. Handy, and Philip S. Watson.

Of the faculty members of the Boston University School of Theology, William C. Moore did substantial research on church school materials, and Donald T. Rowlingson assisted in the reading of Southern periodicals. Members of the committee have used the opportunity of exploring aspects of the project in seminars. The following students of the School furnished resource materials in the form of term papers, research memoranda, and, in a few instances, doctoral dissertations on related topics: Donald W. Anderson, C. Philip

Bosserman, John C. Campbell, John H. Cartwright, Lloyd E. Chorpenning, Ivan N. Clark, John T. Dahlquist, James B. Darcy, Richard L. Deats, Dewey R. Findley, Harold W. Garman, Ronald H. Goetz, John H. Graham, Hugh E. Haggard, Richard L. Hamilton, Donald H. James, Pierre M. Kempf, C. Travis Kendall, C. Eric Lincoln, Robert Paul Lisensky, Robert C. Mezoff, Leslie H. McKown, Orloff W. Miller, Ralph T. Mirse, Charles H. Moore, Robert W. Musil, Joseph A. Perez, Charles M. Prestwood, F. Warren Rempel, C. Allyn Russell, Robert L. Shelton, John J. Shephard, James A. Smith, Robert E. Snyder, Henry J. Stonie, Duane F. Stroman, Harry G. Swanhart, Alfred H. Tracy, Mark C. Trotter, John G. Wall, Douglas E. Wingeier, and J. Philip Wogaman.

The voluminous material thus assembled is deposited in the library of Boston University School of Theology, which has established a repository of documents and publications on Methodism and society. A portion of the data has also been transcribed and coded in a punched-card file.

The committee wishes to express its deep gratitude to all those, named and unnamed, who in various ways so generously contributed to this undertaking. Special thanks are due to the librarian of Boston University School of Theology, Jannette E. Newhall, who, with her staff, not only unsparingly assisted the committee in its researches but also provided office space in a congenial atmosphere.

NILS EHRENSTROM
PROJECT DIRECTOR

Foreword

THIS VOLUME IS PART OF A LARGER STUDY OF "METHODISM and Society" undertaken by the Board of Social and Economic Relations of The Methodist Church in co-operation with the faculty of the Boston University School of Theology.

It is the hope of the Board that the four volumes of the project will serve as a foundation for study and action in the church, with the aid of forthcoming study guides and interpretive materials, and also will be used extensively by professors and students in colleges, universities, and seminaries, and by scholars doing independent study. The volumes should find their place as a significant contribution to ecumenical interests and research in the broader reaches of the total Christian impact upon society.

The interest of The Methodist Church in social matters goes back to its founder, John Wesley. It was an integral part of the thought, life, and activity of early Methodism. This interest in the welfare of people and the direction which society takes has been of increasing concern to The Methodist Church in the United States of America.

"The Social Creed" of the Methodist Church was adopted by the General Conference of the Methodist Episcopal Church in 1908. This was a turning point in the life of Methodism and for all the churches associated together in the Federal Council of the Churches of Christ in America. For it was the "Social Creed" of The Methodist Church which was adopted with little change as the social ideals of the Federal Council of Churches in 1908.

The Board of Social and Economic Relations was established by the General Conference of The Methodist Church in 1952 and received as its mandate the implementation of the "Social Creed."

13

As the new board began its work in race relations, economic life, and social and civic welfare, it soon became apparent that there was no systematic, objective survey and evaluation of the historical involvement of Methodism in the United States in social issues and the realization of social justice by the society.

Such questions as the following seemed to require answers:

Has The Methodist Church actually been a determining factor toward achievement of social justice in the United States?

Has The Methodist Church largely reflected advances made by secular and political institutions or has it actually been a pioneer for social justice which is the assumption that most Methodists make?

What has been the relationship of Methodist social action to Methodist theological beliefs?

Is there a well-defined Methodist theology for social action?

What has been the relationship of Methodist social action to that of other churches?

What have been the special social action emphases characteristic of Methodism in the United States?

What should Methodist social action be and do in the future?

The board decided to undertake a study of Methodism and the social scene in the United States of America and applied to the Fund for the Republic for a grant to undertake the project. The Fund made a grant which has been supplemented by the board's own funds and by a research grant from Boston University to bring the project to conclusion. We are grateful to the fund for its support.

The board consulted with various educational institutions of our connection and decided that the project would be well done at the Boston University School of Theology. We are especially glad that Nils Ehrenstrom, professor of ecumenics at Boston, and for many years the director of studies for the World Council of Churches, consented to become the chairman of the committee and project director. The other members, appointed by the faculty, were Dean Walter G. Muelder; Paul Deats, Jr., associate professor of social ethics (secretary of the committee) Richard M. Cameron, professor of church history; Allan K. Chalmers, professor of preaching and applied Christianity; S. Paul Schilling, professor of systematic theology; and Herbert E. Stotts, professor of church and community. They have

14

discharged their responsibilities with imagination and diligence and have worked in the closest co-operation with the board and its sub-committee for the project.

The board's own committee consisted of:

MR. SAMUEL W. WITWER, CHAIRMAN

MRS. T. J. COTTINGHAM, SECRETARY

BISHOP LLOYD C. WICKE

BISHOP WILLIS J. KING

DR. GEORGIA HARKNESS

THE REVEREND FRANK M. TEMPLIN

They were the responsible representatives of the board in the formulation, organization, and carrying out of the undertaking.

The board extends its deepest thanks to each member of the committee for doing so well a task which consumed many hours of detailed and hard work. We are especially grateful for the work of Mr. Witwer who spent many days with the faculty committee to bring the project into formulation and fruition.

The books were written by members of the faculty committee as follows:

Volume I *Methodism and Society in Historical Perspective*—
Richard M. Cameron

Volume II *Methodism and Society in the Twentieth Century*—
Walter G. Muelder

Volume III *Methodism and Society in Theological Perspective*—
S. Paul Schilling

Volume IV *Methodism and Society: Guidelines for Strategy*—
Herbert E. Stotts and Paul Deats, Jr.

To these authors we express our thanks and commend their work to the church.

Another group of persons actively participated in the undertaking. These were the expert critics who reviewed the books. At least four critics were chosen for each book (including one non-Methodist). These critics examined and evaluated the books carefully from the vantage point of their own specialized technical skills. To these critics

15

we are indebted for incisive, objective, and constructive suggestions which improved the early drafts of the manuscripts greatly.

We are especially happy to acknowledge the work of Charles H. Seaver of White Plains, New York, who for many years has worked in similar projects and who in this connection edited for style and content and prepared several of the indexes.

All concerned with the project are conscious of the special responsibility which the office staff, both in Boston and in Chicago, assumed in bringing the entire undertaking to completion.

The board and the faculty of Boston join in hoping that this project will be a forerunner of other larger and more penetrating analyses of the total social scene and the part of Methodism in it.

Above all, it is the earnest desire of all those who participated in any way in the project that the work will be an honor to the Lord whom we serve and be one of his instruments to sharpen the social witness of his Church in the world.

The Board of Social and Economic Relations was merged with the Boards of Peace and Temperance by the General Conference of 1960 into the Board of Christian Social Concerns. It is hoped that this new board will find these studies useful as it begins its work.

The project has been a co-operative one. The gathering and selection of the material, the interpretations and evaluations, and the method of presentation have been the primary responsibility of the faculty committee and the individual authors to whom the board extended great freedom. In no sense, therefore, can or should any statement in the books of this project (except direct quotations from official actions) be regarded as an official declaration of The Methodist Church or of the Board of Social and Economic Relations or the new Board of Christian Social Concerns.

Alfred Dudley Ward
General Secretary
Board of Social & Economic Relations
and General Editor of the Project

Author's Preface

IT HAS BEEN SAID THAT HE WHO DOES NOT THINK OF HIS future cannot have one; it is equally true that he who is ignorant of his past cannot transcend it. In this series of studies, the purpose of which is not to accumulate information for its own sake, but to point to ways in which The Methodist Church can more adequately face its social tasks, a historical volume has more than an antiquarian function. By pointing out Methodism's successes and failures in its past grapplings with social problems, it presents lessons, both positive and negative, which can be utilized, it is hoped, by those who seek to apply the mind of Christ to the society of our own crucial times.

Although this is a history of *Methodist* social thought and action, and has been written by a Methodist, it has been written not in a spirit of denominational glorification, but in an ecumenical spirit. Though certain features of the Methodist heritage are unique, and make certain aspects of its story unique, yet its main outlines are reproduced in the stories of many other denominations. Boasting is excluded, if only because the battles in the struggle for social righteousness that lie ahead are greater than those which lie behind us, and we have come to realize how necessary it is for all denominations to pool their resources in the fight. The aim of this book, then, is to recount as accurately as possible the way Methodism has attacked social problems in the past, so that not only Methodists themselves, but others as well, can take heed and take hope as they face future struggles together.

This work has relied heavily on the results of previous researchers. The writer has made forays into the vast field of original

17

material but is acutely aware of their partial and tentative nature. He wishes gratefully to acknowledge the wide extent of his indebtedness to previous work in the field. The footnotes will itemize that part of the debt which can be accounted for.

RICHARD M. CAMERON

Contents

19

21

Abbreviations

Books

AJL   Clark, Elmer T., Potts, J. Manning, and Payton, Jacob S. (eds.). *The Journal and Letters of Francis Asbury*.

BHMM   Barclay, Wade Crawford. *History of Methodist Missions*.

Discipline   *The Doctrines and Discipline of the Methodist Episcopal Church*.

EJW   Edwards, Maldwyn. *John Wesley and the Eighteenth Century. A Study of His Social and Political Influence*.

JGC   *Journals of the General Conference of the Methodist Episcopal Church*.

MAC   *Minutes of the Annual Conference of the Methodist Episcopal Church, for the Years 1773-1828*.

MFC   *Minutes of Florida Conference*.

MHC   *Minutes of Holston Conference*.

MLC   *Minutes of Louisiana Conference*.

MNC   *Minutes of North Carolina Conference*.

MNGC   *Minutes of North Georgia Conference*.

SHMEC   Stevens, Abel. *History of the Methodist Episcopal Church in the United States of America*.

SMAH   Sweet, William Warren. *Methodism in American History*.

WCP   Wearmouth, Robert F. *Methodism and the Common People of the Eighteenth Century*.

WIR   Warner, Wellman J. *The Wesleyan Movement in the Industrial Revolution.*

WJJ   Curnock, Nehemiah, (ed.). *The Journal of the Rev. John Wesley, A.M.*

WJL   Telford, John, (ed.). *The Letters of the Rev. John Wesley, A.M.*

Periodicals

ChAp   *Der Christliche Apologete.*

MM   *The Methodist Magazine.*

MMQR   *The Methodist Magazine and Quarterly Review.*

MP   *The Methodist Protestant.*

MPFV   *The Methodist Protestant and Family Visitor.*

MQR   *The Methodist Quarterly Review.*

MR   *The Mutual Rights of the Ministers and Members of the Methodist Episcopal Church.*

MRMP   *Mutual Rights and Methodist Protestant.*

NWCA   *The Northwestern Christian Advocate.*

NCA   *The Nashville Christian Advocate.*

QRS   *The Quarterly Review of the Methodist Episcopal Church, South.*

RCA   *The Richmond Christian Advocate.*

WJ   *The Wesleyan Journal.*

SCA   *The Southern Christian Advocate.*

VCS   *Virginia Conference Sentinel*

WCA   *Western Christian Advocate.*

WCAS   *Wesleyan Christian Advocate. New Series.*

WJ   *Wesleyan Journal.*

WR   *Wesleyan Repository.*

WRI   *The Wesleyan Repository and Religious Intelligencer.*

ZH   *Zion's Herald.*

CHAPTER ONE

Methodism in England

It is the task of this volume to set forth the social thought and activities of the Methodists in England and America in the eighteenth and nineteenth centuries and to trace out some of the observable ways in which it affected the society in which it grew, and in turn was affected by it. The Evangelical Revival in England, the matrix in which the Methodist bodies were born and nurtured, was primarily a *religious* revival; one, moreover, which stressed a religious experience of a highly personal and individual sort. This study, then, will be concerned primarily with but one phase of Methodist history, and one which admittedly was not the chief concern of its early leaders. It can be justified, however, not only by the increased attention given by our own generation to the social aspects of every human activity, but also by the vivid awareness of its first leaders that no matter how individual and personal the reborn Christian's experience of redeeming grace might be, its results could not help being social results, just as the redeemed man cannot help living in society.

John Wesley, who more than any other single man molded the outlook and activities of the Methodists, never departed from his early conviction that "The Gospel of Christ knows of no religion but social; no holiness but social holiness." [1] This oft-quoted phrase has shown itself capable of indefinite expansion. Taken in its context as written in 1739, it meant little more than a characteristic Protestant reiteration of the position that one need not flee "to the desert" to live a life of holiness. But, as Wesley's career unfolded, he found many and varied ways of working out the social implications of the gospel he

[1] John Emory (ed.), *The Works of the Rev. John Wesley, A. M.* (New York, 1831, reprint of 1850; hereafter cited as *Wesley' Works* [Emory]), VII, 593.

25

preached. His spiritual descendants, therefore, though they have transcended Wesley's own conceptions, quite legitimately see there a justification for preaching the social gospel. They are but continuing along a way he began to walk in. Granted that his primary purpose was the saving of individual souls,[2] still he was concerned to save not only souls, but bodies also; that is, to save men, not only for the next world, but for this one as well. An early attempt to formulate the purpose of the Methodists (it comes from one of the first Conferences) reads as follows:

Q. What may we reasonably believe to be God's design in raising up the preachers called Methodists? A. Not to form any new sect; but to reform the nation, particularly the Church, and to spread scriptural holiness over the land.[3]

This was in part a reaffirmation of the Methodists' tenacious loyalty to the Anglican Church, but its first importance lies in their recognition that it was part of their religious duty to change certain conditions in the life of their time and place. Their loyalty to the church itself was not of the uncritical sort, for they conceived that it too, indeed first of all, needed reforming. We, who are far enough away from the time to take advantage of a better perspective, can now see in society certain glaring injustices which they overlooked. But the important thing is that they did not fully share the complacency so general at the time. So they set about their task of reform—truly it was great enough as they envisaged it—and their successors enlarged its scope.

Methodists in America were to conceive their task in the same spirit. Their first printed *Discipline* (1785) carried an answer to the same question in terms adapted to their new situation. There was no reference to reforming the church (for the American Methodists had by 1785 begun to become a church themselves) but their intent was the same: "to reform the Continent and to spread scriptural Holiness over these lands." [4] Thus the declared purpose of reform, though it

[2] He told his preachers in an early Conference: "You have nothing to do but save souls. Therefore spend and be spent in this work" (*Ibid.*, V, 219).
[3] *Ibid.*, V, 212.
[4] *A Form of Discipline for the Ministers, Preachers, and Members of the Methodist Episcopal Church in America*, 1785 (Reprint by Charles Nutter, of the Methodist Historical Society, Concord, N. H., Republican Press Association, 1887), p. 3.

was at first conceived in primarily moral and religious terms, came to embrace more and more aspects of the life of this world.

Nor were the Methodists, with John Wesley at their head, content with uprooting evil conditions. They wrought valiantly at the task of helping human need. There were, in "the age of philanthropy," many who strove to alleviate the sufferings of their less fortunate fellows, before Methodism was born—witness the Charity School movement, and such ventures as Oglethorpe's making Georgia a haven for imprisoned debtors—but the growth of Methodism added considerably to the numbers of the concerned. Wesley himself set the example, which was followed with singular persistence and intensity by his disciples. Their varied philanthropy, which took the form of personal relief of those in need and employed certain organizations formed for the purpose, considering the smallness of their numbers and the slenderness of their resources, was indeed an impressive effort.

Reform and philanthropy, then, were among the avowed objectives of Wesley and his Methodists from the very beginning of the movement. It will be our task in this chapter to survey the nature and extent of these aspects of Methodism during the eighteenth century in England. As an aid to our understanding them, we must first sketch in, though but sparsely, the main features of the society within which they operated.

A. England in the Eighteenth Century

In England the eighteenth century was a century of contrasts. During its course were laid the foundations of the empire, and of the world-wide market which made of it a nation of manufacturers and carriers to the world, and governors of a large portion of it. It produced a galaxy of thinkers and writers which would have graced any firmament in human intellectual history and has found enduring recognition as constituting a new "Augustan Age" in letters. It was an age of relative stability at home and peace with other nations. The ruling oligarchy was quite satisfied with things as they were, the writers gave literary form to their complacency, and the thinkers elaborated theoretical justification for maintaining the blessed equilibrium free from change. But this imposing superstructure was built on a foundation of poverty and wretchedness which was none the less real for being inarticulate. Insofar as the governors and thinkers took the

27

masses into account, it was to say that the prosperity of the nation presupposed a permanent pool of poverty to sustain it, and that it was a providential arrangement which had decreed that the many poor should serve the interests of the few rich. The contrasts in the social life of the eighteenth century in England can be made vivid by comparing a portrait by Sir Joshua Reynolds of an affluent upper-class family with the savagely satirical depiction of the miseries in "Gin Lane" by William Hogarth.

Two revolutions overtook England during the century. First came the agricultural revolution, which increased the output of food enormously. It became profitable to run large-scale farms; but since they required more capital than a small landholder could muster, the increase was given to those who already had the most. Many small farms were thrown together to make a few large ones; the landowners with sufficient political backing were able to "enclose" profitable tracts of arable and grazing land which had before belonged to whole villages in common. Both processes pushed agricultural laborers off the land. Then came the Industrial Revolution, which drew the dispossessed to the manufacturing and mining centers to live out their toilsome lives in greater poverty and under conditions even more unwholesome than before.

The most grievous moral plagues of the age were drunkenness, gambling, and sexual promiscuity. They were not confined to the lower classes by any means. The social tone of the upper classes was set by the court life under the first two Georges, where marital fidelity was a matter of jest, and gross self-indulgence lacked even the thin mantle of grace that the Restoration court had known how to throw about its excesses. It would be easy, did space permit, to assemble specific cases of low life in high places. The chief difference was that the rich could afford to drink brandy from France and were carried home by servants to bed, while the poor drank the cheap gin which had recently begun to be manufactured in England and had "clean straw to lie on for nothing" in the "pubs." If Charles James Fox spent twenty-two hours at a single gaming session "at the trifling cost of five hundred pounds per hour," in a much shorter time Oliver Goldsmith gambled away the fifty pounds given to him to start him out as a student of law.

Crimes against property and person could be committed with im-

28

punity five times out of six; but society exacted fierce retribution from the unfortunate sixth who was convicted. At one time during the century two hundred crimes, including the theft of two shillings from a shop, were punishable by hanging. Conditions in the prisons were unspeakably bad.

Government itself was carried on by the few in their own interests. Sir Robert Walpole, the first prime minister in the modern sense of the word (1721-1742), governed on the cynical principle that every man had his price. Beyond the salutary action taken by Parliament to regulate the traffic in gin by raising taxes on it, no one in the government seemed to care that the masses lived in unspeakable misery from which the only surcease was to find troubled forgetfulness in drink.

There were notable philanthropies, carried on by concerned individuals and voluntary groups, which shone as lights in the darkness of a public indifference which held "that government was best which governed least." Fundamental steps in education for the poor were undertaken in the Charity Schools carried on by religious societies and individuals like the evangelist Howell Harris. Thomas Coram and Jonas Hanaway built foundling homes for the waifs abandoned in appalling numbers. These waifs were uncared for and sometimes deliberately starved to death for the small sums paid by the parishes for their maintenance. General Oglethorpe and John Howard interested themselves in prisoners, and in prison reform. These men, and others like them, shouldered work for the unfortunate which only later came to be recognized as the responsibility of organized society.

What of the churches? In the dissenting churches (Baptist, Presbyterian, and Independent or Congregational), the strenuous loyalty generated by the persecution of Restoration times had relaxed under a toleration just broad enough to remove the danger, but not the annoying disabilities, which had been imposed by the Clarendon Code. The Baptists and the Independents had maintained their Calvinistic orthodoxy firmly enough; but that orthodoxy was devoid of religious feeling or social passion. The English Presbyterians, on the other hand, had suffered from the inroads of the low theology of Deism, and the low Christology of an eighteenth-century form of Arianism. As for the established Anglicanism, being closely connected with the state, it suffered the defects of the governmental outlook. If the government cared not a whit for the sufferings of the poor, how should a state church do better? A single vivid passage from the jurist Blackstone, though not wholly fair, is perhaps more representative than any other of the tone of its preachers.

He says that he did not hear a single discourse which had more Christianity in it than the writing of Cicero, and that it would have been impossible for him to discover from what he heard, whether the preacher were a follower of Confucius, or Mahomet, or of Christ.[5]

Though there were some good men in its bishops' chairs, many were chosen not because of religious or moral fitness, but because of political, or even military, service to the party in power. There were good men, too, in the parish churches; but too many of the better livings were held by place-hunters, or pluralists, or absentee incumbents, who left the work to humdrum curates while they enjoyed the income. In such circumstances the spiritual life of Anglicanism could not be expected to reach high levels—nor did it.

Perhaps the severest judgment on the English Church of the time falls on its failure to manifest any concern for the increasing pressure of need among common people facing changing social conditions. The parish lines, set with the rigor of a long history, did not bend to include areas like Kingswood, where great settlements of miners lived uncared for in an ecclesiastical no man's land. Except in London, no new churches were being built to accommodate the increasing population. Methods of caring for souls and for ministering to the poor which had been fairly adequate in an earlier day were allowed to persist unchanged long after they had ceased to suffice. The Anglican Church made few claims on the people beyond the payment of their rates, a passive conformity, and attendance on service from time to time. Certainly it made little effort to go beyond the prescribed formulas to meet their spiritual and physical needs. The historian Gibbon reveals a great deal about the Anglican Church of his day when he records a passing regret that he had not, when young, chosen among several lucrative careers "even the fat slumbers of the Church." [6]

[5] Charles J. Abbey and John H. Overton, The English Church in the Eighteenth Century (Revised ed., London: Longmans, Green and Co., 1896), p. 300.
[6] Quoted in Trevelyan, English Social History (London: Longman's Green and Co., 1942), p. 359.

B. John Wesley, the Molder of Methodism
1. THE MATRIX OF THE REVIVAL

Just as the evangelical movement in England was larger than Methodism, so the eighteenth-century revival as a whole was larger than the movement in England. How can we account for the fact that in three places, as widely separated geographically as Germany, England, and the Colonies in America, revivals of evangelical Christianity sprang up, if not simultaneously, at least nearly so? It is true that we can trace personal and literary links between them, yet when we have done all we can in this way, we still must say: "The wind blows where it wills, and you hear the sound of it, but you do not know whence it comes or whither it goes; so it is with every one who is born of the Spirit" (John 3:8). The revival as a whole is usually traced to the movement within German Lutheranism, where, during the latter part of the seventeenth century, Philip Jacob Spener and August Hermann Francke were the most conspicuous leaders in what came to be called Pietism. During the eighteenth century, the Pietists who had the greatest influence in England were that part of the "Unitas Fratrum" usually called Moravians, under the leadership of the Lutheran Count Zinzendorf. We remember how, even as early as his missionary trip to Georgia, Wesley was impressed by the Moravians' faith and fervor, and how he was led to his conversion experience by the Moravian Peter Boehler. Meanwhile, what is known as the Great Awakening sprang up in the American Colonies. Though Jonathan Edwards of Northampton, Massachusetts, is the best-known leader of the Great Awakening, he received help from the English Methodist George Whitefield; and Wesley in turn was influenced by the reading of Edwards' *Narrative of Surprising Conversions.*

Having thus described the larger sweep of the revival, we can now turn to that part of it which spread through England. It is usually described as consisting of three divisions: Calvinistic Methodism, led by George Whitefield and Lady Huntingdon; the Anglican evangelical movement, which stayed in the Anglican church; and Wesleyan Methodism, which, though it began in the church and continued there as long as Wesley lived, became a separate body soon after his death. Without pausing here to note the relations between them,[7] we turn immediately to Wesleyan Methodism.

[7] See pp. 78 (and n.120), 79.

John Wesley, more than any other man of the eighteenth century, gave the Methodist movement its form and tone. Both the size of the body of Methodists which looked to him as their founder and the dominance of his influence in the Methodist societies warrant our considering his religious experience and thought, and their outworking in the social context. As he was born in 1703 and lived until 1791, his life extended into every decade of the century. Augustine Birrell, nineteenth-century English man of letters and cabinet minister, wrote, "No other man did such a life work for England." [8] The influence of that life work has extended not only beyond its century, but also beyond England to lands halfway around the globe.

2. The Warmed Heart and the Quest for Holiness

Very near the beginning of Wesley's long and unremitting activity in the Revival is the famous conversion experience of May 24, 1738, at the meeting of a religious society in Aldersgate Street in London.

About a quarter before nine. . . . I felt my heart strangely warmed. I felt I did trust in Christ, Christ alone for salvation; and an assurance was given me that He had taken away my sins, even mine, and saved me from the law of sin and death.

I began to pray with all my might for those who had . . . despitefully used me and persecuted me.[9]

This inpouring of divine grace and assurance of forgiveness resolved a struggle which for months before had made of Wesley a man divided against himself. It released the energies which had been consumed in the search for the salvation of his own soul for a new objective: the salvation of others. It was a repetition of that classic form

[8] Quoted from W. V. Townshend, H. B. Workman, and George Eayrs, A New History of Methodism (2 vols. London: Hodder and Stoughton, 1909), I, 371.
[9] WJJ, I, 475-76. Fr. Maximin Piette (in his John Wesley in the Evolution of Protestantism [London: Sheed and Ward, 1938]) and Umphrey Lee (in his John Wesley and Modern Religion [Nashville: Cokesbury Press, 1936]) have concluded that the real turning point in Wesley's religious life came in 1725 when he was still under Anglican influence and he "set in earnest upon a new life"; and that the Aldersgate Street experience under Moravian influence was secondary in importance and mystical in nature. I am constrained to agree with the traditional appraisal, as defended by George C. Cell (The Rediscovery of John Wesley [New York: Henry Holt, 1935]), and J. Ernest Rattenbury (The Conversion of the Wesleys [London: The Epworth Press, 1938]). The inescapable conclusion to which the evidence brings us is that the conversion experience of May 24, 1738, was epochal in importance for Wesley's own religious experience and for the Revival in England; and that it was evangelical, not mystical, in nature.

of conversion known as evangelical, in which the struggle is won when it is given over and replaced by trust, "trust in Christ alone for salvation." Before Wesley arrived at this point, he had, again like other Christians before and since, traveled a long road, desperately searching for salvation through self-achieved holiness. After Aldersgate Street he felt that he was traveling a new road but the travels already endured were not lost. Ever since he had read, while still an undergraduate at Oxford, books by holy men of Roman Catholicism and Anglicanism (Thomas à Kempis, Jeremy Taylor, and William Law), he had been zealous for living a holy life. The nickname of the "Holy Club" of which he had been the guiding spirit, though applied in derision, was accurate enough in essentials. Its members fasted, prayed regularly, lived sparingly, and gave to the poor both of the time and the substance thus saved. They visited the sick, preached in prisons, and kept a school for poor children.

After Aldersgate, the passion for holiness persisted, and expressed itself in much the same ways, though with less emphasis on austerity and with more attention to works of mercy. There was a greater difference still, which lay in the realm of motive. Whereas the earnest University students undertook their regime of self-denial and "social service" as steps on the way to justifying themselves in God's sight, the later Methodists undertook the same steps out of the joyous assurance that their sins were already forgiven, not of their own desert, but of God's grace. They were not the roots, but the fruits of salvation. They sprang not out of anxiety for self, but out of compassion for others and love for God.

3. THEOLOGICAL EMPHASES

This is not the place to give a complete account of Wesley's doctrine,[10] even a summary one. We can notice only those features of it which had a special bearing on the Methodists' sense of social responsibility. Wesley always contended that Methodism was nothing else than "plain, old Christianity." But inevitably there were emphases and even matters of content which were characteristically Wesleyan. He put the doctrine of salvation at the center of his system, and related to it the other doctrines—of God, of man, of sin, and so forth. No man was excluded from access to this salvation, either by his

---

[10] See Volume III of this series.

own sinfulness or by an immutable decree of God. Whosoever will may come. Though salvation was the gift of God, a man was not without responsibility in the matter, either before or after he came face to face with the proffered grace. He was to expect it in watchfulness and prayer, in reading of God's word, in attendance on the means of grace, and in actively doing good to others. He had freedom either to accept or to reject the proffered grace. In these matters Wesley diverged with Arminius from the teaching of Calvin. It must be said in this connection, however, that both Wesley and Arminius accepted the Luther-Calvin formulation of the doctrines of original sin, total depravity, and the absolute necessity of divine grace in salvation.

Characteristic of Wesley himself was the emphasis on the doctrine of assurance—his insistence that the redeemed could rejoice in the certainty that his sins were forgiven, and that he was a child of God. Moreover, salvation was great enough to include salvation from all sin. The emphasis put on holiness of heart and life was likewise characteristic of Wesleyanism. "Holiness, without which no man will see the Lord" (Heb. 12:14) was a very important text for Wesley. He insisted that the moment a man was born again, his growth in holiness began. Wesley had many ways of describing this growth, but the simplest was by saying that it was growth in love—love to God and toward one's fellow men. A Christian—any Christian—could reach a stage of maturity in which this love could be called perfect; in short he might attain to Christian perfection. This, too, was a gift from God, and God might grant it at any moment. For this new gift the Christian should live in constant expectation; that is, again, in watchfulness, in prayer, in attendance on the means of grace, and in doing good to all men. Further, we should notice that this quest for Christian perfection should be pursued not in retirement, but in the midst of society, and while following one's ordinary business. Again, growth should not cease once perfection had been attained, for Wesley insisted that there must be progress both toward and in perfection. Wesley never allowed his Methodists to think they had "arrived." Moreover it had as its special matrix the Methodist societies and their subdivisions— but of the Methodist organization we shall speak later.

Whatever one's attitude toward the expediency of a man's claiming that he had been made perfect in love (and Wesley never did so for himself), one cannot help seeing how his insistence on the doctrines

34

of assurance and of Christian perfection would generate a pervasive sense of social responsibility, and a tremendous dynamic for the relief of suffering men, as well as for the reform of the abuses that made them suffer. For it put emphasis on the activity of love in society as the truest expression of the Christian's life before he gets to heaven.

4. THE METHODIST ORGANIZATION

Wesley was not content with the proclamation of the gospel. He followed it by binding his converts into an organization admirably calculated to keep alive the good impulses aroused by the preaching. There was a pyramid of organizations, from the band with eight members or so, through the class with a dozen, and to the society, which might be of almost any size. At the top in geographical spread and in authority, if not in size, was the conference, composed of preachers only. For each of these groups there was a leader or leaders to keep the whole functioning smoothly. Behind these several units lay the three purposes basic in any group organized for religious purposes: discipline, edification, and benevolent activity. Wesley was not an inventive man in the matter of organization, but he showed great capacity for adopting and adapting devices which others had already used. The rapid growth of the movement rather caught him by surprise. As a consequence, the formative period of Methodist organization was filled with expedients, some of which proved their worth and were retained, others of which did not and were discarded.

a) *The Society*

The Society became the basic and characteristic unit of Methodism for administration and worship. The model at Wesley's hand was the considerable number of religious societies composed of earnest Anglicans, which had been in existence since the last quarter of the seventeenth century. Canon Overton, a sympathetic Anglican historian of Methodism, has pointed out that the Wesleys' first work was done in such societies, and that the first ones they themselves established were modeled on them. Indeed the Holy Club at Oxford was one such. The use of certain terms in both the old and the new societies illustrates their continuity. The purpose of the older societies was declared to be the cultivation of "holiness of heart and life"; that phrase was often heard in the Methodist meetings. Just as the earlier

35

societies had had "stewards" chosen from among their membership to look after their money concerns, so did the Methodist societies. Still, the innovations in the Wesley societies were more important than the continuities. Perhaps the greatest single novelty was the absoluteness of Wesley's personal authority. We must return to this later; for the time being it is sufficient to note that, ultimately, dissidents had either to submit or to depart on Wesley's word. This was quite different from, say, the Fetter Lane Society,[11] where a majority vote decided that Wesley was no longer to be allowed to preach among them. We can here barely mention those two innovations without which the revival would never have grown so swiftly. The example of preaching in the fields was set by Whitefield. Wesley followed it reluctantly at first, but soon recognized how essential it was to the spread of the work. Of equal importance was the use of laymen as preachers. The importance of these two innovations lay in their providing ways of continuing the evangelistic work in spite of the indifference or hostility of the parish clergy. Men who would never have gone to the church came to hear sermons in the fields; and they came in greater numbers than could have got into most churches if they had wished.

The relation of the societies to the established church was a complex one. Wesley's first concern was the prosperity of the work; but he endeavored to make it contributory to the welfare of the church rather than a competitor with it. He continued to preach in other men's parishes. But he long insisted on asking the incumbent's permission to preach in the church. Only if this was refused (as it usually was) did he preach outdoors. It was in justification of this practice that he first used the famous phrase, "I look upon all the world as my parish."[12] It was only well on in the 'eighties that he reluctantly allowed a few of the societies to hold meetings at the hours of church services. Certainly he was adamant in his determination to keep them

---

[11] The Fetter Lane Society was founded shortly before the conversion experience. It was a joint enterprise in which the Wesleys participated as equals with others. It went beyond the "old line" societies in dividing the members into "Bands" for mutual examination and edification; but it kept the old democratic form of procedure. On the other hand the Foundery Society was begun toward "the latter end of 1739" by a number of persons submitting themselves to Wesley's sole guidance and control. The rest of the Wesleyan Societies followed the pattern of the Foundery, not that of Fetter Lane.

[12] WJL, I, 286.

from becoming churches themselves. To this end, he insisted all his life that his Methodists take the sacraments regularly in their parish churches. Nevertheless, he could not prevent a good deal of overlapping. In one way or another the Methodists exercised all the functions of a church save the sacramental one. In the matter of doctrine, one of the early conferences arrogated to itself the authority to review the Thirty-nine Articles, to see whether or not they were in accord with Scripture;[13] and long before Wesley's death the only preaching permitted in the Methodists' "preaching houses" was that which conformed to the Methodists' own doctrinal standards, which were Wesley's Notes on the New Testament, and the "first four volumes of sermons." In matters of discipline, the "Rules of the United Societies," to which all who would retain their membership in the societies had to conform, appeared as early as 1743; furthermore, the annual meetings of conference added almost every year to the list of regulations for preachers and people alike. Finally, the Methodist meetings could not help engaging in common worship, filled as they were with scripture reading and exposition, prayer, and hymns. Thus, as time went on, in spite of Wesley's declared purpose to keep his Methodists good Anglicans, more and more of them looked not to the church but to the society for all their edification and all their worship save the sacraments.

When the societies were numerous enough, they were grouped into circuits, served by a "group ministry" in the sense that all the preachers were ministers to all the points in the circuit. They exercised their ministry under the supervision of a senior minister who was called first an assistant, and then a helper.

b) Bands and Classes

Because they were smaller units, the bands and classes were the groups in which, week by week, the intimate work of examination, edification, and discipline went on. Wesley adopted the device of the band from the Moravians. The classes were of Methodist origin. The functions of the two groups overlapped to so large an extent that gradually the classes all but superseded the bands in the Methodist scheme. Consequently we shall pause over the bands only long enough

[13] J. S. Simon, John Wesley and the Methodist Societies (2nd ed.; London: The Epworth Press, 1937), p. 211. Simon adds: "It is significant that the decisions of the Conference on the points in question are not recorded in the Bennet 'Minutes.'"

to say that, in general, they were for those who had made some progress in the Christian life; and that there were some bands for special purposes: penitent bands for those who had lapsed from standards of conduct, and were undergoing a period of trial before readmission to full participation in the societies; and there were select bands, usually composed of those who were so mature in their devotion and living that they "walked in the light of God's countenance," and could be of special help to Wesley when he needed counsel. Conversely, he turned to them in solving the intricate problems which confront those far advanced in Christian experience. I mention these to show the enormous thought and care Wesley bestowed on the best means of fulfilling the pastoral needs of his people. Having said this much about the bands, we turn to the classes, remembering that the function of the two was at bottom the same: mutual edification and discipline in small groups of Christians who took their calling seriously.

The classes, it is not too much to say, became the most important working unit for the discipline and edification of the members. Every member of a society had also to be a member of one of the classes into which it was divided. The class originated simply as a device for paying a debt on property at Bristol. It consisted of a leader and eleven other people, living usually in one neighborhood. The leader was to visit the members of his class weekly, to collect a penny from them. But this visitation soon took on a pastoral significance when the leader noted that some were not living as they ought. Wesley seized on this expedient with alacrity, as a chance to use the class leaders as lieutenants in the pastoral oversight which was rapidly assuming proportions too large for him. The next step in the evolution of the class meeting was to gather the members all together in one place at a set time during the week. Wesley's comment on the usefulness of the classes indicates how highly he esteemed them.

It can scarce be conceived what advantages have been reaped from this little prudential regulation. Many now happily experienced that Christian fellowship of which they had not so much as an idea before. They began to "bear one another's burdens," and naturally to "care for each other." As they had daily a more intimate acquaintance with, so they had a more endeared affection for each other. And "speaking the truth in love, they grew up into him in all things, who is the Head, even Christ." [14]

We do not have a great deal of information on the steady functioning of the class meetings—their proceedings were not the sort to be put down in documentary form. Obviously much depended on the wisdom and sympathy of the leader. This class meeting could be rather inquisitorial or merely perfunctory; but with a good leader it would be more like a family council, the steady and benevolent pressure of which trained up young Christians, kept mature ones from extravagance, encouraged the remorseful, rebuked the wrongdoers, and above everything held before them all the ideal of Christ the Head. From the social point of view, the great virtue of the class was that it gave each individual a sense of "belonging"—that there were eleven other persons who cared for his welfare as they did for their own. That was no small factor in their success, especially in the teeming towns, where it was so easy for one to feel lost in the multitude.

Here must be mentioned one feature of the scheme on which the classes were operated—the "tickets." The tickets may be regarded as the material symbol *par excellence* of the seriousness with which the early Methodists took their discipline. Very soon after the establishment of the class meeting, every member was given a ticket as a sign of his membership. Each quarter, moreover, his character was reviewed, and, if passed, a new ticket was given him. But if he was found guilty of some fault which brought scandal on the societies, or which was considered unworthy of his profession, the ticket was denied him till he displayed suitable repentence and gave evidence of his sincere desire to mend his life. Thus continued membership in a class, and hence in the society, depended in a very real way on continued conformity with the standards of conduct delineated in the General Rules and in the disciplinary *Minutes*. Thus, also, the difference between Methodists and "the world" was kept sharp and clear, and the moral life was taken much more seriously and maintained at a much higher level in the societies than in the national church. The state church, being nearly coterminous with the population, could not maintain an ethical standard much higher than that of the population as a whole.

[14] *The Works of John Wesley* (ed. John Emory; New York: Lane and Scott, Reprint of 1831 edition, 1850) V, 180.

39

The societies, on the other hand, being voluntary organizations, could and did require conformity to a much stricter ethical code, enforcing it by expulsion when necessary. The tickets were the visible symbol of this strictness.

c) The Conference

Composed of preachers only, the Conference met annually. It performed a triple function in the discipline, the education, and the "stationing" of the preachers. It also was the deliberative body in which the doctrinal and disciplinary standards for the whole "connection" were drawn up. Full and free discussion of all issues prevailed, according to the decision of the first Conference (held in 1744) that every question should be "bolted to the bran." The personal dominance of Wesley, however, was such that his ideas, and even his phraseology, are easily discernible in most of the minutes.

Most of the preachers, it must be remembered, were laymen, and from the humbler walks of life. The men of the Anglican church continually objected that unlearned men ought not to be entrusted with the ministry of the Word. Wesley stoutly defended them:

Some of those who now preach are unlearned. They neither understand the ancient languages, nor any of the branches of philosophy. And yet . . . in the one thing which they profess to know they are not ignorant men. I trust there is not one of them who is not able to go through such an examination in substantial, practical, experimental divinity, as few of our candidates for holy orders, even in the university . . . are able to do.[15]

Along the line of education, the conferences often resolved themselves into what might be called seminars in Christian doctrine. The results of their "conversations" were recorded in minutes, which as they accumulated were gathered together in the "Short Minutes." These formed a body of doctrinal statement which, if it was not systematic, was at least pertinent to their needs. As for discipline, the character of each of the preachers was reviewed every year; only if it was "passed" was he allowed to continue in his ministry. Otherwise, he had to manifest a change of heart and conduct before he could resume his labors.

[15] Ibid., V, 155-56.

5. THE SOCIAL STATUS OF THE METHODISTS

Because of Wesley's constant insistence that the gospel must be preached to the poor, it is safe to conclude that they formed the bulk of the membership of Methodism. The upper classes, who were inclined to think that even degrees of sinfulness corresponded pretty closely to the existing class distinctions, were less likely to be attracted by the Methodist preaching that all mankind was shut up under sin. The Duchess of Buckingham, for instance, said: "It is monstrous to be told that you have a heart as sinful as the common wretches that crawl on the earth." [16] It was the common people who heard the Methodist preaching gladly. Yet from the beginning, there were some from the middle and upper classes in the societies, and in the course of the eighteenth century the proportion grew. This came about in two ways: more people above the lowest classes were attracted to the movement, and many Methodists moved up in the scale by their own efforts. The humblest leave few records behind, and we cannot give statistical evidence for assuming that the poor predominated. However, Warner has selected at random a number of early class leaders and those who founded new classes or societies, and given their occupations. He names a poor pedlar, an impoverished widow, a family servant, a carpenter, a schoolmaster-shepherd, a retired soldier, an upholsterer, a tailor, a tanner, a piecemaker, a hand loom weaver, a cordwainer, a cooper, a grocer-breadbaker, and a brazier.[17] Among the first generation of local preachers, the following occupations were represented: a collier, a brass cutter, a toymaker, a farmer, a baker, a cabinetmaker, a printer, a schoolmaster. But there were some from the professions, too, and as time went on, an increasing number of more or less successful businessmen.[18]

Almost none of the regular preachers came from the upper classes, and, contrary to the current opinion, almost none from the lowest. A

[16] Townshend, op. cit., I, 20.
[17] WIR, p. 263. The impression of the poverty of the majority of the first Methodists is heightened by the unwitting evidence in the account of the founding of the class meetings: there were objections to requiring a penny a week from each member; and the class leaders (who numbered, say, one in twelve) had as one of their duties making up the amount their class members could not give. Here too must be considered the difficulties in the way of the leader's visiting each member in the place where he lived: "Many persons lived with masters, mistresses, or relations, who would not suffer them to be thus visited. At the houses of those who were not so averse, they often had no opportunity of speaking to them but in company." (Wesley's Works V, 179).
[18] WIR, pp. 259-60.

survey of sixty-three biographies of preachers disclosed the parents' occupation in about half the cases.

Six were farmers, three were simply labourers, two were clothiers, two were shopkeepers, two were in a building trade, two kept public-houses, and each of the following claimed one representative: husbandry, gardening, woolen manufactory, pilchard-fishery, baker, mason, tradesman, cutler, tanner, carpenter, barber, "tradesman and farmer," shoemaker, school teacher. . . . Practically all of the regular preachers, therefore, during this period of more than fifty years, were drawn from a single social stratum, located between "unskilled labour" and the "middle class.[19]

For the first thirty years, apparently, most of the preachers engaged in some form of gainful occupation to help support themselves and their families. In 1768 this was definitely forbidden, though it was realized that it would work some hardship. The reason assigned was that it was easier to draw the line before any such work started than to discriminate between those preachers who might and those who might not do outside work, or to assign a place where such work, once begun, must stop.[20] One cannot but admire the self-denial of these men in the interest of whole-hearted service to the gospel; and one notices a genuine Franciscan tone in the "Twelve Rules of a Helper" drawn up in an early Conference. The first edition had as its ninth rule:

Take no money of any one. If they give you food when you are hungry, or clothes when you need them, it is good. But not silver or gold. Let there be no pretense to say we grow rich by the Gospel.[21]

6. John Wesley's Political Views

We can sum up Wesley's political views in a very short phrase: John Wesley was a Tory. The source of his Toryism was probably the political outlook of the Epworth Rectory, the lord and master of which was both Tory and High Church. Wesley started out as both too—but because his High Church views hindered his work, he modi-

---

[19] *Ibid.*, pp. 249-50.
[20] John S. Simon, *John Wesley the Master Builder* (London: The Epworth Press, 1927), p. 227.
[21] John S. Simon, *John Wesley and the Methodist Societies* (2nd ed.; London: The Epworth Press, 1937), pp. 216-17. This rule was omitted from later editions of the "Twelve Rules."

fied them. His Toryism, however, as Maldwyn Edwards points out, was subject to no such strain, and remained unaltered.[22] Yet it would be wrong to suppose that Wesley's political views were merely an uncritical inheritance from the past. He did not change them much, but he did read and think about them, and he could give reasons for what he believed. The reasons, as we might expect, were religious and moral ones.

Wesley repudiated the doctrine that the people were the source of power as it was stated by Rousseau, though he had some emotional affinities with what the latter had to say about the state of nature, and certainly was sympathetic with the place he allowed to emotion in the workings of the human spirit. He was also familiar with the contract theory of the origin of government, as propounded by John Locke, but his familiarity only bred contempt, and he rejected it on grounds both historical and moral. Wesley contended that in all history there was but one instance of the people giving sovereign power to any one, i.e., to Massaniello of Naples.[23] As for English history, seven hundred years of it contained not a single instance of such a transfer.[24] He was very scornful of the use made of the contract theory to support the Revolution of 1688. It was not the *people* who put William III on the throne, but a mere handful of lords and gentlemen. But Wesley's chief reason for denying that the people had the disposal of authority in their hands was simply his opinion that they were incapable of wielding it. They were not trained for it, but above all they were morally unqualified.

In his positive suggestions, he was neither clear nor original. He believed that "the greater share the people have in government, the less liberty, either civil or religious, does the nation . . . enjoy." [25] This would seem to commit him to the conclusion that the nation under an absolute monarch has the most liberty. Yet he pointed instead to the liberty England's subjects enjoyed under her limited monarchy. He was never tired of singing the praises of the British Constitution and pointing out how grateful the people who lived under it should be for the liberties they enjoyed. To the contention

[22] EJW, p. 13. I am indebted to Mr. Edwards' treatment for much of the substance in this section.
[23] Ibid., p. 24; Wesley, Works, "Calm Address," VI, 300.
[24] Ibid., "Some Observations on Liberty," p. 310.
[25] Ibid., p. 311.

that the people were the source of power in government, he replied, in words of scripture, "There is no power but of God." This doesn't quite answer the question, which is, so far as civil government is concerned, who shall be regarded as the repositories and interpreters of that power in the state? Wesley's answer meant two things to him. Since power is of God, it devolves from the top down, that is, in England, through the King and Parliament; and it must be administered in such a way as to secure the maximum expression of morality and justice. This excludes the people, whose political incompetence and incapacity for self-discipline are obvious to all observers. When it was pointed out to Wesley that, as a matter of fact, the members of the Commons were elected at the polls, he replied that, once elected, they were no longer responsible to the voters, but to God and their conscience alone.

The criterion of morality which he applied so rigorously in the case of the people, he quite inconsistently failed to apply to the governing oligarchy. This man, who was entirely devoted to the interests of the common people, excluded them from any share in the direction of the government under which they lived because they were unregenerate. At the same time, though he had very little sympathy for aristocrats (he once said, "One needs great grace to talk with great people"), he was ready to entrust the whole divine authority of government to their hands.

Wesley's position, anomalous as it was, was so positively held that it set the tone of the political thinking in all the Methodist societies. He rallied the societies so well to the support of the Crown that he was charged, wrongly, to be sure, with seeking the political reward he was several times offered, but as often refused. In this respect, he was quite different from the two leading writers among the dissenters, Drs. Price and Priestley, who were very Whiggish in their politics. The dissenters furnished many of those who constituted a radical party by welcoming the doctrines of the French Revolution. But the Methodists, because of Wesley's influence, opposed them almost to a man.

Wesley lived through the American Revolution, and on into the middle of the French Revolution. After a period when he favored the aspirations of the American colonists, he faced about quickly and completely when they sought to gain independence by forcible means.

In his "Calm Address to our American Colonies," he endeavored by arguments both scriptural and political to convince them that they were wrong. They were not being treated unjustly in being taxed without representation, for they had forfeited the right to representation when they emigrated. In fighting against the King, they were disobeying God's word commanding that every man should be in subjection to the higher powers. They would find themselves under the greatest tyranny of all if they succeeded in establishing the rule of the people. Wesley's pamphlet did not succeed in preventing American independence; nor did it prevent him from recognizing it as an act of providence, once it was attained.[26] But it did sorely embarrass his American Methodists and compromise their situation in the midst of their neighbors, most of whom whole-heartedly supported the Revolution.

Wesley did not live long enough to participate in the controversy which arose in England over the French Revolution, but we can imagine which side he would have taken. His detestation of its "Republicanism" would have been aggravated by the deistic, or even atheistic, doctrines which accompanied its later stages. In any case, he heartily rejected the Republicanism which was in the air in both America and France during the second half of the century. Certainly he regarded such doctrines as bad when applied to the government of the societies he had created. It was while justifying his refusal to allow the people any voice in choosing their stewards and class leaders that he said "We are no republicans, and never intend to be."[27] In 1789, he wrote in the *Arminian Magazine*: I am convinced a republic spirit is injurious to religion among Methodists, as I find most fallen Methodists (and perhaps some who are not fallen) are Republicans.[28]

The claim has been made (by non-Methodist as well as Methodist historians)[29] that Methodism saved England from a French Revolution. Such a claim cannot, by its very nature, admit verification. The inclination at present is to think that England would not have had such a revolution even though Wesley had never lived. It has been

---

[26] In 1784 he described it as "that liberty wherewith God has so strangely made them free" (WJL, VII, 239).

[27] WJL, VIII, 196 (Jan. 13, 1790).

[28] EJW, p. 93.

[29] Among the non-Methodist historians who have taken this position are Elie Halévy, the French writer on English history, and the rather rationalistically inclined Lecky.

45

pointed out, for instance, that England had already had her revolution—the bloodless one of 1688—in which despotism had been successfully overthrown. In spite of the fact that some Englishmen welcomed the revolutionary ideas from France, and some Jacobin clubs were formed, on the whole the reverberations in England were not very great. Though it is true that Methodism had many more adherents than it had names on its membership rolls, yet we must remember that they numbered fewer than 75,000 members at the time of Wesley's death. It hardly seems possible that so small a body of humble people could have swayed the destiny of the nation in such dramatic fashion. Indeed it has been said that it was a characteristically English resistance to Jacobin ideas which helped the growth of Methodism along, rather than *vice versa*.[30] Leaving this interesting but rather futile speculation on one side, however, we cannot but recognize (as did King George III himself) that the influence of Wesley's teaching was always upon the side of loyalty to the Crown and Constitution. It could not but have a stabilizing effect on the public mind in the disturbed days around the turn of the century. The conservative tendency of the conference increased, if anything, after Wesley's death. Still, as Mr. Edwards points out,[31] such was not the ultimate effect of Wesley's influence upon his followers. His religious message gave men a sense of their own worth based on considerations quite different from their immediate political and economic situation. It gave them the patience to wait for changes in it till they could be peaceably accomplished. It gave them practice in thinking seriously and speaking in public. In other words, it prepared them for participation in the political arena as Christian men, content when the opportunity presented itself, to use Christian means to secure their political and economic rights. Thus Wesley's teaching had by-results in the democratization of England which he did not foresee, and which, could he have foreseen them, he might even have deplored.

7. WESLEY THE REFORMER

At the outset of our consideration of Wesley as a reformer, let us recall that early conference statement which declared the purpose of

[30] G. M. Trevelyan, *op. cit.*, p. 494.
[31] EJW, p. 52.

46

the Methodists to be to reform the church and the nation, and to spread scriptural holiness throughout the land. We should be aware of what was, and what was not, involved in Wesley's conception of reform. This will prevent us from blaming him for not hitting a mark at which he did not aim. We have raised our sights since his time to include reforming evil *institutions* and we unhesitatingly resort to legislation to that end. Only in a very minor degree did Wesley include either policy. He found most of the meaning of reform to consist in the spread of scriptural holiness. That is, in more concrete terms, he did denounce certain specific evils, and he sought first of all to develop scruples in his converts against participating in them. In this sense, his strategy of reform was to multiply the number of people with such consciences. Beyond this, where transformations in "the world" could be made, they were to be made by men on fire with a vision of a holy life; that is, by the loving activity of the saints in the world.

Wesley's ideal in this respect strikes us as vastly better than that of the one organized attempt at reform which has come to our attention from just before his day. It was projected by one of the specialized offshoots of the religious societies, known as the "Society for the Reformation of Manners." The main reliance of the society is indicated in a pamphlet account of its activities by Josiah Woodward. The first place in the pamphlet is given to a royal proclamation promising to promote officers who by observance and enforcement discourage vice, and threatening to degrade or remove the others. It charged the magistrates

to be very strict in the discovery and the effectual prosecution of . . . persons guilty of excessive drinking, blasphemy, prophane swearing and cursing, lewdness, and prophanation of the Lord's Day.

Some of the results were described as follows:

A multitude of Drunkards and prophaners of the Lord's Day . . . have been made examples of . . . hundreds of Disorderly houses . . . have been rooted out and suppressed; some thousands of Lewd persons have been Imprisoned, Fined and Whipt, so that . . . our streets have been much purged of that pestilent generation of night-walkers that used to infest them.[32]

[32] Josiah Woodward, *An Account of the Societies for the Reformation of Manners* (London: 1699), p. 22.

All this was repressive enough, but still worse was the denunciation by paid informers. This obnoxious feature of the operation, together with the noticeable absence of any positive ideal, doomed the movement to an early decline. Compared with the society's methods, Wesley's reliance on planting an ideal of holiness in the hearts of men seems infinitely preferable.[33]

The most striking example of the strengths and limitations of Wesley's concept is furnished by his attitude toward prisoners and prisons. Since his Oxford days, he had spent much time in relieving both the physical and spiritual needs of prisoners. A moving instance of his work in relieving the sufferings of French prisoners of war comes from 1759:

> I walked up to Knowle, a mile from Bristol, to see the French prisoners. Above eleven hundred of them, we were informed, were confined in that little place without anything to lie on but a little dirty straw, or anything to cover them but a few foul, thin rags, either by day or night, so that they died like rotten sheep. I was much affected, and preached in the evening on Exod. xxiii. 9, "Thou shalt not oppress a stranger . . ." Eighteen pounds were contributed immediately, which were made up four-and-twenty the next day. With this we bought linen and woollen cloth, which were made up into shirts, waist-coats, and breeches. Some dozens of stockings were added; all of which were carefully distributed where there was the greatest want. Presently after, the Corporation of Bristol sent a large quantity of mattresses and blankets; and it was not long before contributions were set on foot at London, and in various parts of the kingdom, so that I believe from this time they were pretty well provided with all the necessaries of life.[34]

He was not unacquainted with the appalling conditions prevalent in the prison system of the time, for he had been preaching in prisons since his Oxford days. Doubtless he was aware, as any man

---

[33] In 1763 Wesley preached a sermon before the Society for the Reformation of Manners (Wesley, Works, I, 457 ff), in which he highly commended their work and praised its results. He denied that the informers shared in the fines levied on those they denounced. But it is noteworthy that he included a long section on the spirit in which its work should be carried on. Characteristic sentences are: "It is highly expedient that all engaged therein have 'the love of God shed abroad in their hearts.'" They should act also on "the love of . . . neighbor," which produces humility (p. 465). "Your manner of speaking . . . to offenders, should at all times be deeply serious . . . showing that you pity them for what they do, and sympathize with them in what they suffer." (P. 467.)
[34] WJJ, IV, 355-56.

of his wide interests would have been, of the ferocious code for punishment of offenders, especially poor ones. Yet both he and Charles, though they spent much time preaching to those "fast bound in misery and iron," seem not to have spoken a word in criticism of the system. We know that John greatly admired the work of the independent philanthropist, John Howard, who was, for a time, high sheriff of Bedfordshire and who spent most of his adult life investigating prison conditions and obtained some ameliorative legislation by means of appeals to Parliament.[35] The Wesleys showed infinite concern to save the souls of those condemned to die on the gallows, but apparently they never asked whether they should have been condemned in the first place. Wesley was aware of how pressing was the need for changes in the administration of the prisons. But it is characteristic of his whole attitude toward the matter that he apparently relied for securing them on the conversion of the jailers. At least the most striking reference to progress in that direction comes in connection with his description of the changes wrought in Bristol's Newgate by its chief jailer, Abel Dagge, who had been converted under Whitefield's ministry. He described how, where filth and brawling and the promiscuous mixing of men and women had prevailed, all was now sobriety, cleanliness, and order, and the men and women were kept apart.[36] His description closes with an appeal: "Meantime, will no one follow his example?"

It has recently been pointed out [37] that John Wesley not only was interested in social and economic problems, but at one point at least recommended government action. This willingness reaches its clearest expression in the little pamphlet he published in 1773 under the title "Thoughts upon the Present Scarcity of Provisions." In it he recommends, as a measure for lowering the high price of wheat, "prohibiting forever that destroyer of strength, of life, of virtue, distilling." To lower the price of oats he proposes "laying a tax of ten pounds on every horse exported to France," and "laying an additional tax on gentlemen's carriages." His remedy for the high price of pork and poultry was "repressing luxury either by example, by laws, or both."

---

[35] See Bready, *England before and after Wesley* (New York: Harper and Brothers, 1938), pp. 355 ff., and WJJ, VII, 295.

[36] WJJ, IV, 427-28; 416-17.

[37] Robert M. Kingdon, "Laissez-faire or Government Controls: a Problem for John Wesley," *Church History*, XXVI (1957), No. 4 (December), 342-54.

49

Here Wesley appeals to the taxing power of the government, and to what would be called sumptuary legislation for the achievement of social ends. Both these kinds of action were obviously within the sphere of Parliament. If his appeal to legislative intervention was not as explicit or as persistent as we might like, at least it was not wholly absent.[38]

Wesley was reluctant to turn to Parliament even in the matter of slavery. In his "Thoughts upon Slavery," he protested on the one hand that the laws permitting it did not make slavery right and just; but in making his appeal he passed over the English nation as a whole and Parliament, to address directly the captains of slaving ships, the dealers in slaves, and the slaveowners themselves. His reluctance was in this instance based on despair of ever moving Parliament to action. His strategy was to appeal to the individual conscience of the participants. In 1784 Wesley again turned to the prohibition of distilling. This time he did so by writing a private letter to William Pitt, then First Lord of the Treasury, asking him to use his influence toward having it made a felony.[39]

All this is by way of saying that Wesley was first of all an evangelist, and only secondarily a reformer; or perhaps it would be better to say that in so far as he was a reformer he relied mainly on evangelism and the appeal to individual conscience as a method. He did not employ the methods used by subsequent reformers, because they had not yet been invented, so to speak. It was only later that Wilberforce, while leading the antislavery fight, adopted for the first time voluntary associations, mass meetings, petitions, and the other devices for appealing to popular opinion and influencing legislatures which have since become commonplace in the presentation of reforms.[40] But having said all this, the way is open to appreciate how quick Wesley was to perceive some of the social plagues of the eighteenth century for what they were, how vigorous he was in denouncing them, and how insistent he was that his Methodists avoid participation in them.

[38] Kingdon notices (*Ibid.*, pp. 345-46) that the original form of this treatise, a letter to *Lloyd's Evening Post* (published Dec. 29, 1772) concludes with this sentence: "How this can be done the wisdom of the great council of the land can best determine"; but the treatise form is less hopeful in its ending: "Will this ever be done? I fear not. . . . It seems as if God must . . . arise and maintain his own cause." (Wesley, *Works*, VI, 278.)

[39] WJL, VII, 236.

[40] Trevelyan, *op. cit.*, pp. 496-97.

a) *Distilled Liquors*

In an age when distilled liquor was regarded as an indispensable adjunct of social life, and drunkenness hardly regarded as a matter of reproach, in either high circles or low, Wesley perceived liquor to be a destroyer of body and soul, one of the plagues of the national life. Distillers he called "poisoners-general." In his remarkable treatise called "Thoughts on the Present Scarcity of Provisions," he observed that the grain which should go to feed the hungry was being turned into this poison instead, and urged that here lay reasons the poor were unable to buy needful sustenance at a reasonable rate. In an age when distilled liquor was regarded as an essential part of the pharmacopoeia, he asserted that it would not often be resorted to "were it not for the unskillfulness of the practitioner." The distillers

murder his Majesty's subjects by wholesale, neither does their eye pity or snare. They drive them to hell like sheep: and what is their gain? Is it not the blood of these men? Who then would envy their large estates and sumptuous palaces? A curse is in the midst of them: the curse of God cleaves to the stones, the timber, the furniture of them . . . Oh thou man of blood . . . there is a God in heaven: therefore, thy name shall soon be rooted out. Like as those whom thou hast destroyed, body and soul, "thy memorial shall perish with thee." [41]

Methodists, then, should not make a living by distilling, for it was carried on only at the expense of their neighbors' bodies. They were not even to drink liquor, for one of the General Rules forbade "drunkenness, buying or selling spirituous liquors; or drinking them (unless in cases of extreme necessity)." [42] The breadth of Wesley's base of attack on the evils of drink is admirable. He brought to bear economic considerations of a highly social sort in his observations as to the effect of the liquor traffic on the nourishment of the poor. He was one of the pioneers in adducing scientific observations on the physiological effects of alcohol on the human body, in that he brushed aside the prevalent superstitions about its "benefits" to label it truly as a poison. But religious and moral considerations were probably the most influential thrust of his attack, because they would carry weight with more people. What mattered most with the people with

[41] Wesley, *Works*, I, 443.
[42] John S. Simon, *John Wesley and the Methodist Societies*, p. 101.

whom Wesley had influence was that they were told that drunkenness, and even the moderate use of liquors as a beverage, was not only a wrong against oneself and one's neighbor, but also a sin against God!

The extent of Wesley's influence in this matter cannot be precisely determined. There were other causes, such as increased taxes, at work in the notable diminution in the consumption of spirits around the middle of the century. But we cannot help thinking that it was more than a coincidence that the decline in the consumption of spirits coincided in time with the expansion of the Methodist Societies.[43]

b) Slavery

Another evil Wesley furiously attacked was slavery. It was a deep-rooted evil, not because there were many slaves in England, but because huge sums were being made by snatching Africans from their homes and shipping them to work in the Colonies across the Atlantic. Wesley depicts in lurid colors the suffering and indignity inflicted on the innocent Africans to satisfy the greed of men. He denied that it was necessary in the economic operation of the Colonies. Even if it were, he insisted, prosperity purchased at such a price was an offense against God. Already the issue was a divisive one among Methodists, for Whitefield, though he was stirred to wrath at the mistreatment of slaves, nevertheless when the welfare of his orphan-house in Georgia was at stake, did not scruple to purchase some fifty slaves to work for its support—and this in spite of the fact that their use in

[43] Perhaps Bready ascribes too much influence to the Evangelicals in bringing the "Gin Age" to an end when he says: "Not till 1751 when the vehement temperance teaching of the Evangelical Revival had already been heard throughout the land, and when groups of converts in every considerable community were committed to total abstinence, was Law of any avail. In that year the famous Act passed by the Pelham Government . . . marked the legislative beginning of Britain's emancipation from the thraldom of the liquor traffic" (England before and after Wesley, p. 150). After all, the revival had been going only about a dozen years, and was still small in numbers, and as yet in influence on social trends. Still, quite apart from the end of the "Gin Age," the presence in England of a growing body of people who were convinced that the trade in and consumption of spirits were harmful and sinful created a climate of opinion in which the grip of the liquor traffic on economic life and the grip of the drink habit on the lives of Englishmen could be loosened, if not wholly broken. It should be noted that the "total abstinence" mentioned above refers only to abstinence from spirituous liquors. Wesley himself did not extend the principle to all fermented beverages such as beer and wine. In 1789 he waged a short letter-writing campaign against the use of beer, not because it was fermented, but because it was made with hops, which he regarded as poisonous! WJL, VIII, 165, 172, 182. "Teetotalism" was a nineteenth-century development.

the Colony had originally been forbidden by the Trustees. Wesley, however, entered the lists among the first, though some others had preceded him. The Quakers had resolved in 1761 to disown all members who engaged in the traffic. In the Church of England, Bishop Warburton had deplored its existence and the dissenter Richard Baxter had also taken a stand against it.[44]

Wesley's "Thoughts upon Slavery" was written in 1774; he preached on it in 1788 in the city of Bristol, central stronghold of slave-traders.[45] The last letter he ever wrote, and one of the noblest, was the famous one supposed to have been addressed to William Wilberforce, in which he laid his hands in blessing, as it were, on the man who was to lead the fight to a successful conclusion. It contained these words: "Go on, in the name of God and in the power of His might, till even American slavery (the vilest that ever saw the sun) shall vanish away before it." [46] The first Conference after Wesley's death requested the Methodists to add their signatures to petitions against slavery. Some 350,000 signatures were obtained in all, though somewhat over a third of them came from other non-conforming bodies.[47] Wilberforce sadly acknowledged that he got little support from the "high and dry" Anglican clergy for his cause,[48] but the Methodists were among his strongest supporters.[49] The Methodists were quicker to join forces with dissenting liberalism in the cause of the slaves than they were in other political movements.

c) War

Wesley had no first-hand experience of war. Though England was at war through much of his lifetime, with France as her chief enemy, most of the fighting was done on the Continent. Of the two attempts to put Stuart Pretenders on the throne, the 1715 one occurred while Wesley was still a lad of twelve, and the one in 1745 just after he had held the first Conference. The former Stuart effort was dissipated without a battle. Though the latter brought the young pretender as far south as Derby, the expected rising did not take place and no actual battle was fought south of the Scottish border. The excitement

---

[44] EJW, pp. 114-15.
[45] Ibid., p. 120.
[46] WJL, VIII, 265.
[47] EJW, pp. 124 and n.
[48] Trevelyan, op. cit., p. 495.
[49] EJW, p. 123.

of 1745 obstructed the Wesleys' work in several ways; but, on the whole, it and the wars abroad left few traces in John's writing. Perhaps the way it affected Methodism most severely was through the activities of the "press gangs" which regarded Methodists (especially the preachers) as in some sense outside the protection of the authorities, and hence as fair game in their attempt to fill up the ranks of the armed forces.[50] The Methodists thus impressed did not leave their religion behind them, but organized prayer meetings and watchnight services in garrison and camp. Wesley was proud of his followers' fidelity to their faith, and no less proud when he heard stories of their creditable performance of military duty.

He did not romanticize war. If he had no close contact with its horrors, he had read widely enough to know what it meant. He used the existence of war in the world to prove the doctrine of original sin.

I gave him a description of . . . ships sunk with a thousand men, twenty thousand killed on each side, dying groans, limbs flying in the air; smoke, noise, trampling to death under horses' feet, flight, pursuit, victory; fields strewed with carcasses, left for food to dogs and beasts of prey; and farther, of plundering, stripping, ravishing, burning and destroying . . .

Now who can reconcile war, I will not say to religion, but to any degree of reason or common sense? [51]

Wesley felt impelled at least to raise the question of the compatibility of participating in war with a Christian profession. The very first Conference, meeting just before the 1745 Stuart invasion, asked: "Is it lawful to bear arms?" We don't know how much debate there was on the question, nor what direction it took; but the answer inclined strongly to the affirmative: We incline to think it is: 1. Because there is no command against it in the New Testament; 2. Because Cornelius, a soldier, is commended there.[52]

The question may have been raised at that time because in the

---

[50] Shortly before the Young Pretender's expedition, an order was issued requiring all Roman Catholics to leave London. Absurd as it seems to us, the Methodists were suspected of being Catholics—and hence subversives. Wesley felt it incumbent upon him to avoid giving color to these suspicions by leaving the capital just as the Catholic exodus was taking place. So he reluctantly gave up a trip he had long planned just at that time.

[51] "The Doctrine of Original Sin," Wesley, Works, V, 512, 511.

[52] The Bennett Minutes of the first Conference (1744), quoted from R. M. Cameron, The Rise of Methodism, p. 360.

preceding spring, John Nelson, the one conscientious objector of whom we read in early English Methodism, had refused to bear arms when impressed for the army. After he had been impressed, he answered a court martial at York:

I shall not fight; for I cannot bow my knee before the Lord, to pray for a man and get up and kill him when I have done: for I know God both hears me speak and sees me act; and I should expect the lot of the hypocrite, if my actions contradict my prayers.[53]

He steadily maintained his position, but in such a way as to gain the respect of his fellow-soldiers; before long he was released at the intercession of an Earl. But he went back to preaching and had worse treatment there: at Ackham, he was knocked down so often he could no longer rise, then dragged along the street by the hair of his head, with half-a-dozen or so trampling upon him "to tread the Holy Ghost out of him." But as one of his assailants said, "We cannot kill him." The next morning he reported:

I was not so sore as I had expected, for I set out for Mr. Wesley [whom the mob had threatened to kill if he appeared there to preach, and who needed warning] and was enabled to ride forty miles that day.[54]

d) Other Abuses

As Wesley traveled up and down the country, in close contact with the people of all parts, he noted many other evils which he straightforwardly denounced, and stringently forbade his Methodists to participate in. One of these was smuggling, an activity so common as to be taken almost as a matter of course. Trevelyan instances the way Parson Woodforde, respectable clergyman that he was, speaks about "Andrews the smuggler" bringing him six pounds of tea late at night, just as he would have spoken of "Andrews the grocer" doing the same thing in broad daylight.[55] Wesley denounced smuggling as robbing the King,[56] and put it among the evils forbidden in the General Rules. Smuggling was especially prevalent in the Southwest of Eng-

---

[53] Extract from the Journal of John Nelson . . . to which is Added an Account of his Death (16th ed., New York: Carlton and Porter, 1856), pp. 124-25.

[54] Ibid., p. 188.

[55] Op. cit., p. 387.

[56] "A Word to a Smuggler," Wesley, Works, VI, 359 ff.

land, particularly in Cornwall. As Methodism gained a foothold there, a conscience on the subject was developed which abated the practice as the laws had not been able to do for generations.

An abuse attending elections then as now was the purchase of votes. If we can regard the second picture in Hogarth's "Election" series as typical, it was done a good deal more brazenly and in the open then than now. Wesley wrote "A Word to a Freeholder," [57] in protest against this form of political dishonesty. It is the duty, he said, of the Christian to vote for the man who loves God and the King, but first and foremost, not to have perjured himself by having received a gift, or the promise of one.

Wesley, not being a "freeholder," did not qualify as a voter, but he regarded it as a matter of conscience that every one who had that vote should exercise it honestly. The less explicit dishonesties of the representational system, with its "pocket boroughs," evoked a much feebler protest from Wesley. He did, in passing, mention the two most scandalous cases: Old Sarum, without house or inhabitant, with two Members; and the small town of Looe, with four. But this was the government's doing, and Wesley's steady loyalty seems to have stood in the way of his making a protest which would seem to us commensurate with the gravity of the abuse.

His protest against enclosure was of the same sort—brief and oblique. It comes in the "Thoughts upon the Present Scarcity," where he speaks of "the monopolizing of farms" as "perhaps as mischievous a monopoly as was ever introduced into these kingdoms." [58] But this brief protest was made without any mention of the rights or wrongs of the methods by which it was accomplished, or of the principles on which it was based; he deplored it simply because of its effects on the price of pork, poultry, and eggs. This is creditable as an instance of Wesley's solicitude for the difficulty the poor were having in getting enough to eat; but it evinces no great awareness of the deeper social problem involved in the acts of enclosure which were then being so freely passed by Parliament.[59] Dr. Warner concurs in this judgment. He says: "With his keen sense of justice it is admittedly

[57] Wesley, *Works*, VI, 372 ff.
[58] Wesley, *Works*, VI, 276.
[59] Bishop McConnell in his *John Wesley* (New York, The Abingdon Press, 1939, p. 251) says: "I think the boldest step, socially speaking, Wesley ever took was his denunciation of enclosures." He is referring to this paragraph in the "Thoughts on

surprising that Wesley did not adopt a more definite stand on the issue of enclosures." [60]

In 1764 Wesley wrote to the Mayor and Corporation of Bristol urging with deferential persistance that they refuse the request of one who wanted to build a new theater in that city. He gave reasons both moral and economic for his stand.

Most of the present stage entertainments sap the foundation of all religion, . . . they naturally tend to efface all traces of piety and seriousness out of the minds of men . . . they are peculiarly hurtful to a trading city, giving a wrong turn to youth especially, gay, trifling, and directly opposite to the spirit of industry and close application to business; and drinking and debauchery of every kind are constant attendants on these entertainments, with indolence, effeminacy, and idleness, which affect trade in a high degree.[61]

Here speaks the Pietistic suspicion of gaiety and trifling, even when the time is not spent in positively wicked ways. It is of a piece with Wesley's frowning on play for children,[62] with his injunction to the preachers to abstain from "all lightness, jesting, and foolish talking," [63] and with the Rule for the Band Societies which required the members to use every vacant hour in study of the Scriptures.[64] In addressing the municipal authorities of Bristol, Wesley also represents gaiety and trifling as the enemy of devotion to business.

In addition to this, of course, he presents the real moral and religious dangers of the eighteenth-century theater. He regarded the plays themselves as destructive of religion. There may be room for disagreement on the plays themselves; but on the fact that the theater attracted immoral persons, we have confirmation from other sources. The magistrate Sir John Hawkins inquired (1787): "How . . . comes

---

Scarcity," as the context makes clear. He gives no specific references; so I cannot tell whether the Bishop had discovered other stronger instances or not. If they exist, I have never come across them, and it seems that McConnell's judgment rates too highly the significance of this one paragraph.

[60] WIR, p. 107.

[61] WJL, IV, 279.

[62] Wesley, Works, VII, 339.

[63] Ibid., V, 219. The first form of this rule enjoined the assistants to avoid "laughing as you would cursing and swearing" (in the Bennett Minutes of the first Conference; see R. M. Cameron, op. cit., p. 356), but this extreme injunction was later modified to read as above.

[64] Luke Tyerman, The Life and Times of the Rev. John Wesley, M. A. (3 vols. New York: Harper & Brothers, 1872) I, 464.

it about that no sooner is a playhouse opened in any part of the kingdom, than it at once becomes surrounded by a halo of brothels?"[65]

Even by today's standards, the playwriting of eighteenth-century England was of low quality. Not much of it is still produced. Sheridan's *School for Scandal* and Goldsmith's *She Stoops to Conquer* are the chief survivors, and they were hardly of the high seriousness Wesley would have approved. On the whole, it may be said that the dramatic art in England had not yet recovered from the excesses of the Restoration period, and that those who, at Wesley's behest, stayed away from the theater did not lose much. Still some of his followers have carried their antipathy to greater lengths than he himself would have done. One of his preachers, John Pawson, out of mistaken anxiety for Wesley's reputation, saw to it that his dead leader's copy of Shakespeare, with notes in Wesley's handwriting, was destroyed.

8. Methodist Philanthropy

It is difficult to find a proper name for the work on behalf of the unfortunate which bulked so large in the life of the early Methodist societies. "Philanthropy" would call to mind the fact that activities for the relief of the distressed were being performed in England before the Methodists came into existence. But it leaves out of account the consideration that the Methodists' work was done in a pre-eminent degree "as unto God." "Christian charity" might be better, but that expression, too, has acquired a connotation of coldness far removed from the spirit in which Methodist work for the unfortunate was carried on.

That spirit sprang from John Wesley's acute observation, quite unusual for that time, that poverty was not the result of some defect in character, or some delinquency which removed the poor man from any claim on the sympathy of those who were better off. In 1753, Wesley told of visiting many poor in garrets and cellars who were

half-starved both with cold and hunger, added to weakness and pain. But I found not one of them unemployed who was able to crawl about the room. So wickedly, devilishly false is that common objection, "They are poor only because they are idle." [66]

---

[65] See J. W. Bready, *op. cit.*, pp. 164-65 and notes.
[66] WJJ, IV, 52. The contrary opinion was held and widely disseminated by Daniel Defoe in his *Giving Alms No Charity* (1704). Wesley was ready enough to believe that public disasters, earthquakes for instance, were punishment for collective sins. But he did not extend this kind of judgment to the economic misfortunes of individuals.

Consequently Wesley insisted that works of mercy be performed not in a spirit of disdain, but with a warm personal concern best expressed in James Russell Lowell's "The gift without the giver is bare." Wesley taught his followers that it was much better "to carry relief to the poor than to *send* it." [67] Even when one is unable to give of his substance, he should refuse without any roughness, only with loving words and looks.[68]

At the bottom of the very considerable charitable outlay of Wesley and his poor Methodists for the needs of others was a conviction that what was done was no cause for glorying, but simply something one owed to God and his needy children. Everything over and above the barest personal necessities *belonged* to them. Wesley later reported of himself at the beginning of his career:

> One . . . had thirty pounds a year. He lived on twenty-eight, and gave away forty shillings. The next year, receiving sixty pounds, he still lived on twenty-eight, and gave away thirty-two. The third year he received ninety pounds, and gave away sixty-two. The fourth year he received a hundred and twenty pounds; still he lived as before on twenty-eight, and gave to the poor all the rest.[69]

At the very end, with a sigh, he gave up accounting for every penny that passed through his hands, and wrote:

> For upwards of eighty-six years [sixty-six would have been more accurate!] I have kept my accounts exactly. I will not attempt it any longer, being satisfied with the continual conviction that I save all I can and give all I can; that is, all I have.[70]

Having given all he could of his own substance, he was not ashamed to beg from others to meet the need which continually pressed upon his heart. This picture is typical, from a time when Wesley was already an old man:

> At this season [January] we usually distribute coals and bread among the poor of the society. But I now considered they wanted clothes as well as food. So on this and the four following days I walked through the town

[67] WJJ, IV, 422.
[68] *Ibid.*, III, 301.
[69] Tyerman, *op. cit.*, I, 71-72.
[70] Quoted in Eric M. North, *Early Methodist Philanthropy* (submitted in partial fulfillment of the requirements for the degree of Doctor of Philosophy, Columbia University, New York, 1914), p. 123.

and begged two hundred pounds, in order to clothe them that needed it most. But it was hard work, as most of the streets were filled with melting snow, which often lay ankle deep; so that my feet were steeped in snow-water nearly from morning till evening. I held out pretty well till Saturday evening.[71]

Henry Moore, with Wesley's account books before him, estimated that he gave away in fifty years considerably more than thirty thousand pounds.[72] Dr. Bebb, from the account book of the London Societies, concludes that in a period of twenty years (between 1770 and 1790), the London Methodists gave away to the poor some fifteen thousand pounds—a remarkable figure when the poverty of most of the members is taken into account.[73]

a) *Opportunities for Self-Help*

Any account of Methodist philanthropy during Wesley's lifetime must include the founding of two institutions designed to help the poor to help themselves. The first was an employment scheme which involved putting women to work in the Society Room in London during the winter months of 1740. They were taught the carding and spinning of cotton, and were able to produce almost enough to pay for the experiment.[74] The following May, the plan was expanded to include employing at knitting women who had no work and wished it. This was but a part of a larger scheme of relief, which included supplementing what they could earn from stores of goods or money collected for the purpose.[75] How many this helped, or how long it lasted, we do not know. No further mention of it occurs in the *Journal*.

Tyerman reports a slanderous misrepresentation of the scheme in the *Scots Magazine* for August 1741, in which the workers were said to be runaway girls and neglectful servants, together with boys. There was mention of several bedchambers next to the spinning room. Wesley was said to be pocketing their surplus earnings. A man interested to test these assertions visited the Foundery and reported that he found neither bedchambers nor spinning wheels and conse-

---

[71] WJJ, VII, 42-43. This was in 1785, when Wesley was over eighty.

[72] E. M. North, *op. cit.*, p. 122.

[73] E. D. Bebb, *Nonconformity and Social and Economic Life, 1600-1800* (London: The Epworth Press, 1935), p. 143.

[74] WJJ, II, 403-4.

[75] *Ibid.*, 453-54.

quently no runaways or discharged servants.[76] Presumably, then, the experiment had been discontinued by this time, possibly as a result of the scandalous article.

More successful than the work scheme was the loan fund. Wesley had a horror of the hold moneylenders were too often able to lay on the poor who came to them in desperation at some sudden emergency with some of their goods to pawn. As an alternative he set up a fund in London to which Methodists might apply under those circumstances. Set up in 1746, the fund stood a long time at twenty pounds. It was loaned out at first in sums not exceeding twenty shillings, to be repaid weekly over a period of three months. There is no mention of interest. Twenty years later, the fund was increased to one hundred twenty pounds, and the maximum amount which might be lent was raised to five pounds.[77] We read of one man at least, who with his five pounds borrowed from this fund and with native business ability made a financial success of a bookselling business.[78] Neither the work program nor the lending stock was a large enterprise; nor were they unique in Wesley's organization.[79] However, they do testify to his willingness to embark on schemes to help the poor help themselves, rather than resting content with gathering and dispensing alms.

b) Health

Wesley had great interest in physical health, perhaps partly because his own health was not very robust. He was deeply concerned because the physicians of the day charged such high fees for consultation and prescribed such expensive remedies, that the poor were unable to get any benefit from them. Wesley's contribution to the solution of this problem took two forms.

The first was his publication of a book called *Primitive Physick; or an Easy and Natural Method of Curing Most Diseases*. First published in 1747, it went through twenty-three editions in Wesley's own lifetime, and was last published as late as 1828.[80] Some of the remedies prescribed in it, and with the greatest confidence too, seem to us to be weird at best, and at worst even hazardous. But compared

---

[76] Tyerman, op. cit., I, 357

[77] WJJ, III, 246, 329; V, 194. Wesley, Works, V, 189.

[78] E. M. North, op. cit., p. 70.

[79] E. B. Bebb, op. cit., p. 136: "Like so many others, he tried his hand at providing employment . . . and he also . . . started a loan society."

[80] North, op. cit., p. 43.

with the prescriptions of the established physicians of the time, they were mild, and at any rate had the merit of cheapness.

The other contribution was the establishment of a free dispensary for the poor, the first in London. Whether the others which were established there soon after were stimulated by Wesley's initiative, we have no way of knowing. But the fact remains that in this field of endeavor, Wesley took the lead in London. He was impelled by the great demand on the dispensary in London to establish another in Bristol. The London dispensary had finally to be abandoned because it was too expensive, and the fate of the one in Bristol is obscure. One good feature of the treatments given was the strict regimen and wholesome habits which Wesley insisted his patients undertake. These were, indeed, for the most part, in line with what has since been learned about the benefits of such devices as simplicity of diet, fresh air, and regular exercises.[81]

c) *Visiting Societies*

Dr. North expressed the opinion that the most important contribution the Methodists made in the matter of organized philanthropy was the visiting societies.[82] As with so many of Wesley's devices, this grew up because Wesley's personal efforts were soon exceeded by the demand made upon them. When this happened in London in 1741, he called for volunteers, who offered themselves in sufficient numbers to make it possible to establish a regular method of visitation.[83] One of the special developments along this line was the Strangers' Friend Societies. These came rather late, and owed their origin to a layman in London by the name of John Gardner. The inevitable "penny a week" was to be carried on the Sabbath to one who must be "a poor stranger having no parish or friend . . . to help them." Wesley approved the venture, and a similar society was established the next year (1786) at Bristol.

The question has been asked whether most of the Methodist philanthropy was not directed toward members of their own societies. It is difficult to tell. Certainly much of it was, and it would have been

---

[81] *Ibid.*, pp. 42-43, 119.

[82] *Ibid.*, p. 119.

[83] WJJ, II, 448. The visitors had a set of rules; and Wesley preached a sermon, "On Visiting the Sick." (*Works*, II, 329 ff.) The characteristic sentence in it as to method was: "Having shown that you have a regard for their bodies, you may proceed to inquire concerning their souls" (p. 332).

strange indeed had it not been so. But we know that one of the objections Wesley raised against the Moravians' benevolent institutions was just that they confined their ministrations too strictly to their own membership. Certainly the Strangers' Friend Societies were specifically for the aid of non-Methodists. Meanwhile the boundaries of the Methodist membership were expanding rapidly those days, and in many instances those who, originally outside, were the beneficiaries of this loving solicitude soon found themselves in a society. So the question has little more than academic interest.

d) Homes and Schools

Not so original as the institutions we have just been describing, but useful nevertheless, were the orphanages, the poorhouses, and the schools maintained by the early Methodists. There was a poorhouse for a time in London. While it was occupied chiefly by infirm elderly people, there were also several preachers; and Wesley assured the readers of his "Plain Account of the People Called Methodists" that when he was in town he shared the fare of these poor people at their table. This was later given up for want of support.[84]

There was an "Orphan House" at Newcastle; and Whitefield maintained one with considerable trouble at Savannah in Georgia. Wesley had greatly admired the Moravian orphanage he saw on his visit to Germany just after his conversion; and probably he modeled the institution at Newcastle on it, as well as taking over the name.

Of the schools at London, Newcastle, and Kingswood, the last named was the best known. It was begun by Whitefield for the miners' children of that neglected area; but the management of it soon fell on Wesley's shoulders. He shaped it too on the Moravian model, which seems to us unfortunate, for the model was a harsh one. The youngsters were treated as small adults as to both their intellectual and their religious training. Nevertheless it furnished education gratis for a number of children who would otherwise have gone without it altogether.

We cannot leave the subject of education without at least indicating the importance of the Methodist movement in the advance of education as a whole. Much of it was what we would today call "adult education," and came about as a result of the intellectual stimulus

---

[84] Wesley, *Works*, V, 188.

imparted to the thousands of people who joined the movement. They had first of all to read the Bible. Then there was the ceaseless flow of treatises and sermons from the pen of John Wesley, to say nothing of the hymns of Charles. Perhaps John's most significant contribution was his "Christian Library," which has been called "the first Five-foot Shelf" of books. Wesley regarded it as one of his functions to be "a gatherer and scatterer of useful knowledge," and the Christian Library was a considerable aid in this direction. It consisted of abridgements of a number of works of edification, history, and so forth, that Wesley thought it worth while for his people to read. Such emphasis on stretching the mental faculties of these common folk doubtless did a great deal to create the demand which was more formally satisfied very much later by the creation of free public schools.

e) Sunday Schools

The Sunday-school movement as such was conceived and promoted by an Anglican newspaper publisher, Robert Raikes, of Gloucester, about 1780. The name in the United States (until it was superseded by "church schools") meant sessions in close connection with the churches' Sunday meetings for worship and to be devoted altogether to religious instruction. But in the eighteenth century, though religious instruction was of course given, the primary purpose was to instruct the children of the poor in the "three R's" on the only day they were free from work; that is, on Sunday. Of course good use was made of catechisms in the instruction. Over a decade earlier than Raikes, a Miss Hannah Ball, of High Wycombe, had started a Sunday school of her own, under Methodist auspices. In 1770, she wrote Wesley:

The children meet twice a week, every Sunday and Monday. They are a wild little company, but seem willing to be instructed. I labour among them, earnestly desiring to promote the interest of the church of Christ.[85]

In his later travels, Wesley came across Sunday schools in increasing numbers, and records his approval of the singing of some, and the cleanliness of others. Probably because of his age, however, and the multitude of other cares, his interest in them never got very far be-

[85] North, *op. cit.*, p. 104.

yond general approval. As he grew older, his delight in the company of children increased, but his contribution to the education of the young was pretty well comprised in the schools he had founded early in his career.

As we try by way of summary to estimate the place of philanthropy in the Methodist movement and its contribution to society, we come to the conclusion that it was tremendously successful in generating a new and vigorous spirit of concern for the needy, which expressed itself in surprisingly liberal giving by even the poor Methodists for people needier than themselves. The resources for it became available because of Wesley's constant insistence on stewardship; but more remarkable than the amounts given was the spirit in which the giving was carried on. It was a spirit of sharing far different from the condescending "hand-outs" of perfunctory institutions. Wesley's wide-ranging concern embraced the needs of the poor, the unwell, the aged, the unemployed, the orphans, and so widened the mental horizon of his people. The establishment of institutions to take care of these problems is an indication of his concern. But it is evident that such activity was merely on the fringes of his main concern, which was evangelism; indeed it could not have been anywhere else. The institutions once begun were not always continued, because Wesley himself didn't have time to supervise them and beg for them. Apparently, in these circumstances, contributions stopped coming, or able personnel was not available, or both. On the institutional side of its philanthropy, the contribution of Methodism was less than on the spontaneous and individual side. The most original of the Methodist organizations was the Visitors' Societies; Kingswood School was the most permanently useful of the philanthropic institutions he founded. The greatest contributions Methodism made were the generation of a spirit of concern for common people, a conviction that need ought to evoke compassion, not scorn; and the creation of a body of people who thus concerned were willing to demonstrate it in practical fashion.

9. The Wealth of Christians

Wesley was quick with compassion for the suffering of the poor he saw as he went to and fro on his gospel journeys. He wrote:

> I have known one . . . picking up from a dunghill stinking sprats, and carrying them home for herself and her children. I have known another

65

gathering bones which the dogs had left in the streets, and making broth of them to prolong a wretched life!

At the same time he noted with indignation the waste in the houses of the great, which he regarded as one of the causes of the poverty he deplored:

Only look into the kitchens of the great, the nobility and gentry, almost without exception . . . and when you have observed the amazing waste which is made there, you will no longer wonder at the scarcity.[86]

It was with pictures like these in his mind that he forbade his Methodists all waste, even all superfluity, in food, dress, and furniture. At one time, setting the example himself, he recommended that they do without tea, both as a method of improving their health and that they might have the more to give to those in need.[87] But in addition to this human compassion, or rather animating it, was a religious idea, according to which the goods at a man's disposal were not his to be used for self-gratification of any kind, but God's to be used for his glory, especially through relieving those who also were his children, the poor. Here we come upon one of the most influential of Wesley's ideas, socially speaking, in all his thinking, the idea of *stewardship*.

This teaching of his appears and reappears in many of his writings, in a hundred different ways; but we find its quintessence in his sermon "The Good Steward." [88] God has entrusted us with our souls, our bodies, and our goods. We are not at liberty to use what he has lodged in our hands as we please, but as he pleases. Of all these things, it is certain, we are only stewards.

The Lord of all will . . . inquire, "How didst thou employ the worldly goods which I lodged in thy hands? . . . In what manner didst thou employ that comprehensive talent, money?" [By] first supplying thy own reasonable wants, together with those of thy family; then restoring the remainder to me, through the poor, whom I had appointed to receive it; looking upon thyself as only one of [the] poor, whose wants were to be supplied out of that part of my substance which I had placed in thy hands for this purpose.[89]

[86] Wesley, *Works*, VI, 274, 275-76.
[87] Wesley, *Works*, VI, 568.
[88] *Ibid.*, Sermon LII, I, 448 ff.
[89] Wesley, *Works*, I, 455-56.

Thus far, the Wesleyan doctrine sounds quite Franciscan. But its further development was built on the Protestant doctrine of the calling rather than a Catholic mystical self-identification with the poor, and so turned out quite differently. Not only is it our duty to regard all we have as God's, it is likewise our duty to increase what we have in order to have the more to use in supplying the needs of others. Wesley's famous trilogy of admonitions contained not only a "Give all you can," but also a "Gain all you can and save all you can." [90]

Thus conceived, Wesley's teaching on stewardship turned out to have singular economic efficacy. The virtues of industry and frugality which he taught as inescapably Christian were also economic virtues much in demand in the business world, particularly at the time when the Industrial Revolution was gathering momentum.

In his sermon "On the Use of Money," he said:

> Use all possible diligence in your calling. Lose no time . . . "Whatsoever thy hand findeth to do, do it with all thy might." Do it as soon as possible: no delay! no putting off from day to day, or from hour to hour! Never leave anything till tomorrow which you can do today. And do it as well as possible . . . Let nothing in your business be left undone if it can be done by labour or patience.

Moreover, it is a mark of a Christian to use all one's intelligence, to be inventive in improving business methods.

> [Use] in your business all the understanding which God has given you. It is amazing . . . how few do this; how men run on in the same dull track with their forefathers. But whatever they do who know not God, this is no rule for you. It is a shame for a Christian not to improve upon *them* in whatever he takes in hand.[91]

So much for *earning* all you can. When it comes to "saving all you can," Wesley doesn't mean to encourage putting money in the bank, still less accumulating wealth which would be as bad for one's children to have as it would be to have it one's self. What Wesley meant by saving was refraining from wasteful expenditure. All expenditure

[90] Wesley, *Works*, "Thoughts upon Methodism," VII, 317.
[91] Wesley, *Works*, "Thoughts upon Methodism," I, 444.

merely to gratify the "lust of the flesh and the lust of the eyes, and the pride of life" was wasteful, and spiritually deadening. He recurs to this theme again and again, not only in his sermons on the dangers of wealth, but also, for example, in that "On Dress," which explained the General Rule against "putting on gold and costly apparel," and that "On Public Diversions," on another General Rule. Thus, by inculcating diligence and frugality, Wesley made of his Methodists "ascetics of the market place," to use a phrase which has already been applied to Calvinist men of business. The motives behind this asceticism were in the first place reasons of health; then a desire of avoiding the idleness and luxury which were enemies of the soul; and finally, to have enough to carry on a large and constant charitable activity. All these were required by God of his stewards.

We must not think that, although Wesley felt it was a Christian duty to gain as much as possible, he thought pursuit of gain was an end in itself, one which justified any and every means. Quite the contrary, just because it was part of the Christian calling, it should be pursued within the limits of the Christian standards of love, which applied to one's relations not only with the poor, but also with those with whom one dealt. Consequently Wesley hedged about his admonition to "gain all you can" with limitations designed to secure its being carried out in a Christian way. If Wesley once wrote to one of the stewards in a society, "I hope you will always be diligent in business, as one branch of the business of life," he hastened to add, "But let *this* [that is, "life"] be still uppermost in [your] thoughts." [92] No one should make his money at the risk of harming his own health, which is the same as risking life. "Whatever . . . reason or experience shows to be destructive of health or strength, that we may not submit to; seeing that 'the life is more [valuable] than meat, and the body than raiment.'" As with health of body, so with health of mind.[93] Certainly one should carefully avoid all forms of cheating and dishonesty.

Also, one is to gain all he can only without harming his neighbor. Not in his *substance*, for instance, by taking unlawful interest or by

[92] WJL, VI, 317.

[93] Wesley gives a rather surprising example of such an occupation. He says he himself could not engage in the study of mathematics "without being a deist, if not an atheist"! (*Works*, I, 442.)

selling below the market price.[94] Nor should one exact more than the real value of what he sells—that is, "the usual price of goods"— especially if his customer is in "pressing want." [95] One should not make his money by dealing in goods which harm his neighbor's body, such as spirituous liquors. And finally one should not make his money by "ministering . . . either directly or indirectly to his unchastity or intemperance . . . [Let] all . . . consider this who have anything to do with taverns, victualing houses, opera houses, play houses, or any other places of public, fashionable diversion." [96]

Thus did Wesley, even in the sermon "On the Use of Money," which was concerned primarily with enforcing the duty of gaining and saving, hedge his admonition about with limitations. His later sermons on the subject, as their titles indicate, were concerned to emphasize the limitations even more than to exhort to gain: Sermon XCII on "The Danger of Riches"; Sermon CXIII "On Riches," preached from the text "It is easier for a camel to go through the eye of a needle than for a rich man to enter the Kingdom of Heaven"; and Sermon CXXX "On the Danger of Increasing Riches." [97]

In addition to these limitations put on the acquisition of goods, Wesley's grand prescription to prevent *accumulation* was, of course, "give all you can." Enough has been said of this as the motive which impelled Wesley to urge the Methodists to gain and to save, to show how different was his ideal from that of the giants of the Industrial Revolution. It is true that he did stress those virtues of individual enterprise which were of particular utility in the industrial growth of the times. But, if some of his flock got caught up in the mammonism which was *its* driving force, it was quite contrary to Wesley's intention, and in spite of his efforts.

One other thrust of Wesley's thought on the wealth of Christians should be mentioned. It was a proposal, made in 1744, that some of the Methodists "have all things in common." It came at a period when Wesley was feeling this way and that, shaping institutions, as need arose, to embody the characteristic impulses of the revival. The master-idea of Wesley during this period seems to have been to

[94] Loc. cit.
[95] Wesley, Works, "Fifth Discourse upon the Sermon on the Mount," I, 229.
[96] Wesley, Works, I, 443-44.
[97] Wesley, Works, II, 248 ff; 396 ff; 486 ff.

bring them as nearly as possible into conformity with the primitive church. The data from Wesley himself are tantalizingly brief. They consist of seven words in the special rules set down for the select societies in the minutes of the first Conference. The third of these rules read: "Every member, *till we can have all things common*, will bring once a week, *bona fide*, all he can spare towards a common stock." [98] So far as this writer has been able to discover, Wesley never referred again to this dream of his. At any rate, four years later, three of the same rules were set down in another place, though probably for the same select societies, *without* the phrase about having all things common.[99]

We do have one further reference to this matter, in the diary of one Richard Viney, who was much in Wesley's confidence in 1744.[100] Viney reports in his diary for Feb. 22 of that year:

He [Wesley] told me of an intention he and some few have of beginning a Community of goods, but on a plan which I told him I doubted could not succeed. 'Tis this; each is to bring what cash they have and put it together. If any owe small debts, they are first to be paid. Then each abiding in their Dwellings and following their Business as they do now, are to bring weekly, what they earn and put into the common box, out of which they are again to receive weekly, as much as is thought necessary to maintain their Families, without Reflecting whether they put much or little into Ye Box.[101]

Wearmouth speaks of this as a plan for "a kind of religious communism." [102] We can accept this designation if we are careful to note its limitations. Like the primitive church's plan of which we read in Acts, it was to be a communism of consumption only, not of production; the participants were to dwell in their own homes, and *make* their money in their accustomed way, as individuals. It is a little

---

[98] From the Bennett Minutes, here quoted from R. M. Cameron, *op. cit.*, p. 355. The first words have been italicized by me.

[99] Wesley, *Works*, "A Plain Account of the People Called Methodists," V, 185.

[100] Richard Viney was a tailor, for a time a leader in the Fetter Lane Society, who later wavered between the Moravians and the Methodists, and at a still later period made some trouble for both bodies. In 1744 Wesley showed him the agenda he had drawn up for the first session of the first Conference, and asked his criticisms.

[101] R. F. Wearmouth, *Methodism and the Working Class Movements of England, 1800-1850* (London: The Epworth Press, 1937), p. 203.

[102] *Loc. cit.*

difficult to tell whom Wesley meant to include in the "we" who were to have all things common. Was it the more advanced Christians of the select societies only, or did he ultimately envisage all his Methodists in the plan? We cannot tell, nor is it worth so much attention as we have given it here, save as a tantalizing indication of a bold dream Wesley dared to entertain, one which, however, flew "forgotten as a dream dies at the opening day."

The history of Methodism around the end of the eighteenth century makes it quite clear, nevertheless, that the Methodists heeded the call to gain and save better than they obeyed the call to give. They proved themselves, in increasing measure, worthy of posts of responsibility in the service of men of property. Many of them became stewards of men with large estates.

One rather undignified but telling witness is to be found in one of the pictures in Hogarth's satirical series called "Marriage à la Mode." It shows a fashionably dressed husband come home in the morning after a night of debauchery, sunk wearily in a chair, with his stockings dangling neglected about his legs. His wife is in a tantrum on the other side of the teapot. An account book lies open on the floor by an overturned chair, and the steward, who, to judge by his sober garb, is intended to represent a Methodist, is throwing up one hand in despair, while holding in the other a sheaf of unpaid bills his master has refused to look at.

Another proof that the Methodists were rising in the economic scale is Wesley's mounting anxiety over the dangers into which increasing riches were leading them. His anxiety, indicated in the sermons, came to a climax in the unpalatable conclusion that it was impossible for any revival of true religion to continue long. For it carried within itself the seeds of its own destruction, in that it inevitably makes men rich as it makes them religious.

Wesley's complaint was not new. In a somewhat different way, medieval monasticism had had to face the same dilemma. "Religion," the monks used to say, "hath brought forth wealth, and the daughter hath devoured the mother." It is noteworthy that even in his disappointment it did not occur to Wesley to change his teaching. "We ought not to forbid people to be diligent and frugal; we must exhort all Christians to gain all they can and to save all they can; that is, in effect, to grow rich!" [103] His answer was not that the Christian should, like St. Francis, identify himself with God's poor, by becoming poor himself; nor should he, like Karl Marx, seek to socialize the productive process and its products; his answer was simply a reiteration of his doctrine of stewardship.

What way, then, . . . can we take that our money may not sink us to the nethermost hell? There is one way, and there is no other under heaven. If those who "gain all they can," and "save all they can," will likewise "give all they can" then, the more they gain the more they will grow in grace, and the more treasure they will lay up in heaven.[104]

C. After Wesley in England

After Wesley's death, what he had so much dreaded and had striven so hard to prevent, the separation of the Methodists from the Anglican Church, inevitably came to pass. It was steps Wesley himself had taken which led to this one. Yet it was accomplished only after a good deal of pulling and hauling, between the "church Methodists" and those whose whole religious life was centered rather in the societies themselves. After some strenuous struggles which centered around the question whether or not the sacraments should be administered in the societies, agreement was reached in 1795 on what was called (rather ironically, as it turned out) the "plan of pacification." This plan, a strange reversal of the "connectional" system which had up to that time dominated Methodist policy, provided that each society should decide for itself whether or not to have its preachers administer the sacraments to the membership. It was only gradually in the course of the next generation that the Conference began to practice the "laying on of hands," first for foreign missionaries, and then for those beginning to preach at home; and the preachers began to call and think of themselves as "ministers." Indeed there were some societies in which, as late as 1870, or even later, the sacraments were not administered. So the emergence of Methodism as a dissenting church was not a matter of institutional schism, but of a gradual accretion of churchly functions to the Methodist societies. The change in their thinking on social questions was

[103] Wesley, Works, "Thoughts upon Methodism" (1786), VII, 317. Italics are mine.
[104] Wesley, Works, VII, 317.

likewise gradual. Its tempo and direction are the subjects of our consideration in this section.

The structure of Wesley's social thought and action, as we have seen, faced two ways. In *politics* an explicit authoritarianism overlaid the individualism implicit in his religious message. In *social* thought an instinctive reluctance to criticize existing institutions was overborne by indignation at certain abuses which cried out for rectification. In *economic* thought, his inculcation of the economic virtues was at sharp variance with his apprehension lest increasing riches dissipate genuine piety. In all three respects it was the conservative facet of his thought which influenced his successors most strongly at first.

Politically, it was half a century before the Methodist realized his individualism with clarity enough to join the liberals' demand for increased civil rights. Socially, Wesley's bold experimentalism contracted into docile support for a few "good causes," of which the abolition of slavery was the most radical. Economically, the rising prosperity of the Methodists (particularly those of the Wesleyan connection) cut them off from the close sympathy with working men which would have enabled them to be *the* church of the Industrial Revolution.

1. METHODISM AND POLITICS

The first part of the nineteenth century witnessed a strong reactionary movement in English politics. It was nourished by the leaders of political thought, by the Anglican Church, and by the Tory party. The political leaders and the Tory party reacted against the republican excesses of the French Revolution. The church reacted against the deistic and atheistic ideas which accompanied them. Wesley's Toryism in politics and devout scriptural evangelicalism dominated the thought of his societies throughout this period. They professed to follow a "no politics" rule; but actually the official neutrality brought them too into line with the reactionary movement.[105] Indeed, the "No Politics" rule was very one-sidedly applied. Jabez Bunting, who came nearer than anybody else to being a successor to

[105] Wesley's own attitude gave support to this position in his followers. In 1782 he wrote a piece just a page long, called "How far is it the Duty of a Christian Minister to Preach Politics?" the substance of which was that they shouldn't do it at all, except when it was necessary to defend the government against slander (Wesley, *Works*, VI, 346).

73

Wesley, ruled the Conference with an iron hand for thirty years during the first half of the century. A high Tory himself, he engaged in considerable activity in support of their candidates, but he censured any participation of the preachers on the other side—even so slight a matter as writing letters in favor of Liberal candidates to the newspapers.[106]

At the turn of the century most Methodists were "church Methodists"; that is, they had so thoroughly absorbed Wesley's loyalty to the established Church that they chose to cast in their lot with Anglicans rather than with dissenters. The tradition was already strong which on the whole made liberals of dissenters and conservatives of Anglicans. The Methodists' prolonged attachment to the national church then meant a prolonged stay in the Tory camp. There is no doubt that Jabez Bunting's long ascendency could not have been maintained, no matter how autocratic his control, had he not in good measure represented the actual beliefs of most Methodists.

It was near the middle of the nineteenth century when the Methodists emerged from under the spell of Wesley's teaching on loyalty to the church and uncritical adherence to the *status quo* in politics. Then they broke the "pontificate" of Bunting and began to join forces, politically and socially, with the dissenters. At last they perceived that the social aspirations and outlook of dissent were fundamentally similar to their own. The Methodists' situation during the first part of the century could hardly have been comfortable, midway as it was between Anglicanism and dissent. The clergy at times made difficulty over administering the Sacraments. An extreme, but all too indicative case was the refusal of Communion to the aged and infirm widow of John Fletcher of Madely by a curate in the very church where "the saint of Methodism" had served.[107] Late in the nineteenth century a clergyman refused to give Christian burial to one who had been baptized by a Methodist minister.

2. PROTESTS IN METHODISM

The latent liberalism of the Methodists repeatedly came to expression in individuals or small groups during the first half-century after Wesley's death. But the pioneers suffered for it by repression and

[106] E. R. Taylor, *Methodism and Politics* (Cambridge: The University Press, 1935), p. 132.
[107] W. J. Townshend, *op. cit.*, I, 388.

expulsion. In these dissident movements, attacks on the autocracy and clericalism in the government of the societies were combined (in different proportions in different cases) with participation on the liberal side of political questions, and with support of the aspirations of the workingmen for better conditions of labor.

The first sizeable schism was that led by Alexander Kilham into the Methodist New Connection (1797). Kilham was accused of "radicalism," but his demands for the liberalization of the government of the societies were in reality quite moderate. He sought to give lay people a share in the admission and dismissal of members, in the choice of preachers, and in the decisions of the district meetings and conferences. The irony of Kilham's expulsion was that most of the changes for which he contended were adopted by the Wesleyans, some of them very soon.[108]

Hugh Bourne led a protest against the tendency to confine Methodist preaching to their preaching houses. He attempted to restore the outdoor preaching of the "primitive" times, but with a different slant due to the promotion, by Lorenzo Dow, of the "camp-meeting" methods lately sprung up in America.[109]

There was no room for this "new" method in the Wesleyan fold, which was by now settled in its preaching houses and on its way to respectability. The result was the formation, in 1812, of the Primitive Methodists, who after severe struggles at birth, survived to minister to the working classes with whom the Wesleyans were losing contact. William O'Bryan formed the Bible Christians in 1815 because the Methodist circuit system had become too rigid to make room for his "irregularities" in preaching, just as the state church's parish lines had been too rigid to accommodate the preaching of Wesley and his laymen in the beginnings of Methodism. At bottom, this movement, like Kilham's, was a protest against government by the preachers only.

3. Methodism and Social Movements

The Wesleyan Conference's attitude toward social and political questions is, on the whole, not misrepresented by Bunting's oft-quoted statement, "Methodism hates democracy as much as it hates sin." [110]

[108] Maldwyn Edwards, *After Wesley, A Study of the Social and Political Influence of Methodism in the Middle Period (1791-1849)* (London: The Epworth Press, 1935), pp. 48-49.
[109] *Ibid.*, p. 53.
[110] *Ibid.*, p. 156.

The Conference, ostensibly neutral, in effect supported the Government in its enactment of the "Corn Laws" which benefited the landlords, but wrought hardship on the poor (1815).[111] The "Tolpuddle Martyrs" were men who had been condemned to seven years' transportation for forming an Agricultural Laborers' Union. Though most of them were Methodists, Bunting refused an interview to a woman who had journeyed up to London on their behalf.[112] The Wesleyan Methodists as a whole opposed the aspirations, both political and economic, of the Chartists. When, at Manchester and Newcastle, meetings were held to agitate for the extension of the franchise, Methodists who participated were warned, and, if unrepentant, expelled. It is possible, though by no means certain, that the same fate awaited those who joined labor unions. Methodists were advised to avoid "associations . . . employing unlawful oaths, and threats and force to acquire new members." Whether this referred to labor unions or not is a disputed question. Probably official Methodism's attitude toward them is most accurately described as neutral.[113]

The Conference bitterly opposed Catholic emancipation. Wesley himself had shown sympathy with individual Roman Catholics, and acknowledged his debt to devotional writings of Catholicism. Yet he opposed any move toward extending the franchise to Catholics. He had himself suffered much from suspicion that he was one of them, and especially at the time of the "Forty-five," when Catholicism involved Jacobitism, and consequently treason, he had felt under necessity of repeatedly protesting his loyalty to the Sovereign. Such experiences not only increased his Tory sentiments; they also increased his aversion to seeing any political power being put in Catholic hands. He would have them protected from overt persecution, but nothing more. He repeatedly and publicly stated that the Catholics, owing allegiance to the Pope, could not be trusted as subjects of the temporal ruler.[114]

Wesley's opposition to the enlargement of the political rights of

[111] *Ibid.,* p. 31.

[112] *Ibid.,* pp. 34-35.

[113] R. F. Wearmouth, *op. cit.,* pp. 248-49. Dr. Wearmouth disagrees with Rattenbury and the Webbs, who believe the "advice" quoted above refers specifically to labor unions.

[114] Maldwyn Edwards, *John Wesley and the Eighteenth Century* (New York: The Abingdon Press, 1933), pp. 99-100.

the Romanists was continued by his followers; untempered, however, by his breadth of personal sympathy.

The influence of Methodism was thrown in 1813 against a mild measure to relieve Catholics of some of their disabilities. It was defeated by a margin of four votes.[115] Animosity against Catholics and Catholicism persisted in Methodism till the middle of the century. An attempt was made in 1832 to disestablish the Church of England. Here again the official Methodist attitude was one of neutrality. Against this apathy, and that of the country as a whole, the bill for disestablishment made very little headway.

We have already spoken of the positive way in which Methodism lent its aid to the antislavery crusade.[116] In addition, it took the initiative in two other activities with beneficial results. The first of these was the promotion of education. Methodists continued to promote Sunday schools, though the Conference tried several times (unsuccessfully) to forbid their teaching writing! Beginning in 1837, they began the erection of a great number of day schools, since education was still regarded as the responsibility of religious, rather than civil bodies. These, says Edwards, "made Methodism in the last century rank with the Established Church as the greatest force for popular education in England." [117]

The second movement we should note is the conduct of missions in foreign parts. Dr. Coke had labored indefatigably through his last years to establish foreign missions. He had attempted, without success in either instance, to get work started in France (during mounting revolutionary excitement!) and in Africa. Somewhat reluctantly, the Conference allowed him to head a mission to India, but he died on the way thither in 1814.

His enthusiasm, however, had been caught at home, and a great public meeting held at Leeds in 1813 is usually regarded as the beginning of the Methodist Missionary Society. Five years later it was an integral part of the conference organization. For the first time in English Christendom, a religious body had followed the example of the Moravians and acknowledged the obligation of the religious community as such to carry the gospel to distant lands. Early *Minutes*

[115] M. Edwards, *After Wesley*, p. 115.
[116] See pp. 52-53.
[117] M. Edwards, *After Wesley*, p. 107 ff.

of the conference show how seriously it took this obligation. They report 111 missionaries at work in France, Africa, the West Indies, India, and the Canadas.[118] Jabez Bunting and Richard Watson ably administered the work as the first two missions secretaries.

4. THE SOCIAL WORK OF THE ANGLICAN EVANGELICALS

The leadership in the great humanitarian reforms of the first half of the nineteenth century came from the evangelical party in the Church of England, chiefly from its laymen. In addition to Wilberforce's and Macauley's leadership of the abolition movement, there was the varied philanthropy of the Thornton brothers, of Hannah More, and the factory legislation of Lord Shaftesbury. Lord Shaftesbury was not ashamed to say of his work for the women and children in the mines, "I have been bold enough to undertake this task, because I must regard the objects of it as being created, like ourselves, by the same Master, redeemed by the same Saviour, and destined to the same immortality." [119]

There has been a good deal of difference of opinion as to the nature of the relationship between the Methodism which ultimately left the church and the evangelicalism which stayed within it. Some would say they had a common origin, others that they were identical; others that the one was the cause of the other.[120] Without trying to be too precise about priority, we can recognize two things about the relationship. First, differences did exist, from almost, if not quite, the very beginning. When confronted with the necessity of choosing between the parish system of the Anglican Church and the itinerancy, the evangelicals chose the former, the Methodists the latter; and in theology, the evangelicals were generally moderate Calvinists (John

[118] W. J. Townshend, op. cit., II, 294.
[119] J. W. Bready, England Before and After Wesley, p. 306.
[120] Overton and Relton's formula is: "The Methodist movement and the Evangelical revival both [started] from the spiritual impulse imparted by William Law." (J. H. Overton and Frederick Relton, The English Church from the Accession of George I to the End of the Eighteenth Century [London: the Macmillan Co., 1906], p. 139). They were identified by a contemporary enemy of both. Sidney Smith lumps Arminian and Calvinistic Methodists and Evangelicals together with a sneer: "We shall use the general term Methodists and distinguish these three classes of fanatics, not troubling ourselves to point out the finer shades and nicer discriminations of lunacy." (Quoted from T. C. Hall, The Social Meaning of Modern Religious Movements in England [New York: Charles Scribner's Sons, 1900], pp. 111-12). J. W. Bready, on the other hand, says: "Almost they may be considered as cause and effect" (England Before and After Wesley, p. 289).

Fletcher was the great exception) while the Methodists were Arminian. Second, there were numerous personal links between the movements.[121] Even though with the passage of time the links became fewer and the lines more distinct, we are justified in saying that the flame tended with such conspicuous success by the Wesleys was one of the sources, indeed the chief source, of the warmth and light carried onto the social scene by the Anglican evangelicals.[122] Methodism made a more direct contribution to the fight for legislation limiting factory work hours through the part some Methodists took in the field campaigning.

Richard Oastler was the son of a local preacher. Whereas the father was active in the struggle for the emancipation of the slaves, the son adapted his phraseology to that for factory legislation by inventing the terms "wage-slave," "factory slave," and the like.

J. R. Stephens was an ordained Methodist minister who was repudiated by his Conference because of the radicalism of his methods. Both he and Oastler advocated resort to violence if other methods failed. Stephens is reported to have said, in one of his fiery speeches, "I will plead for the poor; . . . when . . . pleading and praying are . . . of non-effect, then I will fight for the poor." [123] Another Methodist who joined the cause was Philip Grant, the editor of the *Ten Hours Advocate.*

5. Methodists and the Labor Movement

We have already seen that the official attitude of the Wesleyan Conference, while professedly neutral, did, in effect, militate against movements of workingmen to better their condition, either politically or economically. We also saw that there were Methodists who refused to accept the limitations put on their action by the Wesleyan Conference, and proceeded to act in their own behalf, even though it meant incurring the disfavor of the conference, or even expulsion. Amongst these the Primitive Methodists especially kept close to the workingmen's aspirations, and exerted considerable influence in their movement to organize for higher wages and better working conditions.

---

[121] J. H. Overton and Frederick Relton, *op. cit.,* pp. 140 ff.

[122] T. C. Hall speaks of the "great . . . debt the Evangelical party owes and confesses to the Wesleyan movement" (*The Social Meaning of Modern Religious Movements in England*), p. 93.

[123] Wearmouth, *op. cit.,* p. 101.

For one thing, a surprising number of local preachers became leaders in the unions. As Edwards pointed out:

Men found it easy to step from the pulpit onto the platform. The story of the Miners' Association in Durham and Northumberland, is, in measure, the record of local preachers, who, by their probity of life, and their capacity for speaking, were able to lead the miners.[124]

Twelve of the leaders of the miners in Durham and Northumberland in the early 1830s and the mid-forties have been identified as Primitive Methodist local preachers.[125] During one of their strikes the twelve men they picked to go up to London to win sympathy for their cause were known as the "twelve Apostles."

Sidney Webb has paid high tribute to the influence of Methodism among the miners of Durham in the second quarter of the eighteenth century:

The "Ranters" [that is, the Primitive Methodists] did great work from village to village. . . . From the very beginning of the Trade Union movement among the miners, of the Co-operative movement among all sections of wage earners, of the formation of Friendly Societies, and of the attempts at adult education. It is the men who are Methodists in Durham County, especially Primitive Methodists, who take the lead and fill posts of influence. From their ranks have come an astonishingly large proportion of Trade Union leaders, from check weighers and lodge chairmen to county officials. . . . Trade Unionism was itself largely a result of the elevation of character brought by religious conversion on individual leaders.[126]

The Methodist influence in unions other than the miners' is not so easy to identify. We do know, however, that the founder of the Agricultural Laborers' Union was a Methodist, and that at the Union's Congress of 1872 "half the speakers . . . were preachers of various denominations." [127]

Another interesting evidence of Methodist influence appears in

[124] M. Edwards, After Wesley, p .45.
[125] Robert F. Wearmouth, Some Working-Class Movements of the Nineteenth Century (London: The Epworth Press, 1948), p. 299. A correspondent in a newspaper of 1831 blames the agitation on the "Ranters," which was the favorite nickname for the Primitive Methodist. "Tommy Hepburn, their most notable leader, always counseled moderation and patience, even after a thousand miners' families had been turned out on the street. (Wearmouth, Methodism and the Working-Class Movements, pp. 228-29.)
[126] Sidney Webb, Story of the Durham Miners, in M. Edwards, After Wesley, p. 56.
[127] Wearmouth, Methodism and the Working-Class Movements, p. 270.

the adaptation by the Chartists of devices used in Methodism: the "class meeting" and the "camp meeting." The latter was, as has been noted, much in use among the Primitive Methodists. Hymn-singing parades were also much used.[128] Wearmouth, in a chapter on "Religio-Trade Unionism," concludes as follows:

Many Trade Union leaders were evangelists and local preachers, fervent members, for the most part of Methodist Congregations. . . .

On the other hand the early Trade Unionists desired to see religion as an ally. . . . The first fifty years were troubled . . . with a series of defeats and disappointments. . . . They were passing through the wilderness and the story of Israel came close to their pulses. . . . The New Testament fed them as with the manna of hope. [But with the attainment of success toward the close of the century], their thoughts and ambitions may be said to have turned from the Bible to the Statute Book.[129]

6. SUMMARY

By the middle of the nineteenth century, Methodism had found its place as a social leaven in English life. John Wesley had come preaching a gospel of the grace of God for all who would accept it. He had preached that the acceptance of his grace should work transformations in men beginning forthwith, not merely in some future state of blessedness. In persuading men that God cared for them, he persuaded them that they should care for themselves. He set out to reform the nation by converting individual men. He made several brave beginnings at improving the organization of life about him. Not all of these became a force in the community, but his transformed Methodists, organized in societies and classes, did begin, tentatively and indirectly, but effectively nonetheless, to permeate and elevate social institutions.

At first the Methodists exerted a greater force on society by what they were as individuals than by what they were able to do collectively. Aside from the remarkable philanthropy exercised by individual Meth-

---

[128] Wearmouth, *Some Working-Class Movements*, pp. 126 ff., 144 ff., 309. The Chartist movement, begun in 1836, was at bottom an economic movement, with a purely political program. Its principal objectives were manhood suffrage, the abolition of property qualifications for M. P.'s, and equal electoral districts (G. D. H. Cole, *A Short History of the British Working-Class Movement, 1789-1947* [new ed., rev., London: George Allen & Unwin, 1948], p. 98).

[129] Wearmouth, *Some Working-Class Movements*, pp. 320-21.

odists, the first great beneficent changes in society were wrought by the evangelicals who stayed in the Church of England. The Wesleyan Conference, after Wesley's death, fastened on the conservative side of Wesley's teaching and withdrew into a *laissez-faire* attitude which, except for their espousal of a few reforms, made rather for the maintenance of the *status quo* than a bold transformation of existing abuses.

But there were many Methodists who refused to stay within these limitations, and, sometimes at the cost of expulsion, advocated radical political and economic demands. They brought considerable aid, by their numbers, and by their capacity to take responsibility and discharge it dependably, to the Trade Union Movement. Even the Wesleyans found themselves, by the middle of the century, allied less with conservative Anglicanism than with liberal dissent, and ready thenceforth to play their part with their fellow dissenters in subsequent liberal movements.

CHAPTER TWO

The Methodist Societies
in the American Colonies

THE COLONIES TO WHICH THE FIRST METHODISTS CAME AS immigrants were still very much dependent on England in every way. They were able to furnish valuable raw materials, it is true, but these were exploited, according to the mercantilist theory of the day, for the benefit of the mother country. Politically, the colonies, even those which had originally been founded by chartered companies or proprietors, had become Crown colonies, and, though they had legislative bodies elected by themselves, were ultimately responsible to governors sent out by the Colonial Secretary. Physically the colonies were a thin series of small settlements hugging the sea-coast, and creeping up the river valleys toward the West. It was still difficult for them to communicate with each other. Travel by water was slow, but it was better than by way of the rough roads.

Culturally, provincialism prevailed. There were perhaps colleges in which European books could be read by those who were interested; but individual interchange with intellectual centers in Europe was for the most part by letter. The century and a quarter of isolation had begun to get in its work. The new colleges could not really make up for the inaccessibility of Oxford and Cambridge. For every Benjamin Franklin (who had not been to college at all), who after the Revolution could move easily in European circles, there were hundreds of backwoodsmen who were overawed when they visited Philadelphia which, though the largest town in the country, had fewer than twenty-five thousand inhabitants!

Outside Boston with its busy port, New England was a land of villages built around small mills. Power for these mills was supplied by near-by streams. Most of the inhabitants depended for a living in whole or in part on their own farms. Quite different were the large plantations in the Southern colonies. They were so broad and so far apart that they had to become as nearly economically self-sufficient as possible. The "big house" was surrounded by a cluster of outbuildings, storehouses, a forge, a cobbler's shop, and the cabins of the slaves who worked in them and on the land. The South had its flourishing ports like Charleston, from which the products of the plantations were shipped, and a few sons sailed for an Oxford or a Cambridge education.

A momentous factor of American life, which subtly pervaded its temper and its economic and political institutions, was the vast empty tracts of land, empty—or almost so—of inhabitants, which stretched away to the Mississippi. The claims of European nations to it were either extinguished or rendered virtually inoperative with the recognition of our independence. Ways were soon found to extinguish the claims of the Indians, too often by extinguishing the claimants themselves. Land hunger possessed the people of the new nation. They *would* take up land, if an enforceable government policy was ready, within the bounds of that policy; but if it was not, they took it up anyhow. Even before peace was signed with England, the westward trek had begun. After it, the frontier moved with astonishing rapidity. Its mobility posed many of the problems the churches and the government had to face. Both took a hand in keeping the institutions of a settled society abreast of the frontier's progress.

Before the Revolution nine of the colonies had established churches supported by the state, the three in New England being Congregationalist, and the other six Anglican. The battle for toleration of other forms of worship had progressed further in some than in others; in none of them was it so complete as in Rhode Island and Pennsylvania. Nevertheless, the proportion of the population which had an active connection with the churches was very small. The "Great Awakening," of which George Whitefield and Jonathan Edwards were the most widely known heralds, and which reached its height around 1740, had added considerably to the number of churches (chiefly Presbyterian and Baptist), supported by voluntary adherents. After the Great Awakening, revivals were to be a permanent feature of American religious life.

Though Methodism came comparatively late onto the Colonial scene, it came at a time of crying religious need. Moreover, it came with gifts well suited to fill those needs. It was born in a revival, and was prepared to use the revival as a method of advance. In the "era of the common man," it preached a gospel eminently suited to the common man. It had a discipline which was to prove a restraining influence in a land of few restraints. It had a disciplined yet flexible organization, well fitted to keep up with the march of the frontier. And it came just soon enough to feel at home in the American scene before it was called upon to bear a large part in the ministry to the swiftly growing nation.

A. The Social Status
of the First American Methodists

We have already seen that the first generation of English Methodists included people from the lowest income brackets up through the class of small tradesmen.[1] The very first Methodists in America, however, came from Northern Ireland, and were artisans or lease-hold farmers. Philip Embury, the first local preacher in New York, was a carpenter; he had worked on a preaching house in Ireland with his own hands, and was to do the same on Wesley Chapel in New York. The five men who signed the deed for the land on which the John Street preaching house was soon built, presumably members of the society, must have already accumulated some property before taking that responsible step. Two of the five were merchants, one a "gentleman" (this was Captain Thomas Webb of the British Army), one a shopkeeper, and one a hatter.[2] Robert Strawbridge, the first Methodist preacher in Maryland, also came from Ireland. How far his coming was motivated by a desire for economic betterment is difficult to say. He had preached in Ireland, and continued to do so after arriving here. From what we know of his activities, he was more zealous in preaching than in furthering his worldly estate. He spent his last days on a farm lent to him by a generous friend.[3]

Most of Wesley's American evangelists came from humble circum-

---

[1] See pp. 42-43.

[2] J. B. Wakeley, *Lost Chapters Recovered from the Early History of American Methodism* (New York: Published for the Author by Carlton and Porter, 1858), p. 59.

[3] *Cyclopaedia of Methodism* (Matthew Simpson, ed., Philadelphia: Louis H. Everts, 1880), p. 837.

85

stances. The great George Whitefield himself was the son of an inn-keeper, whose widow was able to give young George a good early schooling; but, to use the modern phrase, he had to "earn his own way through college." Francis Asbury's parents were "poor but godly." He was, after some schooling, apprenticed at a forge. Before Richard Boardman and Joseph Pilmoor could come over, the preachers at the conference at Leeds in 1769, most of them poor men themselves, generously collected upwards of fifty pounds toward their expenses. Robert Williams sold his horse to pay his debts; a friend paid his passage.

Pilmoor says of Williams that he came to America about business. He undertook to sell Wesley's books, but both the English and the American conferences intervened to put a stop to it, fearing he was doing so for his own profit.[4] Thomas Taylor in his famous letter begging Wesley to send over a preacher to help the New York society, which had sprung up spontaneously, as it were, tells a great deal about both the economic circumstances and the zeal of its members when he says: "With respect to the money for payment of a preacher's passage over, if they could not procure it, we would sell our coats and shirts and pay for it."

In these days when the word "servant" and the institution itself have nearly died out in our country, we are surprised to find that Barbara Heck could and did have one.[5] Embury, once here, turned his hand to several other things besides carpentry and preaching; he taught school for awhile, and his name is on a petition to the governor for a grant of land for a linen company.[6] After a move from New York City to Ashgrove, he became a magistrate.[7] Richard Sause, who had come to New York from Dublin, established a cutlery company. His friend, Charles White, also from Dublin, was a donor to the New York building fund. A loyalist in sympathy, he went first to Nova Scotia, then "westward, where Francis Asbury found him later, "without property and without grace." [8] M. Molloy was a barber. P. van Pelt of Staten Island, in whose house several Methodists preached, was of an old Dutch family and a prominent citizen. Captain Webb

[4] W. W. Sweet, *Men of Zeal*, p. 80. *Cyclopaedia of Methodism*, p. 951.
[5] AJL, I, 9.
[6] W. W. Sweet, *op. cit.*, p. 59.
[7] *Ibid.*, p. 70.
[8] AJL, I, 10, n. 21, and 11, n. 22.

and William Lupton were able to lend money for the purchase of the original New York property.[9]

Before the end of the century, Asbury mentions in his *Journal* men of substance and position like Judge White who protected him in Delaware; Henry Gouch, owner of Perry Hall, whose ample rooms sheltered a half-dozen preachers while they were doing the planning preliminary to the Christmas Conference; Philip Barratt who built Barratt's Chapel; and Judge Bassett, who became governor of Maryland. Nothing like what would be considered complete statistics today is available for that early period; but the quick glance we have just taken leaves us with the impression that, though the very first Methodists in this country were humble folk, it was not long before the middle class was represented among them in about the same proportion as in the population as a whole. Presumably this process moved even faster here than in England, since economic lines were easier to cross here, and the "economic virtues" inculcated by Wesley could produce their well-known effects more easily. In other words, Methodists who began poor could accumulate possessions faster here. It would seem also that the message they preached appealed to sufficient numbers of people already partly up the economic ladder to raise the relative economic position of the Methodists.

Methodist congregations were from the very start diversified racially as well as socially and economically. Barbara Heck's Negro servant was present at Embury's first sermon in New York; Peter, the slave of a tobacconist, was converted in the Rigging Loft by the preaching of Captain Webb.[10] Asbury early mentions the Negroes among his hearers.[11]

B. The Social Outlook
of the Colonial Methodists

1. EVANGELISTIC ZEAL

It is to be expected that, while the societies were just a-borning, the Methodists' concern for their neighbors should express itself chiefly in preaching the gospel to any who would listen. While they

[9] *Ibid.,* I, 8, n. 12; 9, n. 18.
[10] AJL, I, 9, n. 19. When Peter's master returned to England, the trustees purchased him, and allowed him to work out his freedom as sexton of Wesley Chapel. He became one of the founders of the A. M. E. Zion Church, toward the end of the century.
[11] AJL, I, 9, et passim.

87

were small in numbers, inconsiderable in influence, and led for the most part by recent arrivals on these shores, their direct impact on the social fabric of pre-Revolutionary America could not, in the nature of the case, be great. But they did preach the gospel, all of them. The official missionaries sent over by Wesley numbered eight in all; [12] perhaps ten others continued after arriving here the preaching they had begun in England, either with or without the express permission of Wesley, and in more or less close co-operation with the conference system.[13] The official missionaries all left during the years between 1774 and 1778; that is, with the saving exception of Francis Asbury. At the end of the period just mentioned, the Methodists numbered over eighty-five hundred. Of these, forty-nine were preachers, most of them native-born.

Such a rapid spread can be accounted for only by supposing that the lay people did a good deal of evangelizing in their personal contacts, as they went about their daily work, and by testimony in society and class meetings. The system of making the more responsible and able lay people class leaders, exhorters, and local preachers was continued here as in the homeland. Their part in the day-to-day evangelizing and carrying on the societies' work in the absence of the preacher on his rounds can hardly be overestimated. Direction, example, and encouragement the English preachers certainly gave; but others did much of the evangelization. Spurred by a sense of responsibility, and by confidence in the inherent expansiveness of the gospel they bore, they spoke with a sense of ultimate triumph. Two short sentences extracted from Thomas Taylor's letter are instructive here: "Mr. Webb and Mr. Embury . . . have none to *direct* them. . . . I doubt not but, by the goodness of God, such a flame would be soon kindled as would never stop, until it reached the great South Sea [i.e. the Pacific Ocean!]"[14]

---

[12] They were: Richard Boardman and Joseph Pilmoor, who arrived in 1769; Francis Asbury and Richard Wright, 1771; Thomas Rankin and George Shadford, 1773; and James Dempster and Martin Rodda, 1774.

[13] Robert Williams, John King, Joseph Yearbry, and William Glendenning had Wesley's permission to preach. Robert Strawbridge, Philip Embury, Captain Webb, Robert Lindsey, Edward Dromgoole, and (in a class by himself!) George Whitefield were volunteers. It is curious that Whitefield, who had been preaching powerful awakening sermons on extensive voyages through the colonies ever since 1739, had not founded a single Methodist Society. The fruit of his labors was visible in increased interest in the churches already in existence.

[14] BHMM, I, 16. Italics mine.

2. Methodists and the State:
The War for Independence; Religious Liberty

We have already seen[15] how Wesley's Tory pamphleteering embarrassed the American Methodists. It put them in the dilemma of having to choose between their loyalty to Wesley and their solidarity with their fellow colonists. They clung to their leader's views for a long time,[16] but by the end of the Revolution had whole-heartedly embraced the cause of independence. It is true that Wesley, early in the same year in which he had published the *Calm Address*, had written to Rankin, advising him to stay above politics, and to persuade the preachers to do the same.[17] But because Wesley failed to follow his own advice, he made it almost impossible for the preachers so to do. Undoubtedly, the sympathies of some of his missionaries were with England. Martin Rodda, for instance, got himself into trouble by distributing a royal proclamation in Delaware. Thomas Rankin spent the winter of 1777-78 in Philadelphia, which was then occupied by the British, and sailed away for home the next spring.

But no matter how they felt, or how quiet they might keep about their feelings, their usefulness in the service of the revival in America was over after the publication of the *Calm Address*. Freeborn Garrettson, though American born, was threatened by a mob in Delaware, and would have been hanged but for the intervention of some friendly gentlemen. Philip Gatch was given a coat of tar by a mob in Maryland, and in the process one of his eyes was permanently injured. Francis Asbury, believing that he as a minister should not bear arms, refused to sign an oath presented to him by the authorities in Maryland where anti-Tory activities were especially intense. Having determined to ride out the storm for the sake of future usefulness to Methodism here, he took refuge across the Delaware border, and his traveling was severely restricted for some time. Judge White, who

---

[15] See p. 45.

[16] During the British occupation of New York, while other churches were burned, Wesley Chapel was protected and used for Methodist meetings on Sunday evenings. "These facts—possibly quite as much as anything said or done by the preachers—created trouble for the Methodists." (BHMM I, 46.)

[17] It is your part to be peacemakers, to be loving and tender to all, but to addict yourselves to no party. . . . [Some there were who] would set one of you against the other." The Wesleys evidently felt the matter to be a serious one, for Charles wrote under the same date and in the same sense (WJL, VI, 142-43).

hospitably took him in, was arrested on account of his suspicious guest, so Asbury had to leave even that shelter for a month.

The rest of the eight English missionaries left for England as they had occasion.[18] Asbury felt more alone with each departure. By 1778 only George Shadford, Asbury's best friend, and the ablest of the eight, was left. Early in the year the two appointed a day on which they were to fast and pray together to discover God's will for their future. At the end of the day, Asbury was convinced that he should stay; Shadford, that he should go. "One of us must be in error," said Asbury. "Not necessarily so," said Shadford, "I may have a call to go and you to stay." [19] Soon after Shadford's departure, Asbury's Journal has this entry:

> I was under some heaviness of mind. But it was no wonder: three thousand miles from home—my friends have left me—I am considered by some as an enemy of the country—every day liable to be seized by violence and abused. However, all this is but a trifle to suffer for Christ, and the salvation of souls. Lord, stand by me! [20]

As yet "home" is England; he does not say of America, "my country," but service to the cause of Christ and the salvation of souls is paramount. He alone of Wesley's missionaries had managed to subordinate politics to the gospel, and he was able in the years to come to imbibe and appreciate the spirit of America.[21]

The sympathies of some of the native-born Methodists, preachers and rank-and-file members alike, fell in the same direction. Jesse Lee tells us about Methodists who were conscientious objectors, but nothing about enthusiastic fighters for independence. This may have been because he himself was a conscientious objector; but the impression left by what he says no less than by what he leaves unsaid, in his Short History, is that he was less interested in the winning of

[18] A number of Methodists who for one reason or another did not want to take up life in the British Isles again, yet found it difficult to remain in the Colonies after they had taken up arms against their king, went to those Colonies north of the St. Lawrence which were content to remain under the Crown. How many of these there were we have no way of knowing. We do know that several Hecks and Emburys went thither from New York.

[19] SMAH, p. 92. The incidents related just previously come from Sweet's excellent Chapter V, "During the War for Independence."

[20] AJL, I, 263-64.

[21] In 1783, Asbury wrote to Shadford (now back in England): "O America! America! it certainly will be the glory of the world for religion! I have loved, and do love America." (AJL, III, 29).

independence than he was in the effect of the war on religion in general, and on the Methodist cause in particular.

Asbury, as we have seen, was unwilling to fight because he was a minister. Jesse Lee, too, gives that as a reason for his unwillingness to fight, but he ultimately rests his position simply on his being a Christian. "As a Christian and as a preacher of the gospel I could not fight. I could not reconcile it to myself to bear arms or to kill one of my fellow creatures." [22] Vividly, he tells the story of his being drafted, and refusing to hold a musket, in spite of the arguments of his superior officers. He seems to have been fairly well treated, in spite of his unco-operative attitude. This may have been partly because of his own ready and vigorous friendliness, and partly because some of the battles for "soul-liberty" had already been fought in Virginia by the Baptists.[23] At any rate, Lee preached and sang from his guard-house cell, and we can read between the lines that it was the opportunity to do just this which had determined him to obey the draft, "to go and to trust in the Lord." Though he would not bear weapons, he decided he would do anything else in the army, and was finally assigned to a baggage wagon, the driver of which was also a Methodist.

Some of the early Methodists may have objected to warfare on grounds of conscience, but, like the early Christians, they had no objection to the employment of military terms to express the Christian's warfare. We are told that it was as a result of Asbury's "recruiting" language that Lee finally "enlisted" as a member of the Conference. It was in 1782, at the conference session, that, while the preachers were standing out in front of the building where the conference was meeting, Asbury called out, as he saw Jesse nearby: "I am going to enlist bro. Lee." A preacher, falling into the figure of the moment, asked, "What bounty do you give?" Asbury said, "Grace here, and glory hereafter will be given him if he is faithful."

Not immediately, but at the next Conference session, Lee was taken in on trial. Freeborn Garrettson and Philip Gatch were likewise conscientious objectors.[24] Lee tells us, without giving particulars, about

---

[22] Minton Thrift, *Memoir of the Rev. Jesse Lee, with Extracts from his Journals* (New York: Bangs and Mason, 1823), p. 26.

[23] Sweet (SMAH, p. 89, n. 12), quotes from one of the early preachers, Philip Gatch, these words: "Baptists had preceded the Methodists in all this region, and had rolled back the wave of persecution."

[24] Garrettson said, "I was quite drawn away from a belief in the lawfulness of shedding human blood under the gospel dispensation. . . ." BHMM, I, 48.

others. "Some . . . were bound in conscience not to fight; and no threatenings could compel them to bear arms or hire a man to take their places." [25] It might be suspected that these men were refusing to fight either because they did not sympathize with the cause of independence, or because they were more or less blindly following Wesley's direction to stay above party strife, or his exhortation not to take up arms against the king. But, so far as they gave their motives, it was none of these, but simply a conscientious conviction that the shedding of blood in any cause was incompatible with their Christian profession.

On the other hand, Thomas Ware, who later became a preacher, enlisted at the age of eighteen, giving this reason in his autobiography: "This cause I held to be just . . . the principles for which we were contending . . . worth risking life for." [26] Men like Ware must have been fairly numerous, for we hear nothing of reprisals on the Methodists as "collaborationists" after the war was over. The Methodists accepted the outcome of the war as indication of the divine will (as we have already seen, Wesley himself set the tone here), and seem to have been conscious of no disadvantages as over against others when it came to participation in the life of the new nation. They ordered a day of thanksgiving at the war's end; and their two Bishops made a grave address of congratulation to the newly elected President Washington, which was as gravely welcomed by him.

Lee's anxieties all through this period were centered not on the precarious cause of independence, but on the damage the war wrought on the religious and moral life of the time, and on the fortunes of Methodism in particular. "Many [Methodists] were drafted . . . some of them lost their lives, some made shipwreck of the faith, and but few of them returned home with as much religion as they formerly possessed." [27] His interest seems to have been shared by the rest of the Methodists. The Conference of 1783 appointed two days of public thanksgiving throughout the connection, not for having won the

---

[25] Jesse Lee, A Short History of the Methodists, in the United States of America (First printed in Baltimore, by Magill and Clime, in 1810. The quotation above was taken from a much later reproduction limited to 1200 copies, by the Cokesbury Press, n. p., n. d.) p. 72. He goes on to tell what befell these conscientious men: "In consequence some of them were whipped, some were fined, and some imprisoned; others were sent home, and many were much persecuted."

[26] Quoted from BHMM, I, 49.

[27] Jesse Lee, op. cit., p. 72.

war, nor for the achievement of independence, but for "temporal and spiritual prosperity, and the glorious revival of the work of God." [28] The address presented in 1789 to President Washington was not a specimen of "Fourth of July oratory," as it might very easily have been. Bishop Asbury read it, but by his side was the other Bishop, Dr. Coke, who was still a subject of the English king.

The message, in the name of the Methodists, congratulates George Washington on his election as civil head of the new nation. It is confident he will preserve those civil and religious liberties which have been transmitted to it by the providence of God. It commends him for his piety in that he has acknowledged God as the source of "the most excellent Constitution of these states." It expresses confidence that he will be "a faithful and impartial patron of genuine, vital religion," and promises the fervent prayers of the Methodists on his behalf.

The President thanked them, hoped not to disappoint them in their hope that he would be "a faithful and impartial patron of genuine, vital religion," and implored the divine benediction on their "religious community." [29] It seems that there was resentment on the part of some that the Methodists should have undertaken thus to address the new chief executive; but it may have been connected with regrets that they hadn't thought of it first. At any rate, in this way the Methodists assured the nation of their loyalty, and were apparently accepted without prejudice as citizens with a valuable contribution to make in the strenuous years ahead.

The eagerness manifested in the address for impartiality in the government's attitude toward religion represents, of course, acceptance of the "hands-off" attitude of the constitution-makers. The Methodists, in order to come to this position, had had to shake off the remnants of a habitual fondness for an established church, left over from the time when most Methodists were also Anglicans. In 1776, George Shadford, in behalf of all the Methodists in Virginia (there were nearly three thousand of them at the time), presented a petition to the Assembly protesting against disestablishment.[30] They were not

---

[28] *Ibid.*, p. 78. The note in the *Minutes* for 1783 has also "for our public peace" (MAC, p. 19).
[29] SHMEC, II, 501 ff.
[30] BHMM, I, 50.

then willing to regard themselves as "common dissenters." They rallied slowly to their Baptist and Presbyterian brethrens' fight against a measure which would have had the stipends of ministers of all denominations paid by the state. It was the Baptists and Presbyterians who won this fight, and went on to insist on complete separation of church and state, both in the State Constitution of Virginia and in the National Constitution itself.[31] Obviously, by the time of the address to Washington the Methodists were not only reconciled to, but enthusiastic about the doctrine embodied in the First Amendment to the Constitution: "Congress shall make no law respecting an establishment of religion or prohibiting the free exercise thereof."

3. SLAVERY

The Dutch vessel which (more or less by accident) landed a shipload of slaves in Virginia in 1619 brought what was probably the first trickle of that fateful stream which was to bear so many miseries both in itself and to the shores it touched. But we must remember that even without this "accident," the inundation would have come, for slavery was already a part of the economy of the British Empire, and already flourished in the nearby British West Indies. The trade in men which had for some time been enriching the merchants of Bristol would before long be enriching those of Newport, R. I.,[32] and furnishing laborers for the rapidly spreading plantations of the South.

Christian nations had accepted the enslavement of non-Christians as a matter of course, though it had always been held wrong to make slaves of other Christians. For this reason, some consciences were troubled over whether the process might be reversed, and slaves made Christian. Some suspected that once they were converted, the only right thing to do was to emancipate them. Not so, said the Bishop of London in a famous letter of 1727.[33] Aside from scattered voices, it

---

[31] See William Warren Sweet, *The Story of Religion in America* (New York: Harper & Brothers, 1950), p. 191 ff.

[32] Edward Channing, *A History of the United States.* (6 vols.; New York: The Macmillan Company, 1919-1925), I, 214-15.

[33] Christianity, and the embracing of the Gospel, does not make the least Alteration in Civil Property, or in any of the Duties which belong to Civil Relations. . . . The Freedom which Christianity gives is a Freedom from the Bondage of Sin and Satan . . . but as to their *outward* Condition, whatever that was before . . . their being baptized, and becoming Christians, makes no manner of Change in it" (P. G. Mode, *Source Book and Bibliographical Guide for American Church History* [Menasha, Wis.: George Banta Publishing Co., 1921], p. 551).

94

was not till about the middle of the eighteenth century that protests against the slave traffic began to be heard in any volume.

These protests got their inspiration from two sources, one religious, the other secular. A secular humanistic emphasis on the "rights of man," uttered by such men as Diderot and the Encyclopaedists, was supported by a romantic exaltation of the "natural" man, as by Jean Jacques Rousseau. These ideas were widely prevalent among the agitators for American independence, including Tom Paine (who had spent some time in France), and finally were crystallized in the Declaration of Independence and the preamble to the Constitution. Men like Thomas Jefferson and George Washington probably owed more to the secular than to the religious libertarian thought of their time. But it was broad enough to lead them to the logical conclusion that the "rights of man" applied to the black as well as the white man. Though involved in slavery during their lifetime, they were opposed to it in principle, and both Thomas Jefferson and George Washington were among the many who expressed these convictions by drawing up in their wills acts of emancipation for their slaves.

The other root of antislavery sentiment was the Christian tradition. Among evangelical Christians on this side of the water, the voices of two eminent Congregationalist ministers of New England, Ezra Stiles and Samuel Hopkins, began to be heard. It took more courage for them to speak out, as they were both preaching to Newport congregations, many members of which had been enriched by the very trade the preachers were denouncing. There were others, too, but the van was led by the Quakers. The patient, persistent, personal exhortations spoken and written by John Woolman are well-known. The work of "Friend Anthony Benezet" also was behind the emancipation of many slaves before the Revolution. The Philadelphia Yearly Meeting had come so far in antislavery sentiment that in 1776 they agreed to "disown" any of their members who did not emancipate their slaves.[34] The Pennsylvania Friends had formed the world's first society for the abolition of slavery two years earlier. It was soon followed by others.[35]

[34] See Rufus M. Jones, The Quakers in the American Colonies (London, The Macmillan Company, 1911), Chap. VII. Allen C. Thomas, and Richard H. Thomas, History of the Society of Friends in America. (In Vol. XII of the American Church History Series, New York: Christian Literature Co., 1894), p. 245.

[35] Leonard W. Bacon, A History of American Christianity (New York: Charles Scribner's Sons, 1901), p. 204.

The abolition movement was to be vastly accelerated in the 1830's, but it was beginning thus early, and provided a part of the background for the Methodist attack.

Influenced by the forces just described, and, of course, animated by the zeal of Wesley, which, though distant, was powerful, some Methodists had thought and acted on the matter even before it was a part of the Discipline. Freeborn Garrettson, for instance, soon after his conversion in 1775, and as a result of it, announced one day at family prayers: "It is not right to keep our fellow-creatures in bondage. . . . It was God, not man that taught me. . . ." He then pronounced his servants free. Philip Gatch, another early American-born preacher, likewise emancipated his slaves.[36] Asbury's references to the question in his *Journal* are rather discreet, but there is no doubt as to where his sympathies and his convictions lay. For June 8, 1783, there is an entry which shows him protesting, at the cost of considerable discomfort to himself, against the mistreatment of a slave.[37] In 1798, while too ill to travel, he brooded over the question, and came to the conclusion that compromising with slavery was inconsistent with Christian perfection.[38] In 1785, Coke and Asbury went together to ask General Washington for his signature to the petition of the conference to the Assembly of Virginia requesting a measure to permit emancipation. Washington did not see fit to sign the petition, but said he shared the sentiments of the two men on emancipation.[39]

We must remind ourselves at this point that the center of gravity of Methodism was in the South. Of the native-born Americans among the ninety-eight men who were admitted to Conference during the eleven years from 1774 to 1784 inclusive, all were from the South. There were nearly fifteen thousand members in the Methodist So-

[36] SHMEC, I, 354, 380.
[37] "I went to John Worthington's; but I beheld such cruelty to a Negro that I could not feel free to stay; I called for my horse, delivered my own soul and departed" (AJL, I, 442).
[38] "If any had asked the Lord on the subject of slavery, as on polygamy [the reference is to Matt. 5:31, on divorce, which he here equates with polygamy rather than adultery], he must have said, Moses, as a man, suffered this, a less evil, to prevent a greater; but it was not so from the beginning of creation: it is the fall which hath done this, not a holy God. It is man's work, of two evils to choose the least. . . . Christians of two evils should not choose or use either, if they would be like God" [evidently a reference to the concluding verse of Matt. 5: "Be ye therefore perfect as your heavenly Father is perfect"] (AJL, II, 149).
[39] AJL, I, 489 and n.

cieties in 1784; of these only about twenty-five hundred lived north of Maryland.[40] Keeping this in mind will demonstrate more forcibly how much courage was involved in the initial Methodist position on slavery.

The first mention of slavery in the Conference Minutes appears in 1780:

Does this Conference acknowledge that slavery is contrary to the laws of God, man, and nature, and hurtful to society; contrary to the dictates of conscience and pure religion, and doing that which we would not that others should do to us or ours? Do we pass our disapprobation on all our friends who keep slaves and advise their freedom? Yes.[41]

During the same Conference, probably in response to protests against unregulated assemblies of slaves, it was agreed that the preacher in charge of the circuit should see to it that meetings for Negroes were held only under the supervision of himself or some proper helper, and that their meetings were not allowed to continue late.[42] Already the tension had appeared in Methodist documents between the desire to evangelize the slaves and the fear that the meetings for evangelization would foster united and insubordinate action.

One other step taken by this Conference has been called the first written rule of American Methodism on slavery: "Ought not this Conference to require those traveling preachers who hold slaves to give promises to set them free? Yes." [43] Having disapproved the holding of slaves by laymen, the preachers were now required to promise they would set free their slaves. This regulation still lacked sanctions; it probably presupposed not so much a double standard of morality, one for laymen and another for preachers, as a practical recognition that the usefulness of the preachers would be impaired in some parts of the "connection" if they were slave owners. The "traveling preachers," of course, were practically, if not in theory, ministers of the whole connection in a way that laymen were not.

The legislation of the Conference of 1780 just considered took place, it is true, during the first schism in American Methodism. The "Virginia brethren" had decided at their Conference at Broken Back

[40] BHMM, I, 52, 72.
[41] MAC, p. 12.
[42] Loc. cit.
[43] Loc. cit.

97

Church in Fluvanna County to answer the pressing needs of their people for the sacraments, and to that end had appointed a committee who had ordained each other, and then the rest of the preachers. This was a case of the preachers on the ground having recognized a need and being prepared to meet it in advance of the distant Wesley. Asbury was doing all he could by post (which was more uncertain than usual because of the war) to press the matter on Wesley's attention, but meanwhile he was adamant that no steps should be taken before his permission was obtained. The Virginia brethren were, it is true, the southernmost part of the connection, but that was a mere accident. The division was not between "North" and "South," nor between slaveholding and non-slaveholding sections, but between a territory where the vacuum created by the collapse of the Anglican Church was severely felt, and one where it was not nearly so strong; or, to put the matter in other terms, a section where connectionalism was weak, and one where it still prevailed.

This latter formulation might be further explained by saying that Asbury with his strong sense of "connection" had for over two years been confined to Delaware, with occasional incursions into Maryland; so he had not been present to restrain the centrifugal tendencies among the far from submissive brethren of Virginia. One of their leaders was James O'Kelly, always a notable individualist, on whom the claims of co-operation rested very lightly. But it goes to show that this schism had little or no connection at all with the slavery question, that this same O'Kelly was later one of the greatest champions of the antislavery position in Methodism. The stand of the Baltimore Conference of 1780, though taken during the absence of the sacramental party, was later reiterated and strengthened by the whole body of preachers.

In 1783 local preachers were required to free their slaves where the laws of the state permitted, under threat of suspension.[44] There was, according to Asbury's report, a good deal of antislavery sentiment at this Conference. Asbury reports briefly of it: "We all agreed in the spirit of African liberty and strong testimonies were borne in its favor in our love feast." [45]

In 1784, at the regular Conference sessions the legislation, and also

[44] MAC, p. 18.
[45] AJL, I, 441.

the exceptions, were elaborated. Buying slaves, with intent only to hold them, was forbidden under penalty of expulsion, and none were to sell them on any condition whatever. Local preachers were evidently reluctant to emancipate their slaves, even where the laws permitted it, for the question came up again. It was decided to suspend those in Maryland, Delaware, Pennsylvania, and New Jersey, but to give those in Virginia another year.[46] Jesse Lee comments that some slaves obtained their freedom by this rule, but he also notes that the rules on slavery were a disservice to the societies.[47]

It was in 1784 that the famous "Christmas Conference" was held, at which the Methodist societies were constituted a church. This very fact made this Conference a fountainhead from which momentous social consequences flowed. Some of these we will examine later. We are at present concerned only with the position it took on the slavery question.

Its rule was sweeping, and intended to be applied to preachers and laymen alike. It required emancipation by all Methodists without distinction of status, save the inevitable one made between Methodist citizens of states where civil law permitted it and those where it did not. The preliminary declaration ran:

We view it as contrary to the golden law of God, on which hang all the law and the prophets, and the inalienable rights of mankind, as well as every principle of the Revolution, to hold in the deepest abasement . . . so many souls that are all capable of the image of God. We therefore think it our most bounden duty to take immediately some effectual method to extirpate this abomination from among us.

All Methodists were then required to draw up, within the year, an instrument emancipating their slaves at specified ages. The preacher was to exclude those who had not complied within the period. No one was to be admitted to membership thereafter who held slaves.[48] This was more drastic than anything that had gone before. Even that troublesome distinction between preachers and people disappeared, for the time being at least. But the other one—more fateful still— survived: the distinction between states where the laws permitted

[46] MAC, p. 20.
[47] Jesse Lee, op. cit., p. 82.
[48] SHMEC, II, 199-200.

emancipation, and those where they did not. The Christmas Conference exempted the latter from the application of this rule. The Conference had (in 1780) declared slavery to be contrary to the laws of God and man; but in fact it was buttressed by the laws of man in some states. Here, where the nascent Methodist Episcopal Church found the two laws diverging, it chose to submit to the laws of man rather to those of God.

The reaction to this requirement was swift, intense, and hostile, and the attempt to enforce it was abandoned within six months.[49] The rule was kept in the Discipline, however, at least in an attenuated form, and served as an ineffaceable ideal and as a rallying point for those who refused to relinquish the "extirpation" envisaged in the preamble.

In the months which followed, the preachers courageously proclaimed the stand of the Conference on slavery. The opposition they met must have made the preachers think of the tense times of the Revolution, but this time the threats came from their own members. Asbury tells us of one occasion from which he was thankful to come off "with whole bones." [50] Dr. Coke, who went on a preaching tour for the five months or so between the Christmas Conference and his return to England, tells us of some who, at great cost to themselves, as he admiringly notes, did emancipate their slaves; but he also has several stories of being met with staves and clubs.[51] Once, after some "principal friends" had demanded repeal of the slavery rules, a counterthreat to withdraw from the circuit made them "draw in their horns," as Asbury said, indicating that their Methodism meant a great deal to them indeed.[52] But the struggle was too intense and too

[49] Jesse Lee commented: "These rules were short-lived, and were offensive to most of our southern friends; and were so much opposed by many . . . that the execution of them was suspended at the conference held in June following, . . . and they were never afterwards carried into full force. . . . [At] the . . . general conference in 1808 . . . the greater part of the rule . . . was abolished, and no part of it was retained respecting private members" (op. cit., pp. 97-98).

[50] AJL, I, 488. This was at a Conference in Virginia, which, in spite of all, and probably at Coke's urging, sent a petition to the General Assembly asking for the emancipation of slaves. "The Colonel used some threats: next day O'Kelly let fly at them, and they were made angry enough."

[51] SHMEC II, 247-48. "A high-headed lady also went out [from a barn where he had been preaching] and told the rioters . . . that she would give fifty pounds if they would give that little doctor one hundred lashes . . . but [they] only had power to talk."

[52] SHMEC, II, 249-50.

constant for them to bear. Coke heaved a sigh of relief when he got out of Virginia into a state where laws forbade emancipation and he was free not to enjoin it.[53] He resumed it courageously when once more in Virginia, but the end of his stay was drawing near. At a Conference which met at Baltimore on June 1, he and Asbury conceded the suspension of the rules on slavery.[54] The minutes of the Conference for 1785 read:

It is recommended to all our brethren to suspend the execution of the minute on slavery till the deliberations of a future Conference; and that an equal space of time be allowed all our members for consideration, when the minute shall be put in force.

N.B. We do hold in the deepest abhorrence the practice of slavery; and shall not cease to seek its destruction by all wise and prudent means.

4. Ministerial Support

The sparse indications given us in the documents of these early years about the provisions for the support of the preachers and their families tell a tale of heroic self-denial when we think of the small amounts involved; but we are even more impressed by the *method* of granting the support. They carried their spirit of brotherhood so far as to share not only the hardships as equally as possible, but also the tangible resources accruing to them from their ministry. They did not use the word salary—"quarterage" at first and "support" later were the terms—and tried to avoid even the idea that what they received was compensation for their work, or in any way tied to its amount or quality. They would have said, if the phrase had been invented then, "from every man according to his ability," and they would have also said "to every man according to his need," except that there was never enough to go around, and they had to practice a rigid equality in dividing what there was. The conference was the collecting and dividing agency. They admitted the "need" principle to the extent of making an allowance equal to the preacher's own to his wife, if he was married, and for a time, an additional amount for each young child. If "creeping socialism" has affected the Methodist ministry since those days, it has been creeping out, rather than in.

[53] *Ibid.*, II, 248.
[54] *Ibid.*, II, 252.

In 1778, the preacher's "quarterage" was eight pounds, Virginia currency.[55] The Christmas Conference set the allowance at sixty-four dollars for each preacher, and an equal sum for the wife of each one who was married. For each child under six, sixteen dollars was allowed; for each one between six and eleven, $21.33. The allowance for the children was "not pleasing to our societies," and was discontinued in 1787.[56] At the same conference, provision was made for superannuated preachers and their widows and orphans. To a fund for this purpose, each traveling preacher was to contribute two dollars a year. In 1796, this became the "Chartered Fund." The Conference made a valiant, but losing effort to keep this equality, by requiring the preachers to put even contributions made to them individually into the common stock. At first seeking money gifts was altogether forbidden; in 1779 the Conference at Fluvanna asked "In what light shall we view those preachers who receive money by subscription?" The answer was categorical: "As excluded from the Methodist connection." [57] Soon after, it was decided that all gifts, whether of money or clothing, should be brought to the quarterly meeting, and the amount given to each deducted from his "quarterage." [58] Some of the preachers objected to dividing equally a sum to be devoted to the preachers' wives, for which differing amounts had been contributed by different sections. But Jesse Lee stated the reason for treating the matter as a concern of the connection as a whole, rather than of one section, when he said: "The Methodist cause is but one in every place; and he who loves his neighbour as himself will feel for every circuit, every preacher, and every preacher's family." [59] Receiving fees for the performance of ministerial acts such as the performance of marriages, baptisms, and burials was strictly forbidden here, as it had been in England, where Wesley had said: "Let there be no pretence to say we grow rich by the Gospel." [60]

---

[55] MAC, p. 9.
[56] Jesse Lee, op. cit., p. 96.
[57] MAC, p. 11.
[58] Jesse Lee, op. cit., p. 74.
[59] Ibid., p. 77.
[60] In the "Twelve Rules of an Assistant." Quoted from John S. Simon, John Wesley and the Methodist Societies (2nd ed.; London: the Epworth Press, 1937), p. 217. It is Jesse Lee who tells us about the prohibition: op. cit., p. 98. In 1776, Asbury records refusing a funeral fee because his "quarterage" was paid in full (AJL, I, 202).

Before long, however, it was permitted to the preacher to receive a fee for performing the marriage ceremony, provided it be applied (by the steward of the circuit) to the quarterage of the preacher who had received it, if that had not yet been paid in full (which it usually was not). Otherwise it was to go to those preachers whose support had not been paid in full. The attempt to preserve this equality died with the eighteenth century; in 1800, the preachers were allowed to keep wedding fees without giving account of them.[61] The faint echo of these early rules is heard today when a minister comes home from performing a wedding, kisses his wife, gives *her* the fee, and says: "Now, my dear, get yourself something with this you've wanted for a long time." The principle of equality of payment, however, was prolonged into the nineteenth century in the equal payment given to all presiding elders and to all bishops.

If the preachers were not separated from their people by having a greater income, they were likewise kept close to them by express intention. The *Rules of a Helper* taken over bodily from the "Disciplinary Minutes" of the English Conference have the following provisions: "Do not affect the gentleman—a preacher is the servant of all. Be ashamed of nothing but sin; not of fetching wood (if time permit) or drawing water: not of cleaning your own shoes, or your neighbor's." [62]

5. EDUCATION

From the time Methodism became a church, and even before, she manifested an interest in the development of the young. Before there is any mention of a Sunday school or a church school by that name, the preachers were bidden: "Where there are ten children whose parents are in society, meet them at least an hour every week." After three other directions for the spiritual nurture of children, occurs this one: "Preach expressly on education." 'But I have no gift for this.' "Gift or no gift, you are to do it, else you are not called to be a Methist preacher." [63] Behind this is the story of the beginning of Cokesbury College. This is not the place to tell in any detail the story of its

---

[61] Jesse Lee, *op. cit.*, p. 99. Another notice (*ibid.*, p. 270) reads, "The preacher might receive any present, and not give account thereof."

[62] *Ibid.*, pp. 94-95.

[63] *Ibid.*, p. 99.

short and troubled life. But enough must be said about it to indicate how earnestly the early Methodist leaders, confronted already with a task beyond any human performing, shouldered the additional burden of providing institutions of learning where the intellectual horizons of its young might be broadened as well as their spiritual life nurtured. Asbury conceived the idea of a school before the Revolutionary War was over. With Coke's enthusiastic help, he got it started by 1787. As originally projected it was to include an orphanage. Wesley chided them for calling it a college, but at Coke's insistence it was chartered as such and granted the privilege of awarding degrees. They found it difficult to maintain a faculty capable of teaching on that level, however, and it finished its days at Abingdon as it had begun them, a preparatory school only. Fire put an end to the undertaking, and an attempt to reconstitute it in Baltimore met the same fate. In that, as in many subsequent Methodist schools, revivals were regarded as a normal part of the life.

In general it must be said that the leaders of the school were better at recognizing that young people had a claim on the attention of the church than they were expert in meeting it; they treated them as small adults. The discipline was rigorous, having been modeled on a poor pattern. The regime sounds much like that of Kingswood School: The boys' day began at five in the morning. Seven hours were devoted to study; morning and evening prayers were daily parts of the schedule. There were periods for *recreation*, but no *play* was tolerated: Wesley had written, "He who plays as a boy will play as a man," and shut it out completely from the scheme of things at Kingswood. Asbury seemed almost relieved when the project finally ended, and Jesse Lee's tone as he tells of the venture seems to indicate his unspoken verdict that the Methodists had taken on something outside their true province, and should profit by the lesson in its failure.[64] But Methodism had made a beginning in what was to be one of its great contributions to our national life.

6. OTHER SOCIAL ATTITUDES

In other matters as well, the *ethos* of the Methodists reflected the disciplinary provisions which had been carried across the Atlantic;

---

[64] *Ibid.*, pp. 113-14. For a fuller account of the college see the art. "Cokesbury College," *Cyclopaedia of Methodism;* SHMEC II, 253 ff.

and it is apparent that those were most emphasized which were most appropriate to the new situation. The matter of superfluity of dress is a case in point. In England, it was adhered to because of Wesley's insistence that everything over and above necessity be saved for giving to those in still greater need,[65] and also because of the poverty of the first Methodists. Here it comes up several times in the early conferences. In 1784 the Conference urged the preachers to set the example, and to speak frequently and faithfully to the people on superfluity of dress.[66] The Christmas Conference enlarged on this: "This is no time to give any encouragement to superfluity of apparel. Therefore, give no tickets to any, till they have left off superfluous ornaments . . . . [such as] high heads, enormous bonnets, ruffles, or rings." [67] To deprive a Methodist of his ticket as a class-member was in effect to exclude him from the society; so the Conference was very much in earnest about it.

Doubtless, as Methodism moved out on the frontier, such a rule would survive as a reflection of the frontiersman's distaste for display; while in the older settlements where some were more affluent than others, enforcing this rule would be a way of preventing disparity of dress in meetings and the consequent humiliation of those unable to afford the "ruffles or rings." The Methodists of these days took seriously other rules which have not so much as been heard of for generations—for instance the rule passed in 1784 which allowed "no exception" . . . to the rule which had "the men and women sit apart" in meetings.[68]

In accordance with another of the Rules which forbade "brother going to law against brother," the Conference of 1781 devised a scheme for choosing a committee to settle disputes in the societies. Its decision was to be accepted under the pain of expulsion. Expulsion was also the penalty for marrying an unawakened person, but this rule also was moderated in 1804.[69]

---

[65] "Putting on of gold and costly apparel" is forbidden in the "Rules of the United Societies," and so in our own General Rules, as one of the things "we know is not for the glory of God" (See John S. Simon, *John Wesley, and the Methodist Societies*, p. 102), that is, it constituted a kind of self-glorification akin to idolatry.

[66] MAC, p. 20; Lee, *op. cit.*, p. 82.

[67] *Ibid.*, p. 92.

[68] *Ibid.*, p. 102.

[69] *Ibid.*, p. 302.

A fast day proclaimed to be observed "with sabbatical strictness" in 1796 was to awaken Methodists to contrition over their covetousness and love of the world, their breaches of promise, making contracts without so much of an intention to keep them as honest heathen have, profanation of the name and the day of the Lord, drunkenness, and the vassalage still deep-rooted throughout the land.[70]

A passage in Asbury's Journal during 1785 is illuminating as to his conception of the relation between worldly success and spiritual progress, and which was to be sought first:

Some of our principal members here are men who have not been successful; had they prospered in their pursuits, perhaps they would never have sought the Lord: being now in possession of religion, there is the less of danger in prosperity; I therefore counseled them to go to the western country, where the means of rearing a family, and advancing in the world, were the more within the reach of the inhabitants.[71]

[70] MAC, pp. 63-64.
[71] AJL, I, 497.

CHAPTER THREE

The New Church in the New Nation

THE DOMINANT FEATURE IN THE LIFE OF THE NATION during its first period was *expansion*. Even before and during the Revolution there had been trickles of population flowing across the Appalachian Mountain dam. Once the war had been over long enough to allow a recovered equilibrium, the trickles became a stream, and the stream a flood. Between the years 1790 and 1820, ten new states were added to the Union. The War of 1812, which brought distress to the seaboard, served rather to increase than to diminish the flow. A European observer said in 1817: "All America seems to be breaking up and moving westward." [1]

There was need for an aggressive religious body such as Methodism. There were bright spots, but the religious situation in general may be described as dark. The Great Awakening did not die out as suddenly or as completely in Virginia as in New England, and a slow recovery began with the new century. But in the East, the religious spirit characteristic of the first four decades of the century had been dissipated by theological wrangling, by the dominance of political concerns, and finally by the War for Independence. Most authorities concur in describing the end of the eighteenth century as a period of low religious interest. [2]

This being the case in the more settled portions, we are prepared to encounter a still more attenuated state of religion in the "back country." Peter Cartwright's description of his boyhood home in Logan County, Kentucky, as "Rogues' Harbor" is well known. [3]

---

[1] SMAH, p. 153.
[2] See BHMM, I, 102-4.
[3] "Although there was law, yet it could not be executed . . . Murderers, horse thieves, highway robbers, and counterfeiters fled here until they combined and actually

107

Doubtless this situation was worse than most, but the circuit riders' accounts show how prevalent was the spiritual and moral destitution of the frontier. Not all the migrants were people who went out to begin a stable life in a new place where they could rear families and make a more decent livelihood. Many went west to get away from something—debts, for instance, or even their families.[4]

Expansion characterized this period of Methodism's history as well as the nation's. In several fundamental respects, Methodism as it came from England was well adapted indeed to fit into the new environment, and to expand with the new nation. It had been born in a revival, and it had come to a country where revivalism was to be even more a part of the religious scene than in its homeland. It made a large place for lay activity in evangelization and in the conduct of the societies, at least on the local scale. It preached a doctrine for plain men: a doctrine which insisted that free men's choice had a role to play in their salvation, and that self-help was approved of God in the economic sphere. Moreover, the doctrine was preached not only for, but by plain men; free from theological subtleties, it was readily applicable to the momentous issues of everyday life. In matters of church government, even the dictatorial control of the leaders was an asset in evangelizing a highly mobile population.

In certain other respects the Methodism "made in England" needed modification in the interest of usefulness on the American scene. Its being a society, rather than a church, was a real handicap throughout the whole Colonial period. It was vastly more difficult for Methodists to take the sacrament here than it had been in England. In some parts of the colonies the Anglican Churches were few and far apart. The other churches had severe requirements for par-

formed a majority. . . . They . . . put all law at defiance . . . a very desperate state of things" (*Autobiography of Peter Cartwright* [Charles L. Wallis, ed., Nashville: Abingdon Press, 1956], p. 30).

[4] Dr. Barclay, in his *History of Methodist Missions*, quotes a paragraph from Thomas Ware, "one of the most able of the early itinerants," descriptive of this element of the frontier population: "there were many . . . refugees from justice. Some there were who had borrowed money, or were otherwise in debt, and left their creditors and securities to do the best they could. Persons of such principles cannot be expected to exert themselves in promoting order in society. But there were others whose influence was much more pernicious, especially against the introduction and progress of Methodism. These were such as had been guilty of some heinous or scandalous crime, and fled from justice. Some of them had left their wives and were living with other women." (BHMM, I, 86.)

ticipation in the sacrament which put them out of reach of most Methodists. Anti-English feeling in the colonies before the Revolution extended to the English Church and her sacraments; the war itself decimated the number of churches, thus compounding the difficulty. The true significance of the schism of the "Virginia brethren," as has been mentioned above,[5] lay not in tension between North and South over slavery, but in just this matter of the crying need for the administration of the sacraments in the societies.

The lack was made good at the "Christmas Conference" of 1784. At that Conference Dr. Thomas Coke transmitted to Francis Asbury Wesley's commission to act as Superintendent in the new Church; likewise Coke, Vasey, and Whatcoat transmitted to some of the American preachers Presbyterial orders which had been transmitted to them by Wesley and other Presbyters of the Church of England. Thus, simply and solemnly, the American Methodists, who had up to that time been "societies," became the Methodist Episcopal Church, and began the ministration of the sacraments.

Though the American Methodists welcomed Wesley's provision for their administering the sacraments, they were not so hospitable to his proposals for a liturgical form of worship. He had sent over his own abridgment of the English Book of Common Prayer with recommendations for its use. His wish was that the Morning and Evening Prayer be read "every Lord's day," the Litany on Wednesdays and Fridays, and that the Lord's Supper be administered weekly. The Christmas Conference provided permissive legislation on the subject; but such a procedure was too uncongenial to the temper of the Americans to endure for long. The modified Anglican forms for the Communion service and for the other "occasional services" were kept; but by 1792 all attempt to read Morning and Evening Prayer from Wesley's Prayer Book was abandoned. The impatience of the free spirit of the new land which identified form in worship with formalism was too strong to be ignored, and the old tradition yielded to the new.[6] Another striking instance of the same tendency was the quick

[5] P. 98.

[6] Jesse Lee describes the process and the disposition which brought it about: "In the large towns, and in some country places, our preachers read prayers on the Lord's day; and in some cases the preachers read part of the morning service on Wednesdays and Fridays. But some of the preachers who had been long accustomed to pray extempore were unwilling to adopt this new plan. Being fully satisfied that they

disappearance of the traditional gown and bands as the garb of the ministers while conducting services.[7]

Here we shall merely mention two other changes in the Methodist scheme which may be reckoned as responses to the demands of the new environment. We shall treat them both more in detail later on.

The first was the adoption of the greater part of the disciplinary provisions formulated in the twenty years during which the British Conference had been meeting, and embodied in their Long Minutes. So far as administrative regulations are concerned, they embodied pretty thoroughly Wesley's highly autocratic method of control exercised "from the top down." One modification so significant that it may be called revolutionary was introduced on this side of the water. Once Asbury was here long enough to sense the temper of the preachers, and he concluded that in the circumstances Wesley's appointment to the superintendency would not suffice. He resolved that both he and Coke must likewise be *elected* by the suffrages of the preachers. This was forthcoming at the Christmas Conference, and constitutes the precedent according to which the Methodist Superintendents (or Bishops as they now have long been called) have been elected ever since. It is noteworthy that the Protestant Episcopal Church embodied a like provision in their Constitution. Both instances represent a modification imposed by the democratic spirit on the procedures which had been followed in the old country. In the case of the Methodists, it was not long, as we shall see, before a protest was

could pray better and with more devotion while their eyes were shut than they could with their eyes open" (*op. cit.*, pp. 102-3).

[7] A tradition which was recorded later, but which nevertheless has the ring of authenticity, adds somewhat to Lee's explanation: "Extra services on the Sabbath, especially love-feasts, frequently consumed time needed for the liturgy, so that it gradually fell into disuse. Wesley's Sunday service, though mentioned occasionally in successive *Disciplines* until 1792, is not officially referred to after that date" (J. M. Buckley, *A History of Methodists*, p. 247). The American Methodists apparently weren't objecting to the *length* of services (many of them had come a long distance to attend them), but they wanted to spend their time in a kind of worship more spontaneous, and more congenial to their temper, than that provided by Wesley's *Sunday Service*. "The Superintendents and some of the Elders introduced the custom of wearing gowns and bands, but it was opposed by many of the preachers, as well as private members, who looked upon it as needless and *superfluous*. Having made a stand against it, after a few years it was given up, and has never been introduced among us since" (Lee, *op. cit.*, pp. 102-3). Lee doesn't say so in so many words, but from his tone, one can easily gather that he himself approved these changes, which he ascribes impersonally to "many of the preachers as well as private members." As a matter of fact, he personally remonstrated with Asbury for wearing gown and bands while preaching at the headwaters of the Yadkin in North Carolina in 1785 (AJL, I, 481, n.).

110

raised that the revolution had not gone far enough. But, as far as it went, it was a step toward democracy, and it must be reckoned as one of the many great services of Asbury that he insisted on it from the beginning.

The other instance of radical modification of the English discipline under American conditions is a far less happy one—the relinquishing of the high antislavery provisions within six months after they had been incorporated in the American discipline by the Christmas Conference. It was a lamentable capitulation to the pressure exerted by a social wrong which had already deeply permeated American society.

Thus, by the time English Methodism was required to face the task imposed upon it in the new nation, while preserving those of its features which were to be useful to it, for weal or woe, it had modified others which would have hindered its expansion. It had kept much of its heritage; but it had likewise undergone certain adaptations which facilitated its expansion.

Of this expansion only the sketchiest indication can be given here. One good index is the addition of new conferences toward the west in the early years of the church's existence. In 1788 a conference session was held in Beesontown, Va., a town which later came to be known as Uniontown, Pennsylvania, right in the Appalachian Mountains. In 1796, the Western Conference was organized. It included the new states of Kentucky and Tennessee. Methodism also expanded against the current of migration into New England, in the last decade of the century.[8] A story which is indicative from the dramatic, if not the statistical point of view, is told of Richmond Nolley, the circuit rider:

In a remote section of Mississippi one day he saw fresh wagon tracks and overtook a settler just unloading his goods and placing his family on a new homestead.

After learning who Nolley was, the settler exclaimed in disgust: "Another Methodist preacher! I left Virginia for Georgia to get clear of them. There they got my wife and daughter and I came here, and here is one before I get my wagon unloaded!"

"My friend," said Nolley, "if you go to heaven, you'll find Methodist preachers there; if you go to hell, I'm afraid you'll find some there; and

---

[8] For fuller notes of this sort, see BHMM, I, 121, 140-41.

you see how it is on earth, so you had better make terms with us and be at peace." [9]

During the first quarter of the nineteenth century, the Methodists increased more than fivefold. In 1800, there were 63,961 members and 287 preachers; in 1825, there were 334,269 members and 1,197 preachers.

One of the reasons the common people heard the gospel as preached by the Methodists was that it was preached to them by plain men like themselves. This advantage the Methodist propaganda shared with the Baptists, who along with them were the most successful evangelists on the frontier. Where the number of Baptist churches multiplied because their congregational polity made it comparatively easy to organize a new one, with a farmer-preacher as its pastor, the Methodists expanded under the quite different regime of connection-alism, led by a disciplined and mobile corps of preachers, drilled to take the hardest circuits by turns, and taught by their forms of church government to make good use of the promising laymen in the various communities where they established churches. To the role of this itinerating ministry we must now turn.

A. Authority and the Preservation of the Itinerancy

The itinerancy, of course, was an inheritance from Wesley, who was himself a tireless itinerant, and who, finding it peculiarly useful in the prosecution of the revival in England, maintained it strictly there. If it was useful in England, it was to be even more so here. Asbury was aware of this from the very beginning, and acted accordingly. One of the first things he inveighed against after his arrival here was the tendency of the other preachers to "abide in the cities and live like gentlemen." [10] Indeed, before he had been here a month, he wrote: "I have not yet the thing which I seek—a circulation of preachers, to avoid partiality and popularity . . . My brethren seem unwilling to leave the cities, but I think I shall show them the way." [11] Jesse Lee said of him and Wright: "They . . . did not spend their time in

---

[9] Quoted from Halford E. Luccock and Paul Hutchison. *The Story of Methodism* (Nashville: Abingdon Press, 1926), p. 293. Nolley worked in Georgia, Mississippi, and Louisiana from 1811 to 1815 (MAC, p. 275). His travels in that country might be described as a "ordeal by water." He died of exposure in the open after being separated from his horse while fording a cold raging creek—he got across, but his horse didn't.

[10] AJL, I, 85 (under date of July 14, 1773).

[11] *Ibid.*, p. 10.

the cities as the other preachers had done. Mr. Asbury spent most of his time among the people in the country, and . . . he soon found their labors were more visibly owned of God in the country than in the cities." [12] Asbury made these observations before he had any other authority than such as could be exerted by "showing the way"; indeed, in 1773, Rankin was, by Wesley's appointment, his superior. Asbury was vested with Wesley's authority, however, and he unswervingly pursued the same course, and insisted last, as well as first, on "the Methodist plan."

We have already had occasion to notice the authoritarian character of Wesley's control of his societies.[13] But once the American Methodists had become a church, Wesley's "sons in the gospel" became restive under such measure of control as he attempted to exercise from three thousand miles away. The Christmas Conference made a statement of filial devotion: but the Conference of 1787 repudiated the earlier position, and refused to elect one of their number to the superintendency on Wesley's command.[14] The principle of the "consent of the governed" was so deeply ingrained as to make some such result inevitable.

Asbury himself had correctly foreseen this tendency in the American preachers, and, whether willingly or not, had by his own decision woven it firmly into the polity of the new church. When he heard the news from Coke that he was to act as general superintendent, Asbury wrote determinedly in his *Journal*: "If the preachers unanimously choose me, I shall not act in the capacity I have hitherto done by Mr. Wesley's appointment." [15] The result of his determination was to make the Annual Conference (which has since become many conferences) the fountainhead of authority in Methodist polity.

---

[12] Lee, op. cit., p. 31.

[13] See p. 45.

[14] Lee, op. cit., p. 124. In 1784: "During the life of the Rev. Mr. Wesley, we acknowledge ourselves his sons in the gospel, ready in matters belonging to church government, to obey his commands." But in 1787: "they did not feel ready now to obey his command."

[15] AJL, I, 471. A penetrating analyst of Methodist affairs wrote a generation ago, in comment on the significance of this decision of Asbury: "The government of the Methodist Episcopal Church in the United States is founded not upon a principle of legitimacy, namely the pure transmission of authority, but upon a revolutionary principle, namely the consent of the governed" (from an unpublished lecture, in this author's possession, by George Croft Cell, late professor of historical theology in Boston University School of Theology).

It is equally clear, however, that certain features in the government of the new church were far from democratic. The lay people of the societies had no voice in the choice of their leaders in the congregation, not even the class leaders. That was all done "from the top down." Still less did they have a voice in conference affairs. Not even the local preachers were allowed to vote there. The bishops, once chosen by the preachers, aside from the fact that their character was subject to the same scrutiny as that of all the preachers, exercised their authority from an almost impregnable position, especially in the matter of their appointive power, for there was no appeal from their decisions. The "consent of the governed" could not be exercised below the level of the itinerancy. Even there it was limited to a voice in the framing of disciplinary regulations and the choice of governors; it had very little scope in the working decisions in the operation of the system. What saved it from being an intolerable tyranny was the devotion of bishops, preachers, and people to the common cause. This has been formulated most aptly as consisting of two principles and only two: "to preach the Gospel, and to keep its ministers in circuit." [16]

Bishop Asbury had perhaps made it harder to "keep the ministers in circuit" when he had admitted the preachers to a vote in the Conference. Human nature being what it is—and Methodist preachers were then, as now, human—it was inevitable that there should be protests against what sometimes seemed the excessive appointive power of the bishops. But the majority felt that the itinerancy must be preserved at all costs, and that, for the good of the whole, it must be protected against any who would abridge the appointive power of the bishops. That is why the preachers, as a sort of self-denying ordinance, not out of servility, ultimately rejected all attacks on it in the conferences, both annual and general.

Concern for the preservation of the itinerancy, then, is the reason why, in opposition to the prevailing currents in political life, and indeed in the life of the other denominations, the Methodists restricted control to a comparatively small group of preachers, and put the highest authority into the hands of the Episcopacy, which consisted at first of only two men. All the denominations with congregational

[16] Peter G. Mode, *The Frontier Spirit in American Christianity* (New York: The Macmillan Co., 1923), p. 133.

114

polity were far more democratic in their government; so were the Presbyterian churches. Even the Protestant Episcopal Church, with its much higher conception of the *spiritual* authority of its clergy, made room in its new constitution for a much larger voice of the congregation in the polity of their church, and from the beginning allowed laymen to sit in their general convention. In contrast to these, the Methodist system, though not a sacerdotalism, certainly was a clericalism.

I. THE FIRST SCHISMS OVER POLITY

a) *James O'Kelley and the "Republican Methodists"*

Persons were not lacking, however, who felt that the Methodist system was quite out of harmony with the spirit of American institutions, and not to be borne. The first man to lead a charge against the appointive power of the bishops was James O'Kelley. O'Kelley was a man of considerable ability, and had served as a Presiding Elder (as the District Superintendents were then called) in Virginia, a state in which, at the time "republican" sentiments flourished. Feeling that the church should be run on more republican principles, or perhaps, as several accounts intimate, professing these principles to mask other reasons for dissidence,[17] he proposed in the first general conference (1792) that any preacher feeling himself dissatisfied with the appointment he had received from the Bishop might appeal to the conference for a change. O'Kelley had succeeded in attaching a number of the preachers to his cause, including William (later Bishop) McKendree.[18] The debate was warm, and lasted several days; but when the vote was finally taken, O'Kelley found himself very much in the minority. Accordingly, he left the conference, with a number of his adherents. Not long afterwards, he formed a new body which he called the "Republican Methodists." Later, however, as his support waned, he threw in his lot with the churches of congregational polity which called themselves simply "Christian," and under the leadership of Barton W. Stone coalesced with the followers of the Campbells to form the "Disciples of Christ."

---

[17] The article on O'Kelley in the *Cyclopaedia of Methodism* suggests a difference with Asbury; Jesse Lee suggested that he used this cause as an expedient to escape charges of irregularity on the doctrine of the Trinity (*op. cit.*, p. 178).

[18] SMAH, p. 134.

b) *The Methodist Protestants*

Fending off the attack of the O'Kelleyites on the Bishop's appointive powers resulted in some loss in numbers and some bitterness in the region affected. The next attack, motivated by a more single-minded devotion to the cause of democratic government in the church, and with a more genuine grievance at the way their plea was received by the official powers, was even more serious. It rose during the decade between 1820 and 1830, and eventually led to the establishment of the Methodist Protestant Church.

This second surge of protest against the authority of the bishops may be regarded as a renewal of that begun by O'Kelley; but the "Reformers," as its supporters soon were called, had more strings to their bow than the Virginia preacher had. The movement began by trying to curtail the powers of the bishop by making the presiding elders less dependent on him and more dependent on the body of the preachers in the conference. It eventually abolished both episcopacy and presiding eldership, and admitted laymen (including unordained preachers) to a voice in the conferences.

One line of the reformers' argument stressed the discrepancy between the democratic principles on which our civil government was based and those followed in the church. The New Testament was cited as furnishing the charter for democracy in both. Since the polity of Methodism was so undemocratic, its source was evidently to be found somewhere else than the New Testament. A favorite polemical device was to find this source in the Roman Church.[19] Presumably the word "Protestant" in their title got its point from this protest against the "Romanism" in the government of the Methodist Episcopal Church. Nathan Bangs, then Book Agent, wrote a rebuttal in which he denied that the government of the church should be patterned after the civil government, alleging the difference between spiritual authority entrusted to the ministers of the church and the authority with which civil officers were endowed. The effect of his argument was to maintain the idea that, though in civil government

[19] "Whence are derived unequal forms of church government? It can never be supposed that the New Testament affords principles of equal government in political matters, and the reverse in ecclesiastical affairs. Whence, then, are illiberal forms of church polity derived? From the Church of Rome? Yes, from the Church of Rome." (WR, I [1821-22], 207-8.)

authority might proceed from the people upward, in the church it proceded from the top downward.

But the "protestants" remained unconvinced. One of their writers in the *Wesleyan Repository* commented: "And what could his holiness the Pope have said more?" [20] Another argument of the reformers was that the episcopacy and the presiding eldership were innovations, not only on the New Testament but on Wesley's own plan for American Methodism. Much was made of the inconsistencies of Wesley's ordinations; and repeated reference was made to the letter in which he had scolded Asbury for having assumed the title "bishop." [21] The objection to Presiding Elders was chiefly that the office was "unscriptural," but also that their contribution did not justify their cost to the church.[22] The basic grievance, though they might state it in historical, scriptural, or financial terms, was the arbitrary power in the hands of officials against whom the preachers and people, especially the local preachers and laymen, had no recourse.[23]

When it became inescapably clear that their cause had no future in the Methodist Episcopal Church, the reformers now took the next step—the formation of a new body called the Methodist Protestant Church. Its constitution was the result of the labors of General Conventions in 1828 and 1830. It is significant that the former year was the year of Andrew Jackson's election to the White House; the following years saw the triumph of "Jacksonian democracy" in the national government. We may see in the contemporaneous writing of the Methodist Protestants' constitution an analogous revision, in the ecclesiastical sphere, of an older and more

---

[20] See *Ibid.*, 2, 373. What Bangs said was: "The government of the church of God is somewhat different from 'civil society' and . . . those ministers whom God selects . . . possess the right of governing themselves in religious matters, and all those committed to their care."

[21] *Mutual Rights of the Ministers and Members of the Methodist Episcopal Church.* (Baltimore, 1824 ff.; hereafter cited as MR) 3 (1824-25): 154. "Our whole system of episcopacy in the United States is . . . an 'innovation' upon the genius and plans of Wesleyan Methodism and one expressly disapproved and disavowed by Mr. Wesley." See also *Ibid.*, 4 (1827-28), 344.

[22] "We wish presiding elders taken, as respects name and office, out of the Methodist world as a creature of which we have no account in the Word of God and entirely unnecessary. . . . Are not [the deacons and elders] competent to take care of themselves? Hence, we regard presiding elders as living upon the labor of others and as a mere burthen to the church." (*Loc. cit.*).

[23] One writer objected to the authority to cast a member out of a Society without a trial for non-attendance at class-meeting.

authoritarian tradition. The new constitution carefully preserved the features of government for which the reform movement had contended. Episcopacy and presiding eldership were both rejected. The annual conference was presided over by a president elected annually, and was composed of an equal number of ministers and laymen, as was the General Conference. The line between ordained ministers and unordained preachers was kept; [24] but the equality of all elders was insisted on.[25] The ministerial vote in the annual Conference was restricted to itinerants only,[26] but the "local" preachers had their representation as a part of the "laity." The preachers "not under the stationing power of the conference" participated as laymen in the election of representatives to General Conference and presumably were themselves eligible for election to it.[27] Class leaders were normally to be elected by the class; only in case of failure to elect were they to be appointed by the superintendent.

There were, however, limitations on the democracy thus achieved: the franchise was limited to adults who were also male and white.[28] These lines were to be transcended later, but thus far the reformers embodied their objectives at the very beginning in the working constitution of the Methodist Protestant Church. Thus they infused into their church organization a more democratic principle, and brought it nearer to the spirit which animated our civil institutions. Thus they kept before the Methodist Episcopal Church the ideal which was, in time, approximated in it also.

After a period of rapid increase, the new church's growth slowed, and failed to keep up, in percentage, with Episcopal Methodism. So many factors enter into the speed with which the American churches grew during the nineteenth century, it would be impossible to say how much the Methodist Protestant Church was retarded by its adoption of the more democratic scheme. Insofar as the "time-limit" on pastorates may be said to coincide with the itinerancy, the itinerancy was maintained in the Methodist Protestant Church since the three-

---

[24] *Constitution and Discipline of the Methodist Protestant Church* (Baltimore: published for the Book Committee, 1830), p. 19.

[25] *Ibid.*, p. 14.

[26] *Ibid.*, p. 20. The "Itinerants," included "all ministers properly under the stationing power of the conference." The term "Local Preacher" does not appear in the new *Discipline*, but the designation "Exhorter" does (p. 19).

[27] *Ibid.*, p. 23.

[28] *Ibid.*, p. 29.

year time limit was written into their Constitution. On the other hand, one gets the impression that their "stationing committees" never worked so smoothly or with such regard for the good of the whole as the Episcopal appointive power, with the weight of almost autocratic authority behind it. The Methodist Protestant historian, Drinkhouse, stoutly maintained that Episcopal Methodism's more rapid rate of growth was due, not to a better appointive system, but to "the gravitation that gives attractive power of large bodies over smaller; the pull of large numbers congregated in all the centres against small numbers segregated and scattered." [29] We may put the question this way: which of the two churches was able better to keep up with the frontier? To the question thus put, Drinkhouse, without realizing it, gave an answer when he complained of the numbers his church lost by migration to new communities "where no organization of the new church existed." The loss he put at ten to one.[30] Episcopal Methodism, on the other hand, far from complaining of migration as a source of loss, regarded it, and rightly, as a means of expansion.

B. Spreading the Gospel: Revivals

It is impossible, within the scope of such a volume as this, adequately to treat either revivals or missions from the historical point of view. Yet both were among the most effective ways in which the

---

[29] Edward J. Drinkhouse, *History of Methodist Reform* (2 Vols. Baltimore and Pittsburgh: Board of Publication of the Methodist Protestant Church, 1899), II, 692 ff. There is no doubt that in church membership it is true that "to them that have, shall be given," and that Episcopal Methodism had the uninterrupted benefit of the resources of a Missionary Society which it took the Methodist Protestants some time to establish. Indeed Drinkhouse denied that Episcopal Methodism had the better rate of growth. In proof, he gives a series of statistics by decades which lead him to the conclusion that in the first fifty years (1790-1840) the Methodist Episcopal Church achieved a net gain of 2,049 per cent; the Methodist Protestant Church, during its first fifty years made a net increase of 2,220 per cent (1828-1878). A good deal depends on what years one takes. In 1878 the Methodist Protestants had just consummated a union with "the Methodist Church." If one not only picks other years, but compares the two churches with each other, a different picture emerges. Comparing the membership of the Methodist Protestant Church in 1846 with that of the Methodist Episcopal Church in 1844 (the last year before the great split over slavery), we get 64,944 to 1,171,356, which makes the Methodist Protestant Church about 5.5 per cent as large. In 1910, the Methodist Protestants counted 188,437 members to the Methodist Episcopal Church, North's, 3,489,696, a proportion of not quite 5.4 per cent. If we combine the membership of the two Episcopal Methodisms, we get a total of 5,372,739 in the same year. To this total, that of the Methodist Protestants bears a proportion of 3.5 per cent.

[30] *Ibid.*, II, 334.

churches in general and Methodism in particular exercised their influence on society. Fortunately it is less necessary to treat them extensively here because of the good work which has recently been done in both fields.[31] We must on that account content ourselves with a brief appraisal of the social factors involved.

The Great Awakening, which reached its height in the decade after 1734, raised a controversy between pro- and anti-revivalists. They were, in general, divided into parties distinguished by cultural differences. This division has persisted into our own time; though the parties have changed their names, or have had no names at all, the issues have been pretty much the same. Those who favored the revivalist methods, have in general had less, and those who opposed them have had more of a stake in their culture, academically, institutionally, and economically speaking. Notable exceptions to this general statement will occur to everyone—indeed many of the *leaders* of revivals have been such exceptions. Methodists will doubtless think of the Wesley brothers, Presbyterians of Charles G. Finney, and so on. But the exceptions will serve rather to enhance than to diminish the usefulness of the distinction.

The Great Awakening disappeared almost as suddenly as it arose in New England. In the South, however, though it abated, it never completely disappeared. During the last years of the eighteenth century and the first of the nineteenth, arose what has been called the Second Awakening. It, too, affected all parts of the nation, but the homogeneity of the Great Awakening had made way for a differentiation in form and intensity which corresponded to different sections of the country, and to some extent to denominational differences as well. Revivals had come to stay in American life, but they would henceforth change their form from place to place, and from time to time.

---

[31] Notable among recent works on revivalism are: Edwin S. Gaustad, *The Great Awakening in New England* (New York: Harper, and Bros. 1957); Charles A. Johnson, *The Frontier Camp Meeting: Religion's Harvest Time* (Dallas, Southern Methodist University Press, 1955); William G. McLoughlin, *Modern Revivalism: Charles Grandison Finney to Billy Graham* (New York: Ronald Press Co., 1959); and Timothy L. Smith, *Revivalism and Social Reform in Mid-Nineteenth-Century America* (Nashville: Abingdon Press, 1957). On Methodist missions, mention should again be made of the projected six-volume *History of Methodist Missions*, the first three volumes of which are now published. Ably written by W. D. Barclay, they have frequently been cited in the present work.

The Second Awakening along the seaboard, and especially in New England, was attended with relatively little excitement. This was especially true of that phase of it which flourished in the colleges, notably at Yale, under President Timothy Dwight. On the frontier, however, a ruder, more intense revivalism prevailed, and came to be associated with that characteristically American institution, the camp meeting.

The camp meeting was born with the nineteenth century, and was a striking instance of the modification of religious institutions to fit the peculiar needs of a new social situation. For the camp meeting filled a social as well as a religious need in the lives of the frontier folk. The typical frontier family was isolated from its neighbors, engaged from dawn to dark in an exhausting, often brutalizing struggle to wrest a living from a recalcitrant wilderness and security from a hostile environment. There was little provision for sociability, as there was little opportunity for it. The camp meeting gave occasion for men to meet their neighbors, brought some excitement into their monotonous lives, and provided an outlet for their pent-up emotions. These were not the only functions they performed, but they cannot be ignored in any account of the swift rise to prominence of the camp meeting in the religious life of the early nineteenth century in America.

It is a striking fact that, though the first camp meetings were led by Presbyterians, it was not long before most of them repudiated their own invention. They were repelled by the extravagant demonstrations of emotion; they deplored the moral dangers accompanying the meetings; they preferred to insist on the comparatively high educational standards of their ministers; and finally they feared the dilution of their theology by contact with revival Arminianism. They bore their witness, and it was a needed one; but their choice involved leaving the Methodists and Baptists to use the method best adapted to carry the gospel to the common man on the frontier, and to an expansion in numbers they could not achieve.

Camp meetings were never an *official* part of Methodism, in the sense of being written into the *Discipline*. But they were early adopted and encouraged by Methodists from Asbury down. The conferences, both annual and quarterly, which in those days were devoted quite as much to fervent religious exercises as to administrative matters, formed nuclei with which camp meetings easily coalesced. Indeed, it is not always easy to tell, in some passages in Lee's *History*, whether he is talking about conferences or camp meetings.[32] It must not be supposed that in adopting camp meetings so heartily, the Methodists were oblivious of the dangers. Peter Cartwright made every effort to discourage "the jerks" (as some of the more extreme physical manifestations of excitement were called), and assured us that most of the preachers did the same.[33] The rowdyism, drunkenness, and sale of liquor which accompanied the camp meetings were carried on around the fringes of the assemblies by those who had come for those purposes; those who were attending for serious reasons did their best to exclude them by making strict codes to that end.[34] That the religious excitement attending the camp meetings multiplied offenses against chastity must remain a matter of surmise rather than a proved assertion. To the emotional manifestations and the claims to conversion growing out of the camp meetings, the Methodists tried to apply what might be called the "neighbor test." Jesse Lee was one of these:

It will likely be asked, were not many of these converts deceived? Perhaps they were. . . . But the Christians who were acquainted with the people while they were careless about their souls, and were present with them while they were under conviction, and at the time they professed to be converted, can tell pretty well whether they were deceived or not.[35]

Furthermore, we must disabuse ourselves of the notion that the Methodists relied *solely* on camp meetings and revivals as methods of operation. The fact is, and we shall enlarge on it later on,[36] that discipline and instruction were regarded as equally important, if not equally spectacular, ways of bringing influence to bear on their constituency.

Having adopted camp meetings, and having surrounded them with such safeguards as they could, the Methodist leaders of the time leave

---

[32] For example, see the *Short History*, p. 304: "Another quarterly-meeting was held . . . in Bottetourt county, which continued for five days; during that time eighteen professed to be converted. The next noted meeting was on Indian Creek . . . which continued four days, and . . . 30 souls were . . . delivered from their sins."

[33] Charles A. Johnson, *The Frontier Camp Meeting: Religion's Harvest Time* (Dallas: Southern Methodist University Press, 1955), p. 46.

[34] *Ibid.*, p. 90 ff., where several sample sets of rules are given.

[35] Lee, *op. cit.*, p. 315.

[36] See pp. 128-31.

us in no doubt that they put high value on them. There is an exultant note in their reports of how the glorious work "broke out," and souls were saved. Peter Cartwright takes up the tale where Jesse Lee leaves off. He says of a camp meeting in Logan County, Kentucky:

> It was supposed that this was one among the best ever held [there] . . . where there had been many, very many, glorious camp-meetings. . . . The fruits of this camp-meeting I hope to see with pleasure in vast eternity.[37]

Cartwright was sure the most successful part of his ministry had been exercised in camp meetings, and asserted, "There the word of God has reached the hearts of thousands that otherwise, in all probability, never would have been reached by the ordinary means of grace." [38]

The balance of judgment on camp meetings clearly falls on the favorable side. Their adoption in America accelerated the spread of Methodism here just as the adoption of field preaching and the employment of lay preachers had hastened it in England. The Methodists in both places were using methods in consonance with popular needs, and became, as a consequence, a church of the people.

C. Spreading the Gospel: Missions

Missions may be defined, for our purposes here, as transcultural evangelism. Missionaries may, and do, differ as to how far they should try to transmit the "sending" culture along with the gospel they preach, but the difference can be only one of degree, for they cannot, no matter how hard they try, eliminate the cultural factor altogether.

The Methodists of the early nineteenth century were somewhat later than the older American denominations in the development of a "missionary" as distinct from an "evangelistic" consciousness. We may with propriety allow the formation of the Methodist Missionary Society in 1819 to stand as marking the transition point. In that year the first voluntary missionary society in the United States, the New York Missionary Society, was nearly a quarter of a century old; and the best-known society for foreign missions, the American Board of Commissioners for Foreign Missions, had been in existence for a decade. These two were interdenominational in composition, at least

---

[37] *Autobiography* (ed. Wallis), p. 159.
[38] *Ibid.*, p. 339.

at first; but the Congregational Association of Connecticut had formed a society of its own as early as 1797.

Among the Methodists, there had been opposition to the formation of a special missionary society on just the ground that the whole church was a missionary society. The promoters of the new organization, however, not only stressed the greater outreach it would have, but, with considerable frankness, urged that the Methodists should have their own society instead of channeling their contributions through others. The objections of the society's opponents are understandable in the light of the remarkable expansiveness of their church, and because the society at first envisaged only what later came to be called home missions. Indeed, there was considerable difficulty in distinguishing between the regular work on the frontier and the missions there. Without bothering too much about the theoretical niceties of the situation, the conferences, the bishops, and the society co-operated strenuously at the task. On the other hand, it is significant of the transcultural factor we have noted that the Methodist Missionary Society rose out of interest in the evangelization among the Indians.

If we use the word distance in both its geographical and its sociological sense, we may say that a missionary is an evangelist who is sent a long distance to his work. Taking the geographical sense of the word first, we can illustrate it by noting that Asbury regarded himself as a missionary his whole life long. Those Methodist preachers were called missionaries who were sent to the frontier either from "back East," or when they were supported by money which came from Methodists in other places than their fields of labor. Illustrations of the "social distance" which the nineteenth-century Methodist missionaries traveled is found in the special groups for which they worked. During the early part of the century, in addition to the work for the Indians already mentioned, they strove to evangelize the Negroes (still slaves for the most part), the French and German-speaking immigrants, and the seamen of the ports.

Ultimately the two kinds of "distance" we have mentioned were combined in missions which traversed the oceans. There were combined the factors that made the missionary society necessary. The bare existence of a missionary society, and much more the complex operations of a modern one are testimony to the recognition that some fields of labor are harder to reach than others, and that they require special methods of operation and a personnel specially selected and trained. But fundamentally the purpose of the Missionary Society was, and has remained, the same as that of the church: evangelization.

Space forbids our going into the story of the manifold missions carried on at home and abroad. The story is a long, a variegated, and a thrilling one. Simply for purposes of illustration, however, we must include the stories of two, one at home and one abroad, stressing the social significance of each. The famous mission of Jason Lee to Oregon, undertaken in 1834, has been credited with some (perhaps too much) influence in arousing the United States government's interest in securing the territory for this country. The romantic beginning of the mission in response to a reported call from some Flathead Indians who wished to learn about "the white man's Book of Life" issued in a distressing failure, but a failure which carried a lesson with it. Lee came, in the course of planting the mission along the Willamette, to a conception of his task broader than that with which he started. Originally his sole purpose had been to bring the Christian message to the Indians. That remained, it seems, his primary purpose, but he came to believe that in order to accomplish it he would have to make farmers and craftsmen of the Indians first. This position is accepted as a commonplace today; and indeed it had been explained by the Jesuits two centuries before him, in their famous *Relations*. To Christianize the Indians of the St. Lawrence Valley, they argued, you must teach them to read; before you can teach them, you must get them to settle down by the schoolhouse; to get them to settle down, you must wean them from their hunting; before you can wean them from their hunting, you must teach them other ways of getting the necessities of life—chiefly by farming. But Lee's progress toward this position, though much slower than the Jesuits', was faster than the society's; the unwillingness of the society (and, it must be added, their financial inability) to support him in his plans brought on the ultimate breakup of the enterprise.

It was 1832 before the Methodist Missionary Society found a man willing to go to Africa as their missionary, though they had had money to send him for some time. Melville Cox did not long survive his arrival in Liberia, whose pestilential airs were long the terror of all white residents. He made a good beginning, but had no time for more. "Let a thousand fall before Africa be given up!" he cried, while dying. He had a sure insight into the value of the Christian mission for Africa, a value which is, in mid-twentieth century, being forcibly impressed upon us by the headlines of each day's newspaper.

D. The Discipline

The Discipline is, of course, in American Methodism, a book. In the book, which has grown by accretion, quadrennium by quadrennium, we find an accumulation of historical statement, doctrinal formulation, forms for worship, codified administrative regulations, and ethical standards. Our Discipline grew out of the English Conference's annual enactments in conference, known as the "Long Minutes." As the "disciplinary minutes" accumulated faster than the doctrinal ones in England, so did they here, till now the administrative code occupies by far the larger part of the book. But this should not be allowed to obscure in our minds what the very name of the book points to—that its central purpose consisted in the moral discipline of the Methodists.

The nucleus, the animating center of the whole vast accumulation, is found in the "General Rules." Wesley was too wise and too spiritual a man to make the General Rules a mere list of "don't's." The introduction to the General Rules breathes a lofty sense of the relation of Christian behavior not only to an awareness of the divine moral government (the desire to flee from the wrath to come!), but also to a yearning for "salvation from sin." Wesley was animated in part, it is true, by the desire to remove reproach which might arise around his infant societies by reason of scandalous conduct in its members. In such matters he proceeded along the lines laid down by the text which had been the classic reliance of the church's governors since primitive times:

If your brother sins against you, go and tell him his fault between you and him alone. If he listens to you, you have gained your brother. But if he does not listen, take one or two others along with you that every word may be confirmed by the evidence of two or three witnesses. If he refuses

126

to listen to them, tell it to the church; and if he refuses to listen even to the church, let him be to you as a Gentile and a tax collector.[39]

Compare with this the concluding statement of the General Rules: "I will admonish him of the error of his ways. I will bear with him for a season. But if, then, he repent not, he hath no more place among us." [40] Deeper, however, than fear of scandal swirling about his societies, deeper even than the fear that the wrath of God might fall on erring members of the flock, was the longing that they all might attain to holiness of heart and life. The inward temper having been changed through a sense of the forgiveness of sins, and the beginnings of holiness having been wrought in the believer, he was expected to go on to perfection, to freedom from inward and outward sin. There really are only *three* General Rules: Do no harm; do good after every kind; attend on all the ordinances of God. All the rest were specifications under those three. The whole, then, was far more than a legalistic code; it was spirit as well as rules. But the rules were to be enforced, under pain of expulsion; and so, for the most part, they were. Thus *The Discipline* showed how a real *discipline* was to be administered.

American Methodists, as we have seen, continued to cherish the moral standards of the English Wesleyans, and the religious outlook which animated them. Technically speaking, the General Rules were not requirements for *joining* a society; but conformity to them was expected of all who wished to *remain* in one; so in practice, the difference was not great. The original status of the General Rules in the Methodist Episcopal Church is somewhat obscure, for they were not printed as part of the *Discipline* till five years after its organization; that is, not till 1789.[41] When they did appear, it was with some modifications to suit American conditions.

Nevertheless, all writers from Jesse Lee on down assume that the standards of English Methodism were accepted unless and until they were repudiated, explicitly or by implication, by action of the Amer-

[39] Matt. 18:15-17.
[40] The text of the General Rules as originally written by Wesley is given in John S. Simon, *John Wesley and the Methodist Societies*, pp. 100-103. Wesley's "I" was soon changed in the American *Discipline* to "we."
[41] BHMM, II, 29. Actually, they were printed in 1788, but as a "useful piece annexed." See Charles Nutter's note to his reprint (1888) of the fourth ed. of the Discipline, and the title page of the same.

ican Conferences. This was certainly so in the days before the organization of the church, and it would seem natural to suppose that the authority of Wesley's General Rules prevailed without interruption until they appeared in print as revised in 1789. Certainly since that time they have been regarded as part of American Methodism's disciplinary standards. Lee had this to say in his *Short History*, writing of the events of 1770: "The Rules by which the societies were then governed were the same that Mr. Wesley had previously drawn up in England, and have with very little alteration been continued among us ever since." [42]

Especially on the frontier the disciplinary action of Methodism was a powerful force in restraint of the unruly *mores* of the community as a whole, especially valuable during the period before the civil society had had opportunity to organize its apparatus of legal codes, courts, and law enforcement. The Methodist Church of course was not alone in this situation. The other frontier churches also were engaged in this same task: the Baptists, the Presbyterians, the Congregationalists, and others. Each church after its special fashion performed the valuable service of bridging the interval before the coming of the state's machinery for preserving law and order. But it is perhaps the more useful to insist on the Methodists' part in this process because they are usually thought of as exercising their influence on society chiefly through camp-meeting revivals. These latter were much more spectacular, to be sure; but it would be a mistake to suppose that they were the sole reliance of even frontier Methodists. On the contrary, their disciplinary system was quite as effective an influence, though much quieter.

1. DISCIPLINARY ORGANIZATION AND PROCEDURE

In the United States, the summit of the pyramid of Methodist governing bodies has been, since 1792, the General Conference. It is the supreme legislative body, and may hear appeals of ministers from their annual conference. The annual conferences are the intermediate bodies, and the source of the authority for the General Conference above it, as well as for the local units below it. In the Methodist Episcopal Church both the annual and general conferences

[42] Jesse Lee, op. cit., p. 21.

consisted only of ministers throughout most of the nineteenth century; in the Methodist Protestant Church, however, laymen had a voice in them from the very beginning.

Below the annual conferences were the "quarterly meeting conferences" embracing a number of adjacent societies or churches. The societies in turn were divided into the classes, the smallest unit of all. These smaller bodies were composed, of course, largely by laymen in both Episcopal and Protestant Methodism, and they were the important bodies in the disciplinary action of the church so far as the laymen were concerned.

The class meeting was, throughout much of the nineteenth century, a tremendous force for edification and discipline. It never exercised the functions of a court, but exerted a steady pressure of group training and sanctions nevertheless. It had all the advantages of a small group which are being rediscovered as in our own times. It utilized the techniques of "group dynamics" before that dreadful term had been invented. The existence today of cell groups in many churches is testimony to a growing realization that, with the passing of the classes, Methodism lost something with a very real potential for the spiritual and moral growth of its members, something not achieved by the agencies—like the church school, the young peoples' fellowship, and so forth—which displaced it. It was in the classes in America as in England, that the basic work of training and discipline went on.

When the class failed to keep a member on the path of virtue, the society would take a hand. The spirit of Christian love prevailed in the "higher courts" too, but inevitably they had to pay more attention to the good name of the society and its influence in the community. With these ends in view, and without ever losing hope for the ultimate reclamation of wrongdoers, they did not hesitate to impose fitting penalties on the guilty, amounting, in obdurate cases, and as a last resort, to expulsion from the society.

Minor offenses brought only reproof for the first two times; the third time meant a trial. Trials were held either before the society, or before a committee drawn from its membership, and in the presence of the minister. Failure of the culprit to appear was construed as evidence of guilt. Every effort was made to follow the regularly prescribed procedures. One of the interesting features of the trials was the willingness of the accused to appear for trial. Apparently good standing in the religious community was too precious to be abandoned without a struggle.[43] Particularly in the smaller communities of the West where everybody knew everybody else, moral deviations were usually followed by rumors, and in the wake of rumors investigation was started. The whole matter was taken very seriously by all the parties concerned. The bodies charged with the responsibility for enquiry and judgment hewed to the line; they did not spare the guilty, either ministerial or lay.

According to the *Discipline* of 1808, elders, deacons, and preachers, whether itinerant or "local," were summoned by the presiding elder or the preacher of the circuit for examination before a committee of his peers. If the examining committee believed a trial was called for, the members of conference would be tried by that body, a local preacher by the quarterly meeting.

The following case of a woman offender occurs in the minutes of the Quarterly Meeting of the Carrollton circuit (Illinois Conference) in 1843:

> The case of sister .... Murphy who was charged of lying and slander, who found guilty by a select committee and expelled, and who appeals to this conference, the conference after hearing the specifications, the evidence in the case, and the decision of the committee read considered the same, and confirmed the decision of the said committee.[44]

Legislation supplementary to the General Rules was binding on Methodists too. Especially this was true of ministers, who were held to be examples of even stricter behavior than lay people. Indeed, possibly because the records of the conference before which they were tried were more carefully drawn up and preserved than those of lesser bodies, more instances of trials of ministers than of lay people are available to us.

The *Discipline* of 1808 required "The preachers . . . to execute all our rules fully and strenuously against all frauds, and particularly of dishonest insolvencies, suffering no one to remain in our society . . . who are found guilty of any fraud."[45] The ministers themselves, however, in their eagerness to supplement their meagre "support"

[43] W. W. Sweet, *Religion on the American Frontier* (4 vols., Chicago: University of Chicago Press) IV, 664-45. Copyright 1946 by the University of Chicago.
[44] *Ibid.*, pp. 667-68.
[45] *Ibid.*, p. 642.

sometimes violated this rule. James Gilruth reports in his journal an item from the session of the Ohio Conference of 1835: "Employed in the trial of Francis Wilson and J. P. Taylor for taking up goods without a probability of paying for them." [46] In 1839 a lay preacher by the name of Meacham was tried and found guilty of immoral conduct by a committee of the Shelbyville (Ill.) quarterly conference. The charges were brought by the father of a young woman whose bed Meacham had twice sought to enter.

A record of the San Augustine Circuit (Texas Conference) shows the disposition of a case of ministerial violence:

It appeared that the Revd W. D. Ratliff was charged with gross immorality—the specifications are 1st shooting and wounding Mr. Banks Burrow 2nd an attempt and design to his Burrows life. . . . Resolved that Brother Ratliff is considered by this Conference as not guilty under all of the Circumstances of the Case as charged—Resolved that Brother Ratliff remain suspended in his ministerial capacity—

By order of Conference Brother Ratliff have the privilege at his request to withdraw from Conference and not stand as a suspended member.[47]

2. TEMPERANCE REFORM

Americans inherited their forebears' addiction to the use of alcoholic beverages. American Methodists also inherited the tradition of Wesley's abhorrence of the traffic in spirituous liquors and his disciplinary provisions against it and against "dram-drinking." The two legacies conflicted with each other for some time before a movement toward the ideal attained such proportions as to make a noticeable dent on the actuality. In the 1830s the protest assumed the proportions of a movement, not only among Methodists, but in the country as a whole, so that, in 1842, a writer in *The Methodist Quarterly Review* could speak in glowing terms of "the temperance reformation in our own day." [48]

There was need for it. Not only was the free use of whisky socially acceptable, it was regarded as indispensable. The distillation of

[46] *Ibid.*, p. 455.
[47] *Ibid.*, p. 601.
[48] MQR, 14 (1842), 91. The first Temperance Society of which record has come to us was founded in 1808 in Saratoga, N. Y. (art. "Temperance," *Encyclopaedia Britannica* [11th ed.], 26: 579). In this matter it was America which set the example and Britain which followed.

potable spirits was an invention of the late Middle Ages when chemistry and its products were associated in the popular mind with all sorts of superstitutions. Brandy was regarded as a kind of divine essence, with special life- and health-giving properties. The name given to it, *aqua vitae* (water of life) is testimony to this attitude. Probably because the wish was ever father to the thought, this view died hard. In the absence of scientific scrutiny, "ardent spirits" were regarded as the sovereign remedy for every ill, the reviver of drooping courage, the strengthener for every difficult task. The cheap and abundant supply of gin, domestically distilled, devastated social life in eighteenth-century England. The making of rum from the molasses of the near-by West Indies and soon the making of whisky from domestic grain had the same effect on American life.

Our Puritan predecessors frowned on drunkenness, of course, but accepted the use of spirits as a normal, even essential, part of life. One of the legal enactments of the Colony in Massachusetts Bay *required* the setting up of a tavern within easy distance of the meeting house. Travelers on the frontier, Methodist itinerants among them, agree in testifying to the copious flow of whisky that accompanied all activities. It was the essential attraction at every social function; barns could not be "raised" without it, business deals were sealed with draughts, it was indispensable at weddings and funerals. Store owners kept handy an open keg, in order to attract customers with free drinks. Under such conditions drunkenness became appallingly prevalent; abstinence on principle was rare indeed.

In 1788 a Dr. Trotter of Edinburgh published books attacking the popular view that the drinking of spirits was beneficial to the body and the mind. In the same year the admirable Dr. Benjamin Rush, a Philadelphian of Quaker parentage (who had studied in Edinburgh), began the attack on the use of spirits from the medical point of view. The task of freeing the public consciousness from the half-superstitious misconceptions as to the effects of alcohol on body and mind was to take a long time. Indeed it is a perennial one. More effective at first was the moral and religious approach, which stressed the devastating effects of heavy drinking on men as spiritual beings, as sons of God.

A quick survey of the history of temperance reform in this country discloses that it has passed through three phases in each of which a different method of approach predominated—without, of course, excluding the other two. In the early nineteenth century it was the moral-religious approach; after the middle of the century, political action to secure regulation and prohibition came into prominence; since the repeal of the Eighteenth Amendment, the scientific-educational approach has come to the forefront. Of course each approach needs, and has had, in varying degrees, the support of the other two.

To anyone aware of how strenuously Methodists have for generations opposed the use of alcoholic beverages and the traffic in them, it will come as a surprise to learn that it was not always so. But early conference legislation shows quite clearly that not only the members, but also the ministers, drank, distilled, and sold liquor. In this they were at one with their time; and, if there were attempts to get them to change their habits, which argue a higher standard of behavior, there was also resistance to the reform which strikes us as incongruous in the Methodist temper.

a) *The Liquor Problem in the* Discipline

According to Wesley's original General Rules, among the evils "in every kind" to be avoided were "drunkenness, buying or selling spirituous liquors; or drinking them (unless in cases of extreme necessity)." [49]

As we have seen,[50] the General Rules were not printed in the American *Discipline* till 1789. Before that date, there were some regulations in the conferences. In the early 1780's, the emphasis was on preventing the making, buying, and selling, rather than the use of spirituous liquors. A provision of the Conference of 1780 required exclusion of members who distilled them. In 1783, "selling and drinking in drams" was included in the rule, but the penalty of exclusion had disappeared.[51] As for the preachers, the first *Discipline* put it thus in Question 23: "May our Ministers or traveling-Preachers drink spirituous liquors? A. By no means, unless it be medicinally." [52] The

---

[49] John S. Simon, *John Wesley and the Methodist Societies*, p. 101.

[50] P. 127 and note.

[51] MAC, pp. 12, 18.

[52] In 1887, Charles S. Nutter, of the Methodist Historical Society with headquarters in Boston, had reissues made by the Republican Press Association of Concord, N. H. of the two earliest editions of the *Discipline*, i.e. those of 1785 and 1786. In 1888 the fourth and fifth editions were likewise reproduced. Finally Mr. Nutter succeeded in finding a copy of the 3rd ed. which was reprinted in 1890 (the last-mentioned three were printed by the News-Letter Press, of Exeter, N. H.). The five thin pamphlets in the New England Methodist Historical Society's Library have been

final form of the question asked of ministers stood from 1788 to 1844 as follows: "Do you chuse and use water for your common drink? And only take wine medicinally or sacramentally?" [53]

The next year, when the General Rules were included for the first time in the American *Discipline*, a form even more drastic than Wesley's was used. It forbade "drunkenness, buying or selling spirituous liquors, or drinking them." [54] There must have been a protest against this, perhaps from a feeling that the rule had been included *ex post facto*, for it was watered down the next year, to read: "Drunkenness; or drinking spirituous liquors unless [in] cases of necessity." The prohibition against buying and selling had fallen out. Apparently this gave rise to some scandals; but in spite of several attempts, it could not be restored. The farthest they could get was legislation in 1796 which made it possible to discipline Methodists in whose houses *disorders* arose as a result of their selling liquor. [55]

In the country at large, the low point in this matter was reached in the second decade of the nineteenth century. Then the conscience of the concerned began to awaken to the damage caused by the almost universal and often excessive use of spirits. The first of a number of Temperance Societies appeared in Massachusetts in 1813. [56] A national society was formed in Boston in 1826, called The American Society for the Promotion of Temperance. Leadership in the early stages of the movement came chiefly from the Congregationalists, Presbyterians, and Unitarians—clerical and lay alike. [57]

The American Society relied heavily, as did the Anti-Saloon League later, on support from religious bodies as such. Methodism as a whole did not respond readily. A list of thirty-four such bodies in the society's second Annual Report shows only one Methodist body—the New England Conference. [58] However, several individual champions

---

bound together in a single volume, in the order of their original appearance. The title-page reads: *A Form of Discipline for the Ministers, Preachers, and Members of the Methodist Episcopal Church in America*. The above quotation is from the 1785 *Discipline* p. 10.

[53] BHMM, II, 29, and the *Discipline* for 1788 (Nutter's reprint), p. 18.

[54] *Discipline* for 1799 (Nutter's reprint), p. 48.

[55] BHMM, II, 30.

[56] *Encyclopaedia Britannica* (11th ed.) 26, 579.

[57] BHMM, II, 36.

[58] *Ibid.*, p. 37.

had appeared to lead the cause in both the annual and the general conferences. Timothy Merrit and Wilbur Fisk led the movement in New England. James Axley, a presiding elder in the Western Conference, carried the fight for temperance several times to the floor of the General Conference. He had only moderate success before the slavery question became paramount; by that time the General Conference had interest in little else.

In 1812 Axley failed to secure passage of a resolution to condemn ministers who sold "spirituous or malt liquors." The only word to issue from that conference on the question was in the address to the church, which deplored the prevalence of the excessive use of strong drink, and urged a stand against it in the annual conferences by precept and example. Four years later, Axley returned to the charge, and succeeded in getting the Conference to decree that any local preacher who distilled or retailed spirituous liquors should be deprived of his license. In 1820, an attempt to repeal this provision was defeated.[59]

b) *The 1830's: Temperance Becomes a Movement in Methodism.*

In the 1830's, the interest in temperance, having spread widely amongst church people as a whole, began to permeate the Methodist Churches too. A number of the church papers began to ask for the restoration of the original form of the General Rule, as it had been formulated by Wesley. *The Western Christian Advocate*, for instance, reported the action of the Kentucky Conference by which it "unhesitatingly resolved to request the General Conference to restore this rule." The editor believed it would pass, and urged its enforcement. "If this is done, it will mean that no person who either makes, buys, sells, or drinks ardent spirits can legally continue as member of the Methodist Episcopal Church." [60]

In spite of the *Advocate's* optimism the attempt failed in the General Conference of 1836. Legislation was passed at that Conference, however, forbidding ministers of all grades to distill or retail spirituous liquors, under penalty of forfeiting their standing.[61]

---

[59] BHMM. II, 31.
[60] WCA, 2 (1835): 94. While the agitation to restore the Rule was on, a Methodist distiller wrote anxiously to the *Christian Advocate* and *Zion's Herald* asking whether he would be deprived of his membership if it succeeded. The editor was unequivocal in his reply: yes he would; moreover the movement would probably succeed in 1836. CAZH, 7 (1832), No. 9 (Oct. 26), p. 34.
[61] BHMM, II, 32.

In the *Mutual Rights and Methodist Protestants'* first volume appeared a communication headed "Ardent spirits, an Enemy of Religion." The writer had observed the tendency of heavy drinkers who had been converted in revivals to relapse into their evil ways, and proposed that "no intemperate person should be received into the Christian church immediately upon a profession of religion," and that a pledge of abstinence from ardent spirits be required of such as a condition of receiving the Communion.[62] The General Conference of the Methodist Protestant Church in 1834 passed a resolution highly approving of "the great effort now being made to promote the cause of temperance," and recommending that their Church "use all [her] influence to aid in the formation and extension of temperance societies." [63]

C) Methods and goals

Before the middle of the 'forties, the temperance movement in Methodism, as in the country as a whole, had adopted, at least in rudimentary form, all the methods it was later to use, and even aimed at all the goals it was later to achieve. Societies were formed; they developed the kinds of persuasion which were to be in evidence all through the history of the movement: the urgent calls for signatures on pledges of abstinence; issue of material, written and spoken, on the harmful effects of alcohol on the human body and mind, and on society. They went beyond persuasion to steps in the political field, steps toward not only regulation, but, even thus early, toward prohibition.

Perhaps the most important factor in the growth of the movement was the formation of societies. We have already noticed the earliest non-Methodist ones. The first Methodist temperance society, so far as this writer has been able to discover, was formed at Bangor, Maine, at the end of 1831.[64] The New England Conference Temperance Society was founded in 1833.[65] The next year the Tennessee Conference formed itself into a temperance society "on the broad principle of total abstinence from the use of ardent or intoxicating spirits, ex-

[62] MRMP, 1 (1831), 236.
[63] *Journal of the General Conference of the Methodist Protestant Church,* 1834, p. 35.
[64] CAZH, 6 (1832), no. 22 (Jan. 27), p. 86.
[65] BHMM, II, 37.

cept as medicine," and each preacher was to form societies in his own charge.[66] Other conferences followed.

"Abstinence" at first meant abstinence only from distilled liquors; but it was not long before "teetotalism" appeared, and signers were pledging to abstain from *all* alcoholic beverages. The American Temperance Society was calling on ministers to take the lead in severing "all connection with this destroyer." Three thousand ministers, the society said, had already taken a pledge of total abstinence.[67] The annual meeting of the Ohio Temperance Society in 1835 noted that pledges to abstain from ardent spirits didn't always prevent continued drunkenness. They therefore resolved to ask for pledges to abstain from *all* intoxicating liquors.[68]

An early note of a tenuous connection between the temperance movement and political pressure appears in 1832. The members of the quarterly meeting conference for Munroe circuit resolved not to vote for any candidate who offered ardent spirits to his constituents for the purpose of influencing their choice.[69] Already dissatisfaction with licensing by the government was being voiced by the movement in Ohio, which seems to have moved swiftly along the path that others took more time to tread. A temperance convention there (not Methodist, but held in a Methodist church) declared that the licensing system was wrong, and should be abolished, and the traffic should be prohibited.[70]

In 1833 the *Methodist Magazine and Quarterly Review* printed an article by David M. Reese, M. D., entitled "A Brief Essay on the Medical Use of Ardent Spirits, being an attempt to show that alcohol is as unnecessary and mischievous in sickness as in health." [71] *Zion's Herald* carried a contribution which traced the connection between insanity and pauperism and indulgence in strong drink: "The increase of pauperism, of late, has excited much public interest, and the cause has been diligently sought for, and, if I mistake not, found in the *rum bottle.*" Dr. Reese's article, cited above, anticipated the view

[66] Cullen T. Carter, *History of the Tennessee Conference* (Nashville: printed at the Parthenon Press, copyright by the author, 1948), p. 87.
[67] The *Virginia Conference Sentinel* (Richmond, 1836), 1 (1836), 124.
[68] WCA 2 (1835), 98.
[69] CAZH, 7 (1832), no. 9 (Oct. 26), p. 34.
[70] WCA, 1 (1835), 162.
[71] MMQR, 15 (1833), 294 ff.

which has prevailed widely only recently, that alcoholism is a disease. He phrased it otherwise than we would, but he regarded the habitual drunkard as "an object of pity, rather than of blame. His sin consisted in drinking at first moderately . . . [but] he is now a monomaniac."

The appeal to Scripture was of course indispensable in the Methodist attack. The Address of the General Conference of 1832 on the subject of temperance was written by Henry B. Bascom, professor of moral science in Augusta College, Kentucky. This address shows that the use of wine and spirits is "broadly and unsparingly condemned in the scriptures of the Old and New Testaments as directly inconsistent with Christian character." [72] The appeal by the opponents of temperance to Paul's advice to Timothy (1 Tim. 5:23) was refuted now as a special case of illness, the prescription for which cannot be taken as a safe general practice, and again by flatly denying that it was alcoholic wine which Paul had prescribed.

By 1844, the writer of an article in Zion's Herald, while admitting that much still needed to be done, could exult in the progress of the temperance movement in the preceding fifteen years. "The time has gone by when a vindication of temperance societies is called for. Their good results have been so apparent as to silence the objections of their bitterest enemies." [73] The temperance movement had gained momentum swiftly in the country at large. The scales had been removed as it were from eyes which could now see alcohol not as a benefit but as a destroyer of health, both physical and spiritual, and of values both individual and social. Beginnings had been made at writing measures of control into the legal codes of the land. Prohibition had been set as a goal, the attainment of which was not to be delayed for long. Flourishing societies existed in most parts of the states, which could work at the unfinished tasks with vigor increased by past successes.

The Methodists had put in their Discipline a regulation according to which a minister of any rank must forfeit his ministerial standing if convicted of making, selling, or drinking spirituous liquors. As to the membership, the movement to restore "Wesley's Rule" had not succeeded as far as the law of the church was concerned. Nevertheless,

[72] The address is given in MMQR, 15 (1833), 90 ff.
[73] ZH, 15 (1844), no. 36 (Sept. 4).

the church was being swept by a tide of sentiment which had impelled thousands of Methodists to undertake a voluntary pledge to avoid all implication with alcoholic beverages, whether by way of manufacture, sale, or use. If in the East Methodism had followed, rather than led the movement, and if official Methodism had "dragged its feet" in resistance to church legislation, in the West the enthusiasm of volunteers was soon to put Methodists in positions of leadership.[74] and the code of the church soon yielded to their impact.

[74] See BHMM, II, 38. "The Methodist preachers were the most active of any group. So preponderant was the Methodist influence in some sections of the West that enemies of temperance charged the Methodist Church with using the reform as a cloak for proselytizing, thereby gaining members among temperance advocates in other denominations."

CHAPTER FOUR

Slavery

Since slavery was such an important factor in economic life, it was inevitable that it should trouble political waters as well. The attempts to still the turmoil took the form of a series of compromises. The first of these was written into the Constitution itself, a compromise permitting the abolition of the slave trade, but not before 1808. For a time the Missouri Compromise of 1820 held the line between free and slave territory at latitude 36° 30′ north. But the Missouri Compromise was itself "compromised" out of existence by the Kansas-Nebraska Act and the Dred Scott decision of the 1880s.

Over these issues, the lines were drawn for the most part, but not wholly, between the North and the South. Rear-guard actions were fought against the institution in even some of the southern states—principally those near the Mason and Dixon line. It is an important, but little-remembered fact that a bill for gradual emancipation was introduced into the Virginia Assembly as late as 1832, and occasioned lively debate. During the preceding year a bill for the deportation of free Negroes was defeated in the House of Delegates by *only one vote.* The purpose behind the bill had been to encourage private emancipations.[1]

During the same period of time, slavery won a victory in Southern thinking more complete than those it won in legislative halls. Whereas in the eighteenth century idealists, both secular and religious, both Southern and Northern, had almost universally deplored the existence

---

[1] Channing, *A History of the United States,* V, 142 ff. What later became the separate state of West Virginia was then included in the representation in the Assembly; but the preponderance of voting power lay in the eastern counties nevertheless.

of slavery, by the early nineteenth century, though still regarding it as an evil, they came to think of it as a *necessary* one. Beginning with the 1830s, even religious men in the South capitulated still further: they elaborated a justification for it on religious grounds.

The reasons for this change may be briefly adduced. The success of the abolition movement in Britain (1833) gave rise to a vigorous abolition movement in the Northern states here. In its most militant form, it centered about William Lloyd Garrison, his outspoken paper *The Liberator*, and the American Anti-Slavery Society which he controlled. Concurrently, an expanding European demand for raw cotton, and the increased ease of preparing it for shipping made possible by Eli Whitney's "gin" had made cotton king in the South. Because the actual raising of cotton was still a matter of hand labor, the need for slaves increased tremendously. A measure of this increase may be found in the market price of slaves. In 1790 a good slave might be purchased for $300; the same slave in 1830 brought $1,200, and in 1860, $1,500 to $2,000.[2] The Southern defense of slavery, then, may be regarded as both a consolidation of defense against abolitionism and a result of its growing economic importance.

In the churches, as in politics, there were some protests against this capitulation of conscience. In 1835 the Kentucky Conference of the Methodist Episcopal Church, while taking a stand against abolitionism, at the same time described slavery as "morally wrong, and mischievous in all its tendencies."[3] The next year the Baltimore Conference took an almost identical stand.[4] A brief, but effective, witness to the refusal of some to capitulate to the new arguments for slavery appeared in the *Virginia Christian Advocate* in 1847. It is a bitingly ironic account by one who had been listening to W. A. Smith, "Orator," who accomplished in his hearer's spellbound ears what Clay with all his eloquence had not been able to do:

Never [before] in my life did I feel . . . that there was a prescription that hallows . . . usurpation. That a principle wrong in the abstract could be right in the concrete. That the importation of the African slave was a missionary enterprise, fraught with immeasurable good . . . which would . . . releaven Africa. . . . Powerfully did he silence that squeamish dogma

[2] Sweet, *The Story of Religion in America*, p. 294.
[3] WCA, 2 (1835), 102.
[4] ZH, 7 (1836), no. 16 (April 20).

of Mr. Jefferson's "that in a contest between the white and the black the *Deity* had no attribute that could take sides with the white." [5]

Such protests as these, however, dwindled away and ceased altogether during the 'fifties. In 1857 a Northern writer could remark on the very noticeable retrogression of public opinion on the question of slavery in the South:

The public bodies, the political guides, the popular press, the leading theologians stand almost uniformly committed to the "Great Apostasy." . . . Washington, Jefferson, Patrick Henry, Madison, Monroe, Lee, not to speak of their great northern contemporaries, uttered sentiments against slavery which, if now asserted in the South, would be retorted with proscription and violence.[6]

Social pressure which did not boggle at threatening physical violence pushed the last dissenter into line, silencing, if it did not altogether convert him. A late nineteenth-century church historian thus described the situation:

It was less perilous to hold Protestant opinions in Spain or Austria than to hold, in Carolina or Alabama, the opinions which had but lately commended to universal acceptance by the unanimous voice of great religious bodies, and proclaimed as undisputed principles by leading statesmen.[7]

A. The Southern Apologia for Slavery

The new defence of slavery was elaborated voluminously, with passion and ingenuity, if not with cogency. It is not possible to consider here all the variations and elaborations; we must focus our attention on the main lines of argument, which may be reduced to four. The first is the argument from Scripture. The second is that the Negro is better off as a slave than when free. The third argument is economic, and compares the condition of the slave with the free laborer's to the advantage of the former. The fourth was drawn from political philosophy, and, probably because of its inherently self-contradictory character, was not dwelt on very long: that slavery is the only true safeguard of a permanently republican government.

[5] RCA (successor to the *Virginia Conference Sentinel*; the "new series" began in 1847), 1 (1847), 161.
[6] *The Methodist Quarterly Review*, 39 (1857), 262.
[7] Leonard W. Bacon, *A History of American Christianity* (New York: Charles Scribner's Sons, 1901), p. 278.

1. THE ARGUMENT FROM SCRIPTURE

The general conclusion which emerged from the re-examination of scripture was that since slavery is not anywhere condemned and is in several places allowed by implication, or even explicitly, it is therefore good and right. In the Old Testament slavery was practiced by the patriarchs, and permitted to the chosen people by Levitical precept; hence it should be accepted as an arrangement of Divine Providence for the government of the world, with which it is obligatory to comply. This is further shown in the New Testament by the constitution of the primitive Christian church, which was, we are bound to suppose, a perfect society, and included slaves in its membership. When Paul sent the slave Onesimus back to his master Philemon, it was not with instructions to the latter to release him, but to treat him "as a beloved brother." Moreover, Paul elsewhere enjoins on the slaves submissiveness and obedience to their masters. The classic verse in the Old Testament was Lev. 25:45: "You may also buy from among the strangers who sojourn with you, and their families that are with you, who have been born in your land; and they may be your property." In the New Testament, there are three passages in Paul's letters, chief of which was Eph. 6:5: "Slaves, be obedient to those that are your earthly masters, with fear and trembling, . . . as to Christ." Col. 3:22 is very similar, and, in the letter to Titus, Paul enjoins him to "bid slaves to be submissive to their masters, and to give satisfaction in every respect." [8]

Slavery, moreover, was a part of the divine economy for Negroes, because it was a punishment visited upon them for the sin of Ham in beholding the nakedness of his father Noah (Gen. 9:22, 25-27). He who fights against slavery, then, fights against God. God saw that slavery would be a blessing to both master and servant. Our omniscient Savior and his apostles instituted rules for the perpetual institution of slavery.[9] William Winans, replying to the charge of an abolitionist that the religion of the South was "idolatry," said:

[8] The above quotations are taken from the Revised Standard Version. In this case, the translation is even better for the defense of slavery than the King James Version, for it uses "slave" where the earlier version used "servant."

[9] "A Southern Clergyman" (pseud. for Iveson L. Brookes) *A Defense of Southern Slavery against the attacks of Henry Clay and Alexander Campbell* (paper, 48 pp. Hamburg, S. C.: printed by Robinson and Carlisle, 1851), p. 6. Brookes also speaks of God's beneficent institution of slavery (*Ibid.*, p. 8).

The religion of the South . . . does . . . just what the Saviour and his Apostles did, when they preached the whole of . . . true religion in countries where slavery prevailed. . . . It condemns slavery as clearly and as strongly as any one or all of these ever did, and it goes no farther toward sanctioning the abuses of slavery than they did. . . . The religion of the South is stainless of the guilt of mobbing and lynching. It would deprecate these things, though directed against the most malignant abolitionists. . . .[10]

2. SLAVERY IS THE BEST STATE FOR NEGROES

In another phase of their apologetic, the slaveholders kept insisting that the Negro's lot was much better when he was a slave than when he was free. Whenever they are left to themselves they are in misery; they cannot manage themselves. This is the reason why the colonization scheme in Liberia has failed.

Have our slaves then . . . been wronged, in being raised, through the institution of slavery, to a condition of moral, intellectual, and civil improvement, and to a state of protection, comfort, and happiness never elsewhere . . . known? [11]

3. THE SLAVE IS BETTER OFF THAN THE FREE WHITE LABORER

This argument, like the preceding one, was elaborated in reply to the antislavery men's insistence on the miseries of the slave's lot. There was much justification for this *tu quoque*, for the industrial societies of Europe and the North were far too complacent about the injustices under which their own working classes had to labor. It was a case of the pot calling the kettle black, and vice versa, each only pointing out another job of cleaning that needed to be done, without becoming any less sooty in the process.

One clerical apologist for slavery starts even his economic argument

[10] SCA, 1 (1838): 119.
[11] I. L. Brookes, *Defense of the South Against the Reproaches of the North* (Hamburg, S.C.: printed at the Republican Office, 1850), p. 9. "This feature in slavery [i.e., having absolute property in slaves] seems to be especially obnoxious to the abolitionist, only because his vision has become too morbid to allow him to see it correctly. The truth is that the ownership of the Southern slave holder . . . is under God, the highest safeguard of protection and happiness to the slave. . . . Now . . . it . . . bespeaks this institution to be founded in benevolence, showing it to have its origin in divine authority (*Isdem, Defense of the South*), p. 12.

with scripture. Free labor is "hireling." But the Bible says "the hireling fleeth." And indeed we find that in the West Indies he goes off leaving complicated machinery idle, and so causes much waste.[12] In his book entitled *Sociology for the South*, George Fitzhugh argues:

Employers of free laborers, like the riders of hired horses, try to get the most possible work out of them for the least hire. They boast of the low rates at which they procure labor, and still hold up their heads in society, uncensured and unreproved. No slaveholder was ever so brutal as to boast of the low wages he paid his slaves, to pride himself on feeding and clothing them badly, neglecting the young, the aged, the sick, and infirm. Such a man would be hooted from society as a monster.[13]

Mr. Brookes goes further and says that what is called free labor is really slavery:

And, Sir, this thing slavery, in accordance to God's fixed appointments, now exists throughout the civilized world . . . notice in Spain and France (now republican) and haughty England, their porters, boot cleaners, washer women and cooks, ah, their tenants, who, after they pay their rent and taxes are scarcely able to live from hand to mouth. . . . Finally go to intrusive New England and look not to the "Black Nancies and Scipios," but at what they modestly call their helps, and what, we ask, is seen in all this circuit but a state of slavery under other names it is true, but, for the most part, far worse than our state of negro slavery.[14]

---

[12] I. L. Brooks, *Defense of Southern Slavery*, p. 22.

[13] Quoted from a review of the book by G. F. Holmes, esq. in QRS, 9 (1855), 200.

[14] Brookes, *op. cit.*, p. 12. In the same vein, a correspondent of the *Richmond Christian Advocate* writes from a sojourn in England: "There are estates belonging to Lords tenanting thousands . . . who are as verily slaves to their masters as the negro of the Pampas. . . . Can they set any price upon their labor, any bounds to their toil? . . . [As for] slaves in the South . . . [their] masters are obliged to feed and clothe, and in every way provide for them. . . . Where is the essential difference between the slave in name and fact, and the slave in fact only? . . . The money-aristocrat has ever been a greater tyrant than the landed lord" (*The Richmond Christian Advocate*, 1 [1847], 44). In 1825 the Hon. James Barbour, Secretary of the Department of War, said in effect: Providence has given us many slaves. We must treat them as well as we can. Permitting them to do nothing brings ruin on owner and slave alike. They should be given plenty of food (bread, bacon, etc.) and drink, such as milk and cider. A central place and a good person should be appointed for the care of the children.

Such a system would challenge "without fear, a comparison with the laboring classes in some of the civilized countries of Europe" (WJ, 1 [1825], no. 11 [Dec. 10], first page).

Few slaves were made to labor as hard or as long in the day as most free whites were compelled to work for the support of their families. Statements like these, and accounts of the seamy side of factory capitalism's effect on the workers, sometimes amounting in effect to "atrocity stories," were retailed to counter the bad impression of slavery left by the lurid descriptions of the abolitionists, and especially, it would seem, by *Uncle Tom's Cabin.*[15]

4. SLAVERY IS THE ONLY TRUE SAFEGUARD OF FREEDOM

In defense of the position that slavery was the best guarantee of permanent republican institutions, the examples of the republican city-states of Greece and other historic communities were called upon; and, with a certain amount of "wresting," Scriptural arguments were adduced. The Genesis story (14:14 ff.) of Abraham's slaves rescuing Lot from the four kings was cited as an instance of slavery's buttressing freedom. The argument from the New Testament again assumed *a priori* the perfect republican nature of the primitive church. Since it indisputably included slaves among its members, it was obvious that slave-holding and true freedom are quite compatible with each other.

B. The Antislavery Movement in the Northern Churches

In the churches in the North, antislavery sentiment not only did not yield before the about-face of the South, but it became stronger and embodied itself in a movement. Gradually, as the colonization scheme's impotence became apparent, this movement adopted abolition, more or less immediate, as its objective. Even a cursory study of the growth of abolitionism in the various denominations in the North discloses the fact that it came to influence in spite of discouragement from the various denominational organizations. In some, this discouragement amounted to official censure and obstruction. As it turned out, when certain denominational organizations vigorously

---

[15] See the account of the "overlookers" of child-workers in English factories, RCA 1 (1847), 19. The reviewer of the above-mentioned *Sociology for the South* says that book purported to be a "calm and philosophical analysis" intended to dissipate the effect of Harriet Beecher Stowe's famous book (QRS 9 [1855], 180).

opposed the accelerating momentum of the abolition movement, it was they, not it, which broke apart.

Whence came the momentum of the movement? The antislavery societies provided the organization, to be sure; but the momentum came from the revivals of the first half of the nineteenth century. Gilbert H. Barnes and others have spoken of "The Great Revival" of 1830, led by Charles G. Finney and his co-workers, and shown how powerful a force it was in turning its converts' reforming energies into abolitionist channels.[16] Timothy L. Smith's recent study shows that the revival did not die out between 1840 and the annus mirabilis 1858, another notable revival year. It changed its form somewhat, becoming naturalized in the growing cities of the North, through the efforts of Baptists like Jacob Knapp, Congregationalist city pastors like Leonard Bacon and Edward N. Kirk (who perpetuated the movement by converting Dwight L. Moody), Presbyterians like Albert Barnes, "foremost among the group of revival men who dominated the New School Synods," and the Lutheran Samuel S. Schmucker. These men were not only revivalists but also antislavery men. Some of them were ardent abolitionists, and innumerable converts of their revivals followed in their train.

The connection between the revival and the abolition movement can best be illustrated by citing the career of Theodore D. Weld, a new-school Presbyterian converted by Finney to revival evangelicalism, and by Charles Stuart to abolitionism. Weld was much less conspicuous than Garrison (being as determined to avoid publicity as the latter was skillful at attracting it), but more effective in winning both other leaders and rank-and-file adherents. He converted nearly the whole student body of Lane Seminary to the abolition cause, and that in spite of the opposition of its president, Lyman Beecher. This was done after long "debates," which, accompanied as they were by prayerful and intense exhortation, were more like revival meetings than conferences depending on logical persuasion. One of his converts was William T. Allan, the son of an Alabama slaveholder. It was Weld who persuaded James G. Birney, later to be twice the Liberty

---

[16] Gilbert Hobbs Barnes, The Antislavery Impulse 1830-1844 (New York: D. Appleton-Century Co. 1933). The first chapter is entitled "The Great Revival, 1830."

Party's presidential candidate, to become an Abolitionist.[17] One of Beecher's own daughters came over to Weld's side. Later when, as the famous Harriet Beecher Stowe, she was challenged to prove that *Uncle Tom's Cabin* was not overdrawn, she had recourse to the reservoir of facts collected by Weld and published in his *Slavery As It Is*.[18]

During the time that Weld was field agent for the Antislavery Society, he astonished its officials by the pertinacity and persuasiveness with which he would stay a week or more in the small towns of Ohio, Pennsylvania, and New York, making several addresses a day, discussing the question with small groups, until he had inspired them with the fervor of his "gospel" and organized them into an active local auxiliary of the Society. But, as one writer remarks, the officials needn't have been surprised; Weld was just following the methods and spreading the spirit he had caught from the preachers of the revival. Though he had collected a fat volume of clippings and stories of the cruelties involved in slavery (most of them from Southern sources) and used them effectively, his central conviction was that all these cruelties were incidental to the central evil, the "destruction of [the slave's] personality." His message was that of a preacher of righteousness: slaveholding is a *sin*, and as such to be eradicated.[19] Timothy Smith thus formulates the doctrinal service performed by the Northern revivalists to the antislavery cause:

> By making the law of love the key to the Scriptures and subjecting them to a Christian version of the doctrine of progress, Northern evangelicals escaped the strait jacket of literalism in which proslavery preachers were fatefully binding the conscience of the South.[20]

THE ABOLITION MOVEMENT AND THE DENOMINATIONAL STRUCTURES

The story of the partition of the denominations into proslavery and antislavery sections is a sad one. For the most part it is the story of

[17] *Ibid.*, pp. 64-69.

[18] *Ibid.*, p. 73.

[19] *Ibid.*, p. 79. Weld adopted the rather confusing Garrisonian conception of "immediate abolition," according to which it was to be "gradually attained." The economic aspects of slavery scarcely interested him. He was hardly more interested than Garrison in practical proposals for steps to be taken toward the goal. He too was content to be an "agitator" in the sense of believing that if sufficient abhorrence for this sin were aroused in the public mind, ways would be found to bring it to effect.

[20] Timothy L. Smith, *Revivalism and Social Reform*, p. 219.

an officiary concerned primarily to preserve the unity of their churches, attempting to keep the abolitionists from "rocking the boat," and failing in the end. In some cases doubtless such a stand was the result of a not very creditable institutionalism; but in others it was due to a genuine conviction that it was the church's business to save souls; hence anything which threatened its effectiveness in this respect was to be deplored, and, if possible, repressed.

The decision was attended with subtle difficulties in the case of the Baptists, whose only "denominational" organization was a missionary convention. The convention's officials could quite plausibly say: "It is our business to conduct missions; our supporters expect us to do that; we have no *right* to divert their gifts or to stultify our cause by rash pronouncements in a matter outside our province."

Interdenominational agencies such as The American Bible Society had to face the same question. Most of them ended by adopting a "hands off" policy. The rending of the purely ecclesiastical structures was attended with conflict and pain in proportion as their membership was distributed over both the North and the South, and as their polity was centralized. Because Methodism was both ubiquitous in the United States and connectional in polity, their split was attended with more pain than the others.

The Presbyterians were already divided over doctrinal questions into old and new schools, the former with most of its members in the South, the latter predominantly Northern in its constituency. The new school's general assembly was agitated by the slavery question for a number of years before it declared in 1845 that, though it regarded slavery as "intrinsically unrighteous and oppressive," it was unable to make a clear-cut pronouncement upon it without creating division. In spite of this policy of reticence, however, they came to division in the end. In 1856 some Presbyteries south of the line, disturbed over the growing number of their Northern counterparts which were making antislavery pronouncements, withdrew to form a United Synod.[21] The greater and more decisive break came in 1861,

[21] Timothy L. Smith, *op. cit.*, pp. 196, 197, 198. The United Synod did not join with the predominantly Southern Old School Presbyteries, because the latter were not explicit enough in their proslavery testimony!

149

when forty-seven Southern Presbyteries formed the General Assembly of the Presbyterian Church in the Confederate States of America. It was in 1865 that these Presbyteries and those of the United Synod joined to form the Presbyterian Church in the United States.[22]

The Baptists were more evenly distributed in the two regions than the new-school Presbyterians, but their tenacious hold on congregational independence made the organization of a Southern Baptist Missionary Convention, in 1845, comparatively easy. The Congregationalists were not only decentralized in government; they were also so predominantly Northern in distribution that they were almost completely antislavery in their stand. Such differences as they experienced rose up between parties which espoused "gradualism" and "immediacy," without going deep enough to cause any real schism.

We shall turn in the next pages to a consideration of the process by which the Methodist Episcopal Church was ultimately split on the rock of the slavery question. At this point let us consider the rupture of Methodism simply as the first of a series of denominational splits and the relation of the series to the political strains which ultimately broke the Union apart. Henry Clay's expression of perturbation at the split among the Methodists is well known:

> I will not say that such a separation would necessarily produce a dissolution of the political union of these States; but the example would be fraught with imminent danger, and, in cooperation with other causes unfortunately existing, its tendency on the stability of the confederacy would be perilous and alarming.[23]

Thus did the statesman who had anxiously sought a formula which would keep the Union together find in the division of the Methodist Episcopal Church not only an indication that his labors might end in failure, but also a causal significance. It was in his eyes the snapping of one of the ties which still bound the sections of the nation together.

Other denominational unities were broken in the years between the Methodist schism in 1844 and the political rupture in the Union, but they did not all have the same significance for the political break. The earlier ones, the Methodists and the Baptists, were primarily

---

[22] Frank S. Mead, *Handbook of Denominations in the United States* (rev. ed., Nashville: Abingdon Press, 1956), p. 172.

[23] Quoted in Buckley, *A History of Methodists in the United States* [4th ed., "American Church History Series," vol. V.] New York: Charles Scribners' Sons, 1900), p. 475.

breaks over the slavery question. The later ones, the Episcopalians and the Lutherans, were among the results, rather than the causes, of the political tension: they split over the issue of loyalty to the government. In the case of the Episcopalians, the schism lasted only a very little longer than the secession of the Southern states. In between were the Presbyterians. It has been pointed out that the later schisms, those actuated more by political considerations, occurred in those churches which had the greatest state-church tradition. The earlier ones, those in which the "sectarian" tradition was stronger, were unable to exorcise the protest over the moral aspects of slavery, which was consequently more potent than the political issue in bringing about the break.[24]

C. The Slavery Question in the Methodist Churches

1. The Status of the Negro in Methodism

In the period after the organization of the church in 1784, as before it, Methodists manifested concern for the salvation of the soul of the Negro; and, as we have seen,[25] the Missionary Society carried on special missions to the slaves beginning in 1828, in spite of the opposition they met in some quarters. In 1831, James O. Andrew of Georgia was insisting: "The slave has a soul, and needs the faithful preaching of the Gospel as much as his master. . . . We . . . look forward . . . to the time when a proper course of religious instruction for the slaves shall be deemed indispensable by the planters of every neighborhood." [26]

As for stated services of worship, the Negroes worshiped in the same building with the whites, but in a specially designated part of it only. This was true in the North as well as the South, as the stories of the beginnings of the African Methodist Episcopal and the African Methodist Episcopal Zion Churches show. Discrimination of some sort was responsible for the formation of both those separate Negro groups. The African Methodist Episcopal Church grew out of an

---

[24] H. R. Niebuhr, *Social Sources of Denominationalism* (New York: Henry Holt & Co., 1929), p. 191 ff.

[25] P. 124.

[26] MMQR, 13 (1831), 314, 322. These sentiments of the future Bishop occur in a review by him of an address made by Charles C. Pinckney, who was one of the first and most influential supporters of the missions established by the South Carolina Conference. Presumably the opinions were those of Mr. Pinckney as well, and are approvingly retold by Mr. Andrew in his review.

incident in St. George's Church of Philadelphia. It has been said that the Negroes "were violently dealt with as they knelt at prayer in some part of the church they mistakenly supposed themselves privileged to occupy." "So," wrote their founder, Richard Allen, "we all went out of the church in a body and they were no more plagued by us in the church" [27] The beginnings of the African Methodist Episcopal Zion Church were due to a secession of Negroes from the John Street Church, New York, because "caste prejudice forbade their taking the sacrament until the white members were all served." [28]

In both cases we may assume that the Negroes felt freer in their worship and had easier access to positions of leadership after the separation than before. Richard Allen seems to have tried for a while to stay in the Methodist Church—he was the first Negro to be ordained (in 1799)[29]—but the friction continued, and finally his Bethel Chapel was given its independence. He established the African Methodist Episcopal Church in 1816; the African Methodist Episcopal Zion Church was begun in 1820. In 1835 there was a secession from the church in Charleston, S. C., because Francis Asbury had arranged for some of the aged and infirm Negroes to sit on the floor, without going to the gallery, though they were restricted to a special place on the floor. The larger part of the congregation maintained the usefulness and respectability of the colored members, and said besides: "They are our brothers." [30]

In 1800 the General Conference passed a measure permitting the ordination of Negroes to the office of local deacon under certain rather exacting conditions; but the possibility was not often realized—indeed it was not even widely known, because the objection of the Southerners against it was so strong as to prevent its publication.[31]

---

[27] H. Richard Niebuhr, *The Social Sources of Denominationalism.* The quotation is from Allen's own account. Another student implies that the details are not fully known: "The full story would probably include a greater recognition of the part played by the personal ambitions of Richard Allen." See also Dwight W. Culver, *Negro Segregation in the Methodist Church* (New Haven: Yale University Press, 1953) p. 44, n.

[28] H. Richard Niebuhr, *op. cit.,* p. 261.

[29] SHMEC, IV, 174.

[30] Reprinted from *Zion's Herald* in WCA, 1 (1835), 194.

[31] Jesse Lee, *op. cit.,* p. 272; JGC, I, 44. Another Janus-like action of the General Conference (of 1804) was its authorization of the printing of the "spiritual" part of the discipline (i.e., the part without the section on slavery) separately "for the use of the south" (JGC, I, 65; AJL, II, 440, n.).

Though not many were able thus to be ordained, a goodly number of them became useful as preachers.

In 1824 a special paragraph was inserted in the *Discipline* which (with the usual exception of places "where the usages of the country . . . forbid it") accorded "our colored preachers and official members . . . all the privileges which are usual to others in the district and quarterly conferences." Where their numbers warranted, the presiding elder might hold a separate district conference for them; the annual conferences might employ them to travel and preach, after they had been duly recommended.[32] The McKendree Church of Nashville reported to the Tennessee Conference of 1841 more Negro than white members. These and the Negroes of several other churches were organized provisionally, after the separation of 1844, into "African Missions." [33]

While we are considering the status of the Negroes in the Methodist Episcopal Church, at least brief allusion should be made to a subject which reveals one of the disabilities under which they stood in some conferences—the matter of the validity of testimony of Negroes against white men in trials in the church's courts. The question was hotly discussed in the General Conference of 1840, where the struggle assumed the aspect of a preliminary trial of strength between the sections—one of the votes on a substitute motion was sixty-nine to sixty-nine.[34] Ignatius A. Few introduced a resolution to the effect that it was inexpedient and unjustifiable for any of the preachers to admit colored testimony in church trials against white persons in any slave-holding state or territory where colored persons are not permitted to testify in trials at law. This resolution was passed, as was a long supplementary resolution introduced by Bishop Soule, to the effect that the adoption was not to be interpreted as prohibiting the admission of such testimony in states where it had been the custom to admit it, and that it was not intended as a reflection on

[32] *Discipline*, 1824, p. 190.
[33] Cullen T. Carter, *op. cit.*, pp. 101, 110.
[34] The debate over this question in the General Conference might be likened to that in Congress over the Wilmot Proviso—though to be sure the subject matter was quite different. In both debates, preliminary battle lines were drawn, and in both, threats of division were heard. In the General Conference "W. Winans . . . talked loudly of a division of the church if [M. Few's] resolution were rescinded! 'If the moment of separation must come,' he said, 'the sooner the blow was struck, the better for his feelings.' " ZH, 11 (1840), no. 24 (June 10), p. 93.

"the Christian piety or integrity of the numerous body of coloured members under our pastoral care. . . ."

Bishop Soule balanced this by an interpretation of another case. Silas S. Comfort had been convicted by his own (the Missouri) Conference of maladministration because he had received the testimony of colored persons against white, and had appealed to the General Conference. This body had refused to affirm the decision of the Missouri Conference. Bishop Soule's resolution on this matter (it was likewise passed) declared that the General Conference's refusal to affirm the original action on comfort did *not* imply that it was either expedient or justifiable to receive Negro testimony where the laws of the states forbade it in civil trials.[35]

2. THE QUESTION IN THE GENERAL CONFERENCES, 1796-1832

As already noted,[36] the declared intention of the Christmas Conference to disown all members who did not emancipate their slaves, where they were not forbidden by law to do so, had to be abandoned in the face of prevalent objection. The extirpation of slavery continued to live on as an ideal, but hopes for its realization dimmed as sanctions disappeared, and "affectionate addresses" took their place.

The General Conference never abandoned its opposition in principle: it continued to assert that "we are more than ever convinced of the great evil of slavery"; but a committee reported to the General Conference of 1816 that they were "of opinion that . . . little can be done to abolish a practice so contrary to the principles of moral justice." [37] The battle was kept up, but more as a "holding action," counterattacks on small sectors, than an assault along the whole line, animated by hope of ultimate victory.

The Methodists already had before them the example of two nations which had distinguished between slave trading and slave holding, by prohibiting the former while allowing the latter to continue. What Great Britain and the United States had done on an international scale, the American Methodists undertook to do within their own church. The result was that the sector on which they were most successful was in preventing trading in slaves by their members;

[35] JGC, II, 57, 60, 109.
[36] Pp. 99-100, 111.
[37] JGC, I, 169.

they were least successful in the repression of slave-holding among their membership as a whole. They were moderately successful in keeping their ministry clear of both.

When, in 1789, the General Rules were first printed as part of the *Discipline*, one on the slave trade was added to the Rules taken over from English Methodism. It read at first: "The buying or selling the bodies and souls of men, women, or children, with an intention to enslave them." [38] The wording, but not the intent, was soon changed. By 1808 it read: "The buying and selling of men, women, and children, with an intention to enslave them." [39] So the Rule stood, until the separation, and beyond it, in both Northern and Southern churches.

The General Conference of 1796 provided that a member proved guilty of selling a slave should be excluded forthwith. One purchasing a slave, however, was to be allowed to retain him long enough to compensate himself for the purchase price, after which he was to emancipate the slave. The children of a female slave born during such a period were likewise to be set free at specified ages.[40] There must have been leaks in this dyke, however. In 1804 the General Conference took cognizance of the possibility of justifiable sale of slaves by providing that a committee from a local society should determine whether or not the sale had been carried out "at the request of the slave, in cases of mercy or humanity." If not, the member was to be excluded. The provisions of 1796 regarding purchase were re-enacted almost unchanged, but this time the states of North Carolina, South Carolina, and Georgia were excepted from its operation.[41] In 1808 even this attempt at regulating the slave traffic was abandoned by the General Conference, and the principle of localism prevailed. It was moved "that the General Conference authorize each annual conference to form their own regulations relative to buying and selling slaves. Carried." [42]

As might be expected, this liberty led to a great deal of diversity in the annual conferences, so much so that in 1820 it was rescinded—without anything being put in its place.[43]

---

[38] *Discipline* of 1789 (Nutter's Reprint), the General Rules.
[39] *Discipline* of 1808, the General Rules.
[40] JGC, I, 23.
[41] JGC, I, 63.
[42] JGC, I, 93.
[43] BHMM II, 83; JGC, I, 205. The Virginia Conference in 1813 voted to continue

Since the General Rule forbade the slave traffic only, it was understood that it did not forbid the *holding* of slaves. Where the holding of slaves was forbidden to Methodists it was not by the law of the church, but by the laws of the states in which they resided. It must be remembered in this connection that there were two categories of slave states. In one category, not only was slaveholding legal, but further, emancipation was forbidden. In the other, slaveholding was legal, but the slaves might legally be manumitted. The difficulties of the General Conference in legislating on slaveholding by its members stemmed from this dilemma: such legislation would have been *superfluous* in the free states; it would have been *impotent* in the slave states where emancipation was forbidden; and it was regarded as *undesirable* in the others.

It was in these states where there was no legal obstacle to emancipation that the discrepancy between the church's profession and its practice was most glaringly apparent. It was obvious that the legal impediment was not the only, perhaps not even the chief reason for permitting Methodists to own slaves. As yet, the majority of Methodists were too deeply involved in it to shake themselves free, or even to want to do so.

The church was slower to allow members in official station to be slaveholders. The legislation of the general conferences on this subject was confused, imprecise, and self-contradictory. Probably this confusion was a result of the contending strains of thought in the church as a whole.

In 1800 the ruling on traveling preachers was:

When any of our travelling preachers become owners of a slave or slaves, by any means, they shall forfeit their ministerial character in the Methodist Episcopal Church, unless they execute, if it be practicable, a legal emancipation of such slave or slaves, agreeably to the laws of the state wherein they live.[44]

the policy of expelling members engaging in the traffic in slaves. There was inevitably a tendency to appeal to the motive of mercy to justify a transaction. In 1813 in the Tennessee Conference a local preacher was suspended for selling slaves; his defense before the Conference was that he had "made the condition of the slave much better." But the Conference sustained the Quarterly Conference's action. In both the Tennessee and the Ohio Conferences, antislavery sentiment, strong at first, declined as time went on (BHMM, II, 87-90).

[44] JGC, I, 44.

Four years later, much the same rule was retained for the traveling preachers, but at the same time a regulation was adopted which looks in the other direction:

We do fully authorize all the yearly conferences to make whatever regulations they judge proper in the present case respecting the admission of persons to official stations in our Church.[45]

The legislation on those in official status came to its resting point in what came to be known as the "Compromise law" of 1816, and which was to be invoked in 1844 in defense of Bishop Andrew:

No slaveholder shall be eligible to any official station in our Church hereafter where the laws of the state in which he lives will admit of emancipation, and permit the liberated slave to enjoy freedom.[46]

This rule was adopted because of the divergent courses taken by the respective annual conferences under the localism allowed by the legislation of 1804. Evidently the general conference felt it should regain control of such legislation as was made on the subject; but just who was included in the term "official station" is not made clear. As it turned out, it was applied chiefly, if not exclusively, to the traveling preachers. Because it was rightly felt that the preacher was a prominent representative of Methodism in the public estimation, and because his itinerancy might take him to parts of the country where differing attitudes on slavery prevailed, it was felt that he should keep himself as clear as possible of involvement in it. How successful the attempt was is difficult to determine; but the Methodists thought the attempt was worth making, and the indications are that the ministry was, in comparison with the laity at least, much less deeply involved.[47]

These then, were the principal measures enacted by the early general conferences for the regulation of slavery in the Methodist Church. The equilibrium thus attained was at first a dynamic one.[48] But the

[45] JGC, I, 63.
[46] JGC, I, 170.
[47] See BHMM, II, 99-100. Dr. Barclay's formula is: "An earnest attempt was made by the Church to keep its ministry untainted—on the whole, considering the complications involved, a reasonably successful effort."
[48] Witness this extract from a single page of the Journal of the General Conference for 1800:

"FRIDAY MORNING, MAY 16.
"Brother Snethen moved, that this General Conference do resolve, that from this

equilibrium tended to become static as hopelessness overcame the antislavery faction. Thus it remained until abolitionism once more made the question a live one in the church. The Conference of 1824 said:

All our preachers ought prudently to enforce upon our members the necessity of teaching their slaves to read the word of God; and also . . . give them time to hear the word of God preached on our regular days of divine service.[49]

The next quadrennium a resolution that cases of inhumanity to slaves be treated as other cases of immorality was tabled, and never considered.[50] No action at all was taken on the question of slavery in 1832.

During all this time, and even beyond it, the Bishops manifested no disposition to give positive leadership to the antislavery cause. From Asbury to Simpson, they were concerned first and foremost with the effect it would have on the church's growth and unity.[51]

3. The Question in the General Conferences of 1836 and 1840

In the three General Conferences yet to be considered, a definite

---

time forth, no slaveholder shall be admitted into the Methodist Episcopal Church. Negatived.

"Brother Bloodgood moved, that all negro children belonging to the members of the Methodist Society, who shall be born in slavery after the fourth day of July, 1800, shall be emancipated—males at _____ years, and females at _____ years. Negatived.

"Brother Lathomus moved, that every member of the Methodist Episcopal Church, holding slaves, shall, within the term of one year from the date hereof, give an instrument of emancipation for all his slaves; and the quarterly meeting conference shall determine on the time the slave shall serve, if the laws of the state do not expressly prohibit their emancipation. Negatived.

"Brother Cooper moved, that a committee be appointed to prepare an affectionate address to the Methodist Societies in the United States, stating the evils of . . . slavery, [and] the necessity of doing away the evil as far as the laws of the respective states will allow. . . . Agreed to.

"Brother M'Kendree moved, that this General Conference direct the yearly conferences to appoint a committee to draw up proper addresses to the state legislatures, from year to year, for a gradual abolition of slavery. Agreed to" (JGC, I, 40-41).

[49] JGC, I, 294.
[50] BHMM, II, 84; JGC, I, 337.
[51] BHMM, II, 87, n., which gives a quotation from an address by Asbury to the Western Conference in 1808: "Would not an *amelioration* in the condition and treatment of slaves have produced more practical good to the poor Africans than any attempt at their emancipation?" He deprecated the effect talk of emancipation was having on the slaveholders' disposition to keep slaves away from the ministrations of the Methodists.

progression can be observed, or perhaps two different sets of progression. In each of the three, we can note a strengthening of the *opposition to slavery*. The *results* might be charted, but on a crooked, rather than a straight line. In 1836, though the revived opposition caused some brisk skirmishing, there was no change in the official position of the church. In 1840, the opposition was markedly stronger, but the results were, by way of reaction, rather on the pro- than the antislavery side. In 1844, the opposition achieved a preponderance, and the result was separation.

The question which had seemed dead in 1832 showed a surprising degree of reinvigoration in 1836. The year of the former General Conference had seen the formation of the New England Antislavery Society. The first *Methodist* Antislavery Society was formed during the same quadrennium, in 1834.[52] The New England Conference's general conference delegation of seven was solidly abolitionist, and was joined by one of equal solidity and equal size from the New Hampshire Conference.[53] But abolitionism was still confined to New England, as can be seen by the fact that other conferences were condemning it. The Ohio Conference, for instance, in 1835 was still supporting the program of the Colonization Society; and passed a resolution in which they regretted "the proceedings of abolitionists and antislavery societies." James Gilruth, a presiding elder in the conference, from whose journal this information was taken, was himself an ardent abolitionist, and recorded the conferences with a pious ejaculation of distress—in parenthesis—"O God!" [54] The abolitionist memorials sent up with the New England delegates were among the several factors that set off the exciting discussion. How vigorous the movement was in the Northeastern states of its origin is shown by the fact that at the session of the New England Conference in Springfield, Mass., in 1836, Sunderland, arraigned for defamation of character in some of the expressions in his abolitionist paper, *Zion's Watchman*, was nevertheless passed in character.[55]

[52] This was founded in New York in 1834, by Le Roy Sunderland, a member of the New England Conference. The second was the Wesleyan Antislavery Society, founded at the session of the New England Conference at Lynn, Mass., in 1835 (James Mudge, *History of the New England Conference of the Methodist Episcopal Church* [Boston: published by the Conference, 1910], pp. 280-81, 284.

[53] *Ibid.*, p. 282.

[54] W. W. Sweet, *Religion on the American Frontier*, IV, 460 and n.

[55] Mudge, *History of the New England Conference*, pp. 284-85. Sutherland was,

Some resentment was caused in the General Conference by the fraternal address of the British Wesleyan Conference, which affectionately but frankly set forth its opinion that slavery was inconsistent with the spirit of the gospel, and intimated that the American Methodists ought, on that account, to take a step toward the position they (the Wesleyans) had already occupied.

A rather noncommital reply was devised, in which the sentence occurred: "Had you been as well acquainted with this subject as we are . . . your tone of sympathy for us would have been deeper and more pathetic." [56] In the first heat of resentment at Britain's "interference," there was sharp opposition to printing the fraternal address. The vote was evenly split, 59-59; Bishop Soule, who was in the chair, cast the deciding vote against bringing up the subject.[57]

Requests were heard for a restoration of an earlier and stricter form of the rule on slavery; but that move roused a reaction which, according to Peter Cartwright, both threatened secession and proposed to have the rule stricken out altogether.[58] These proposals came, it is true, "in private caucus" rather than on the floor of the conference, but they evidenced the growing strife nevertheless.

During the sessions of the conference, two members absented themselves from the session to address an abolition meeting. Inasmuch as the conference was being held in Cincinnati, where the population was divided between slavery and antislavery feeling, the conference regarded their act as both disrespectful to the conference and capable of inflammatory results. The conference passed a resolution which rebuked the two members, and stated that the conference

are decidedly opposed to modern abolitionism, and wholly disclaim any right, wish, or intention to interfere in the civil and political relation between master and slave as it exists in the slave-holding states of this union.[59]

The determination of the conference to make no change in the part on slavery in the *Discipline* came as a resolution proposed by the

as Mudge put it, "a sharp thorn in the side of all who leaned Southward." The *Virginia Conference Sentinal* took the New England Conference to task for letting Sunderland off so lightly (VCS, 1 [1836], 94-95).

[56] VCS, I, (1836), 69.
[57] ZH, 7 (1836), No. 20 (May 18), p. 28.
[58] Charles L. Wallis (ed.) *Autobiography of Peter Cartwright*, p. 238.
[59] JGC, I, 447.

committee on slavery in response to memorials asking that "certain rules on the subject of slavery, which formerly existed in our Book of Discipline, should be restored." They reported,

That it is inexpedient to make any change in our book of Discipline respecting slavery, and that we deem it improper further to agitate the subject in the General Conference at present.[60]

During the quadrennium between 1836 and 1840, the struggle intensified. In almost all the annual conferences it came up in one way or another. On one side were the abolitionists led by Orange Scott of the New England Conference and Lucius Matlack, both men of courage and ability. The Abolitionists were few save in the New England and New Hampshire Conferences, but determined. Their leaders presented their cause in many of the annual conference sessions. At all they attended, they were opposed by the bishops, who assumed the task of repressing "radical abolitionism" in the interest of the unity of the church. At the end of the quadrennium, the abolitionists found themselves with much to discourage them, for the ensuing General Conference was able to counter all their moves. Nevertheless they kept at their task, with the courage and optimism born of conscientious conviction.

The tactics of the abolitionists were aimed at getting discussion of their cause, sometimes by introducing resolutions into the annual conferences, sometimes by discussion over "passing the character" of the members of conference or applicants for full membership. They proceded along this latter line at the New Hampshire Conference by moving the appointment of a committee to consider the case of those members who had attended an antislavery convention in Lowell in 1837. Every minister who had so participated was challenged by another abolitionist, and in defending himself presented "the cause" at length. At such length, indeed, that the impatient conference finally resolved that attendance of a member at the convention did "not militate against his ministerial character." [61]

Lucius Matlack himself was unable, because of his abolition activities, to get full membership in the Philadelphia Conference. In

[60] JGC, I, 475.
[61] Charles Baumer Swaney, *Episcopal Methodism and Slavery, with Sidelights on Ecclesiastical Politics* (Boston: Richard G. Badger, 1926), p. 81.

1837, when he was presented, with high recommendation, one of the presiding elders said:

> Mr. President, the abolitionists are radicals. This young man is a radical. These radicals deny your authority and the authority of the General Conference. He has been spoken of as a young man of talents and piety. If he were as pious as St. Paul and as talented as an angel, he should never enter this conference as an abolitionist if I could prevent it.[62]

When the abolitionists presented resolutions in the annual conferences, they met such consistent opposition from the presiding officers, whether presiding elders or bishops, as to make it clear there was a concerted effort for repression on the part of those officials. One case which attracted a good deal of attention, and was brought up for review at the next General Conference (1840), was that of a quarterly conference meeting at Springfield, Mass. The presiding elder, Daniel Dorchester, refused to allow the passage of an antislavery resolution, and abruptly adjourned the quarterly conference. A convention of laymen was summoned through the columns of *Zion's Herald*, which not only requested the withdrawal of the presiding elder, but suggested several candidates who would, in their opinion, make acceptable replacements.[63] Needless to say, their proposals were not accepted.

Bishops presiding at conferences also refused to receive memorials to the General Conference urging abolition. Bishop Waugh refused to put such a motion in the New England Conference; he would not allow an appeal from his decision, and refused to put a motion asking for an expression as to whether the memorials were in possession of the conference. Similar conflict beset the presiding officer at the New Hampshire Conference.[64]

The "radicals" found it difficult to get access to expression in the church papers. *The Christian Advocate* closed its columns in 1837 to discussion of the slavery question.[65] *Zion's Herald* alone remained open. As in the case of that other dissident movement of the 'twenties, which had resulted only a few years before in the founding of the Methodist Protestant Church, the abolitionists had recourse to found-

[62] J. M. Buckley, *A History of Methodists in the United States* (New York: Charles Scribner's Sons, 1900), p. 388.

[63] *Ibid.*, p. 399.

[64] *Ibid.*, pp. 387-88.

[65] BHMM, II, 99.

ing their own publications. *Zion's Watchman* (New York, 1836), published by Le Roy Sunderland; the *Wesleyan Quarterly Review* (1838, by Orange Scott), and the *New England Christian Advocate*, (Lowell, Mass., Luther Lee, editor) were all organs of the movement at one time or another.[66]

In almost every Northern conference an exciting struggle took place during 1838 and 1839. The conservatives won most of them.[67] It must be said that both sides exceeded the bounds of truth and charity. Matlack and Scott were accused of slandering the bishops in their papers. The bishops and the presiding elders justified their actions by saying that the motions they refused to put were irrelevant to the business of the conferences over which they were presiding.

Bishop Hedding was the special target of ill-considered animosity. He and Mrs. Hedding were made the objects of burlesque slave auctions acted out in some of the abolitionists' addresses.[68] So bitter was the feeling against them that the Heddings felt compelled to move their residence from Lynn, Mass., to New York State.

The attitude of the Southern proslavery forces was, as was to be expected, uniformly unfavorable to the abolitionists. An extreme instance of this was the declaration of a meeting of slaveholders in Mississippi which declared that any person circulating abolition papers in the state was "justly worthy, in the sight of God and man, of *immediate death.*" [69]

The officials undoubtedly discriminated against the participants in abolition activities; their status in conference was often determined by their stand on this one matter, regardless of their character and devotion as ministers. Some were cut off from all relation to their conferences; some were suspended till they promised to fulfill certain conditions, such as ceasing to go to abolition meetings or to lecture on the subject, or refraining from circulating abolitionist papers. Sometimes they were sent to "poor" appointments as evidences of official displeasure.[70]

[66] Buckley, *op. cit.*, p. 387.
[67] C. B. Swaney, *op. cit.*, p. 79 ff.
[68] *Ibid.*, p. 89.
[69] Quoted in *Ibid.*, p. 88.
[70] For the decade between 1837 and 1847 every candidate for admission to the Philadelphia Conference was asked, "Are you an abolitionist?" Unless the answer was "No," he was rejected. In 1838 the Pittsburgh Conference discontinued a man on trial for giving two lectures on Abolitionism (BHMM, II, 98). All of this amounted,

In appearance, the battle had nearly everywhere gone against the abolitionists. In actuality, when to the antislavery convictions of the minority were added convictions that they were being unfairly treated by the officiary of the church, their future predominance was assured. But the time was not yet.

In the General Conference of 1840, the supremacy of the anti-abolitionist forces was demonstrated by the legislation. Indeed, this legislation became, in a higher degree than ever before, proslavery.

There were in this, as in the preceding general conference, but two abolitionist delegations—from the New England and New Hampshire Conferences. Their program was, as before, to agitate for a "restoration" to the *Discipline* of what they described as an earlier and more Wesleyan form of the regulations on slavery—one which would forbid not only trading in slaves but also the holding of them, as sinful, and hence unlawful for Methodists. The Episcopal Address anticipated them by declaring against any change in the General Rule.[71]

A still further similarity to the proceedings of the General Conference of 1836 is to be seen in the content of the Fraternal Address of the British Wesleyan Conference, and the response to it. The Wesleyans, after referring to their previous letter, said:

Far be it from us to advocate violent and ill-considered measures. We are, however, strongly . . . of the opinion that it is . . . the paramount Christian duty of the ministers of our most merciful Lord . . . to maintain the principle of opposition to slavery with . . . unflinching firmness.[72]

---

in practice, to a denial of free assembly and speech and press to one faction, admittedly a partisan one, in the Methodist Episcopal Church. For further examples of trials and disciplinary action by Annual Conferences, see Lucius C. Matlack, *The Antislavery Struggle and Triumph in the Methodist Episcopal Church* (New York: Phillips and Hunt, 1881), p. 100 ff. One of these ends as follows: "He [Paul R. Brown, after trial before the New York Conference in 1838, and refusing to cease agitating for Abolitionism] was publicly rebuked by the Bishop, and his appointment was in a distant field, where he suffered much inconvenience and many privations. Special contributions during the year were made by personal friends among the Abolitionists." (p. 114). At the sight of these undeserved sufferings, Matlack says, "More enemies of abolitionism became its friends than contrariwise" (p. 115).

[71] JGC, II (1840), 134 ff. The ground of the bishops' reproof was that their agitation had been carried on in "such a spirit . . . as to disturb the peace of the Church." The results of the action of the New England Conference had not been such as to contribute to the objective of freeing the Methodist Episcopal Church from the "great moral evil of slavery."

[72] JGC, II (1840), 152-53.

The reply was concerned to controvert the implication that the standards of the American church had changed, to point out the differences in the political situation between England and the United States, and finally, to remind the British Conference that they themselves, before the abolition of slavery in the West Indies, had advised their missionaries there to follow a course identical to that which the American church was now following, namely, evangelization of the Negroes without going beyond to interfere in their civil status in contravention of civil law.[73]

The anti-abolitionist forces gained a good deal of ground because of an antislavery petition presented over eleven hundred signatures, from New York City. The Committee on Slavery, headed by Nathan Bangs, reported that it had discovered that most of the signatures should not be counted: some had been obtained by deception, others had been put down without obtaining the consent of the persons named; others were duplicated; still others were females; and the signatures had been obtained for the most part by people who were not members of the Church! [74] Scott's defense was that he was innocent of any attempt to deceive, and had received the petition from persons whom he felt he could trust. He was not allowed to regain possession of the petition to verify the work of the hostile investigators who had asserted the fraudulence of the greater part of the signatures.[75]

The conservative position of the Conference was made clear by its favorable action regarding the Colonization Society. It adopted entirely a long report of a committee entrusted with the question of the Society's suitability as a channel of antislavery activity. The action commended the success hitherto attending the activities of the society, which were a "blessing not only to the colonists themselves, but also to the vast population of Africa now enveloped in heathen darkness." The work of the society was then commended to the annual

---

[73] JGC, II (1840), 154-55. "We have adopted no new principle or rule of discipline respecting slavery. . . . In our General Rules . . . which are of constitutional authority in our Church "the buying and selling of men, women and children with an intention to enslave them is expressly prohibited. . . . And the extract of part ii, section 10 . . . is still of force. . . ."
[74] ZH, 11 (1840), no. 23 (June 3).
[75] C. B. Swaney, op. cit., p. 96.

conferences, and it was proposed that a collection for its work be taken up on or about the fourth of July of each year.[76]

The Conference's approval of the course pursued by the bishops and district superintendents with regard to antislavery measures proposed to their respective conferences was obtained by a large majority. This was accomplished through the adoption of the report of the Committee on Itinerancy under the chairmanship of William Winans of Mississippi. The important provisions were to the effect that

The President . . . has the right to decline putting the question . . . when in his judgment, such a motion . . . does not relate to the proper business of the Conference. . . . The President . . . has the right to adjourn the Conference . . . when, in his judgment all the business prescribed by the Discipline . . . shall have been transacted.[77]

The report of this committee originally contained an action of the Georgia Conference declaring that "Slavery as it exists in these United States is not a moral evil." [78] A motion to delete this part was tabled; but when the final report was adopted the provision did not appear.

The action of this General Conference which most clearly showed the growing impatience of the pro-slavery forces under the restrictions which the history of the church had placed upon them was the adoption of the report of the Committee on the Westmoreland Petition.[79]

Westmoreland was a circuit in the Baltimore Conference, but lay within the bounds of the state of Virginia. The petition asked for redress of grievance for certain preachers who had been refused election to and ordination in the Conference solely on the ground of being slave owners. Their contention was that Virginia should be included among those states for which exception was made in Methodist law, since it was, in fact one in which "the laws . . . relating to slavery forbid emancipation, except under restrictions and subject to contingencies amounting, to all intents and purposes, to a prohibition." [80]

The resolution of the committee implied acceptance of the petitioners' contention as to the law of Virginia. As adopted it read:

The simple holding of slaves, or mere ownership of slave property, in

[76] JGC, II (1840), 59-60.
[77] JGC, II (1840), 121. Cf. also the action on the report of the Committee on the Episcopacy (ibid., p. 99).
[78] JGC, II (1840), 106.
[79] JGC, II (1840), 129, 167 ff.
[80] JGC, II (1840), 167.

states or territories where the laws do not admit of emancipation, and permit the liberated slaves to enjoy freedom, constitutes no legal barrier to the election or ordination of ministers to the various grades of office known in the ministry of the Methodist Episcopal Church, and cannot therefore, be considered as operating any forfeiture of right in view of such election and ordination.[81]

Insofar as this resolution was an enunciation of a general principle, it but recognized the practice which had been followed perforce in those states whose laws forbade emancipation. Its general result was further to breach the early policy of keeping the ministry as clear as might be of implication in slavery. The General Conference hesitated to apply the general principle to the Westmoreland petitioners because of insufficient evidence that they had been refused election and ordination because of their slaveholding; and the introductory remarks of the committee make it clear that they felt the right of any annual conference to elect or reject freely should remain inviolate. On the other hand, in spite of the hesitant tone of the report, it would seem as though the committee wished to bring Maryland, a border conference, to an observance of the Southern practice. If this was their wish, it was disappointed, as the sequel (in the General Conference of 1844) was to show.

The results of the General Conference of 1840 were received with satisfaction in the South, and with resignation in the North. Zion's *Herald*, to be sure, protested vigorously its action on the testimony of colored people,[82] but so far as the church periodicals were concerned this was an exception. At this juncture it was the refusal of the "last-ditch" abolitionists to give up which turned the tide. At first they were but a small minority. They were held at arm's length by loyal Methodists, because of suspected separatist tendencies. The suspicion was correct, as the matter turned out, but paradoxically this suspicion was the very factor which made it possible for the "tail to wag the dog," and brought about an astonishing growth of overt and aggressive antislavery sentiment in the whole Northern part of the Methodist Episcopal Church.

It began with a call by Scott and Matlack and others for a Methodist

[81] JGC, II (1840), 171.
[82] C. B. Swaney, *op. cit.*, p. 104, citing ZH, 13 (1842), 152 (Sept. 21), and 156 (Sept. 28).

antislavery convention, which met in New York in the fall of 1840. The convention said nothing about leaving the church, but it was severely critical of the actions taken at the General Conference the preceding spring. The points in its criticism touched the following: that it did not disapprove the resolutions of the Georgia and South Carolina Conferences declaring that slavery was not a moral evil; it resolved to reject the testimony of colored people; it recommended the Colonization Society's program; and it refused to restore the earlier and stricter rule on slavery.[83]

An interesting feature of the convention was its correspondence with the editors (Bond and Coles) of the *Christian Advocate and Journal,* in the same city. The convention asked the editors if they would print antislavery material. The editors' reply was that they would receive personal communications from the members of the convention, and any organization that might result therefrom, but they could not receive *official* communications from an organization not authorized by the *Discipline.* Moreover, they raised a question which has been heard more recently in Methodism: whether it was legitimate for them to use the word "Methodist" in such an unofficial organization.[84]

The convention accordingly organized itself into a society under the name "The American Wesleyan Anti-Slavery Society," and proclaimed its object to be the "entire extinction of slavery in the Methodist Episcopal Church in America."[85] In view of the oblique but definite refusal of the *Advocate* to print its material, the society went so far as to recommend to its members to choose their own periodical. This was construed as disloyalty to the *Herald* as well, and, together with the other critical and incipiently separatistic tendencies, roused the suspicions of some antislavery, but loyal Methodists.

Witness this letter to *Zion's Herald,* by a man who had put his hand to their petitions, but turned back:

I sign[ed] a call for another Methodist Antislavery Convention . . . thinking . . . it would promote the enterprise; [but I now think] the course Br. Sunderland is pursuing with the New England Conference, and Br. Scott's course with the Herald are daily weakening the confidence of

[83] Report in ZH, 11 (1840), no. 38 (Sept. 16), p. 151.
[84] ZH (1840), no. 45 (Nov. 4).
[85] Report in ZH, 11 (1840), no. 46 (Nov. 11).

abolitionists in each other. . . . I had as lief Mr. Garrison would lug into the abolition cause the woman question, and non-resistance, as to have Bro. Scott lug church reform into the same cause.[86]

The Annual Conferences to which the leaders of this movement belonged, noting these refractory tendencies, disciplined the leaders, but the discipline served merely to accentuate the tendencies. By June 1841, Orange Scott was saying: "There is, therefore, no alternative but to submit to things as they are or secede." [87] Secessions had, as a matter of fact, begun in Ohio *before* the General Conference, that is in 1839; there had been others in the Michigan and New York Conferences in 1841. The American Wesleyan Anti-Slavery Society did not live long as such; [88] its leaders, and many of its members coalesced with these small fragments to form the Wesleyan Methodist Connection of America, at a convention held in Utica, N. Y., in 1843.[89]

If Matlack represents the matter correctly in his *Antislavery Struggle*, the Northern Methodists started a backfire by calling some antislavery conventions of their own; one of these met in Maine, one in New Hampshire, and one in Boston. The one in New Hampshire said: "The only way to prevent an entire dissolution among us as a Church, is an entire separation from the South." [90] This sounds like a self-contradiction till one reflects that what they were probably proposing was some such arrangement as the present jurisdictional system.

The Boston convention's utterance represented the growing conviction in the North: "Slave-holding is a sin." Those who had already organized themselves into a new church rejoiced at such proceedings in "the old Church," but made no move to rejoin it. It boasted six thousand adherents at its first organization, including twenty-two traveling ministers from the Methodist Episcopal Church, some from the Methodist Protestants, and some from a smaller body known as the "Reformed Methodists." At their first General Conference (at the end of 1844 or the beginning of 1845) they reported fifteen

[86] ZH, 11 (1840), no. 40 (Sept. 30).
[87] *Cyclopaedia of Methodism*, p. 791.
[88] Lucius Matlack, *Antislavery Struggle*, p. 146.
[89] *Ibid.*, p. 141.
[90] *Ibid.*, p. 151-52.

thousand members. Their general rule on slavery prohibited the *holding* of slaves, or claiming that it was right to do so; the other respect in which they differed most widely from the church they had left was in having abolished the Episcopacy. A restrictive rule forbade introducing distinctions into the ministry on account of color.[91]

Other factors probably concurred, but Charles B. Swaney is, in the main, correct in saying:

"What the agitation of a decade had failed to accomplish, the secession of those who had formed the Wesleyan Methodist Church brought to pass. The policy of the Methodist Episcopal Church changed immediately when the secession movement began to gather momentum." [92]

The New York and Genesee Conferences asked for new forms of the rule on slavery. The former asked for a restoration of the early rule; the latter's proposal was that no slaveholder could be a member where it was possible for him to emancipate his slaves. The attitude of the Baltimore Conference, however, was to stand pat on its original position, which was to keep slaveholding ministers from membership in the Conference, but to resist any change in the rule.[93]

Dr. Bond of the *Christian Advocate and Journal* opened the columns of his paper to discussion of the subject, and even began taking a stand himself. True, this stand was rather conservative, so far as the church itself was concerned; but he roused the fears of the Southerners by a forthright attack on an attempt in the Maryland Legislature either to compel free Negroes to leave the State, or to reduce them once more to servitude. One Southern writer questioned whether the *Advocate* could circulate in the South.[94]

In spite of the fact that the General Conference of 1840 had specifically approved the course of the bishops and presiding elders in refusing to entertain antislavery motions or resolutions,[95] these

---

[91] *Ibid.*, pp. 141-43. Matlack does not mention it, probably because it was an embarrassment to him and to his cause, but the new "Connection" also made a declaration against secret societies (Charles B. Swaney, *Episcopal Methodism and Slavery*, p. 107).

[92] Swaney, p. 109.

[93] *Ibid.*, pp. 110-11.

[94] *Ibid.*, p. 111. His stand amounted to "the sinfulness of slavery depends on the case."

[95] See p. 166.

officials, seeing which way the tide was running, ceased to put difficulties in the way. In these new circumstances, the antislavery expressions of the conferences multiplied with astonishing rapidity, and, by the time of the General Conference of 1844, reached the proportions of an inundation.

4. SLAVERY IN THE METHODIST PROTESTANT CHURCH UP THROUGH THE GENERAL CONFERENCE OF 1842

The decade which witnessed the first great surge of abolitionism was also the first decade of ecclesiastical existence for the Methodist Protestants. If sound church growth was the chief concern of the officials of the Methodist Episcopal Church, it was even more natural for it to be so with the Methodist Protestants, who had just won a cause supremely dear to them, and were embarked on the venture of embodying it in a new church. So intent were they on this achievement, that they had time for little else. One reads their church papers throughout this whole decade without finding much beside accounts of institutional experimentation, defining the boundaries of power, establishing a system of checks and balances, trying and rejecting, or trying and developing new institutions. One would scarcely suspect from reading these same sources that there was an abolitionist controversy raging in the country at large, in other religious bodies, and in their own denomination.

Nevertheless, it finally caught up with them, and brought about a separation in their body too. It was not so painful a wrench as in the case of the Methodist Episcopalians, nor did it last so long. The central concepts of the controversy were very much the same as those we have already reviewed: a struggle between the authority of the General Conference and the Annual Conferences was settled with less reluctance in favor of the latter; the question of whether slaveholding was sinful, and under all circumstances, was warmly debated. The determination of the nonslaveholding conferences to hold no fellowship with slaveholders finally brought about the schism so much deprecated by the leaders of the young church.

It is not altogether true that the Methodist Protestants had no thought for affairs beyond getting their own body functioning smoothly. There were other interests, of course. A Home Missionary

171

Society was established in 1831.[96] A Board of Foreign Missions consisting of a dozen persons, with headquarters at Baltimore, was constituted in 1834.[97] In 1836 the Board sponsored a meeting in that city in the interests of a mission at Cape Palmas in Africa. But the mission failed (if tradition be correct) because of the word "white" in the church's constitution.[98] The church was not unmindful of the temperance movement. Drinkhouse describes the resolutions passed by their Conferences as "pronounced and prohibitory." [99]

The status of the Negro in their church was pretty well determined by the limitation of the franchise (already noticed),[100] to white male adults. Much of the disciplinary struggle was to get this word "white" stricken from the constitution. The Genesee Conference early rebelled at this restriction, and in 1831 resolved that "all the colored members belonging to the Church within the bounds of this Conference be entitled to the same rights of suffrage and membership as the white members." [101]

It does not appear that the slavery question disturbed the Methodist Protestants in their General Conference of 1834. There was at this time a fairly even balance of conferences as between slaveholding and free territory. In 1835 the Book Committee was being pressed to open the pages of the periodicals to the controversy, but refused. "On the subject of slavery and abolition, we intend to be silent, for reasons that must on all hands, we think, appear to be just and indispensable." [102]

The interval between general conferences had at first been set at seven years; but there was a call for one but four years after that in 1834; at this one the regular interval was reduced to four years thereafter. The slavery question could not be suppressed at this Conference of 1838; it was aggravated by an attempt to get the Book Committee to move the concern from Baltimore to Pittsburgh. Asa Shinn was the antislavery champion, but the general conference could do noth-

[96] Edward J. Drinkhouse, *History of Methodist Reform* II, 283.
[97] Ancel H. Bassett, *A Concise History of the Methodist Protestant Church* (Pittsburgh: Press of Charles A. Scott, 1877) p. 109.
[98] Drinkhouse, *op. cit.*, II, 303-4.
[99] *Ibid.*, II, 305.
[100] See p. 118.
[101] Drinkhouse, *op. cit.*, II, 283.
[102] *Ibid.*, II, 300.

ing but compromise, leaving the matter, in essence, where it was.

Thomas H. Stockton was elected the new publisher for the denomination; he took up the task only with the understanding that he should have freedom from restriction over what he was to print. With this understanding he proceeded to Baltimore to take up his duties. Once arrived there, however, he found that the conservative Book Committee's understanding of the freedom of the press differed from his; on the subject of slavery at least, they had gagged the paper. They pleaded it was a matter of its life or death, but Stockton felt unable to continue as editor in these circumstances.[103] This led to a demand for a paper for the North and West, which was granted later.

There was a good deal of abolitionist sentiment among the Methodist Protestant delegates to the General Conference of 1842. The New York Conference's delegates were instructed to press for a rule condemning slavery in its principle and practice as antispiritual, and "consequently a moral evil"; also that some provision be made for disengaging the Northern Conferences from all complicity in the evil.[104] This and many similar memorials were referred to a Committee on Memorials which reported its opinion that the General Conference should express itself on the subject; that the distinctions of color be erased from the constitution; and that an insertion be made in the General Rules prohibiting not only trading in slaves, but holding them as well. The minority of this committee objected strongly to "the introduction of any measures . . . which are calculated to disturb . . . the order and stability of the church [which] we regard . . . with paramount . . . interest." [105] The ultimate judgment of the General Conference, however, was simply that it had no jurisdiction in the matter; it remanded such judgments to the respective annual conferences.[106]

5. The Methodist Episcopal General Conference of 1844 and Its Aftermath.

The General Conference of the Methodist Episcopal Church in 1844 turned out to be the last one for ninety-five years in which all Episcopal Methodists were to meet together. Before it was over they

---

[103] Drinkhouse, op. cit., II, 310.
[104] MPFV, 8 (June 4, 1842), fourth page.
[105] Loc. cit.
[106] MPFV, 8 (1841-42), June 4, 1842, fourth page.

had divided into two separate churches. The church's guides began the conference with fascinated reluctance. The question which was uppermost in their minds was avoided as long as possible. The Episcopal address did not even mention slavery, though it spoke at some length on missions to Negroes. No committee on slavery was appointed at the beginning. But it was not possible to avoid it for long. The current below, hurrying them along, could not be denied. On the third day a motion to appoint a committee on slavery survived a motion to table and was carried; the committee itself was appointed the next day; to it were referred the memorials on the subject too numerous to be read before the Conference.[107]

Once the subject had shouldered its way to the center of attention, it was not displaced for the rest of the session. Other things were done, but everything was pervaded by the great question—even the election of bishops, which in more normal times creates an interest all its own. Peter Cartwright had, in 1840, advised against the election of bishops, though there was need of it to lighten the burden of the six existing ones. He feared that, if an election were held, what he called the "ultras" of both sides would force a choice between slaveholders and nonslaveholders, and that a split would certainly result. He took credit to himself and those whom he persuaded for having avoided schism in 1840.[108] In 1844, two new bishops—both Northern men—were elected; but the fat was in the fire, for instead of a slaveholder becoming a bishop, a bishop had become a slaveholder.

The first test of the strength of the two factions—for that is what they obviously were—centered around the appeal of Francis A. Harding, a minister of the Baltimore Conference, a slaveholder, who had

---

[107]A sample is here extracted from a form urged by the Springfield District of the New England Conference: "1. We earnestly entreat you to take such action as shall effectually destroy that . . . resolution [taken at the last General Conference] prohibiting the reception of the testimony of colored persons . . . and secure to all our members equal rights and privileges, whether as parties or witnesses. 2. We . . . believe that the interest of the whole church . . . requires that you . . . [elect] no man to fill the Episcopal office . . . who is a slaveholder. 3. We . . . petition you . . . to take such constitutional measures as shall effectually separate the Methodist Episcopal Church from all connection with the practice of slave-holding" (ZH, 15 [1844], no. 2 [Jan. 10]). The most extreme position is taken up by the ninth resolution of an antislavery convention in Vermont: "We as Christians can have no fellowship with any man, whether he be a Methodist or otherwise, who can hold and treat a fellow-being as a slave . . . (ZH, 15 [1844]: no. 8 [Feb. 21]).
[108]Charles L. Wallis (ed.), Autobiography of Peter Cartwright, p. 246.

been suspended by that conference because he had refused to emancipate the slaves belonging to him and Mrs. Harding. The issue was debated for a week before the vote was taken. The similarities of his case to that of Bishop Andrew were always in the delegates' minds, and the very able arguments were presented in the consciousness that the positions stated would set a precedent for future and more crucial action. The Baltimore Conference, as will be recalled from the earlier treatment of the Westmoreland appeal,[109] had a settled policy of admitting only ministers who were unencumbered by slave property, or who were willing to engage to manumit them.

The arguments of the Baltimore Conference were that this had long been a settled condition of membership with them, a condition which Mr. Harding knew when he was taken into the conference; that it had been possible in spite of the Maryland law for numbers of people to emancipate their slaves, and for the latter to live in peace in the state thereafter. The arguments for reversing his conference's decision were: that whether emancipation of slaves and their enjoyment of liberty had actually been carried out in Maryland or not, it was an infringement of the law to attempt it; that whatever the "settled policy" of the Maryland Conference was, the written code of the church at large excepted the dwellers in such states as forbade manumission from any requirement in the matter; and that the exception ought to be as jealously protected where it was applicable as the mandate to emancipate where it was not.

When the matter was put to a vote, the General Conference refused to reverse Baltimore's decision, by one hundred and seventeen votes to fifty-six. Only two Southern delegates voted with the majority. On the other hand, nine Northerners, and all the border delegations, voted with the Southern minority for reversal. Maryland, of course, voted with the majority;[110] this set a precedent for her cooperation with the North in the case of Bishop Andrew.[111]

The case of Bishop Andrew began on May 20 with a resolution requesting the Committee on Episcopacy to investigate the report

---

[109] See pp. 109, 166.

[110] JGC, 2 (1844), 33-34; and C. B. Swaney, op. cit., p. 119.

[111] Even Abel Stevens, editor of Zion's Herald was surprised at the outcome. During the trial he wrote back to his paper, "I presume the General Conference can hardly sustain the Baltimore Conference . . . the provisional exception in the Discipline covers him" (ZH, 15 [1844], no. 20 [May 5]).

that "one of the Bishops of the M. E. Church" had become connected with slavery. The committee elicited a full and frank statement from Bishop Andrew which revealed that he had by bequest become the owner of two slaves, whom he could not legally emancipate, unless and until they were as willing to leave the state as he was to have them go. The only voluntary move in the direction of involvement was that he had recently married a second time, to a woman who was then the owner of several slaves. His statement concluded: "It will be obvious . . . that I have neither bought nor sold a slave; that in the only two instances in which I am legally a slaveholder, emancipation is impracticable." [112]

Never during the whole debate over his status was the suggestion once made that Bishop Andrew was anything less than a godly man of stainless personal character, one who was zealous for the spiritual welfare of the Negroes, and compassionate and friendly in his personal dealings with them. The Bishop was taken by surprise to find all this storm raised around his head. He offered to resign to preserve the peace and unity of the church; but the Southern delegates persuaded him that this would never have the effect he intended, so he stayed on.

The first motion after the receipt of the facts in the case was a straight-out request that he resign;[113] this was later modified by the Finley substitute. On the ground that Bishop Andrew's being the owner of slaves would embarrass the exercise of his office as an itinerant general superintendent, it resolved that "it is the sense of this General Conference that he desist from the exercise of this office so long as this impediment remains." [114]

The debate was able and the arguments intricate, involving inevitably questions as to the powers of the General Conference with respect to the Episcopacy, which in turn were further complicated by the traditional Methodist unwillingness to decide whether it is merely an office, or in some sense also an order. The South thought that the "Compromise Law" of 1816 should govern all further procedure

[112] JGC, II (1844), 63-64.
[113] JGC, II (1844), 64.
[114] JGC, II (1844), 65-66.

in the matter; the North insisted that the settled policy of the church to keep its itinerant ministry as free from slaveholding as possible ought to be determinative.[115] The form in which the rebuke to Bishop Andrew was worded gave rise to many misunderstandings; was it advisory, or mandatory? was it administered because of slaveholding per se, or had Bishop Andrew rendered himself liable to discipline because of improper conduct? The Southern states avowed their intention of seceding if any reflection, however light, was cast on Bishop Andrew's fitness to exercise the duties of a bishop; on the other hand, the New England Conferences indicated quite as clearly their intention to leave the church if Bishop Andrew continued so to act.

In this deepening crisis the bishops proposed a postponement of the whole matter for another quadrennium, thinking thus to avert a seemingly inevitable split. Several of the bishops who had originally concurred in this proposal later withdrew their names, having discovered that it would not accomplish its purpose. The motion to table the bishops' proposal won, ninety-five votes to eighty-four.[116] Immediately thereafter, the vote was taken on the Finley substitute; it passed, one hundred and ten votes to sixty-eight.

Several days later the delegates of the slaveholding conference made a declaration to the effect

[115] The truth seems to be that the extremists on either side were determined on a split, and managed to force it on the moderates. Swaney's view is that fear lest the New England Conferences should go off to the Wesleyans stiffened the North's attitude; and perhaps even that of the Baltimore Conference, which voted with the North (*Episcopal Methodism and Slavery*, p. 126). As to the radical Northerners themselves, one wishes they had concentrated more on the plight of the slave, and ways of extricating him, and less on ridding themselves of complicity in the evil. The South would seem to have had somewhat the better of it from the constitutional point of view—the anomalous action of the General Conference respecting Bishop Andrew left too many questions unanswered from that point of view to have made the most satisfactory occasion for the break. The present writer has never come across a hint of such a motive in the sources, but a glance at the statistics gives room at least for the hypothesis that the Southern extremists were forestalling the statistical trend. in some such way as the Beards suggested that the Confederacy fought its war "against the Census." In 1816, when the "Compromise Law" was passed, there were five Northern conferences with fifty-nine delegates; there were four Southern conferences with forty-four delegates. In 1840 the Northern conferences had ninety-one delegates, the Southern thirty-nine. By 1844 the Northern conferences increased to one hundred six, while the Southern ones increased only to fifty. The list of conferences and their representatives to these general conferences may be found in JGC, I, 123, 23; II, 5 ff. (1840); and II, 5-6 (1844).
[116] JGC, II (1844), 82-83.

that the continued agitation on the subject of slavery and abolition in a portion of the church; the frequent action on that subject in the General Conference; and especially the extra-judicial proceedings against Bishop Andrew, which resulted . . . in a virtual suspension of him from his office as Superintendent . . . renders a continuance of the jurisdiction of this General Conference over these conferences inconsistent with the success of the ministry in the slaveholding states.[117]

Within a few days there were committees representing both factions at work drawing up an equitable division of the assets of the Book Concern. In 1845 a Convention of the Southern Conferences met in Louisville to organize the Methodist Episcopal Church, South; the next year it held its first General Conference. Both North and South thought the General Conference of 1844 had exceeded its powers: the grievance of the South was that it had reprimanded Bishop Andrew; the North's that it had undertaken to divide the church and the Book Concern. The Northern conferences as they met during the next quadrennium repudiated the agreement as to the division, and the General Conference of 1848 confirmed their repudiation. This action understandably embittered the Southern church, and the estrangement was aggravated by the competition of the allegiance of the border conferences. Nearly a century was to elapse before animosities cooled sufficiently to allow a reunion.

It is clear that moral revulsion against slavery in the Northern section of the church, together with the conviction that it was the church's business to speak out on the matter, was at the bottom of the matter. The South took the other side on both questions. It had allowed itself to be misled by economic considerations into a tragic approval of slavery, and it was likewise convinced that it was no business of the church to express itself as such on the matter, especially if by so doing it jeopardized its evangelistic success. They were willing to leave the matter to the states and their laws.

The Northerners' decision does them credit, but any tendency to self-righteousness will have to be qualified by the recollection that it was a good deal easier for them to make the decision, for it not only did not counter, but actually coincided with their economic interests.

[117] JGC, II (1844), 109.

In addition, it must not be forgotten that for long decades they too resisted making the decision out of consideration for the institutional welfare of the church as a whole, and the supposed harm it would do to its evangelistic work.

After the division, the effort of both churches to attract the border conferences played an influential role in the official statements on slavery. The Southern church kept the disciplinary provisions unchanged for some time after the break; the North, too, was slow to change. The changes, when they did come, were in opposite directions; and it can be said that the official statements changed more than did the practise in the respective churches.

In the Northern church, the agitation of the extreme wing took the form of seeking a change in the General Rule, to include prohibition of slaveholding as well as slave trading, and a penalty of exclusion for failure to comply. The abolitionists had hoped that, once the necessity of considering the South was ended with their departure, the Northern church would proceed to a clear statement on the sinfulness of slaveholding. They were disappointed. The border states remained to put the same brake on decisive action. Only in 1864 did they achieve their purpose of having slaveholding declared a sin. This was two years after it had been made illegal by civil action.

The desire not to alienate the border conferences probably combined with the excitement over the affair of the Book Concern to divert attention from the question of slaveholding in the Northern church.[118]

The General Conference of 1848 extended its jurisdiction over eight slaveholding conferences; and gave point to the *Nashville Christian Advocate's* complaint that the Methodist Episcopal Church, South, was continually being blamed for doing something that the Northern church was still doing.[119] The request of Baltimore Negroes for ministers of their own race, and for a Negro Conference, was rejected.[120] Much the same story was repeated in 1852. The number of memorials asking for a change in the rule increased; the border conferences resisted any change, nor were they alone in that. The

---

[118] Lucius Matlack, *op. cit.*, p. 189.
[119] Charles B. Swaney, *op. cit.*, pp. 199, 240.
[120] *Ibid.*, p. 197.

sentiment of the greater part of the Northern church was not as yet abolitionist. Most of the church periodicals were still antiabolitionist.[121] In 1854, Theodore Parker, speaking of the Protestant ministry of the country as a whole, said there were only a very few "true men" among the whole twenty-eight thousand. There was not, he said, a single Methodist antislavery Sunday school in the land.[122]

After 1852, the tide turned, and the pressure to change the rule increased. The Troy, Erie, and North Ohio Conferences were among those desiring it. But the Episcopal address reminded the General Conference in 1856 of the extent of the membership which still lay in slaveholding states.[123] The attempt to change the rule at that time failed of the necessary two-thirds affirmative vote; but the antislavery forces were able to pass a resolution requiring the church's Tract Society to print antislavery tracts. There was some resistance to this directive, however. The *Northwestern Christian Advocate* complained that tracts on slavery which had been published by the Book Concern and ordered put on the tract list had not appeared. The editor wondered whether Dr. Elliott, the author, had "become too much of an abolitionist for the New York folks." [124]

In that year, Dr. Durbin, then Missions Secretary, wrote a letter widely copied in the church press, which said the best course for the church to take in the extirpation of slavery was to keep the slaveholders in the church, and exercise her influence over them to that end. He argued that the New Testament church had set the example in this regard. The Editor of the *Northwestern Christian Advocate* however, was not impressed. He said: "Our fathers hoped to hasten its extirpation in the country by proscribing it in the church. And it is what the church of today must do if she wishes to do her duty." [125]

The continued existence of slaveholding in the Northern church was the paramount question at the General Conference of 1860. One

[121] *Ibid.*
[122] *Ibid.*, p. 209.
[123] NWCA, 4 (1856), 79.
[124] *Ibid.*, p. 21.
[125] NWCA, 4 (1856), 5. A further editorial on the same letter says (p. 10): "Our whole review has had the effect upon our mind to impress us more and more with the moral and logical impossibility of the attempt to defend a slaveholding church membership from the Bible, and yet to declare that, in so doing, we are not the apologists of slavery."

hundred thirty-seven memorials asked for keeping the rule unchanged, as against eight hundred and eleven asking for the elimination of slavery.[126] There were two schools of thought among those who wished a change: one thought the best way was to change the General Rule; the other thought it would be easier to make the change by interpretation. The majority of the Committee on Slavery reported in favor of changing the Rule; but it failed by only four votes to receive the necessary two-thirds. The conference then proceeded to change the interpretive legislation to include the holding of slaves, along with their sale, under the reprehension of the church:

We believe the buying, selling, or *holding* of human beings, as chattels, is contrary to the laws of God and nature, inconsistent with the Golden Rule, and with that rule in our Discipline which requires . . . us to do no harm. We therefore affectionately admonish all our preachers and people to keep themselves pure from this great evil.[127]

There was a good deal of uncertainty as to the exact bearing of this explanatory chapter. *Zion's Herald and Wesleyan Journal* said that the conference "by vote solemnly refused to call the chapter 'only advisory,'" [128] but other interpreters have concluded that they did just that.[129] In any case, they had gone far enough to cause alarm in the border conferences. The Baltimore Conference rebelled openly. The bishop who presided at the next meeting of their conference gave such equivocal answers to a number of questions as to what penalties could, or would, be meted out to slaveholders under the new paragraph, that they replied with an action itself a masterpiece of equivocation: they declared themselves independent of the general conferences, but still a part of the Methodist Episcopal Church! That is, they did not immediately join the Methodist Episcopal Church, South, in the hope that other conferences would join them, and so constitute the true Methodist Episcopal Church.[130]

The change in the General Rule which had been sought so long was made with scarcely any debate, and with only eight dissentient

---

[126] NWCA, 8 (1860), 86.
[127] Quoted from C. B. Swaney, *op. cit.*, p. 226.
[128] ZHWJ, 31 (1860), 26 (June 27).
[129] C. B. Swaney, *op. cit.*, p. 227.
[130] C. B. Swaney, *op. cit.*, pp. 229-30.

votes, in the General Conference of 1864.[131] But by this time the writ of the Methodist Episcopal Church was pretty well restricted to nonslaveholding areas; and even where, supported by the Union arms, it went beyond, slavery had been abolished by Presidential proclamation over a year before.

The Methodist Episcopal Church, South, during that period of its separate existence which lay before the outbreak of war, not only kept alive but even increased its interests in the spiritual welfare of the slaves. In 1846 was published the report of the South Carolina Conference's Missionary Society. It indicated that of the $14,250 received for missions, $11,000 had been spent on work among Negroes within the bounds of the Conference.[132] Two years later *Zion's Herald* reported on the flourishing state of Negro missions conducted by the Southern church as a whole:

The missions embrace . . . thirteen conferences, in which collectively are established one hundred and twenty-nine missions, who have the oversight of thirty-three thousand, four hundred and ninety members. Of these conferences, South Carolina has the largest membership, viz: 9,103; Tennessee the next, 5,069; and then others range from 1,200 to nearly 5,000. The reports from the Sunday Schools are not complete; those given amount to upwards of ten thousand. The yearly income of this society amounted to $73,667.66.[133]

The Southern church, like the Northern, put off changing the rule on slavery, with the same objective in mind—the wooing of the border conferences. Ironically enough, it took over the rule from the old *Discipline* unchanged: the General Rule prohibiting the trading in slaves, and Section nine, which begins: "We declare that we are as much as ever convinced of the great evil of slavery." [134] The rule against trading in slaves, however, began to be interpreted as applying only to the African slave trade. The general conferences of 1846 and 1850 refused to act on changing the rules. Matlack with some circumstantiality adds that it was Bishop Andrew who advised against the change for fear of losing the border conferences.[135] The Baltimore

---

[131] NWCA, 12 (1864), 161.
[132] C. B. Swaney, op cit., p. 191.
[133] ZHWJ, 19 (1848), no. 1 (Jan. 5).
[134] *The Doctrines and Discipline of the Methodist Episcopal Church South* pp. 24, 195.
[135] Lucius Matlack, op. cit., p. 183.

Conference was determined to maintain its middle-of-the-road course, by which it refused to accept slaveholders as members on the one hand, and, on the other, resolutely refused fellowship with a church which made nonslaveholding a condition of membership. The Philadelphia Conference rallied round the slogan, "The Discipline as it is." [136]

In 1854 the Southern church came within seven votes of striking the rule on slavery out altogether. But it was not finally removed till 1858, by the decisive vote of 140 to 8. It was removed as ambiguous, and because it "might be construed as antagonistic to the institution." [137] In spite of this action, the Southern church continued to refuse to think of itself as a proslavery church. A review of a book by the Rev. Mr. Scaritt says of him:

He then shows that the Southern Methodist Church is slandered when it is called a pro-slavery Church, as it has distinctly and unequivocally avowed that, as a religious body, it will not meddle with the question at all, except to enforce the scriptural duties which grow out of the relation of master and servant.[138]

6. THE METHODIST PROTESTANTS: SCHISM OVER SLAVERY AND REUNION

The split in the Methodist Protestant Church followed the pattern set by the Methodist Episcopal Church in some respects, though in others it was, inevitably, quite different. One similarity lay in the fact that there was a small preliminary break first. The General Conference of 1846 discovered that one whole conference—the Champlain —had broken off and joined the abolitionist Wesleyan Connection.[139] That general conference was not able to transcend the position taken by an earlier one, so far as declarations on slavery were concerned; it got only so far as the cautious statement that slavery might not always be a sin, but it certainly was sometimes.[140] Four years later, there were more resolutions that the word "white" be stricken from

---

[136] *Ibid.*, p. 184.
[137] C. B. Swaney, *op. cit.*, p. 246 ff.
[138] QRS 15 (1861, 134.
[139] Edward J. Drinkhouse, *History of Methodist Reform.* (2 vols., Baltimore and Pittsburgh: Board of Publication of the Methodist Protestant Church, 1899), II, 348.
[140] MP, 12 (1845-46), May 30, second page.

the constitution; but the General Conference again stated that it had no authority to legislate in the premises.[141]

In one respect the course of the Methodist Protestant Church was wiser than that of their sister church: they divided their Book Concern first, and their church afterward. In the General Conference of 1854, the grievances of the antislavery forces against the throttling of the official church papers came to a head in a vigorous demand that a branch of the Publishing House be established at Pittsburgh to give them a channel of expression. It was feared that such a move would be the precursor of separation, and that slavery was at the bottom of it. The proponents of the scheme, however, thought it would contribute to the peace and unity of the church. The permission was in the end granted.[142]

Clearly antislavery sentiment was gaining ground and voice in the Northern conferences. The North Illinois District Conference got its resolutions printed in the General Conference Journal of 1854, though no action was taken on them. These resolutions proposed that slaveholding should be regarded as a sin against God; that it should be extirpated from the church and the world; that it should be regarded as a disqualification from membership in the Church of Christ; and finally that

in our judgment, the fugitive slave law is a most atrocious effort to abrogate the law of God, which we claim to be the *higher* law, binding and controlling our conduct in relation to our fellow men, and we cannot obey it.[143]

Nevertheless, the General Conference again refused to act "in the premises."

The antislavery conferences of the North and West were thereupon convinced that they could hope for no action from the General Conference, nor were they willing longer to be implicated in the slaveholding thus perpetuated.[144] Two years later, then, a convention of

[141] Drinkhouse, *op cit.*, II, 368.

[142] MP, 20 (1853-54), May 27, 1854, first page.

[143] *Journal of the General Conference of the Methodist Protestant Church*, 1854, no. 18, p. 77.

[144] The preamble to their "conditions" presented to the General Conference (Southern) of 1858 read in part, as follows: "We have for a series of years . . . expressed to our Southern brethren our kind remonstrance . . . entreating them to put away for ever this sin and relieve us of a humiliating reproach. But our expostulations have

the Northern and Western conferences met at Springfield, and declared that the disadvantages of adherence to the General Conference were greater than the advantages. The delegates from those conferences to the General Conference of 1858, therefore, instead of repairing to that conference, met in convention in Cincinnati, and agreed on certain conditions to be fulfilled before they would consent to be present. These were, first, the removal of the word "white" from the constitution, and, second, that voluntary slaveholding be declared a bar to membership in the church. Anticipating noncompliance, they resolved to meet again in 1858, to issue a new *Discipline* and constitution, if necessary.[145]

"The Seventh General Conference of the Church convened at Lynchburg, Va., May 4, 1858." [146] The Northern and Western conferences were only scantily represented if at all; the total number of delegates present was thirty-nine—twenty-three ministers and sixteen laymen. The conference, in effect, rejected the request from the section which had met at Cincinnati. There was a resolution (which however was tabled) which would have allowed them to depart freely, and by release; this was offered in the hope of preserving better relations.

The majority pointed to the sad effect the spectacle of divided churches would produce on "scoffers," and said: "We cannot assume responsibility which our Northern and Western brethren would transfer from themselves to us, and thereby place ourselves in the wrong." They pointed out that if the reasons alleged were sufficient to divide the church, the dissidents could not consent to remain even under the political government without sin. "Will disunion be for the glory of God?" [147]

The Northern and Western conferences then proceeded to meet and to justify their existence by declaring the late General Conference (at Lynchburg) a nullity; they struck the word "white" from their

---

ever been deemed not only unacceptable, but highly offensive to our slaveholding brethren. All prospect and hope of their regarding our appeals have well-nigh fled . . . (*Journal of the General Conference of the Methodist Protestant Church*, 1858, pp. 14-16).

[145] Drinkhouse, op. cit., II, 411, ff. cf. MP 24 (1857-58), May 22, p. 1.

[146] *Ibid.*, II, 422.

[147] *Journal of the General Conference of the Methodist Protestant Church*, 1858, pp. 29-30.

constitution, added a strongly worded item against slavery, and took out the provision that the ecclesiastical power should not interfere with the operation of the civil laws—presumably to make room for aid to fugitive slaves in defiance of the Act requiring that they be apprehended and returned to their masters.[148]

The Northern section met next in General Conference in Cincinnati in 1862 in the midst of the War. They declared that the conferences in the Confederate States had violated the Articles of Religion in that they were in rebellion against the civil authorities; and that the General Conference (i.e., themselves) was restored to true and original authority as the Methodist Protestant Church.[149]

The Southern General Conference in 1866 declared the Northern and Western conferences in the state of separation, denying that they held any unkind feelings toward them, and insisting that they would welcome their return as soon as they manifested a disposition to conform to the constitution and *Discipline*.[150] The Northern and Western conferences were for a time after the Civil War united with the Wesleyan Methodist Connection, in what was called simply "The Methodist Church";[151] by 1877, however, the North-South animosities had died down sufficiently to permit the reunion of the Methodist Protestants North and South.[152]

The reasons for the separation having ceased, they very sensibly brought the separation to an end. Two of the embittering factors which had kept the Episcopal Methodist Churches apart for so long were no obstacle here. They had managed to retain the arrangements whereby the assets of their Book Concern had been divided *before* the separation; and the Wesleyans did not exacerbate the division by "invading" the territory of the Methodist Protestant Church, as the Northern Episcopal Church was to do after the War was over.

---

[148] Drinkhouse, *op. cit.*, II, pp. 435-36.
[149] *Ibid.*, II, 452 ff.
[150] MP, 32 (1865-66), May 19, 1866, p. 2.
[151] Bassett points out that this union was a natural one, inasmuch as those Methodists who had become Wesleyans had suffered from the Methodist Episcopalian hierarchy in much the same way as the Methodist Protestants (Ancel H. Bassett, *Concise History of the Methodist Protestant Church* p. 313 ff.) Drinkhouse, however, leaves no doubt that he felt anything a mistake which retarded reunion of the Northern and Southern sections of the Methodist Protestant family.
[152] Drinkhouse, *op. cit.*, II, 428.

CHAPTER FIVE

The Civil War and Reconstruction

FROM THE 1830's ON, THE SLAVERY QUESTION HAD BEEN discussed in the churches primarily as a moral and religious question. As many Christians became aroused to protest against slavery as an evil, so others stirred themselves up to its defense on moral and religious grounds. It is obvious from this distance that the moral judgment of the proslavery men was warped by the pervasive factor of economic advantage; on the other hand, the relative detachment of the antislavery party made for an oversimplification of the issue and judgment expressed in unjustifiably sharp alternatives.

The point here, however, is that in the churches in general, and the Methodist churches in particular, the debate was carried on in moral and religious terms. Political considerations entered the question relatively little—only as the defenders of slavery pointed to the laws of their respective states where they protected the "institution." With the imminence of war, however, politics intruded themselves more and more; and in the end, the military conflict was ostensibly joined over the political issue of preserving the Union. To this issue too, both sides summoned the sanctions of religion and morality; both the preservation of the Union and States' Rights became "sacred" causes.

A. The Methodist Churches and the War

1. POLITICS AND PATRIOTISM IN THE CHURCHES

By the end of 1860, *Zion's Herald* was deploring the imminent break between the States.[1] The next year the *Quarterly Review* of the

---

[1] ZHWJ, 31 (1860), 186.

Methodist Episcopal Church, South, carried an apology for secession, in which Congress' failure to take action on the compromise policy put forward by President Lincoln was held responsible for the break. "The idea of holding any state in the Union by coercion is considered by many . . . too absurd to be entertained for a moment." [2] The Northerners cited the aggressive expansionism of the "slave power," to which the Southerners retorted that they had had to accede to the exclusion of slavery from the northwestern part of Virginia and

from another immense region by the Missouri Compromise—its exclusion from another immense region by the Compromise of 1850—the present attempt to exclude it from all the territory held in common by the North and the South and the denial by the North that the Constitution recognizes its existence outside of the slave-holding states . . . to say nothing about the nullification of Constitutional and Congressional provisions in regard to fugitive slaves.[3]

The *Quarterly Review* of the Southern Methodist Church rallied to the defense of States' Rights:

Our Northern brethren have set forth a political gospel which we seriously believe "another" than that which we received from the apostles of freedom. . . . The thirteen original states were not so fatuous as to abolish their own sovereignty. . . . Among those rights which they reserved was, of course, the right of withdrawing from the partnership if it should fail to answer the ends of its origination; and of this as sovereign States, they, of course, were to be the judges.[4]

Northern Methodist comment had earlier noted the denial of the right of petition in Congress over the matter of abolition petitions.

Governor B[agby of Alabama] ventures to say, and we wonder that he had courage to say it, that *it may be* possible that this subject is embraced within the comprehensive principle of the inalienable right of petition . . . No well-informed man, not under the influence of prejudice of some sort . . . ever doubted this.[5]

Not only the writers, but the preachers too, were drawn into the whirlpool of political contention. Many a fervent prayer went up, "O

[2] QRS, 15 (1861), 318.
[3] QRS, 15 (1861), 294.
[4] QRS, 15 (1861), 463.
[5] ZH, 11, (1840), no. 49 (Dec. 2).

Lord, help the Methodist preachers to mind their own business"; but they were not all answered. In 1860, for instance, J. J. Ferree made a "Republican speech" in Cairo, Illinois. He was greeted with a shower of eggs, one of which struck him full in the face.[6] Complaints in Northern Methodist papers were frequent during the days of the violence over Kansas, partly about the violence itself, and partly because it was directed at the antislavery (if not also political) activity of ministers: "It is these lawless vagabonds" [the "border ruffians"], they said, "that tar and feather preachers and rail-ride men whose dialect betrays a New England nativity." [7] At the outbreak of the war a Methodist's statement went as follows:

We appeal to Heaven for the rectitude of our motives. . . . The war on our side is exclusively and avowedly one of defense—how is it on their side? The Lord be judge. . . . A consciousness of the right makes us strong and indomitable. We have invoked the God of Battles; so have they: He will hear both, and we fear not the results." [8]

This happens to be the statement of a Southern Methodist, but it might stand without change for those made in the Northern church as well. A sermon on a fast day appointed in Evanston, Illinois, toward the end of the war contained these words:

I am aware that grievous doubt exists in the minds of many Christians with reference to God's approval of war . . . but . . . the war in which we are engaged is a holy duty and as obligatory upon Christians as it is to pray. . . . Where there is a . . . great principle of revealed truth to be settled . . . then we do feel that God calls us to the war as distinctly as God called the hosts under Joshua by name to meet the Amalekites in Rephidim.[9]

German Methodism was an exception. The *Christliche Apologete* had no references to the disturbed state of the country in 1860, and only a minimum of such in 1864; in the latter year correspondence with Arkansas appears as well as that from Northern states. The Ger-

[6] ZHWJ, 31 (1860), no. 32 (Aug. 8).
[7] NWCA, 4 (1856), 41. Sweet's verdict is: "The story of the happenings in Missouri throughout the war, as far as the relation of the two branches of Methodism is concerned, contains little of which either side can be proud. . . . Nowhere were greater barbarities practised in the name of the church and religion" (SMAH, p. 282).
[8] QRS, 15 (1861), 464.
[9] NWCA, 12 (1864), 257.

man element in Texas had been great opponents of the continuance of slavery there; we may suppose that their common Germanness was stronger than the sectionalism which was rife in the breasts of their new countrymen of other stocks.

A General Convention of the northern section of the Methodist Protestant Church, held in Cincinnati in the last months of 1862, recommended prosecution of the war to a successful conclusion as a barrier to "anarchy and misrule, . . . and medieval tyranny and vassalage. . . . Resolved, that we heartily endorse the Emancipation Proclamation of President Lincoln; because it strikes at the baleful cause of all our civil and ecclesiastical difficulties, American slavery.[10] Lincoln's commendation of the contribution of the Northern Methodists to the Union's cause is well known: "It is no fault in others that the Methodist Church sends more soldiers to the field, more nurses to the hospitals, and more prayers to heaven than any." [11]

In 1862, nearly a fifth of the preachers of the Tennessee Conference were in the service of the Confederate Army,[12] which is probably not an unfair indication of the devotion of the Southern Methodist ministry as a whole to their cause. One of them, J. B. McFerrin, was elected president of the session of the Conference of 1862, in the absence of a bishop. He was appointed to take charge of the missionary work in the Army of the Tennessee. His war diary gives many vivid glimpses of war conditions, of the sufferings of the army, and of the ministrations of religion carried on in its midst.

I began my work in Shelbyville. I was hailed with pleasure by the officers and soldiers. . . . A great work of grace had commenced in many of the commands, and the chaplains and preachers in the neighborhood were actively engaged in the precious revival that was springing up in almost every direction. On May 17, 1863, . . . I preached in the Presbyterian Church: house crowded with officers and soldiers; serious attention. At three o'clock, I preached in Bates' brigade: a very good time; revival in the brigade. . . . May 22nd, I spoke in General Riddle's brigade: a great work here; already more than one hundred conversions in this command. So the work went on. But in June I was taken sick, and remained unfit

[10] *Proceedings of the General Convention of the Methodist Protestant Church,* 1862, p. 19.

[11] Quoted in SMAH, p. 299.

[12] Cullen T. Carter, *op. cit.,* p. 147.

for work till August, when I joined the army again at Chattanooga, and on August 14th preached in General Wright's brigade. . . . On September 19th and 20th the great battle was fought at Chickamauga, fifteen miles from Chattanooga. The slaughter was tremendous on both sides, but the Confederates held the field. I remained on the battlefield eleven days, nursing the sick, ministering to the wounded, and praying for the dying. The sight was awful. Thousands of men killed and wounded. They lay thick all around, shot in every possible manner, and the wounded dying every day. Among the wounded were many Federal soldiers. To these I ministered, prayed with them, and wrote letters by flag of truce to their friends in the North. They seemed to appreciate every act of kindness. . . . Never before had I been so fully impressed with the cruelty of war, notwithstanding I had witnessed many bloody fights. . . . When I told my wife where I had been, what I had done, what good meetings we had had, how I had waited on the sick and ministered to the well, she rose to her feet and said, "Husband, stay with them to the last!" [13]

Just after the war was over, a writer in the *Methodist Quarterly Review* noted the oft-repeated phenomenon that philanthropic contributions are stimulated by war conditions, and spoke of the high rate of giving to the voluntary organizations, such as the Sanitary Commission and the Christian Commission, which helped in the ministry to the soldiers' physical and spiritual needs during the war.[14]

In the Old Northwest, notably in Ohio, Indiana, and Illinois, Methodism and Republicanism went hand in hand as bulwarks of the Union. So close was the connection there that Peter Cartwright, enjoying a certain immunity because of his long service to the Church, felt called upon to rebuke the members of the Illinois Conference for "political proscription" during its stormy session of 1863. Rather unchristian vituperation was poured liberally upon those who even took and read a Democratic newspaper.

Some Methodists who refused to be dragooned in their political opinions seceded; the fragments sought to unite, but once the centripetal force of the war was loosed they could not hold together; some of them preferred joining themselves to the Southern Methodists

---

[13] Quoted in Gross Alexander, *History of the Methodist Episcopal Church, South,* (in Vol. XI of the "American Church History Series," New York: The Christian Litera ture Co., 1894) p. 71 ff.

[14] MQR, 47 (1865), 65 ff.

over returning to the Northern communion. Meanwhile they smarted under the scornful epithet "Butternuts," which was a local variant of the more general term "Copperheads." [15]

The President's Emancipation Proclamation, which became effective at the beginning of 1863, was more effective in rallying the flagging zeal of the North than in disrupting the social organization of the South. Southerners noted with amazement and gratitude that the slaves thus freed at a time when the South's whole energies were concentrated on prosecuting the war against the North did not resort to violence; nor did they take advantage of the situation to embark on independent careers, let alone execute reprisals on the defenseless mistresses and old masters left behind.

There is no doubt that up to that time, Lincoln's aim as President and Commander-in-Chief had been to preserve the Union, and keep Constitutional guarantees, even for slavery, in force. Emancipation, when it came, was subordinate to the purpose of winning the war, though there is no doubt that it also represented, in Lincoln's own personal view, the righting of an ancient wrong. It was designed to rally foreign support, especially of the English, who, suffering from a cotton famine, were, on a purely practical basis, inclined to favor the Confederacy.

Lincoln's hope was that idealistic pride in her own emancipation of a generation before would revive her support of a similar endeavor in North America. He was successful in rallying the idealistic forces of the Northern churches to his side, at a time when war weariness was beginning to overbear their zeal for the purely political cause of preserving the Union. Toward the end of the war, consequently, we note a frequent recurrence of "fight-on-till-the-cause-is-won" editorials in Northern Methodist papers. The following in the *Northwestern Christian Advocate* must stand for a number in its own and its contemporaries' columns:

Slavery has been sentenced to death by the war power of the nation, but such a sentence must be executed by the sword. And slavery lives *de facto* in every rod of unconquered southern soil. . . . Any reoccupancy

[15] Ralph E. Morrow, "Methodists and 'Butternuts' in the Old Northwest," *Journal of the Illinois State Historical Society*, 49 (1956), 34-47.

of southern territory upon other than an out-and-out antislavery platform merits stern reprobation.[16]

During the war each section of the church was made to feel its importance in the waging of the struggle. Religious and patriotic sentiments became inextricably intertwined—not only in eloquent addresses such as Bishop Simpson's on "Our Country," which he delivered in the Academy of Music in New York just before the presidential election in 1864,[17] but also in many a pulpit in the weekly sermon. "More or less throughout the nation, North and South alike, patriotism crowded religion in all of the churches."[18] Many ministers actively promoted recruiting. At the session of the New York East Conference of 1863, it was voted to have the oath of allegiance administered to the whole body, and a judge of the United States District Court and a major general of the army were called in to administer it .They were given "seats within the altar near the bishop." The

[16] NWCA, 12 (1864), 124. See also *Ibid.* p, 100. The *Christliche Apologete's* tone was much quieter. Twenty years before (after reporting on the general conference and the prospective separation of 1844) it had said: "Even though the Church should split into northern and southern halves, still we needn't fear a division of the German mission work. Since we really have nothing to do with the question of slavery, since, according to the southern brethren, a close connection between the German missions is necessary, and since the greater number of the German missions are situated in the free states, the southern brethren, in the event of a separation from the north, would place no obstacle in the way of the German missions which lie within their territory, if a majority of their members decide for union with the German missions in the northern Church" (ChAp. 6 [1844], 101). In 1864 it said that the war was "God's chastening us for our sins"; the Christians have, however, a great influence to exert, a moral one, not only in the waging of the war, but in bringing it to an end in a durable peace. The war is to decide whether the forces of righteousness or those of evil are to prevail (26 [1864], 154).

[17] Methodists were proud of Bishop Matthew Simpson's frequent visits to the White House and the War Department, and tended to exaggerate his influence on President Lincoln's decisions on policy. The legend that it was the Bishop who suggested the Emancipation Proclamation to the President had wide currency, but the facts are that he was on the high seas returning from the Pacific coast when the decision was made. His previous representations to the President seem to have been directed not toward policy, but toward seeing that the Methodists received their due share of appointments to office. Bishop Simpson co-operated heartily with Bishop Ames in getting from Secretary Stanton permission to occupy Southern Methodist Churches for missionary purposes. He was quite aware of the high value the Government put on Methodist co-operation in the war effort. He enthusiastically encouraged that participation; but never eased, in his relations with high officials, to regard himself as primarily the servant of the Methodist Church and to advance its interests where he could (Robert D. Clark, *The Life of Matthew Simpson* [New York: The Macmillan Co., 1950], pp. 222-23, *et passim*).

[18] SMAH, p. 283.

193

Minutes tell how "the vast audience was moved by emotions of moral sublimity which nothing besides this happy union of religion and patriotism could have aroused." [19]

Thus was Methodism carried closer than ever before to the main stream of politics by the exigencies of the war; and there is little indication that she found it uncongenial.[20]

2. The Methodist Episcopal Church Follows the Army

It was unfortunate that Northern Methodism came to a full realization of her political power at just the juncture when a mood of vindictiveness was settling over the North. The Methodist Episcopal Church's thrust into the South was undeniably productive of some good in the evangelization and especially the education of the freedmen; but its dealings with the Methodist Episcopal Church, South, and their property savored too much of ecclesiastical imperialism, and that at the expense of a conquered foe, to produce anything but resentment among the white brethren in the South.

Bishop Edward R. Ames was the chief architect of the penetration of the South, but he had the backing of the majority of his fellow Methodists. The few Northern Methodists who objected in the name of Christian restraint and compassion were given but scanty attention.[21] As early as 1862 the movement began, with the strong

[19] Quoted in *Ibid.*, p. 284.

[20] Speaking of Methodism's political influence, not in connection with the war only, but during the middle half of the nineteenth century, Hodding Carter in his able book on the reconstruction period has this to say:

"The Methodists were a uniquely powerful sect. The Episcopalians and the Presbyterians in the South and the Congregationalists in New England could count among their members a majority of the upper-class industrial, agricultural, and professional groups. The yet chaotic Baptist expansion, until recently concentrated in the frontier, was most effective still among the least secure and less well-educated citizenry. The ably led Methodist Episcopal Church was the most dynamic, the fastest growing, and, excepting the minuscule Quakers and the sectionally limited Unitarians and Congregationalists, the most dedicated to social reform of the nation's organized churches. . . . When the Methodist bishops and preachers spoke, politicians listened no less attentively than did their congregations." (Hodding Carter, *The Angry Scar, the Story of Reconstruction.* [Garden City, New York: Doubleday and Co., 1959], p. 81.)

[21] Sometimes the protests won hard names for those who made them. The *Northwestern Christian Advocate* copied approvingly an editorial from the *Chicago Tribune*, which said, among other things: "The action of the Methodist Bishop, Ames, in restoring the churches of the South to loyalty and placing in their pulpits men who will not preach treason to the government, has aroused the ire of the Northern copperheads and secession sympathizers. . . . We were glad to see Bishop Ames on his

194

help of Secretary of War Stanton, who ordered Union commanders in occupied districts to turn over to Bishop Ames "all houses of worship belonging to the Methodist Episcopal Church, South" in which a loyal minister "who had been appointed by a loyal Bishop" was not officiating.[22]

There is some indication that Northern Methodists thought many of their Southern brethren would welcome their intervention as a deliverance from the slaveholders' tyranny; but they were doomed to disappointment. The greater part of them saw in the scheme a plan of the Northern church to absorb the Southern secessionist branch.[23] A good many churches in Southern occupied territory were thus turned over to the Northern Methodists, under pretext of putting loyal ministers in place of disloyal ones; some of them, of course, had been emptied by the misfortunes of the war. Finally, word of these doings reached President Lincoln, who wrote to the commanding officer of the department of Missouri, where a Southern minister had been banished from his pulpit: "The United States government must not . . . undertake to run the churches. When an individual, in a church or out of it, becomes dangerous to the public, he must be checked; but let the churches, as such, take care of themselves." [24] Only later did he learn that his Secretary of War had authorized otherwise; he promptly asked him to change the policy. The Secretary, however, complied only reluctantly and in part. With or without the dubious help of the War Department, Northern Methodism was in earnest about its expansion in the Southern states. The Missionary Board at New York appropriated $35,000 for the work,[25] which was prosecuted with energy throughout the period of Reconstruction; some good was done, mostly among the Negroes. Improved relations with the Methodist Episcopal Church, South, were indefinitely retarded by the policy.

---

religious march, having his loins girt about with truth and wearing the breastplate of righteousness. . . . Let him go quenching the fiery dart of ministerial traitors and elevating the church from its slough of treason into the pure light of freedom and religion" (NWCA, 12 [1864], 57).

[22] SMAH, p.295.

[23] Hodding Carter, op. cit., p. 83. A Georgian called Ames's men "missionaries of wrath," among other colorful epithets (Ibid., p. 87).

[24] Ibid., p. 84.

[25] SMAH, p. 295.

B. The Period of Reconstruction

1. THE NORTHERN CHURCH

The close of the Civil War found the Methodist Episcopal Church dominated by two moods: vindictiveness toward the defeated whites of the South, and extravagant hopes as to what might be done for any by the freed Negroes. The vindictiveness was increased by the assassination of Lincoln; the hopes for the Negro paled slowly as the magnitude of the task of his elevation became clear in the course of long and sacrificial effort on his behalf.

A Methodist Preachers' Meeting in Boston in 1865 was but echoing the prevailing sentiment when it resolved:

> That we hold the national authority bound by the most solemn obligation to God and man to bring all the civil and military leaders of the rebellion to trial by due course of law, and when they are clearly convicted, to execute them.[26]

It was not only in Methodist pulpits, of course, that eloquent tributes were paid to the leadership of "the Martyr President" after his assassination. Methodist eulogies were not the only ones mixed with heated demands for punishment not only of the assassin, but also of the "slave power" which had brought on the war and ended in the murder of Abraham Lincoln. It was, however, a Boston Methodist minister, perhaps one who had helped pass the resolution mentioned above, who on the Easter Sunday morning after Lincoln's death preached a sermon containing the following words:

> Abraham Lincoln, our President, whose great heart was as true and loving as a woman's . . . this wise and just and merciful ruler lies murdered in the capital!
>
> What language can express our horror of the blow which struck him down? And what shall we say of the hellish power which prompted and aimed the blow?
>
> We thought we had already seen the utmost reach of barbarism and savagery of which the slave-power is capable. We had seen it trample on the rights of four millions of people, using them solely for its own infernal lusts. . . .
>
> And now, to fill the measure of its wickedness, slavery has done—what?

[26] Quoted in Hodding Carter, op. cit., p. 83.

How shall we characterize its latest deed? What lexicon contains the word by which fitly to call it? . . . This nameless deed slavery has just done to increase and perpetuate its previous record of infamy!

If the old president chastised them with whips, the new president will chastise them with scorpions. . . . I say this: "The halter to intelligent, influential traitors." But to the honest boy, to the deluded man, who have been deceived into the rebel ranks I would extend leniency. . . .

There is hope, therefore, in the bright beams of this Easter sun! Our new ruler knows how to deal with traitors!

Abraham Lincoln is dead: slain by the hand of slavery! . . . "Thou art Freedom's now, and Fame's!" [27]

Methodists in the North joined vigorously in the attack on President Johnson; they thirsted for his political blood because he did not thirst sufficiently for the blood of rebel leaders. In the spring of 1868 Zion's Herald broke out in a rash of violent editorials against him, in which not only his political misdeeds, but also his personal shortcomings, were rehearsed.[28] A nonepiscopal Methodism meeting in General Convention in Cincinnati in 1866 heard a paper in which Mr. Lyle viewed with alarm the attitude of the Chief Executive toward impenitent rebels, and approved the course which Congress was taking.[29] As late as 1876 the Northwestern Christian Advocate was crying out against amnesty for Jefferson Davis.[30]

Gilbert Haven, born into an old New England family, was the most articulate and most consistent advocate of equality for the Negro, social as well as civic, in the church as well as in the state. He joined the New England Conference in 1851. His preaching was marked from the beginning by a lively interest in the ethical aspects of public questions such as temperance and slavery. During his years as editor of Zion's Herald (1867-1872), he was a stanch ally of Charles Sumner and the radical Republicans, and, after he left the editorship for the Episcopacy, he continued to be outspoken in defense of their

[27] From a sermon by William S. Studley, in Sermons Preached in Boston on the Death of Abraham Lincoln (Boston: J. S. Tilton & Co., 1865).
[28] ZH, 45 (1868), Feb. 27: "The days of the despot we trust are ended. He will be driven forth from his seat, and a loyal, just, and capable president take the reins and serve the nation"; and Ibid., Mar. 5, (p. 109): an "execrable libertine, drunkard, and tyrant."
[29] Minutes of the Non-Episcopal Methodist Convention (1866), p. 29.
[30] NWCA, 24 (1876), 4. This was the second editorial on the subject within a few weeks.

policy, even though his episcopal headquarters were in Georgia. One of his most trenchant phrases called the carpetbaggers "the true knight-errantry of the age."

Not only by word, but also by practice, he supported social equality; he entertained Negroes in his home, and mingled freely with them in public. Such a policy raised resentments against him in the hearts of his new white neighbors, who steadily ostracized him, and at times threatened him with violence.

a) *The Southward Extension of the Church*

The "invasion" of the South by the Methodist Episcopal Church, once begun behind the front of the Union armies, was not abandoned. The connections formed during the war by the Methodist Episcopal Church, with a political party and military might, continued for some time during the Reconstruction period, and constituted one of the principal grounds of the Southern church's objection to their presence in the South.

James Lynch, a colored member of the Mississippi Conference, and a presiding elder there, was active in promoting the cause of the Republican party, and was elected to the State Senate, though he never occupied the office. Al. L. Lakin, who was called by Bishop Haven "the head of our work in the South," and by his friends "the best stump speaker in the State" (Alabama), influenced the votes of the Union whites in the northern part of the state. At one juncture when the continued existence of the radical Reconstruction regime was endangered, he prolonged its life by securing the dispatch of a detachment of Federal troops to the danger zone. He strenuously denied that he introduced politics into his sermons, but there is convincing evidence to the contrary. He himself sought political office on several occasions, and was prevented from assuming the presidency of the University of Alabama by the intervention of the Ku Klux Klan.

Perhaps the most conspicuous example of the Negro in Southern politics was Hiram R. Revels, a presiding elder in the Natchez District in Mississippi. He became federal senator for that state.[31] He had been educated by the Quakers, and was conspicuous for his political honesty. He became so disgusted with the corruption of radical Re-

---

[31] Hunter Dickinson Farish, *The Circuit Rider Dismounts, A Social History of Southern Methodism, 1865-1900* (Richmond, Va.: The Dietz Press, 1938), p. 143.

publicanism that "in 1875 he joined the Democrats in overthrowing the Carpetbag-Scalawag-Negro government." He spent later years as the president of Mississippi's Alcorn College for Negroes, and, well liked by the whites of Mississippi, he lived into the beginning of the new century, dying at the age of seventy-nine.[32]

Denominational pride and aggressiveness undoubtedly played their part in Northern Methodism's southward move. The absurdity of some of the justifications offered for the invasion testify to an element of inflation in the plan. For instance, it was frequently charged that the South was determined to restore slavery in a literal sense;[33] or again the hope—rather absurd from any realistic point of view—was expressed that many white Southerners were ready to repudiate the slave-holding oligarchy of the South (because it had dragged them into the long suffering of the war), and to cast in their lot with a Northern church.

It cannot be denied that in this expansionist movement of the Northern Methodist Church into the South, there was an element of institutional pride, a concern for the aggrandizement of the denomination as such. Hopes that the Negroes would one day be the economically successful class in the South were held out as encouragement for work among them while they were still poor. One writer prophesied a golden age "when the planters of the South will be black men . . . a rising class of the community who are destined to possess the wealth of the state." [34]

A quite different appeal pointed out the suitability of Northern Methodism as a "poor man's religion" to the poor whites of the rural South, and to the laborers in the cities.[35] The assumption that it would have more appeal than Southern Methodism was, as the event showed, unwarranted. The class consciousness of those to whom this appeal was addressed was less strong than their sectional loyalty.

In their hopes of doing great work with the whites in the South, the Northern Methodists were woefully disappointed. They did have some success among the whites in the border states. The *Western Christian Advocate* gave some figures (as reported to the General

---

[32] Hodding Carter, *op. cit.*, pp. 260-61.
[33] Farish, *op. cit.*, pp. 126-27.
[34] *Christian Advocate*, April 4, 1872.
[35] Henry J. Fox in MQR, Jan. 1874.

Conference of 1884) on the expansion of the Methodist Episcopal Church in the South since the war, which it introduced with the rather grandiloquent statement that it constituted "one of the marvels of modern church history."

In 1864 it had 332 effective preachers, 71,037 white communicants and 18,770 colored members, all in the four border states. Twenty years later in the sixteen former slave states and the District of Columbia, there were twelve conferences among the whites, with 693 effective preachers and 170,710 communicants; and 13 conferences among the colored people, with 678 effective preachers and 186,326 members. To these must be added three mixed conferences, two in Missouri and one in Florida with 41,054 members.

The concluding flourish of the statement was to the effect that nearly a quarter of the membership was in former slave territory. Less impressive was the fact that in the South outside the "border States" there were only 51,961 white members. It was obvious that the Northern church had not been welcomed with open arms by the white Methodists of the South.

b) *Work for the Negroes*

The Northern Methodist Church's work among the Negroes of the South, on the other hand, finds much larger justification, whether it be regarded from the point of view of the motives which animated it, or the needs it met, or the success which attended it.

Denominational chauvinism, though not wholly absent, played a much smaller part in the work for the freedmen than in the work among the whites. The depth of the Negroes' need was evident—need for help toward a new place in society, toward an education, even toward earning a living. The South was too impoverished to undertake it, even had she been willing, and it was quite obvious that she was not willing to undertake all that the North believed should be done. Some of the hopes entertained by the Northerners were visionary, and some of their methods were questionable, but there is no doubt that they were carried forward to sacrificial and beneficial work by a genuine sense of mission. "The work has been thrust upon us by an imperious Providence," one Northern writer said.

From before the end of the war, Northern Methodists had begun, with other Christians, to cast forward in their minds to what could and should be done for the Negroes so recently and so suddenly given their freedom. They realized their responsibility in the matter, but did not at first realize the magnitude of the task. As yet they did not appreciate the extent of the handicaps imposed on the Negroes by generations of irresponsible servitude; or how great would be the reluctance of whites, so long accustomed to mastery, to see them rise. They approached the work with an idealism which was too lofty to last, but which was necessary, no doubt, to nerve them to the enormous efforts which were to be required. The first General Conference of the newly created Methodist Church (1867) declared with admirable sobriety:

> The slave, freed and clothed with the elective franchise, is to be educated and made a useful Christian citizen. Here is one of the broadest and most promising fields for humane and Christian labor . . . opened to His Church.[36]

The Conference went on to recommend, not the establishment of their own organization for such work, but co-operation with the American Missionary Association, already established (principally by Congregationalists) for the purpose.

Three years earlier, Zion's Herald, still under the spell of wartime exaltation, suggested that the Negro soon would rise in majesty, and the glory of democracy for all would be present.[37]

Gilbert Haven wrote in 1865:

> What then is the service to which the Master calls us? This, and this only: to abolish from the national action and the national heart all distinctions arising from color or origin; all thought and feeling that such distinctions are divinely intended to separate members of the same human family, who are and must ever be one in blood and in destiny, in sin and in salvation, in Adam and in Christ. . . . The medical and the legal bodies have admitted them [the Negroes] as equals; not so the clerical. . . . The Church in America gives itself earnestly to the support of this heaven-hated sin. . . . She separates God's ministers of the least tinged with this complexion into conferences by themselves." [38]

Bishop Haven's advocacy of social equality for the Negroes did not

[36] Minutes of the General Conference of the Methodist Church (1867), p. 23.
[37] ZH, 35 (1864), 158.
[38] MQR, 47 (1865), pp. 268 and 272.

stop short of interracial marriage. He was seconded in his views on this matter by Abel Stevens, the noted editor of several Northern Methodist publications. Stevens deplored the injustice and feared the social results of the Negroes' remaining "forever a caste among us." He said emigration was no adequate solution of the problem. The only way out was amalgamation. He observed that any degeneracy in those of mixed blood was due not to biological but to social factors.

It is often said that degeneration attends the intermarriage of whites and blacks, and there are wise men who oppose it on this ground. The opinion is a fallacy. . . . [the mulatto's] anomalous position amid our unchristian prejudices depresses him in all respects.[39]

The Federal Government recognized its responsibility toward the Negroes by creating the Freedmen's Bureau in 1865. The General Conference of the Northern church had urged the creation of such a bureau in Congress in 1864. It grew out of the need to provide for the immediate needs of those Negroes who fell into Union hands in great numbers during the course of the war, and to administer the confiscated lands.

As such it was an organ of the War Department. Its agents were too often men of little principle who prostituted their position for pecuniary profit and political advantage by manipulating the Negroes and the confiscated lands under their control.

The most satisfactory part of the Bureau's work was done in cooperation with the church societies formed to help the Negroes. The church societies sometimes succumbed to the temptation to engage in political activity too, especially when they thought it essential to secure full civic rights to the freedmen; but gradually they concentrated their efforts on education. When it became apparent that they could not and should not provide educational facilities for the whole Negro population, they turned to the education of teachers and ministers for them in special institutions of higher learning.

Some half-dozen denominations engaged in a noteworthy way in work among the Negroes in the South: the Quakers, the United Presbyterians, the old-school Presbyterians, and the Protestant Episcopalians. Perhaps the most effective of the interdenominational or-

[39]Abel Stevens, "The Problem of our African Population," MQR, 66 (1884), 109-114.

ganizations was the American Missionary Association, which was for the most part Congregational in support and composition, but also included Wesleyan Methodists, Dutch Reformed, and Free Will Baptists. Its most noteworthy foundations were Hampton Institute in Virginia, Howard University in the District of Columbia, both for Negroes, and Berea College in Kentucky for whites.[40]

Next in magnitude after the Association came the Freedmen's Aid Society of the Methodist Episcopal Church. It was organized in 1866, approved by the General Conference of 1868, and completely adopted as official agency of the church in 1872. As its work came to be more and more exclusively educational, its name was changed (in 1888) to the "Freedmen's Aid and Southern Educational Society." By 1869 it had established fifty-eight grammar schools, six colleges and normal schools, two biblical institutes, and one orphan asylum. Among these institutions were Central Tennessee College at Nashville, Clark University at Atlanta, and what is now Rust College at Holly Springs, Mississippi. From Meharry Medical College, originally the medical department of Central Tennessee College, have graduated "more than half of the Negro physicians and dentists now practicing in the United States."[41] In 1895 there were forty-four schools under the Society's supervision, twenty-one of them for Negroes: one theological school, ten colleges and universities, and eleven academies; for whites there were three collegiate institutions, and nineteen academies.[42]

The Society's policy was to exclude none on account of color. In 1878 it declared that none of its schools was exclusively colored. In the 1880's segregation became a vexing problem. The General Conference of 1884 declared specifically that no member should be excluded from worship in any of the church buildings, and that no student should be excluded from instruction in any of the schools under its supervision because of "race, color, or previous condition of servitude."[43]

The issue was sharply joined at Chattanooga University, whose trustees denied entrance to several colored students. The society re-

---

[40] Hodding Carter, op. cit., p. 186 ff.; and W. Walker, History of the Congregational Churches ("American Church History Series," vol. III. New York: Christian Literature Co., 1894), p. 401 ff.

[41] Ibid., p. 195.

[42] BHMM, III, 324.

[43] Ibid., 323.

quested its executive committee "to use all proper means . . . to induce the trustees . . . to rescind the order" and to secure the resignation of one of the professors who, it was alleged, had refused to shake hands with the Negro Methodist minister of a neighboring church. The University was finally persuaded to follow the society's policy,[44] especially after its appeal to the General Conference was not sustained.

This lofty declaration of principle, however, was somewhat impaired in practice by another resolution of the General Conference, and still more by a report of the society, admitting that certain conditions might make it "expedient" to allow room for "the exercise of a free and unconstrained choice in all social relations." [45] What had been withheld by the right hand had been conferred by the left. Evidently the concession was enlarged during the rest of the century, for, as we have seen, in 1895 the society's institutions were described as "for whites," or "for Negroes."

Even in the North, Negroes were not accepted in Methodist educational institutions as a matter of course. When in 1867 a Negro applied for admission to Ohio Wesleyan University, four students asked for his removal. Early the next year, Zion's Herald, in an editorial headed "Ohio Wesleyan puts its foot on caste," pleaded for understanding and hoped for more colored applicants. It even went so far as to suggest that Wilberforce University (then under the patronage of the African Methodist Episcopal Church) be combined with it.[46]

When the society began its work, free, tax-supported education had been making its way through the Northern states, but had not yet reached the South. Above the elementary level, education was regarded quite universally as the responsibility of the churches. Even elementary schools were privately supported.[47] The devastation of the

---

[44] BHMM, III, 323 and n. The "persuasion" was partly economic in nature, and the change was not one of heart. H. D. Farish (op. cit., p. 219) gives the Wesleyan Christian Advocate's version of the outcome which was that the Freedmen's Aid Society "turned out two Negroes while saying they didn't do it."

[45] Dwight W. Culver, Negro Segregation in the Methodist Church (New Haven: Yale University Press, 1953), pp. 56-57.

[46] ZH, 45 (1868), 89.

[47] Although steps had been taken to create a system of common schools in practically all the Southern States prior to the War, the system had never taken deep root" (H. D. Farish, op. cit., p. 239). "Yet some principal communities of the South had created public school systems which rivaled those of the North. By 1860, the South was spending about two and one half million dollars to educate 425,600 white children

war made the resumption of even these private efforts difficult; and of course there were no resources, even if there had been a disposition, to undertake the education of the freedmen. After the war, new beginnings were made in Arkansas, Alabama, and other states; it may be that but for the skullduggery and corruption of the Carpet-bag Era, these beginnings would have grown to greater accomplishments.[48] On the other hand, the establishment of the *principles* of taxation for public education and of education regardless of race has been ascribed to this radical reconstruction movement,[49] corrupt and obnoxious as it was. The combined efforts of the Freedmen's Bureau and the denominational agencies together could not dissipate the heavy cloud of Negro illiteracy. They wisely turned, then, from mass education to the secondary and higher education of those few who were ready.

C) The Status of the Negro Members

The accession, after the War, of so many Negro members to the Northern Methodist Church posed the question of their status in it with increasing insistence. *Zion's Herald* carried the banner for eliminating all distinctions not only in the membership, but also in the officiary and ministry of the church. As early as 1868 it was urging the acceptance of Negroes as regular pastors in white churches, and hoped such an action would close the gap between the white church and the two African churches.[50] In a reply to an editorial in the *Springfield Union* which protested that equality of rights did not mean social equality, the *Herald* replied: "Of course it does. What is the Church but a Christian society?"[51]

Two great questions agitated the church as a whole during the 'seventies and the 'eighties: should it, or should it not, form separate conferences for the colored members? And should it, or should it not, elect a colored bishop? The first impulse, as the church expanded in the South, was to abolish the color line and allow both mixed congregations and conferences,[52] wherever possible. But it was not possible

---

or one in every seven, as compared with one child educated at public expense out of five beyond the South's borders" (Hodding Carter, *op. cit.*, p. 178).

[48] Farish, *op. cit.*, pp. 239, 240. The Arkansas law provided for tax-supported public schools for three months of the year.

[49] Hodding Carter, *op. cit.*, p. 192.

[50] ZH, 45 (1868), 56.

[51] *Ibid.*, p. 103.

[52] Farish, *op. cit.*, p. 212.

everywhere, and the General Conference of 1868 formed a colored conference in Kentucky.

The question was debated for the next eight years. In 1876 the General Conference authorized the bishops to divide the Southern conferences (of the Northern church) along racial lines when a majority of the white and the colored members requested it. By 1890, that portion of the Northern church which lay in the South had yielded to the "atmospheric pressure" of the region, and practically all the conferences there were so divided. There were instances when the initiative for division had come ostensibly from the colored element, but, as Farish observed, "It was obvious that the change had been inspired by no spontaneous demand upon the part of the blacks." [53]

The argument over the election of a colored bishop lasted for over a decade, but it never got far beyond the academic stage. The question seems to have been kept alive so long because of the proposal for union with the African Methodist Episcopal Churches. The very longevity of the question, however, was used in those denominations as an argument against closer union. The General Conference of the Methodist Episcopal Church of 1872 laid down the general principle:

There is nothing in race, color, or former condition that is a bar to an election to the episcopacy, the true course being for us to elect only such persons as are, by their pre-eminent piety, endowments, culture, general fitness, and acceptability best qualified to fill the office. . . . Being of African descent does not prevent membership with white men in annual conferences, nor ordination at the same altars, nor appointment or eligibility to the highest office in the Church.[54]

The changes were rung on the argument for a long time. In 1880, Zion's Herald was suggesting, during the meeting of the General Con-

---

[53] Ibid., p. 215. A communication to the Northwestern Christian Advocate during this process, was headed, "Shall our New South Be Built on Caste or Christ?" and signed by "One who feels deeply." It ran, in part: "The Northwestern of the other week in one of its able editorials suggests . . . that the colored brethren desire separation. . . . Such is not the case. At the Holston Conference, brother Tait, . . . one of the . . . most popular men in that body . . . albeit as black as one can be, begged his brethren with tears in his voice . . . not to pass it. [There follows mention of several Conferences where the separation has been voted down.] Only in the Alabama Conference did they vote for it, and already many are denying that such is their wish. . . . Do in America as we do in India, and refuse to let caste get control of the church . . ." (NWCA, 24 (1876), Apr. 26, p. 1.)

[54] Quoted in Culver, Negro Segregation, pp. 55-56.

ference, that one should be elected; this time union with the Colored Methodist Church was in the air. After the Conference had risen without having done it, the *Herald* said resignedly that if one was not chosen, then it was because they were not ready. It takes time and education to wear down the blight of the caste system.[55]

Thus the hopes entertained by at least some of the Northern Methodists for erasing the color line in the church itself ran against the obstacle of pervasive social custom.

In these circumstances, two other Methodist Episcopal Churches of Northern origin, the African churches, made rapid progress in the South. One of the ways in which Negroes could exercise their new freedom was to choose (or to create) a denomination for themselves, from which feelings of inferiority were banished, and in which the Negroes themselves could exercise leadership. The African Methodist Episcopal Church, after a generation of slow growth, expanded swiftly after the war, so that within fifteen years after the coming of peace it had 400,000 members; the African Methodist Episcopal Zion Church had 200,000.

Even more successful than the Methodists in establishing churches among the Negroes of the South were the Baptists. It was easy to erect a Baptist church, because of the independence of each congregation in that tradition; easy, too, to pick a pastor from among their own ranks. The informality of Baptist worship left room for improvisation on the impulses of the moment in a most congenial way. Again, Baptism by immersion, being more susceptible of dramatic elaboration than mere sprinkling, also had its appeal. To these advantages we may ascribe the rapid multiplication of Baptist churches in the South after the Negroes were free to choose and to act for themselves in church matters.

2. THE METHODIST EPISCOPAL CHURCH, SOUTH

The attempts of the Methodist Episcopal Church, North, to expand in the territory of the former Confederacy could not but arouse the resentment of the Southern Methodist Church. The attempt itself was regarded as unwarranted and superfluous. The military and political means it used only intensified the feeling which had its roots in the belief that the Northerners were trying to make ecclesiastical

[55] ZH, 57 (1880), 204.

capital out of a military victory. Southern susceptibilities, already inflamed by the loss of the war, were not soothed by the attitude which led the Northern church to put "Feegee" and Virginia in the same missionary report.

Since the minority of Northern leaders who wished to do away with the color line in the church were not able to achieve their goal even in their own section, it is no reason for surprise that the still stronger social prejudices of the South prevented that reform in their own section. Even the beneficent results of Northern work among the Negroes met with almost universal resentment in the South. An occasional note of approbation was heard. One Southern minister observed that "the colored Methodists in the South who have had the advantage . . . of your [Northern Methodist] training are far in advance of any colored people in that section." [56] The general attitude of the Southern Methodists was expressed in a comparatively restrained way by their bishops after their meeting of 1866 when they said:

A large proportion, if not a majority, of Northern Methodists have become incurably radical. They teach for doctrine the commandments of men. They have incorporated social dogmas and political beliefs into their church creed.[57]

On the radicalism in the matter of social equality for the Negro, found in the advocacy of racial intermarriage by Bishop Haven and Abel Stevens, the outraged comments were much more vigorous. The *New Orleans Advocate* "regarded Bishop Haven's voluminous indecencies on amalgamation and miscegenation . . . unfit to be quoted or noticed." [58] W. M. Leftwich wrote, in 1889: "The race problem will never be settled upon the basis of social equality. Equality is impossible without amalgamation, and amalgamation is too revolting to be entertained for a moment." [59]

a) *Attitude Toward the Negroes*

If the Northerners (Methodists among others) had doctrinaire

---

[56] Quoted in Hodding Carter, op. cit., p. 88. In 1877, David C. Kelly of Nashville expressed his approval in address before the Central College of that city; and the President of the institution concurred. (Farish, op. cit., p. 187).

[57] Hodding Carter, op. cit., p. 88. Mr. Carter's comment after this quotation is: "Some Southern Churchmen would be saying much the same things and for much the same reasons more than eighty years later."

[58] October 2, 1873. Quoted from H. D. Farish, op. cit., p. 220.

[59] Quoted in Farish, loc, cit., n. 3.

hopes for the Negro's capacity to take advantage of his new opportunities and in too short a time, the Southerners, Methodists included, put equally doctrinaire limits on his capacities and insisted he could never exceed them, no matter how much time he had. The Northerners' attempts to educate the Negro caused one Southerner to exclaim, "Hic, haec, hoc will be the ruin of the African!" [60] Probably he was right insofar as the New England schoolmaster, in his enthusiasm for classical learning, tried to instruct his new charges in it before they had been given a chance to attain a better command of their mother tongue, or even certain rudimentary skills and responsibilities which would enable him to assume a self-respecting place in the body economic and social. But the Southerner was wrong, as subsequent experience has shown, in his assumption that the Negro could never either learn hic, haec, hoc, or make it contribute to the common welfare.

The New Orleans Christian Advocate said in 1867: He [the colored man] is, and must continue to be, the laboring man of the South, because he is not fitted . . . for anything higher.[61] Along with this "closed" estimate of the Negro's capacity for improvement went the conviction that he was socially inferior.

It was taken for granted that all social intercourse with his darker skinned brother, except upon terms of acknowledged inferiority upon the part of the Negro, would be repulsive to the white.[62]

There were certain very definite political disabilities, also. That the fatal opportunism of the carpetbaggers had something to do with it cannot be denied. They posed a cruel dilemma, either horn of which would, for the time being at least, rend the fabric of ordered democratic life in the South: either government by the corrupt leading the incompetent, or a continuation, if only in modified form, of white domination over the black. However that may be, before the election of 1868, the New Orleans Christian Advocate was saying, "Not a Negro at the polls." [63]

Once Southern society had thus lengthened, but not removed, the Negroes' tether, and, to its own satisfaction at least, ascribed once

[60] Quoted in H. D. Farish, op. cit., p. 223.
[61] Ibid., p. 217.
[62] Ibid., p. 209.
[63] Quoted in ibid., p. 221.

more, as in the days of slavery, a certain divine immutability to the limitations thus set, the Southern *churches*, and foremost among them the Methodist Episcopal Church, South, bestirred themselves to help the Negro make the best use of the scope allowed him. H. D. Farish puts it thus:

If it be true, as the Northern Methodists claimed, that the attitude of the Methodist Episcopal Church, South, was responsible in large measure for the Negro being remanded to a subordinate and inferior place in Southern life, the Southern Church nonetheless exerted a strong influence to make possible for the black man "the best opportunity of becoming all that he is capable of becoming" in that status.[64]

As a "man and a citizen" he had certain rights the Southern church would see kept inviolate. The *Nashville Christian Advocate* gave a rather general statement to this in 1883, when it said "as such, he has in common with the rest of us, the full right to 'life, liberty, and the pursuit of happiness.' " [65] More specifically, these "rights" (politically speaking) which the Methodist Episcopal Church, South was willing to maintain inviolate amounted chiefly to the right to a fair trial under the law. "Over his humble cabin the impartial law should spread its protection shield," said the same *Advocate* in 1895.[66] This assertion was made at a time when lynchings were on the increase; the organs of the Southern Methodist church set their face against such extra-legal cruelties. They also maintained for the Negro the same natural right of self-defense as for the white man, and that such a plea should weigh equally in a trial for violence of a man of either race.[67]

With the obtaining of his new freedom from slavery, the Negro had to undergo the great ordeal of the untrained worker in all individualistic economies; namely, the necessity of selling his labor (that is, all he had) on the open market. In the case of the Southern freedman, the ordeal was especially severe, not only because the market for his services was depressed and chaotic, but because, in his inexperience, he had at first but little skill for any but the simpliest kind of labor, and still less of the self-discipline in industry and thrift which

---

[64] *Ibid.*, p. 223.
[65] Quoted in *ibid.*, p. 224.
[66] Quoted in *ibid.*, p. 225.
[67] *Ibid.*, p. 227.

the free laborers of other parts of the world had learned through generations of hazard. He even had such a hazy idea of the meaning of freedom that many believed it meant freedom from work; which is incomprehensible to us till we remember that, hard as he had to labor as a slave, he had never had to work "for a living" before. He worked because someone else compelled him to, and might beat him if he didn't, but in any case provided him with a place to live and something to eat. It took him some time to realize that freedom really meant a connection between work and a livelihood. Under these conditions employers had ample opportunity and temptation to exploit him. The concerned leaders of the Southern Methodist church could appeal not so much to the Negroes' *rights*, as to the sense of Christian responsibility of the more fortunately placed among their white constituency. What they could do along this line, they did.

Will our readers suffer us to remind them that the Bible has special denunciations for those that oppress the hireling in his wages? . . . It is often possible, also, for a generous employer, without much additional expense to himself, to supplement the income of his "hands" in many ways. Land is abundant. To every cabin, therefore, a garden should be attached, and the occupants should be not only allowed, but also encouraged to cultivate it. A cow is no small addition to the resources of a family, and a couple of pigs in the pen will help out the winter's supply of food amazingly. . . . We know that there are difficulties in carrying out such suggestions. But we are not talking to infidels or heathens. Our remarks are addressed to Christian men, who, by the very fact that they are Christians admit that they are in duty bound to be mindful of other people as well as themselves.[68]

b) *Religious and Educational Work for the Negroes*

The work for the religious nurture of the Negroes undertaken by the Methodist Episcopal Church, South, in the *post bellum* nineteenth century, passed through three phases: first, immediately after the end of the War, considerable interest was expressed and plans made to continue the missionary work inaugurated in earlier times; second, during the 'seventies, large numbers of Negroes became inaccessible to the influence of the Southern Methodist Church, and a

[68] Quoted from the *Nashville Christian Advocate* for Aug. 15, 1895, in H. D. Farish, *op. cit.*, p. 225.

corresponding apathy developed in it; the third phase begins in the 'eighties when the denominational situation had solidified, and in that situation aid and support to the Negro work could be undertaken once more.

A noteworthy utterance on the subject in the summer of 1865 appeared in the Baltimore *Episcopal Methodist*. It proposed, as an essential preliminary to religious work among the Negroes, the wholehearted acknowledgment of their civil freedom. The first step should be to collect them together in separate congregations, allowing them to perform for themselves, so far as they were able, the functions of regularly constituted churches. Secondly, judicious white ministers were to fill their pulpits till such time as qualified preachers of their own race could be produced. The third essential was the establishment of Sunday schools, in which the children might be taught to read the word of God. "This we believe to be a solemn debt which the South owes to the African race. It ought to have been paid long since. She ought to claim the privilege of paying it now, and, no doubt, will rejoice to cancel it at once." Fourth, the furnishing of day schools in which "as the intervals of labor would permit," the Negroes might be taught "the ordinary branches of education, to prepare them for the pursuits upon which their secular advancement depends." The last stage will be to furnish them, when they are fitted for it, with ministers of their own color.[69]

The problem was discussed in many of the annual and quarterly conferences soon after the War. The South Carolina Conference, mindful that Negro missions had been originated by them, acknowledged the duty to continue the work; and authorized the quarterly conferences to license local preachers and exhorters.

Just at the end of the War, the Mobile Conference cordially invited the Negroes to attend the services of worship in their churches "as in the past."

The Montgomery Conference acknowledged the duty of continuing missions to the Negroes, but found conditions unfavorable to reestablishing them at once: neither the Negroes themselves nor the Missionary Society were able to bear the burden of the cost as yet. The Montgomery District Conference recognized the change in old habits

[69] Digest made from H. D. Farish, op. cit., p. 164-65.

of thought and action which would have to take place, and faced the responsibility with a sober plea for the divine grace.[70]

These utterances of the Southern conferences reflect a genuine concern on the part of the Southern Methodists for the spiritual welfare of the Negroes, together with the sobering realization that the task had become almost limitless, just at the time when the resources of the church were sadly depleted. They are interesting too, as Farish points out, because they come from the early period before the bitterness caused by the incursion of Northern teachers and preachers had settled over the land. Nevertheless, the element of reluctance to turn the Negroes over to Northern leaders appears early in 1866, and it was thought preferable in some instances to advise them to turn to the African Methodist Churches. The bishops were requested by the New Orleans Conference to negotiate with the African Methodist Episcopal Church for union.[71]

Nothing, however, could prevent an enormous exodus of Negroes from their former masters' churches. "Of the 208,000 colored members in the Southern Methodist Church in 1860, only 49,000 remained in 1866, when the General Conference [allowed them] to organize as a separate ecclesiastical body." [72] In 1870, by mutual consent, it appears, of both races in the Southern church, the Colored Methodist Episcopal Church was organized. The Bishops assisted with the organization; the majority of the colored members went into the five conferences of the new body. Arrrangements were made for the transfer of some property for its use. By the end of the 1880s, the colored members who still remained in the Southern Methodist Church had been put into separate conferences.[73]

These divisions were undoubtedly due in part to discord sown between former master and slave by the missionaries of the Northern church; but not altogether. Such an explanation does not adequately account for the numbers which joined the African churches; nor does it seem improbable a priori that the freedmen already had sufficient aversion to worshiping in the buildings where they had been confined

---

[70] Ibid., p. 165-ff.

[71] Ibid., p. 169. "Why turn them over to the tender mercies of those who neither understand their nature or their wants?" said the Mississippi Conference.

[72] H. R. Niebuhr, The Social Sources of Denominationalism, p. 258.

[73] Farish, op. cit., p. 215; Cullen T. Carter, History of the Tennessee Conference, p. 162-63.

to slave galleries, and an impulse to demonstrate their freedom by worshiping in a communion of their own choice.[74]

After the bitter 'seventies were over, a few bold spirits appeared who were willing to dare criticism and risk ecclesiastical oblivion by calling in clarion tones to the Southern Methodists to rouse them from their lethargy, and summon them to the duty of evangelizing and educating the Negroes in their midst. The prime mover was Atticus G. Haygood, a Georgian of conspicuous abilities, who became president of Emory College and ultimately a bishop in the church. His manifesto was a book written in 1881, which he called *Our Brother in Black: His Freedom and his Future.*

He disposed of the "Northern question" by saying his fellow Methodists had allowed their sensitiveness to criticisms from the North to prevent them from laying some of its truths to heart. But for the teachers from the North, he said, the South would have been dragged down to semi-barbarism by the condition of the Negroes in their midst. A church which had been zealous to send its sons and daughters as missionaries to distant lands was shamed by neglect of a great field untouched on their very doorstep.

Haygood was not content with general exhortations: he proposed work through their daughter church, the Colored Methodist Church, and that a training school should be built in which to train its ministry. The Southern Methodists had stopped Northern contributions to the Colored Methodist Church by reason of their own paternal relation to it, but they themselves had not given help to it. The separate existence of the Colored Methodists Haygood justified by a deep instinctive disposition on the part of both whites and blacks to form church affiliations on a racial basis.[75]

[74] Dr. Farish says, "Perhaps the chief reason for the failure of the Southern Church to regain its following of colored communicants was the interference of the Methodist Episcopal Church" (*op. cit.*, p. 364). Hodding Carter's opinion, on the other hand, runs as follows: "Even had Northern churches pressed for integrated worship, it is unlikely that the mass of Negroes would have gone along during Reconstruction . . . . they had had enough of the white man's churches as slaves." If the preaching to slaves recounted by Molly Finlay, an Arkansas slave, is a fair sample, it would not have increased their desire to stay on in their old churches: "He just say, 'Serve your masters; don't steal your master's turkey; don't steal your master's chicken; don't steal your master's hog; don't steal your master's meat; do whatsomever your master tell you to do.' " (*Ibid.*, p. 89).

[75] A colored minister of the Methodist Episcopal Church by the name of L. M. Hagood took exception to this part of Haygood's argument. He thought "prejudice"

Dr. Haygood was criticized sharply by many in his church who could not be brought to see any good in what the North had done, or who were unwilling to concede that the Negroes might profit by higher education. He was accused of truckling to the North and of "negrophilism." But some forward-looking men of his communion rallied to the cause. The most important of these was the Rev. Morgan Calloway, who was to become the head of the first training school.

The General Conference of the Southern Methodist Church in 1882 received a petition from the Colored Methodist Church for aid in establishing institutions for training its ministry. Some of the *Advocates*, notably the *Wesleyan* and the *Memphis*, came out in support of the plan. The General Conference appointed commissioners to assist in the founding with bishops of the Colored Methodist Church. So Paine Institute was begun at Augusta. Its function was to be the education not only of future ministers, but also of colored young people in general.[76] The choice of a head was simplified by Calloway's voluntary offer to assume charge. The new head's distinguished services to the Southern cause did a great deal to mitigate prejudice against the new venture. Just before entering on his new work, he preached an eloquent sermon on its behalf, called "Our Man of Macedonia," in which he said: "Notwithstanding . . . [the] munificence [of the Freedmen's Bureau, and many missionaries], so gross is the darkness, and so widespread, that it seems that only a few lighthouses have been erected where there should be a light burning in every district and every community." [77]

His work was favorably noticed in the North, and was symptomatic not only of a new era in Southern Methodist work for the Negroes, but also of an epoch in which Methodists of the North and the South could begin to speak appreciatively once more of each other's good qualities and accomplishments.

---

a more accurate term for the basis of segregation than "instinctive disposition" (Dwight W. Culver, *Negro Segregation in the Methodist Church*, pp. 558-59).

[76] WCAS, Nov. 11, 1882. During this year there were frequent articles and editorials in this *Advocate* recommending evangelistic and educational work among the Negroes (see for instance the numbers for January 28, Feb. 4 and 18).

[77] H. D. Farish, *op. cit.*, p. 195. The account of the beginnings of Payne Institute has been condensed from Farish's succeeding pages.

CHAPTER SIX

Methodism's Continuing Social Concerns

DURING THE MIDDLE YEARS OF THE NINETEENTH CENTURY, the most vigorous thrusts of social thought and energy in the churches were directed toward slavery, the relation of the races, and the attendant questions of war and politics. But this does not mean that other problems posed by the impingement of church and society on each other were wholly neglected. In this chapter we shall follow through some of the more important matters in which the churches criticized and sought to influence society, and were in turn, influenced by it.

During the period just after the Civil War these questions were much the same, and were treated in much the same way as before. In the realm of public and private morals, the observance of the Christian Sabbath engaged much attention, and continued to do so up through the early part of the next century. The struggle with the liquor traffic, which became more deeply rooted as it became bigger business, was unrelentingly prosecuted. The church resumed its unfinished task of providing educational institutions in a still expanding country, and began also to provide institutions for the care of the sick, the orphans, and the aged.

As the social situation changed with the waning century, new questions emerged, and thrust themselves on the attention of Christian people. The frontier was passing, and with it the special role the churches had performed in and for it. The shift from a rural to an urban society began; immigration increased from various European countries; and a swarm of problems emerged with the new sprawling cities, problems which were aggravated by the large influx of folk with alien speech and ways. Industries became bigger and finance

216

"higher"; those who had only their work to sell began to combine in order more effectively to protect themselves against exploitation. The wave of industrial violence which characterized the latter part of the century called the attention of the whole country to the inequities under which workmen were suffering.

The churches, the Methodists among them, faced these conditions. Prophetic voices were raised to express Christian compassion with the victims of exploitation; a growing realization of the estrangement of workers from the churches disturbed ecclesiastical leaders. Toward the end of our period, the churches developed more confident procedures, and a more articulate justification for using them. This complex of new methods and its theological justification evolved into the social gospel. As the end of our period approached, more and more Methodist voices were raised to proclaim it, until in 1908, the Methodist Social Creed was adopted by the Northern church. It became the basis of the Social Creed adopted soon after by the Federal Council of Churches.

A. Some Moral Questions

Throughout most of the nineteenth century, however, most Protestants paid more attention to questions of individual morals than to questions of broad social import. In part this was a natural result of the individualistic gospel they preached, hedged about on its moral side by the limitations of view characteristic of a society struggling out of the crudities and violence of frontier life. While some revivalist leaders were able to maintain a lofty conception of the way an experience of divine grace should work itself out into Christian living, not all were so successful in that respect. The attempt, in itself commendable, to maintain the close connection between grace and goodness, to insist that conversion should be discernible in the way a man lived, degenerated too often in practice to making the division between the saved and the unsaved coincide with the line which divided those who did not drink, smoke, fight, swear, gamble, dance, or go to the theater, and those who did such things.[1]

---

[1] What has been said of the religion of certain remote communities of our own time was even more universally true in nineteenth-century America: "Good and bad persons . . . fall into very distinct categories. The significance of religion . . . is that through conversion a person is transferred from one category to the other. The bad men drink whisky, swear, play cards, shoot craps, and are over-ready with the gun.

1. DIVERSIONS

Methodists found the basis of their attitude toward diversions in one of the General Rules cautioning against "needless self-indulgence"; another, more specific, forbade "such diversions as cannot be taken in the name of the Lord Jesus." In the true pietistic tradition, Methodists regarded all worldly delights at the least with distrust, at the most with rather violent aversion. Abstention from them was urged by Wesley as part of his conception of what the completely godly life would be. His conception of the matter might be stated thus: the godly person would not have time for such indulgences and would shun them as dangerous to the entire sanctification of his time and his tempers. His later followers were not always equal to maintaining this lofty conception, this steadfast emphasis on the positive goal.

In their hands Wesley's ways of self-denial, which had always been ancillary, sometimes became the goal itself. What in Wesley's scheme would have fallen away of itself as not worthy of consideration became the center of prohibitory exhortations. Where Wesley would have said "The sanctified person will not indulge in such trifles," his followers tended by a slight, but momentous inversion, to say: "Those who avoid such things are the sanctified, and the only sanctified persons."

This tendency, never wholly absent, increased throughout the nineteenth century, and culminated early in the twentieth in the incautious specification of the "unholy three" diversions, dancing, theater-going, and games of chance, in the "Special Advices" section of the *Discipline*. Having lost the center of the matter precious to their forefathers, the Methodists mistakenly clung to a portion of the periphery.

Methodist papers in America began early in the nineteenth century to express distrust of the effect of amusements on spiritual life. Those singled out at the beginning were pretty much the same as those emphasized at the end: gambling, dancing, the theater, and novel-reading. Nevertheless, the period between the end of the Civil War and the end of the century witnessed increasing eagerness on the part of the American people for amusement, and at the same time an

The good—for the time being possibly—have forsworn such things and believe in the word of God as revealed in the Bible." (Elizabeth K. Nottingham, *Methodism and the Frontier* [New York: Columbia University Press, 1941], pp. 199-200.)

increasing professionalization of large-scale games and facilities for sport. Methodist leaders felt a proportionate anxiety lest their peoples' spirituality should suffer from conformity with "the world" in general, and this tendency in particular. Their remedy was to urge that the line of demarcation between the church and the world be drawn with especial sharpness in this respect. The bishops of the Methodist Episcopal Church, South, in 1870 and again in 1874 noticed this tendency with alarm. In the latter year they said:

> Among our young people everywhere, especially in the towns and cities, there is a tendency to worldliness—to vain and demoralizing amusements. . . . The toleration of these things . . . [in the church and] the loose admission of members adulterate her purity and break down her authority.[2]

It does not appear that the church authorities opposed fun as such, but it does seem at times as though they came perilously close to it. The Y.M.C.A., for instance, was scolded for introducing games into its program—these were regarded as inconsistent with its Christian purpose.[3] Opposition was expressed even to intercollegiate matches in football and baseball.[4] One sympathizes with the fears expressed where damaging associations were inescapably involved in some otherwise innocent games; but feels at the same time that the case was bound ultimately to be lost because it was put too strongly. One sympathizes too with the opposition to professionalized sports, especially those involving brutality and accompanied by gambling, but wishes that the strictures had been directed rather at those evils than at the games themselves. One is struck by the recurrence of such phrases as "fashionable amusements" and "especially in the towns and cities," which indicate that the protests were, in part at least, those of an agrarian outlook against the increasingly complex fascinations of a novel and as yet fearsome city life; or it may be seen as an increasing distrust by Methodists of the effects of their own growing wealth.

a) *Gambling*

Gambling receives comparatively little attention in Methodist periodicals and legislative bodies. As for organized gambling, it has

---

[2] Farish, op. cit., p. 341, n. 3.
[3] BHMM, III, 59. This was done by the Association's own General Convention, made up doubtless of members of all denominations; which indicates that the Methodists were not alone in their deep distrust of such worldliness.
[4] Farish, op. cit., p. 352 ff.

as a rule been forbidden by law, rather than erected into official status as in those countries which have organized national lotteries. Methodists as individuals seem not to have been very much tempted to indulge in that form of vice, if we may judge from the infrequency with which warnings against it appear in their churches' utterances. It may be supposed that the obviously deleterious effects of gambling on economic success made anxious admonition unnecessary.

Early in the century, the Virginia Conference's paper condemned horse racing because of the usual undesirable accompaniments.[5] In 1860 Zion's Herald attacked the habit of gambling on the outcome of elections.[6] In 1878 the Wesleyan Christian Advocate protested towns' spending more money for race tracks than for sidewalks.[7]

State laws had banned public lotteries in New York in 1833, and her example was followed by other states till the only surviving one was in Louisiana. Nevertheless Alabama chartered one in 1866 stipulating that part of the proceeds should go to the rebuilding of the State University of Alabama. Bishop McTyeire, of the Southern church said, "Better its walls should never rise from their ashes; better its foundations were sowed with salt and plowed up, than that by such means it should be helped." [8] The charter of the Louisiana lottery was due to expire in 1890. The Southern church waged a vigorous fight to prevent its renewal. The New Orleans Advocate urged the circulation of petitions against it, carried in its pages a form of memorial to be sent to the state legislature, and urged its subscribers not to vote for any candidate who was under the influence of the scheme's promoters. The renewal was refused; and in the same year Congress passed a law forbidding the use of mails for the transportation of lottery tickets. As a result the Louisiana lottery moved to Honduras.[9]

b) Stage plays and novels

Attendance at the theater might have been considered of value from the cultural point of view, or as broadening one's sympathies

---

[5] VCS, 1 (1836), 183.
[6] ZH, 31 (1860), 191.
[7] WCAS, July 13, 1878.
[8] Farish, op. cit., p. 358 and n.
[9] Ibid., p. 359, and Encyclopaedia Britannica (11th ed.), 17, 21. See also RCA 25 (1890), May 15, second page.

with human suffering or as increasing one's aptitude to help his fellows in need. Not many Methodists, however, looked at it that way. On the contrary, some felt that seeing plays was dangerous, because it roused sympathy for simulated situations but required no active response in the face of the actual need:

> The true task of the Christian is to sympathize with and help those in need. But those who shed tears over the tragedies in the theatre aren't so likely to help those in trouble in real life. The theatre may not lead to ruin, but it is no help in leading a Christian life.[10]

This was one of the milder condemnations of the theater. The writers of articles against the theater made it clear that they thought there was no such thing as a good theatrical performance.

> We will say of the theatre as a late eloquent preacher does of the fashionable amusement of dancing: though we should allow that the entertainment of the theatre is not so pernicious and hurtful as some other practices! "yet nothing more insensibly hardens the heart in wickedness, and betrays the mind to folly. It is a charmer of the fancy, a stealer of the affections, a stifler of convictions, a seducer and leader to the ruin of hell." [11]

The reading of novels was also regarded as dangerous. An American Methodist paper copied an article from the English *Christian Guardian* which said: "It is a matter both of surprise and regret that I so frequently find the Waverly novels in Christian families." They pervert history, for one thing, "[leading one] to imagine that those godly men . . . who fell in the . . . wars in Scotland were little better than loose fanatics and supernatural fools." In the writer's view, they also perverted scripture; but of this accusation no specific supporting instances were given.[12] In 1847 the *Richmond Christian Advocate* spoke of "the baneful influence of fictitious reading." [13] "Novel-reading," said another church paper, "has kept thousands from coming to Christ." [14] Similar were the sentiments of a correspondent of the *Western Christian Advocate*:

[10] ChAp, 22 (1860), 54.

[11] *Zion's Herald*, 3 (1825), 52. Methodists were not alone in such views. A decade later the *Cumberland Presbyterian* contained this word: "To talk of theatre-going Christians is a contradiction in terms. We might as well talk of a sober drunk man, or an honest thief" (quoted [approvingly] in WCA 1853), 118.

[12] VCS, 1 (36), 26.

[13] RCA, 1 (new series, 1847), 45.

[14] Quoted in Farish, *op. cit.*, p. 355.

[Those who] are in the habit of reading novel books never take the *Advocate*, seldom read the Bible . . . cannot bear the cross or deny themselves. . . . Banish this curse at least from our Zion! [15]

c) Dancing

In 1872, in response to many memorials on the subject, the General Conference of the Northern Church included in the chapter of the *Discipline* on "imprudent conduct" the diversions of

dancing, playing at games of chance, attending the theatre, horse races, circuses, dancing parties, or patronizing dancing schools, or taking such other amusements as are obviously of misleading or questionable moral tendency.[16]

In this fairly wide range of diversions, dancing was the most severely reprobated, as the reiteration just quoted indicates. It is on the dance floor, said the *New Orleans Christian Advocate*, that "many a fair maiden and noble youth have betrayed the Saviour." [17] The chief ground for the distrust of dancing was obviously the sexual stimulation it produced by the close contact of dancers of opposite sexes. But the ministers, in the public utterances at least, were hard put to it to say so without offending against the standards of delicacy prevailing at the time. One of them came close to it when he said:

To reduce dancing to a mere physical exercise, an innocent hilarity of action, is to misconceive its true character. It is to be looked at not in its physical aspects merely, but as an emotional action, the expression of emotion by rhythmic, choric movement. It is employed also to give vigor to emotions and to swell their excitement.[18]

But he was outdistanced by a South Carolina minister who said, "Let the sexes promiscuously indulge in this fascinating art, and see at once the tendency to dissipation and lasciviousness." [19]

There was a good deal of pleading and scolding on these subjects, especially when church schools permitted dances at the commencement, or during the school year; but it does not appear that many

---

[15] WCA, 1 (1835), 200.

[16] BHMM, III, 59-60, quoting *Journal of the General Conference of the Methodist Episcopal Church* (1872), pp. 379-80.

[17] Quoted in Farish, *op. cit.*, p. 345.

[18] *Loc. cit.* Quotation from the *New Orleans Christian Advocate* for Sept. 8, 1866.

[19] Quoted in *ibid.*, p. 346.

people were actually disciplined for infraction. It was an exception when, at the General Conference (South) of 1882, a committee was appointed to investigate charges that a lay delegate had "openly violated the general rules of the Church by permitting dancing in his house." [20] The committee reported that the disciplinary provision had been fully vindicated by the pastor, so no action was taken.

2. The Christian Sabbath

The English Puritans had so far out-Calvined Calvin in their insistence on the commandment, "Remember the Sabbath Day to keep it holy," that they had impressed a strict observance of the day on the consciousness of the whole nation, Anglican as well as Puritan. The same concern characterized all the denominations in this country whose origins went back to the British Isles. So prevalent was this attitude here that, at first, little need was felt to justify it. As more immigrants from the continent of Europe arrived, however, bringing with them the "Continental Sunday," the Puritan tradition had to be defended by its heirs, Methodists along with the rest.

The second number of the *Western Christian Advocate* reprinted Wesley's tract "A Word to a Sabbath Breaker," which is a short exposition of the text, "Remember the Sabbath day to keep it holy." [21] In 1833 the *Methodist Magazine and Quarterly Review*, replying evidently to the argument that the Christian dispensation had done away with the Sabbath as a Jewish institution, said that the Sabbath was much older than Judaism, having been instituted at creation, and was therefore a *universal* institution. Though with the beginning of the Christian dispensation it lost its Jewish dress, the Sabbath itself did not pass away.[22] In 1857, the *Methodist Quarterly Review* ran a series of four articles on the same subject, in which the writer insisted that the observance was a moral, not a ceremonial commandment, and hence one which we are bound by the law of love to observe.[23] The *Christliche Apologete* disapproved of the articles in the English language *Advocates* because they scolded too much about travel and amusements. Addressing Germans become Methodists, it stressed rather cessation of gainful toil, and methods to be followed toward

[20] RCA (new series), 16 (1882), May 18, p. 3.
[21] WCA, 1 (1834), no. 2 (May 9).
[22] MMQR, 15 (1833), 394.
[23] MQR, 39 (1857), 237.

spiritual and moral edification. It also insisted that the Sabbath was not abrogated when Christianity superseded Judaism.[24]

In truth, the articles in the *Advocates* are for the most part articles of protest. In the earlier and simpler days appeared a *protest* against "Sabbath cooking . . . in our church." It contains a note of sympathy for "our sisters who are engaged in their laborious domestic concerns during the week"; it bespeaks for them surcease of toil on Sunday, and hints broadly that if the ministers would "but for the sake of humanity desert eating three regular meals of a Sabbath," things would improve in this respect.[25] Later on the list of things Methodists should not do on Sunday grew rather long. The North Georgia Conference in 1898 was especially specific and inclusive in its protest against Sunday excursions, picnics, bicycle riding for pleasure, baseball, football, printing and reading secular papers, and the sale of cigars and beverages on that day.[26] The General Conference of the Methodist Protestants in 1900 added to the list: "buggy riding, letter writing, novel reading, social visiting, and that most baleful feature of our modern civilization, the open saloon." [27]

A good deal of protest was made against public infringements of the Sabbath rest. The railroads were repeatedly criticized for running Sunday trains. [28] In 1887, the *Western Christian Advocate* reported the systematic looting of freight from the Panhandle Railroad by employees, and commented that if the railroad broke one of the Ten Commandments by running their trains on Sunday, they oughtn't to be surprised if their employees broke another by stealing from them.[29]

The next year, the same paper carried repeated exhortations to defeat the Hart Bill, which would exempt all theaters and places of amusement from the compulsory Sunday closing law.[30] Expositions also were held to be included under the law; the *Western Christian Advocate* said: "We record it with joy: the Centennial Exposition in

---

[24] ChAp, 1 (1839), 56, 26.
[25] WCA, 1 (1835), 87.
[26] MNGC, 1898, pp. 38-39.
[27] *Journal of the General Conference of The Methodist Protestant Church*, 1900, p. 61.
[28] See, for instance, WCAS, 1878, numbers of October 5, 12, 26. Also MNGC, 1890, pp. 19-20; 1894, pp. 36-37; 193; 1902, p. 36; 1906, p. 39; 1910, p. 57.
[29] WCA, 54 (1887), 252.
[30] *Ibid.*, 15 (n. s., 1888), Jan. 11 and 18.

this city will not be open on Sunday." [31] In 1892 the General Conference of the Methodist Protestants called upon all Christians to protest against the disposition of the managers of the Columbian Exposition at Chicago to keep it open on the Sabbath.[32] It goes without saying that to have saloons, which should not be open on any day of the week, doing business on Sunday also, was especially deplorable. Representative of innumerable expressions in Methodist papers everywhere was this editorial in the *Methodist Protestant*:

To the members of the Maryland legislature we want to say this: The moral sentiment of Baltimore, the people who are the strength of the city, the people who obey the law, and have to pay the bills for the prosecution of those who violate it, are a unit in favor of perpetuating the Christian Sabbath. It is the saloonist, and the gambler, the greedy tradesman, and the conscienceless money-grabber who want the law repealed.[33]

The next month the same paper ran an editorial beginning: "All honor to the county members of the Maryland Legislature who voted almost solidly against the modification of our Sunday laws." [34]

The campaign to defend the sanctity of the Sabbath increased till beyond the end of our period, if we may judge by the activity of the Methodist Conferences in the Baltimore region. At the close of the First World War, the attacks on it were blamed on anarchism and communism. At the session of one of the Baltimore Conferences in 1924, Sabbath observance was given more attention than any other reform.[35]

The traditional Sabbath was successfully maintained longer in the South than anywhere else. There the active Methodist support of the cause was the chief factor in its success.[36] Doubtless the social factor to be considered is the smaller proportion of immigration from continental Europe which settled there.

[31] *Ibid.*, 15 (n. s., 1888), Feb. 15.
[32] *Journal of the General Conference of The Methodist Protestant Church*, 1892, p. 107.
[33] MP, 70 (1900), Feb. 21, p. 1.
[34] *Ibid.*, 70 (1900), March 7, p. 1.
[35] John Bayley Jones, "The Approach of Baltimore Methodism to Social Problems" (Unpublished Thesis written in partial fulfillment of the requirements for the degree of Master of Sacred Theology, Wesley Theological Seminary, Westminster, Md. [now located in Washington, D. C.], 1942), p. 27.
[36] Farish, *op. cit.*, p. 369.

3. THE FAMILY AND ITS ENEMIES

The family as a subject of discussion from the religious and moral point of view acquired a new focus late in the nineteenth century. The sanctity of the marriage tie, however, a closely related subject, was a perennial one. The reasons for this difference probably are to be found both in the emphases of Biblical teaching and in changing social conditions. The Old Testament conception of the family is much more diffuse than our modern one; its boundaries were indefinite, often including larger groups of kindred than we would today. Throughout much of patriarchal times the family was a polygamous one; even slaves were reckoned as members of the "family." In the teachings of Jesus, and in the New Testament as a whole, while a good deal is said about the relation between man and wife which could be expected of Christians, there is little if any explicit teaching on the family as we know it. In fact, the word (in English) occurs but once in the whole New Testament: then it refers to "the whole family (*patria*) in heaven and earth" (Eph. 3:15).

As to actual social conditions, the family in the sense of parents and their dependent offspring stood out in sharp relief on the American frontier, where isolation made economic self-sufficiency (or as close an approximation of it as could be attained) almost a necessity, and furnished a superabundance of common tasks to be performed for the welfare of all. These conditions of course dwindled as the frontier disappeared and tended to approach the vanishing point in the growing cities, as the father found work away from home, and perhaps the mother too; as the children spent more and more of the day at school; and as multiplying opportunities for amusement took them all in different directions after work and learning were over for the day. We may conclude then, that when religious leaders began to talk about the family they were following a trend, increasingly notable in the latter part of the nineteenth century, to employ a combination of biblical standards and sociological conceptions.

Illustrative of the earlier concern over marriage is a communication, signed "Biblist," and sent to one of the *Advocates* in 1859. The writer urges the strict interpretation of the words of Jesus on marriage and divorce:

Now if there can be any meaning in words, and if Christ was a divine teacher, then there is but one cause for divorcement, and but one justification for remarriage while both the parties are living. . . . All other violations of conjugal rights are so liable to be mutual in their character, and to be misunderstood by the community, it would be extremely dangerous to allow any of them as causes of divorcement.[37]

Somewhat later, attacks on prostitution appear in the church papers.[38] The *Richmond Christian Advocate* expressed concern that the provisions of the trade treaty with China which provided for the suppression of this evil in the "Treaty Ports" be enforced. Prayer is not enough for this, it said; we must see to it that the houses where these vices flourish be suppressed.[39] The church was more vigorously summoned to this crusade in the twentieth century by George W. Shackford of the Methodist Episcopal Church, South. He not only challenged the church to catch up with the accomplishments of commissions appointed by the great nations of the world, but also urged a more positive approach. He bade the church to undertake a reinterpretation of sex life and functions in the light of the Christian ideal. Said he, "The realm of sexual life must be hallowed and made contributory to character, to the home, to social stability and elevation, and to all that is best and noblest in human life.[40]

In the 1880s and after, numerous protests appeared opposing the polygamy practiced by the Mormons in Utah, as destructive of the Christian ideal. The General Convention of the Methodist Protestant Church in 1884 resolved a favor of "a national law to make plural marriage as great a crime in Utah as in any other state, . . . and subject to the same penalties." [41] In 1904 the Address of the Northern bishops

---

[37] NWCA, 7 (1859): 25. In the same year, Dr. Zechariah Paddock wrote an article for the *Methodist Quarterly Review* in which he adduced the sanctions of fear of "the [appalling] effects of [adultery] upon bodily health and human life. . . . It has been maintained that the average length of life, after this course of vice has been fairly entered upon, does not exceed four years." The sin of impurity has a dire effect upon both the individual and the domestic circle not only the body, but the soul is its victim, and its inflictions are eternal. The article goes on to speak of the inequities of the double standard of morality "which condemns a woman, but deals more tolerantly with the man." (MQR, 1859, p. 457 ff.)

[38] For example, ZH, 53 (1876), 364.

[39] RCA (new series), 25 (1890), May 8, p. 1.

[40] QRS (third series), 40 (1914), 280.

[41] *Journal of the proceedings of the General Convention of The Methodist Protestant*

warned the general conference that the evil was as deeply rooted as ever:

> Mormonism has once more reared its hideous head in brazen defiance of the moral sense of the nation and in shameful violation of the pledge which secured statehood for Utah. . . . No palliatives suffice to check the ravages of this cancer, much less to extirpate it by the roots.

More alarm was shown over the increase of divorce than over any other of these enemies of marriage we have just been mentioning. Notice was taken of the extreme divergence of the legal codes in the various states, especially in respect of the grounds allowed to be sufficient cause for granting divorce. For the most part, the treatments begin and end on the New Testament teaching on the subject.[42] Legislation was proposed in the General Conference of the Northern church in 1856, but it was 1884 before provisions were written into the Discipline. The bishops asked the General Conference to provide "more stringent regulations in regard to the solemnization of the marriage of divorced persons." Accordingly the Conference ruled:

> That no divorce shall be recognized as lawful by the Church except for adultery. And no minister shall solemnize marriage in any case where there is a divorced wife or husband living; but this rule shall not apply to the innocent party in a divorce for the cause of adultery, nor two divorced parties seeking to be reunited in marriage.[43]

A treatment of the question of the family by Richard Wheatley holds pretty closely to the New Testament principles, but also follows a sociological approach to the problems of the family.[44] Indeed, his article purports to be a review of a sociological treatment by Charles and Carrie Thwing entitled The Family—An Historical and Social Study. Wheatley professess not to believe that the Thwings were justified in feeling so alarmed for the family; nevertheless, he agrees

---

Church, 1884, p. 50. This resolution came as the adoption of the report of the committee on immorality and crime.

[42] Loc. cit. See also ZH, 57 (1880), 177; a resolution of the General Conference of the M. E. Church, South, reported in RCA (new series), 25 (1890), June 5, p. 2; the Episcopal Address to the Northern Church as reported in ZH, 74 (1896), 293; The Christian Advocate (New York), 74 (1899), no. 43 (Oct. 26).

[43] BHMM, III, 58. Quoting Journal of the General Conference, 1884, pp. 45, 279-80. Appendix, p. 331 ff.

[44] Richard Wheatley, "The Alleged Decay of the Family," The Methodist Review, 69 (1887), 858-882.

that many of the enemies of the family they name are to be feared, and adds others of his own—all of which can be reduced, according to his analysis, to sin.

He gives statistics concerning divorce in some detail, and draws the conclusion: "Legal divorces appear to have doubled in proportion to marriages or population within the last thirty years." [45] The family, he insists, is the fundamental unit of society; moreover it is of divine, not merely civil constitution, as "is obvious from Genesis 2:18-25. It is the parent, not the child, of civil society." [46] Polygamous or polyandrous practices are not primal in the history of the race, but are deformations of the original and divine constitution. Thus marriage is more than a civil contract (Milton and other writers to the contrary notwithstanding), and it is a grievous error for the state to allow by civil law other causes for divorce than those allowed in the divine law. "The state has no more right to . . . nullify the law of marriage underlying the family relation than it has to repeal the decalogue."

Wheatley sets down his own list (though it is not a systematic one) of the enemies of the family. He mentions conditions in the city, especially having to live not in a separate house but in a "boarding house"; a deplorable "passion for social advancement," which leads to late marriages in which wealth, not suitability, is the primary consideration; prenatal infanticide, which is deplorably prevalent. But what Wheatley called the "socialisms" of his day he does not much fear:

Shakerism, Owenism, Fourierism, Noyesism, and all other socialisms . . . are too full of idiosyncrasies, visions, absurdities, injustices, and loathsome vilenesses to threaten permanent danger to the family institution. The same . . . is true . . . of Mormonism. . . . More to be dreaded than they is the ethical rottenness and spiritual depravation . . . which miscegenates the races without the sanctions of marriage.[47]

Along with the "single standard" for man and wife, Wheatley recommended equality of rights and equality of responsibilities for each partner in marriage, in the distinct sphere of each—equality, not

[45] *Ibid.*, p. 875.
[46] *Ibid.*, pp. 858-59.
[47] *Ibid.*, pp. 870-71, 872.

chivalry. He abandons the New Testament in one respect: he is dubious about accepting St. Paul's teaching, "the head of the woman is the man"; [48] but he hews to the gospel line in the matter of grounds for divorce: insanity, even permanent, is no ground, only death or "gross crime." "The doctrines of our Lord and his apostles . . . [are] concordant . . . with deductions cautiously drawn from sociological facts. . . . All deviations from the family ideal are due to depravity, ignorance, and wickedness." Now, as always, the families in which the Christian ideal prevails are happy and wholesome; but there are enough baleful factors present in our society to cause thoughtful men to tremble for the future. Serious and temperate discussion is the need of the time.[49]

B. Methodism and Education

There have been Christians who, though learned in "profane letters," have deliberately turned their backs on the muses, believing that the fascination of their smile was fatal to truly Christian learning and piety. The names of St. Augustine and St. Jerome occur immediately to mind in this connection. The aversion of popular religious movements to education is differently grounded, though it may express the same central concern.

At the opposite pole from an Augustine or a Jerome were the early American Methodists, who likewise distrusted the effect of learning on piety. Another instance of the same attitude is found at the beginning of that Pietism which was the European parent of Methodism. Some students in Leipzig, enthusiastic adherents of the movement, began to turn their class periods into revival meetings, and proposed to leave off the pursuit of "human learning," even in the field of theology, in order not to be hindered in their search for the new birth and the charismatic study of the Scripture. Doubtless social and psychological factors had a part in each of these decisions against "human learning." The pagan learning Augustine absorbed while a boy had originated in, or been fostered by a Roman Empire which

---

[48] *Ibid.*, pp. 864, 880-81, 866. The equality included the right of the wife to her own earnings and property, and equal share in those of the children. It is based on the law of nature, as well as scripture. The author would have "husband and wife . . . meet on a level where each recognizes the complete individuality of the other, and the right of each to rule and the duty of each to obey."

[49] *Ibid.*, p. 879.

was not only hopelessly corrupt, but also on the verge of crumbling before the barbarians. We may surmise that one of the reasons for the Pietist animus against theological learning was the fact that the formal theologians of the day were counted among their enemies.

Methodists came to this country without the tradition of a learned ministry or the opportunity to acquire it for themselves. The English Puritan Presbyterians had been excluded from the universities, but had had the will and the means to build academies for the education of their sons. American Puritans had at least a tradition of a learned ministry, and they respected learning. On the other hand, the Methodists had little learning themselves, and were suspicious of a ministry more learned than themselves. It took time to build the tradition in the new country. And it is worthy of note that whereas among Presbyterians and Congregationalists in America an educated ministry came first, and education for lay people came afterward, it was the reverse with Methodists; with them an educated ministry had to wait on the creation of an educated laity.

Methodism came in for a good deal of criticism for lack of education and indifference to it, especially in New England. Their replies varied between denying the truth of the charge—and proudly accepting it!

Once the resources could be mustered, justification for higher education was not wanting. The only justification for the vigor of the Methodist educational effort the General Conference felt called upon to make boiled down to this: that education could be either "the most powerful auxiliary which infidelity and vice ever won over to their cause," or "a champion for Christianity before whom infidelity, superstition, and bigotry must cower and fall." [50] This was in 1840. Eight years later, the General Conference said in effect that we must educate our children to keep them with us:

When the Church has collected . . . a great population born within [her] bosom, she cannot fulfil her high mission unless she takes measures to prevent this population from being withdrawn from under her care in the period of its youth.[51]

[50] JGC, II (1840), 164.
[51] Ibid., III (1848), 137.

Wilbur Fisk, principal of Wilbraham Academy and later president of Wesleyan University in Connecticut, had this answer to the question about the purpose of education: It is to furnish men "who will be both willing and competent to effect the political, intellectual, and spiritual regeneration of the world." [52]

Indeed, through the early days of our national history, as in colonial days, the churches were not stepping out of their normal role, or providing an extra flourish of "public service" when they concerned themselves with education. In those days most of what educational facilities existed had to be provided by the churches, which were regarded as the proper institutions for such activity. It was not until just before the Civil War that the free public school, even on the elementary level, had begun to take care of the educational needs of a portion of the country. It was not until then that the cry against church schools was raised, and then, of course, it was the Protestants who objected to the Roman Church's continuing to do what all the churches had been doing more or less since colonial days.

As for state support of college and university education, that did not attain noteworthy proportions till 1862, when Congress gave land from the public domain to each of the states, from the proceeds of which they were to maintain colleges—called "land-grant colleges" —in which were to be taught all the arts: liberal, agricultural, mechanical, and military. The notable exception was Virginia, which, on the impulse of Thomas Jefferson, had provided state support from the beginning, though certain other states also anticipated in a limited way the plan of public support.[53]

Thus the brunt of building and maintaining educational institutions up to the Civil War and beyond was borne by the churches. This is noted by William Warren Sweet, who, in addition, stresses the rootage of the institutions east of the Appalachians in the colonial "awakenings." [54] West of the mountains, it was still the re-

---

[52] Quoted in Leland H. Scott, *Methodist Theology in America in the Nineteenth Century* ([Ph.D. Thesis, Yale University, Microcard Theological Studies, vol. 20] Madison, Wis.: The Microcard Foundation for the American Theological Library Association, 1954), p. 60.

[53] *Encyclopaedia Britannica* (11th edition) 27: 776.

[54] "Of the nine colonial colleges, the six established between 1740 and 1769— Pennsylvania, Princeton, Columbia, Rutgers, Brown, and Dartmouth—had some relationship either directly or indirectly to the great colonial awakenings. Previous

vivalistic churches which were responsible for the foundation of the great majority of the colleges during the first half of the nineteenth century.[55]

It was in quite the expected order of things, then, that Methodism should devote part of her energies to this enterprise. She came late to the business, like the Baptists, but, like them, once started, moved zealously forward. By 1830 the Methodists had not established a single college. Between that date and the Civil War, they established thirty-four. In 1834, the Baptists had four; by 1861, twenty-five.[56]

1. THE EARLY SCHOOLS AND COLLEGES

The Methodists began modestly on secondary schools, which came to be known indifferently as "academies" or "seminaries." Francis Asbury drew up a plan according to which each conference was to set up a school and be responsible for its maintenance. One of the most successful of these was at Uniontown, Pa. The plan was reinforced by General Conference action in 1820.[57] This was only a plan for a long time, if indeed it was ever properly carried out. Dr. Bangs, in his *History*, reported that it met with "unreasonable opposition" and "apathy"; and came to the sad conclusion that because of their dilatory tactics, "it became proverbial that Methodists were enemies to learning." [58] Nevertheless, some were established. In 1790, one had already been begun in Bethel, Kentucky. The first permanent one was called Wesleyan, at Newmarket, N. H., which in 1825 became Wilbraham Academy, having moved to the town of that name in Massachusetts. "By 1840, not less than twenty-eight academies, semi-

---

to the colonial revivals, only the two established Churches—the Congregationalist and the Episcopalian—had founded colleges." W. W. Sweet, *Revivalism in America* (New York: Charles Scribner's Sons, 1944), p. 147.

[55] *Ibid.*, pp. 149-50. Of the forty colleges founded between 1780 and 1830, 13 were founded by Presbyterians, four by Congregationalists (one by the two together), six by the Episcopalians, one by the Catholics, three by the Baptists, one by the German Reformed, and eleven by the states. All the state institutions west of the Alleghenies before 1830 were founded under Presbyterian direction.

[56] *Loc. cit.* In addition enough schools below college rank had been founded to bring the total up to two hundred (Sylvanus Milne Duvall, *The Methodist Episcopal Church and Education up to 1869* [New York: Teachers' College, Columbia University, 1928], p. 66).

[57] JGC I, 208: "It . . . is hereby recommended to all the annual conferences, to establish, as soon as practicable, literary institutions, under their own control, in such way and manner as they may think proper."

[58] BHMM II, 401, n., and Sylvanus Milne Duvall, *The Methodist Episcopal Church and Education up to 1869*, p. 26.

naries, and manual training schools had been established under auspices of Annual Conferences." [59]

The "manual labor schools" were an interesting, though not permanent, development in the academy movement. They offered a third possibility between schools maintained entirely by charity, and those which had to charge a tuition fee so high that many were excluded from their benefits.[60] The movement was quite widespread in America between 1827 and 1840. It was either planned or adopted in a number of Methodist schools, including Wesleyan University, Dickinson, and Alleghany. The most successful example of such a school among Methodists was the Maine Wesleyan Seminary, where the plan was carried on for about fifteen years. That school had a sizeable farm on which some of the students worked, while others worked in a shop where various crafts were carried on. The students went to classes all the morning and worked about five hours in the afternoon, being paid according to how much they did. There was a number of older students at the school, which indicates that they had been ambitious for an education, but thwarted by poverty till this scheme gave them their opportunity. The accounts of the success of the plan were quite glowing; nevertheless, it was given up there, as elsewhere. Probably the schools were located with other considerations in mind than closeness to raw materials and markets, and the difficulty of getting proper supervisors for such an enterprise must have been great.[61] Such a venture, however, gives point to Sweet's remark: "That American higher education should be democratic rather than aristocratic was largely a contribution of the revivalistic Churches." [62]

The distinction between academies and colleges was not hard and fast at first. Sometimes an institution founded as a college would perforce sink to the level of a secondary school; or an academy, if it

---

[59] BHMM, I, 222.

[60] It is tempting to think this was a characteristically American development, one which laid the foundation for the willingness of the American student to "work his way through" school, in contrast with the comparative rarity (at least until recently) of such an expedient among European students. But in 1834 a correspondent wrote to the editor of the *Wesleyan Christian Advocate* that the name of Mount Ariel, seat of the Dougherty Manual Labor School of the South Carolina Conference, had been changed to Cokesbury, to commemorate the fact that Coke and Asbury were the founders of the first manual labor school on *this side of the Atlantic* (WCAS 1, 1834, June 27 [italics not in the original]).

[61] Duvall, *The Methodist Episcopal Church and Education*, p. 91 ff.

[62] W. W. Sweet, *Revivalism in America*, p. 150.

prospered, would add a collegiate instruction as it was able. A good many of the church institutions maintained both side by side. The academies were useful as places where the children of missionaries could be sent; and many a man awakened late in life to a call to the ministry, or simply to the need of higher education, could go to school there with boys much younger than himself without being too conspicuous; his preparatory work once out of the way, he would go on through the college and then perhaps to seminary, after such were established. Many of the academies had manual training departments; but the staple offerings of the curriculum were the classical languages, mathematics, and English.

Wesleyan University, oldest of the colleges founded under Methodist auspices, was opened at Middletown Connecticut in 1831.

Education for women was not neglected. At first separate institutions for them was the rule. The Midwest, however, began, after the Civil War, to abandon the segregation of the sexes. This was often done by combining institutions already founded. A "female seminary" would be combined with a boys' college; so that even today in more than one such institution, when a boy goes off to the girls' hall for his date, he learns to speak in as offhand a way as he can muster, of "going to the Sem." Elizabeth Academy at Old Washington, Mississsippi, was chartered as a college as early as 1819. It awarded to its young ladies the degree "Domina Scientiarum." [63] If that degree (which would have fitted Eloise of twelfth-century Paris) is no longer awarded by academic institutions, it seems a pity. But it was not long before the girls became, on graduation, ordinary Bachelors and Masters along with their trousered classmates. Maine Wesleyan Seminary and Female College at Kent's Hill, Maine, one of the first colleges in New England to grant an A.B. to women, is credited with having considerable influence in opening courses leading to Bachelors' degrees to them.[64]

3. MINISTERIAL EDUCATION

The training of ministers was for a long time, as has already been indicated, not at all the same thing as sending them to a professional

[63] S. M. Duvall, *The Methodist Episcopal Church and Education*, p. 74.
[64] *Loc cit.* Duvall here relies on Cummings' *Early Schools of Methodism* (New York: 1886).

school or seminary. The General Conference from a very early date took an interest in their training, and suggested lists of books to be read, which have subsequently developed into the highly organized Conference Course of Study. Though proposed in 1816, the rudimentary form of this course appeared in the *Discipline* only in 1848.[65] By that time the course was designed to last four years; in 1876 one was designed for local preachers also.

The opposition of Methodism to an educated ministry probably has been exaggerated. Most of the utterances on the subject that have come down to us can be reduced to this: it is not *necessary*.[66] To the denominations like the Congregationists and Presbyterians, who had a long tradition of *requiring* a liberal education for their ministers, this doubtless looked more like opposition than it really was. In 1814 Lyman Beecher addressed the Society for the Education of . . . Young Men for the Ministry of the Gospel, using rather scornful terms of those who had not such training. Of eight thousand ministers needed, he said, only three thousand were available.

There may be perhaps 1,500 besides who are nominally ministers of the Gospel. But they are generally illiterate men . . . in some instances unable to read or write. By them as a body, learning is despised. . . .

Religion is the last thing that should be committed to the hands of ignorant and incompetent men.[67]

Nathan Bangs was representative of a number of leading ministers of the Connection, themselves well educated, who approved of a college education for the preachers, but opposed seminaries. It was much better, in Bangs' estimation, to include biblical and theological in-

---

[65] The General Conference of 1816 resolved: "That it be the duty of the bishop or bishops, or a committee which they may appoint in each annual conference, to point out a course of . . . study proper to be pursued by candidates for the ministry; and the presiding elders, whenever a person is presented as a candidate for the ministry shall direct him to those studies which have been thus recommended; and before any such candidate shall be received into full connexion, he shall give satisfactory evidence respecting his knowledge of those particular subjects which have been recommended to his consideration." (JGC, I, 151). See Duvall, *The Methodist Episcopal Church and Education*, p. 45 ff.

[66] See, for example, ZH, 3 (1825): 17. The article, however, goes on to say, "Yet no one can infer from this that they [the Methodists] are prejudiced against education."

[67] Quoted in Duvall, *The Methodist Episcopal Church and Education*, p. 43.

struction in the college curricula, than to found theological seminaries for specialized training.[68]

No account of the founding of the earliest Methodist theological seminaries would be complete which did not include the contribution of John Dempster, who was intimately connected with two of them, and, before his death at the age of sixty-nine, was planning to visit the Pacific coast, in order to start another one there.[69] For most of his adult life, he served the cause of seminary education for ministers with singular persistence. His zeal for the cause is an instance of European devotion to an educated ministry which successfully resisted the solvent influences of American Methodism. He was the son of the James Dempster who had been sent to America as a missionary by Wesley in 1774, and had studied at the University of Edinburgh.[70] The son, smarting under the resistance of his fellow ministers to the cause to which he had devoted all his mature energies, complained in 1856 of "fierce opposition on the part of at least two-thirds of our entire ministry." [71] When in 1853 the *Christian Advocate* printed James Strong's appeal for a theological seminary in the West, the paper was strongly attacked for even opening its columns to so "dangerous" a proposal. Dr. Bond, then editor, defended his paper by saying that it should be open to all points of view; but his own, he said, was uncompromisingly opposed to that way of preparing men for the ministry.[72] The grounds of the opposition to theological seminaries were chiefly that they would be breeding places of heresy, and that they would radically change the character of the ministry of the church.[73]

[68] L. H. Scott, *Methodist Theology in America*, p. 134. Duvall found, rather to his surprise, that almost no courses on the Bible were given in Methodist academies and colleges before the Civil War (*op. cit.*, pp. 80-81.)

[69] *Cyclopaedia of Methodism*, p. 285.

[70] SHMEC, I, 264.

[71] S. M. Duvall, *op. cit.*, p. 47.

[72] *Ibid.*, p. 57.

[73] The *Western Christian Advocate* during its first year printed an article in favor of an educated ministry. "The more sound learning a minister has, the better." But "learning may be bought with too high a price." The article then analyzed the dangers of theological seminaries: first to unanimity of sentiment in doctrine and government, for "theological schools have usually been the hot-beds of these errors, and the starched and laced D.D.'s, their coadjutors, and their pupils, have been the wire-drawers"; and second, to the itinerancy, for the graduates would get the calls to the city churches (WCA, 1 [1835-36], 146). A little later the same *Advocate* replied to a dig in the *Christian Watchman* to the effect that Methodists would have to educate their preachers to keep the influence of the church, by a triumphant exhortation to "look at our recent increase!" *Ibid.*, p. 155.

Nevertheless, the set of the tide toward the best preparation available for the ministry was irresistible. Doubtless the criticism of non-Methodist observers had something to do with this; changing social conditions had more, especially the rising level of the education of the people who sat in the pews.

A great deal of the change is reflected in a letter to the *Northwestern* by N. E. Cobleigh in 1856. First he presents the case made by those who oppose education for the ministry:

They, as is perfectly natural, advise that young men called to the ministry should spend no more time in the college or the seminary, but consecrate themselves at once to the itinerant work. Thus did the early fathers of Methodism—a truly noble race of truly noble men—and behold what God hath wrought by their instrumentality!

But new times require new measures:

Every year, education is becoming more generally diffused among the mass, and more thorough and extensive among the higher classes. . . . In our eagerness to meet fully the present wants of the world, we should not blast our future prospects by disqualifying ourselves to meet the demands of future times.[74]

Infidelity, he added, is using all the logic and learning it can muster. There are all too many young men who never will have the opportunity or resources for seminary training, to make it advisable to discourage those who have them. They should rather be *encouraged* to employ them to the full.[75]

This was the very year (1856) that the General Conference of the Northern church put the stamp of official approval on the activity of theological seminaries; at the same time, and perhaps even more emphatically, rejecting the assumption that educational qualifications were sufficient for the ministry, and taking measures to secure control of the conferences and the general superintendency over such schools.[76]

[74] NWCA, 4 (1856), 13.
[75] *Loc. cit.*
[76] JGC, III (1856), 150. "1. *Resolved,* That this General Conference reject all institutional means for ministerial education which assume the sufficiency of merely educational qualifications for the sacred office. . . . 2. *Resolved,* That the General

Meanwhile, the two earliest theological seminaries had been established without benefit of General Conference sanction. In 1839 a group of people—including laymen—who were concerned with the education of the Methodist ministry met in Boston to consider plans for improving it. This meeting is usually regarded as the beginning of what is now Boston University School of Theology; but an article in Zion's Herald indicates that the discussion goes back at least seven years, to 1832.[77] Then it was decided to open a Biblical Institute at Newbury, Vermont, where the facilities of an already existing Methodist Academy might be utilized. It was two years at least, however, before the funds needed for beginning instruction could be obtained. After a period of struggle at Newbury, the school moved to Concord, N. H., and in 1867 to Boston.

In 1871 it was incorporated into the newly chartered Boston University. The preternatural pertinacity of John Dempster was primarily responsible for keeping the Biblical Institute alive during the difficult Concord period. And it was his impulse that led Elizabeth Garrett to promise help for the second Methodist Biblical Institute in Evanston, Illinois. Garrett Biblical Institute was incorporated in 1855, instruction was begun in 1857 on the same campus as the recently founded Northwestern University. The very term, "Biblical Institute," applied to the two earliest seminaries of Methodism indicates how strong was the unwillingness of the church to have its young men instructed in "theology" or "divinity." By the time the third Methodist seminary was founded in 1867 in Madison, New Jersey, it was possible to call it Drew Theological Seminary from the very beginning.

It is evident that the Methodist Protestants had much the same sort of battle to fight. Their college agent, however, was able to tell their General Conference of 1880:

While . . . many able and useful men . . . did not have the advantages of a college training . . . it must be clear to all that with the facilities now at hand . . . the church should take the position that the first call

Conference looks with approval on those Biblical departments which are in connection with our colleges . . . and upon our Biblical Institutes . . . provided, always, that both these classes of ministerial institutions be encompassed with guards sufficient to protect them from heresy in doctrine and error in discipline."

[77] Cited in Duvall, op. cit., p. 53.

239

of the Divine Master to those who are to work in His vineyard is the call to prepare thoroughly for the work.[78]

The General Conference of 1850 had accepted Madison College at Uniontown, Pennsylvania; subsequently it was opened under the auspices of the whole church. Twenty years later the same patronage was given to Western Maryland College at Westminster, Maryland, which had been founded in 1866 by the Maryland Conference. Other colleges under the supervision of the Methodist Protestants were Yadkin in North Carolina, Bowden in Georgia, and Adrian in Michigan. The last had been begun by the Wesleyan Connection in 1859, and was taken over by the Methodist Protestants in 1868.[79] In Western Maryland College there were, by 1876, enough candidates for the ministry to form themselves into a union called a "Theological Class"; at Adrian there were separate rooms for a "Theological Association," as well as special provisions for instruction in biblical and theological literature.[80] The next year, the joint Convention by which the reunion of the Northern and Southern portions of the church was consummated resolved to recommend to the boards of Adrian and Western Maryland to [66] consider and adopt such measures . . . as may be deemed practicable for the establishment of a full course of theological instruction in connection with these colleges." [81]

The Westminster Theological Seminary was organized by the Maryland Conference of the Methodist Protestant Church in 1881, and was opened for instruction the next year.

In the Methodist Episcopal Church, South, most of the colleges had had to close during the war. One noteworthy exception was Wofford College in South Carolina. In the *Richmond Christian Advocate* at the beginning of 1867 an editorial announced the reopening of others.[82] Among the most useful during the *post bellum* period were Trinity College in North Carolina, which remained the leading college in the state (after the State University fell into "the hands of the Philistines"); and Emory College in Georgia.

---

[78] *Journal of the Proceedings of the General Conference of The Methodist Protestant Church*, 1880, p. 49.

[79] *Cyclopaedia of Methodism*, pp. 604, 607, 629.

[80] *Ibid.*, pp. 930, 12-13.

[81] *Journal of the General Conventions of the Methodist and Methodist Protestant Churches, and of the Joint Convention*, 1877, p. 51.

[82] RCA (new series), 1 (1867), Jan. 10, p. 2.

There had been a cry even before the war for "more culture in the church"; accordingly, just after it was over, the bishops asked the General Conference of 1866 to provide a theological institution. The Conference agreed that more theological instruction was necessary; but because of financial stringency, and the strength of local interests, they provided not a centralized theological school, but "biblical schools" in connection with existing colleges. In initiating this plan, the conference pointed out "the disparity between the intellectual acquisition of our young ministers and the people they are sent to serve," and expressed a fear lest a theological school would harm both the itinerant system and evangelical ardor.[83]

Then began a long struggle for a central theological school, which was realized when Vanderbilt University was established, in 1875, with a theological department. The proponents of the scheme were David C. Kelley, Bishop McTyeire, and Professor Garland of the University of Mississippi. The last-named wrote of the necessity of "enlightened Biblical criticism," which required a knowledge of the languages, and of how inadequate the conference examinations were to secure those ends.

At the General Conference of 1870, a committee reported in favor of the institution, stressing the inadequacies of the Bible departments of the colleges; but again local interests were too strong for them, and, backed by the plea of financial stringency, they succeeded in blocking the committee's proposal. The proponents of the theological seminary then turned away from the General Conference, and called a convention to meet in Memphis in January 1872. They profited by the over-sanguine haste of previous efforts and in their plans for a new central University for Southern Methodism, provided that nothing be commenced till a half-million dollars had been secured; and that subsequent departments should not be added till the sum had reached a million.

In spite of complaints that the church was being levied on for a project which had been rejected by the General Conference, a charter was obtained from the Tennessee Legislature in 1872, and Vanderbilt University was opened in 1875. Bishop Pierce steadily opposed the plan, discounting learned preaching. Vanderbilt suffered at first from the lowered standards consequent upon the competition of the

[83] H. D. Farish, op. cit., p. 261 ff.

too numerous subsidiary institutions; it made a valiant effort gradually to raise its standards. In this effort it had the help of the church Board of Education which was formed in 1894, for the purpose of increasing the educational resources and correlating the work of the various existing institutions. By 1898 Vanderbilt was recognized as the capstone of the educational system of the Southern church.[84]

This uphill struggle was complicated by the dismissal of Alexander Winchell from Vanderbilt, for teaching scientific views which, it was said, militated against the teachings of the Bible. The dismissal was hotly contested; and probably was carried out more from a concern for the stability of the University than from any conviction that Winchell's teachings were actually contrary to Christian truth.[85]

Toward the end of the century, as the state schools became stronger, there was some feeling that the church should get out of the school business. To this, Richard Irby, the historian of Randolph-Macon College, replied that the state systems were still insufficient and that the Bible would not be allowed in the public schools, which were ample reasons for the church's continuing its educational program.[86]

The process we have been describing was carried out at the expense of great sacrifice, both financially and otherwise, in all sections of Methodism. It was both a sign and an acceleration of the cultural maturing of Methodism, now on its way to middle-class status. It would be unrealistic to suppose that Methodists, any more than other people, were oblivious of the fact that "going to college" meant not only a liberal education, but standing in the community, and preparation for professional life—not only in the church but in teaching, in the law, or in medicine, as well.

3. LATER DEVELOPMENTS IN THE EDUCATIONAL POLICY OF THE NORTHERN CHURCH

By the 1850's the Northern church seems to have overreached itself in its zeal to build educational institutions. The committee on education of the General Conference of 1856 reported as "Institutions

[84] See H. D. Farish, *op. cit.*, pp. 263-81, where this story is told at some length.
[85] WCAS, July 6, August 17, and October 5, 1878. In the last article, it was contended (and the sectional strife enters into this matter as well) that the Southern denominational colleges alone were secure against the plague of skeptical speculations from the professor's chair—especially Prof. Winchell's speculative views on the origin of the Negro race.
[86] RCA (new series), 16 (1882), March 9, p. 1.

owned or educationally controlled by The Methodist Episcopal Church, and under the patronage of Annual Conferences"; nineteen Colleges and Universities, with one hundred and five teachers; sixty-eight Academies, Seminaries, Female Colleges, and Collegiate Institutes, employing three hundred and six instructors, and two Biblical Institutes with professors.[87] The results of this overmultiplication of schools must have been severe competition, with consequent lowering of standards, and heightening of claims in prospectuses. At least, such is the impression conveyed by the rather sarcastic article contributed to the *Northwestern Christian Advocate* in 1859:

In the west we are receiving a copious shower of institutions of the *highest grade*. There are no low grades. They are all superb, magnificent and wonderful. Each conference would have at least ten or fifteen universities, fifteen or twenty colleges, and an innumerable number of seminaries, always of the first class. . . . Every county seat would rejoice in a university, every village of fifteen inhabitants in 10,000 vacant lots should have a college and every farmhouse should be built beside a seminary.

Seriously, men of God, men of character, men of means, have we not carried this amiable folly to an extent that demands that we should pause? [88]

The condition complained of in this semifacetious way had already attracted the notice of the committee on education during the previous General Conference, and the conference itself had adopted its resolution "to regard with decided disapproval every attempt to multiply greatly these institutions among us." [89]

Indeed, it was the confusion thus compounded which led ultimately to the creation of the Board of Education in 1868. The Episcopal Address of 1864 for the second time advised some action to restrain "the multiplication of colleges and universities beyond the real demand for them." Yet, it continued, "we cannot but suspect that the

---

[87] JGC, III (1856), 314.
[88] NWCA, 7 (1859), 61. In 1856, this same Journal gave a truly astonishing amount of space to notices of various schools and colleges. In No. 31, of that year, on two consecutive pages were articles on Indiana Asbury, Northwestern University, Illinois Institute, Keithsburg Female Seminary; and that proportion obtained in many of the numbers—some of which tell of prosperous beginnings, but more of difficulties, financial and otherwise. Reading this periodical for these years is well calculated to convey a vivid impression of the tremendous energy and struggle that went into the Methodist educational effort at the time.
[89] JGC, III (1856), 150.

evil complained of is beyond the control of the General Conference." In 1868, the calls for the creation of a board which had been heard for eight years at last came to fruition.

The Board was given the administration of that part of the Centenary Fund which was allotted to the cause of education, as well as the annual collection to be made for the purpose on Children's Day. In addition, it has worked steadily at the co-ordination of the numerous institutions and the development of standards for the institutions of various grades. A truly connectional principle was established in the 1880's; the General Conference of 1892 federated all the colleges and universities of the church, and brought them under the board's control. A senate was formed, which erected educational standards, and provided that only those schools which met them could be called official.[90]

C. The Proscription of Intoxicating Beverages

The initial state of the struggle with the use of intoxicants and the traffic in them has already been described.[91] It was there stated that before 1844 the basic conceptions, convictions, goals, and techniques of the temperance movement had already been defined and put into practice. During the latter half of the century, there was elaboration, intensification, and co-ordination, especially with regard to political action; but the reform proceeded pretty much along lines already laid down in the earlier period.

After the struggle with slavery and the excitements of the Reconstruction period were over, the struggle against intoxicants easily moved into first place in the church's interest. One comes to this conclusion whether one judges by the amount of space devoted to it in the church press, the vehemence of its utterances, or the energy put into campaigning and marshaling votes. But this time all the branches of Methodism were on the same side. In 1876 Henry Wheeler wrote: "The energies of the Church and Nation have been expended in close combat with other evils, which, in the province of God, have been removed. They should now turn attention to the suppression of intemperance." [92]

[90] BHMM, III, 105 ff.
[91] See above, p. 133 ff.
[92] MQR, 58 (1876), 638.

Nevertheless this concentration on one cause likewise had its disadvantages in that it tended to relegate certain other great abuses to a secondary place or to obscure them altogether from the church's attention. It was the old dilemma whether to concentrate on one reform or to champion righteousness and human well-being on a broad front. Near the end of the century, Frances E. Willard, a Methodist, and one of the broadest-spirited leaders of the movement, proposed to broaden the range of the Women's Christian Temperance Union, of which she was president for many years, to include promotion of equal suffrage for women, government regulation of monopolies, direct voting for President, government issue of all money, confiscation of land not used or occupied, and free and unlimited coinage of silver at the ratio of sixteen to one. *Zion's Herald* commented with pained disapproval: "They will not only antagonize hosts of their own supporters, but will endanger their own coherence and usefulness." [93]

Many Methodists entertained an exaggerated idea of the proportion of the kingdom of evil occupied by the liquor traffic, and tended consequently to regard its conquest too simply as the overthrow of the whole kingdom. As a result they concentrated too exclusively on that one front, and were too little concerned with other social ills just as serious.[94] Throughout the last quarter of the century, we find numerous

---

[93] ZH, 73 (1895), 677.

[94] Nowhere was this intense concentration on the liquor problem more observable than in the *Northwestern Christian Advocate*. During the 1850's, editor Watson ran a column every week in which he brought together news of the progress of the reform in various places. In the editorials, week after week, he would start describing some abuse or other in political or economic or social life, but end up, surprisingly, by saying that intemperance is at the root of the whole matter. It was, for him, indeed, the abuse of liquor which lay behind the most varied manifestations of violence, exploitation, and misery in our society. For instance, one editorial maintained that whisky was as necessary to the cause of the border ruffians in Kansas as were powder and shot, and asks: "Is it not an undeniable fact that whisky is the primary moving cause of all our political troubles?" (NWCA, 4 [1856], 112).

In 1876, when Arthur Edwards was editor, the space devoted to the question was increased. In the first number of that year, there are two articles on whiskey; in a third paragraph, he exculpates himself for having allowed a recipe to get into print which specified the use of an intoxicant as one of the ingredients—all this on p. 4. On p. 2, another article, a good column long, had appeared, and on p. 6 was another entitled, "Drunkenness in England" (NWCA, 24 [1876], No. 1 [Jan. 5]).

In 1888 (to choose another instance quite arbitrarily) is an editorial on "How Christmas is Cursed," the burden of which, after some remarks on the intoxication which mars the celebration of the holiday, is: the saloon sets out to destroy the Sabbath

expressions of the feeling of many Methodists that the question of temperance reform exceeded all others in importance. The *Methodist Protestant* said in 1884:

Of political corruption, we have had a sufficiency—the abuse of the ballot and public patronage. One of these has given birth to a distinct issue of growing importance: the reform of the Civil Service. Great as are some of these evils, they are eclipsed by a greater among moral questions —the traffic in ardent spirits.[95]

Four years later, the *Western Christian Advocate* in an editorial headed, "The First Reform," said:

First in importance and first in the order of sequence is the prohibition reform. It is the key to all other moral reforms—the indispensable condition precedent to their success.

The editorial goes on to say that the liquor traffic is the cause of social vice, is a crime-and poverty-factory, and concludes: "There are many other issues of importance in American politics, . . . but the overshadowing issue is the prohibition of the liquor traffic." [96]

A prominent Methodist layman, who had strong personal reasons for his judgment, for he had been so much a prey to drink that he "was on the verge of suicide," [97] said in the course of many speeches he made for the Prohibition Party toward the end of the century:

Of all the worthy suits that press upon the public mind, I chose to champion prohibition. . . . The voice of the Church has declared for but one thing in politics, and that is the suppression of the alcoholic beverage traffic.

—shall such an institution be allowed to exist? (*Ibid.*, 15 [1888], No. 1 [Jan. 4], p. 1).

Ten years later, the same tendency continues: an editorial which starts out by purporting to deal with the question of what the government should do in the way of regulation of trusts and monopolies turns directly to the "rum business" as the greatest monopoly of all. In the same number, another editorial on the role of the state in the education of youth points out the inconsistency of a government's doing something so beneficial for youth which, at the same time, is leagued with an industry which destroys youth (*Ibid.*, 25 [1898], Feb. 9). This attitude is reiterated in practically every issue.

[95] MP, 54 (1884), Sept. 27, p. 4.

[96] WCA, 15 (1888), Jan. 25, p. 2.

[97] *Dictionary of American Biography*, "John Granville Woolley."

At the very end of our period, the *Methodist Protestant* was striking the same note:

We do not seek to prove that there is no other question of importance at the present time, but that temperance and temperance legislation are holding a high place in the thoughts of men and women, we need not pause to demonstrate.[98]

Just at the end of the century, Olaf R. Miller, pastor of the Highlands Methodist Episcopal Church in Holyoke, Massachusetts, reached the highest pitch of single-mindedness when he said: "This is the Christian's great issue. It is God's paramount issue." [99] We may see the fight against the liquor traffic as the successor of that over slavery in this respect also. The very phrase which Wesley had used of slavery, "the sum of all villainies," was, after slavery was gone, transferred by his followers to the liquor traffic; [100] and, to an even greater extent, the reign of righteousness and social health was expected to succeed the exorcism of the "demon rum." We can see, from the vantage point of a later generation, the element of exaggeration in their hopes and the want of balance in their attack. But the important thing is that, though the full fruits of emancipation had not been vouchsafed, those who won it kept alive their hopes and now attached them to prohibition. Exaggerated hopes are better than dead ones, and they carried the Methodists in both North and South forward to the new battle.

Methodists were not alone in this battle, of course. The brunt of it, indeed, was borne by the great interdenominational organizations. In the 1840's rose the Washingtonian movement, perhaps more like the Alcoholics Anonymous of the mid-twentieth century than anything between, because it was founded by reformed drunkards and stressed personal work for the reformation of individuals more than political measures to outlaw the traffic as a whole.

The first state Prohibition law was enacted in Maine in 1851. The

[98] MP, 78 (1908), Feb. 19, p. 5.
[99] In an address, *Methodism and Temperance,* delivered Oct. 26, 1900, and printed soon afterward, p. 14.
[100] See Joseph L. Allen, *The Methodist Board of Temperance as an Instrument of Church Policy* (Thesis [Ph.D., Yale University, 1957, on Microcards], Madison, Wis.: The Microcard Foundation for the American Theological Library Association, copyright, 1958), p. 52, quoting the *Discipline* of the Methodist Episcopal Church, 1900, p. 377.

National Prohibition Party was organized in 1869. In 1874 was founded the Women's Christian Temperance Union, destined to be so effective in the cause for which it was founded, and, beyond that, as a demonstration to the women of America that their influence could be made to count in other fields as well. Last was the National Anti-saloon League, founded in 1895, which enjoyed the co-operation of the churches much more than Garrison's Anti-slavery Society had ever done—so much so, in fact, that it was able proudly to call itself "the Church in action against the saloon."

The personnel and the money, the planning and the work which went into all these organizations came from the great middle strata of American Protestantism. But if Methodism was not alone, surely she was near the van. There was more than denominational pride in what Frances Willard told the Boston Methodist Social Union in 1895: "The Methodists . . . are really the bone and sinew of the temperance movement in this country . . . Our pastors . . . are . . . without exception teetotallers." [101]

1. CARRYING CONVICTION: IDEAS AND METHODS

As was stated above, nearly all the characteristic approaches of the temperance movement were employed early in its history; so that subsequent developments were for the most part either elaboration of ideas already fairly fixed, or the adaptation of methods already employed. One is struck by the tremendous amount of reiteration in the Methodist journals—a few familiar ideas endlessly repeated and illustrated. There was an observable, if not a great, change in emphasis through the century: away from stories appealing to the sympathies, from rhetoric which would not be so effective now as when it was written, to a soberer analysis of what the use of alcohol does to the individual and to society, and of the evils for which the vested interest in the traffic is actually responsible. Revivalistic methods and fervor, never wholly given up in spreading the gospel of temperance, tended to give ground toward the end of the period to a more scientific approach.

[101] ZH, 73 (1895), 83. Roman Catholicism also had its temperance organizations and workers; but the Roman Church in this country never identified itself with the American temperance movement as wholly and as heartily as "the middle" Protestant churches. Occasionally one of the *Advocates* would copy approvingly a note about temperance activities in the Catholic Church, such as: "The County Board of the

The historian of the Tennessee Conference tells us how the most drastic setback the liquor traffic got in the city of Nashville was due to the "impact of the word of God as preached by Sam P. Jones." [102] In 1872 *Zion's Herald*, in the course of an editorial on the evils of alcohol, spoke of the Christians' responsibility for evangelizing the drunkards.[103] A rhetorical denunciation of the reign of "King Alcohol . . . in . . . this sin-stricken and distracted orb" says "famine, and pestilence, and war . . . all three together have probably done much less injury to the human race than has the single vice of intemperance." [104]

Stories of evil-doing by those engaged or interested in the liquor traffic were innumerable. Two examples come from one number of the *Northwestern*: one concerns the burning of the house and belongings of a minister who led the fight to close the saloons in Emmettsburg, Iowa; the other tells about a saloon-keeper who, charged with the double offense of selling liquor to a minor and the rape of a minor, was got off by his lawyer, and gave him a gold-headed cane in gratitude. The article finished by saying, "An adequate characterization of such infamy as this defies the power of all language that we know anything about." [105]

Toward the end of the century a striking evidence of new thinking about the problem appeared in *Zion's Herald*. "My own opinion," wrote a correspondent, "is that intemperance is the symptom of a social disease, and not the disease itself." [106] But such judgments rarely found their way into the Methodist press of the time. In the last year of the century, *Zion's Herald* carried a long review of a book on tem-

---

Federated Catholic Total Abstinence Societies of Chicago, on Sunday last, passed a resolution calling upon the friends of temperance to refuse to patronize groceries where liquor is sold" (*The Christian Advocate*, 73 [1898], no. 4 [Jan. 27]).

[102] C. T. Carter, *op. cit.*, pp. 229-30. The account goes on to describe how the liquor men planned to whip the evangelist, but turned liquor into the river instead, and how the Negro longshoremen caught it in their hats as it poured and were soon drunk. There is not much precise data as to the extent and duration of the changes in the city wrought by the revival—some tabernacles were built and meetings held in support of prohibition.

[103] ZH, 49 (1872), 499.

[104] MQR, October 1847, in a review of E. Nott's lectures on temperance found on pp. 534-57.

[105] WCA, 15 (1888), no. 2 (Jan. 11).

[106] ZH, 73 (1895), 50-51. The correspondent, it should be observed, was Assistant Superintendent at State Reform School in Maine; he was not a Methodist, but a Congregationalist—and a single-taxer.

perance which gave some of the statistics on which the indictment of the use of intoxicants might rest: 25 per cent of the cases of poverty referred to public or private charity result from this habit. A survey of the prisoners in twelve states shows that intemperance was the cause of their incarceration in 50 per cent of the cases. After much more, the conclusion was drawn that over one-third of all the poverty, pauperism, and crime is due to the use of intoxicating drinks. The North Georgia Conference in 1898 pleaded for a law to give scientific education in the schools on the results of the use of intoxicants.[107] A number of articles toward the end of the century by qualified medical and other authorities augmented the number of people who were now ready to believe that spirits were not a help but a hindrance in the treatment of most maladies, including even snakebite—the case in which the popular delusion that alcohol was a good antidote persisted most stubbornly. Another writer maintains that alcohol certainly is not a food.[108]

In *Zion's Herald* is a report of a meeting of the Methodist Social Union at which the need for "rational temperance methods" using a "scientific approach" was stressed.[109] The appeal to the young was not new at the end of the century, but was being freely used in both Sunday school and the Epworth League.[110] Thus, though evangelistic fervor and appeal to the emotions were not left behind in the promotion of temperance, the need was seen increasingly, toward the end of the century, of supplementing it with scientific information and the systematic indoctrination of the young.

2. TEMPERANCE WITHIN THE CHURCH

As the nineteenth century drew on into its afternoon, we find that the legislation of the Methodist church bodies received less attention than formerly; and there was a corresponding increase in reliance on civil legislation. This was due to the fact that civil legislation was more all-embracing and effective than it had been in frontier days; while on the other hand, the ecclesiastical bodies manifested increasing re-

[107] MNGC, 1898, 42-43.
[108] See, for instance the *Christian Advocate* (N.Y.), 74 (1899), no. 5 (Feb. 2) p. 2; *ibid.*, 75 (1899), no. 9 (March 2); *ibid.*, May 17, 1900.
[109] ZH, 78 (1900), 523.
[110] The topic for the Epworth League service for Nov. 18 is the national cost of the liquor traffic (ZH, 78 [1900]), 135-36.

luctance to employ the system of rigorous trials and penalties which had prevailed in the earlier part of the century.[111] What legislation there was did not always look in the same direction: nevertheless, the successive General Conferences and *Disciplines* mark stages of advance toward greater restrictions on the membership's use of alcoholic beverages and participation in the traffic.

Before the General Conference of 1848, the question of restoring "Wesley's Rule" on the use of spirituous liquors had been going the rounds of the annual conferences and obtained the required majority. It was accordingly added to the General Rules by resolution of that conference.[112] The tendency was to include under the term "spirituous liquors" also the less potent beverages like wine and beer, but by a process of interpretation, rather than by actual substitution of the new word for the traditional one. A note in a report to the General Conference of 1868 makes this clear.[113] At the same time, the General Conference of 1848, in a rather unobtrusive way, reduced the seriousness of disobedience to this rule by putting it into the category of "imprudent" rather than "immoral conduct." [114]

As early as 1860, the General Conference called attention to the inconsistency of Methodists renting property to establishments used in connection with the liquor traffic.[115] By 1880 such a transaction, along with signing pro-liquor petitions, was included among the things for which a member became subject to a church trial.[116] The same year the preachers were authorized to appoint a temperance committee in each charge. The General Conference expressed satisfaction with the progress which had been made in repressing the traffic by civil legislation, but its belief that such legislation could not suffice of itself: "Hope for the ultimate success of the Temperance Reform rests

[111] The reluctance of the quarterly conference to bring a member to trial for violations under these laws is mirrored in an editorial in the *Western Christian Advocate*, in which the problem of whether a distiller should be the leader of a church choir or not. The discussion sounds as though it were based on a concrete instance, but one in which no disciplinary action had been taken (WCA, 15 [1888], no. 1 [Jan. 4], p. 1).

[112] JGC, III (1848), 79.

[113] Henry Wheeler, article "The Relations of The Methodist Church to the Cause of Temperance," MQR, 58 (1876), 640: "All classes of beverages known to the trade as intoxicating . . . are intended to be included under 'spirituous liquors' and should be so considered by the . . . Church."

[114] JGC, III (1848), 27.

[115] Wheeler, "The Relations of The Methodist Church," MQR, 58 (1876), 639.

[116] Joseph L. Allen, *The Methodist Board of Temperance*, p. 50, citing the *Discipline* of the Methodist Episcopal Church for 1880, pp. 145-46.

251

chiefly upon the combined and sanctified influence of the family, the Church, and the State.[117] In 1868 the General Conference set aside the last Sunday of every June as "Temperance Sunday," and urged all Methodists to observe it.[118]

Many unofficial statements of Methodist approval of "complete legal prohibition" were sent to the General Conference before its endorsement was forthcoming in 1880. In 1884, the Episcopal Address was still more specific; the General Conference of that year spoke of "Constitutional Prohibition" as "the platform on which we stand as a denomination, and upon which we will battle until [it] is secured in every State and territory in the Union, and finally embodied in the Constitution of the United States." [119]

a) The Board of Temperance

Consequently on numerous suggestions, resolutions for the creation of a church board came before the General Conference of the Northern church some time before action was finally taken in 1892, when a "half-way stage" to a board was created. It took the form of a "permanent Committee of Fifteen . . . with power to act within the authorized declarations" of the church.[120] In 1904, the Committee proposed the creation of a board, with a secretary and certain funds at its disposal, to come from a special collection among the churches. This proposal met with some opposition. The church is a Temperance Society, said many; others, "What we need is more life, not more bureaus." [121] In the end, the Conference compromised: it created the board, but gave it no funds with which to operate. This financial paralysis was cured four years later when the General Conference authorized an annual appropriation of $25,000, and the taking of a special offering in addition. Clarence True Wilson and Alfred Smith

[117]Allen, op. cit., p. 51.

[118] ZH, 45 (1868), 307. This account of the General Conference's action also included the following: "The kindred reform in the use of tobacco was also endorsed. Indulgence in this dissipating and dangerous vice by the ministry was especially condemned."

[119] BHMM, III, 57, quoting the Journal of the General Conference, 1884, pp. 238-39, and Appendix, p. 392.

[120] BHMM, III, 56-57. The General Conference committees on temperance up to this time, like the others, had been operative during the conference sessions only. Their chief function had been to deal with the sections in the Discipline on their particular responsibility (Allen, The Methodist Board of Temperance, p. 55). Many annual conferences and churches had official or unofficial continuing bodies, however.

[121]Allen, op. cit., pp. 57-58.

were engaged as the secretaries. The opposition was not wholly over, however. In 1912, the Episcopal Address questioned the expediency of a board in the church, when it was already supporting the Anti-saloon League and the Women's Christian Temperance Union. But the Conference endorsed the board's work by increasing its support to $50,000 (if it could be collected!).[122]

b) The Appeal to Scripture—the Use of Unfermented Wine in the Lord's Supper

During all this reform movement, its advocates took the rightness of the cause so completely for granted that there was no elaborate effort to buttress it with scriptural sanctions. The General Conference of 1880 included in the *Discipline* a general statement which included the words "Temperance is a Christian virtue, Scripturally enjoined." [123] There were many attempts to avoid or dissolve the embarrassing but obvious references to the use of wine among the first disciples. One special phase of the argument centered on the kind of wine to be used in Communion. Protests against fermented wine were heard early in the century, and grew in volume toward its end. In 1835, Mr. Sprague of Albany preached a sermon in which he asserted the divine foundation of the Lord's Supper required the retention of fermented wine. He insisted that he spoke as a friend of the temperance cause. The *Western Christian Advocate* printed an extract of his sermon, and commented favorably in an editorial. The editorial was even more explicit than the sermon in condemning the extremities the temperance people were running into, as harmful to their cause.[124] Dr. Paddock, in the review of E. Nott's lectures on Temperance already cited, [125] declared flatly: "Alcoholic wine was not used on the occasion of the Paschal supper." In 1864 the general conference included in an appendix to the *Discipline* a recommendation that in all cases "the pure juice of the grape be used in Communion." [126]

c) The Temperance Cause in the Methodist Protestant Church and the Methodist Episcopal Church, South

[122] *Ibid.,* pp. 59-60.
[123] Allen, *op. cit.,* p. 51, with reference to the *Discipline* (1880), pp. 145-46.
[124] WCA, 2 (1835), 57.
[125] The review is found in MQR, Oct., 1847, pp. 534-57.
[126] Wheeler, "The Relations of the Methodist Church to the Cause of Temperance," MQR, 58 (1876), 639.

In general, the attitudes, methods, and goals of the temperance movement in the two sister churches paralleled those of the Northern church so closely that the progress of one might be used as a paradigm for all.

A typical statement made by the Committee on Temperance to the General Conference of the Methodist Protestant Church in 1880 contained the following:

We may well . . . look again upon the stern fact that while, in the United States, $50,000,000 are expended annually for the support of the Gospel, and less than $100,000,000 for education, $700,000,000 are squandered each year upon intoxicating drinks.

Alcohol is a potential poison . . . and the word "intoxicate" indicates a poisoned man. . . . We are of the firm opinion that the word of God, rightly understood and honestly interpreted, does not afford the least support to the theory [that the use of wine is legitimate]. Your committee rejoice in every honest effort made to lessen the evils of the drink traffic, to secure its ultimate suppression, and to increase the number of pledged total abstainers . . . and while we cannot endorse all the ideas and methods of modern temperance organizations, we thank Almighty God for the great good which has . . . been effected by the Gospel temperance movement, by the Women's National Christian Temperance Union; by the Temperance Orders . . . and by the excellent publication of the National Temperance Society.

Resolved, that any member of the church who manufactures, sells, drinks, or rents or furnishes a place for the traffic shall be considered guilty of immorality and should be dealt with as in other cases of immorality. Resolved, that unfermented wine only should be used for sacramental purposes.[127]

The North Carolina Conference in 1874 rejected the proposal placed before it to change the General Rule of the Methodist Episcopal Church, South; but this action was not to be construed, they said, as favoring immoral use of intoxicating liquors. The General Rules and the New Testament furnish sufficient guide in this respect. By 1890, that conference went on record as favoring the "entire prohibition of the liquor traffic." In 1882 the General Conference of the Southern church wrote a new chapter on temperance into its *Discipline* which provided that (1) all preachers and members should avoid

[127] *Journal of the Proceedings of the General Conference of The Methodist Protestant Church*, 1880, pp. 63-65.

drinking unless in case of necessity; (2) cases of drunkenness were to be treated as immorality, and cases of drinking as imprudent conduct; (3) all were to refrain from the manufacture and sale of intoxicating beverages, under penalties of imprudent conduct.[128] The General Conference of the Southern church thus stated its position in 1890: "Voluntary total abstinence from all intoxicants is the sole and true ground of personal temperance, and complete legal prohibition of the traffic is the duty of the government." [129]

D. Political Action Against the Saloon

As has already been suggested, the temperance movement, which began as a movement to recruit voluntary total abstainers, was irresistably propelled, in the course of the nineteenth century, toward political action, and of an ever more drastic sort. John G. Woolley, looking back at the history of the movement from near the end of the century, said: "The total abstinence movement swept the country . . . and the enthusiasm of it was equalled only by the disappointment of it." [130] It was found that shaky converts, even those who started out with great courage and enthusiasm, were not safe when the enticements of the barroom were closely spaced along the streets between work and home, between home and social engagements, along most roads they had to travel. The mildest form of action by governmental forces which was then sought was regulation.

It should be observed that regulation had in some cases been exercised by civil authorities before the reformers brought influence to bear, as a sheer exercise of the power inherent in a government, to take actions necessary to its well-being, or, one might even say, to self-preservation. The government of eighteenth-century England, for instance, alarmed by the enormous increase of gin drinking, endeavored, and with some success, to mitigate the dangers of social deterioration by raising taxes on gin, before the impulse of the evangelical revival was strong enough to aid in the work.

Prohibition is something else again, and was something which waited on pressure generated by the Christian conscience, and applied

---

[128] So the report in the *Wesleyan Christian Advocate* for June 10, 1882; the *Richmond Christian Advocate*, however described engaging in the traffic as subject to the penalties of *immoral* conduct (RCA [new series], 16 [1882], May 18, p. 2).

[129] RCA (new series), 25 (1890), May 22.

[130] ZH, 73 (1895), 435.

through political means. For it depended on a judgment which only the informed Christian conscience dared to make: every use of alcohol for beverage purposes is an abuse—or, if not so strongly put, at least this: every form of traffic in intoxicating beverages, no matter how carefully regulated, is a danger to the community, and in the community's interest ought to be entirely suppressed. So the reform moved from voluntarism through state regulation to state prohibition.

The first wave of the reform's recourse to political methods succeeded quite well between the middle of the century and the Civil War. Following Maine's example, a dozen other states adopted prohibitory laws within four years. This wave receded partly as a result of the large relaxation of morals that followed on the war, and partly because of the impact of the flood of European immigrants which came to our shores in the decades just following. By 1875 only Maine, Vermont, and New Hampshire retained their prohibitory laws.[131]

Thrown back, but not defeated, the temperance forces reformed their lines, and advanced, more slowly this time, and not without setbacks, but irresistibly, through control by license, then by prohibition on a local, a state, and finally on a national scale. The logic of the renewed appeal to political measures was stated in an editorial in the *Methodist Protestant*:

For nearly half the century life of the Republic we have been striving to meet [the traffic in ardent spirits] as most moral questions can be met, by moral suasion. . . . It is with [the] population of foreigners that moral suasion utterly fails—there is no conscience to which you can appeal. They shelter themselves under the license laws of the States and defy public opinion to do its worst. Seeing how they are entrenched, public virtue casts about for a remedy, and finds it in Prohibition.[132]

The propulsion of the movement was irresistibly forward because peculiar difficulties beset each stage. Long experience brought the advocates of temperance to a conclusion expressed in a phrase which was adapted from another frequently heard in the slavery controversy: "The nation cannot exist half wet and half dry."

An observer wrote in 1895:

[131] BHMM, III, 55.
[132] MP, 54 (1884), Sept. 27, p. 4.

The license system has been tried for hundreds of years, but has not succeeded in checking intemperance. . . . Local option is good as far as it goes. . . . Prohibition, like total abstinence in its sphere, is the safe and effectual remedy.[133]

A later justification for the course taken by the temperance forces reads:

Refusing all domestic regulation and control, it [the organized liquor traffic] leaves the American people but two alternatives—the abject surrender of their inherent right of self-government or its national annihilation. . . . We therefore declare for . . . an amendment to the Federal Constitution which shall forever prohibit [it].[134]

For the most part, however, the temperance forces felt the rightness of their cause and the propriety of their methods to be self-evident, or that it could best be made evident by exposing the essential harmfulness of beverage alcohol and the incorrigible lawlessness of the trade in it. The consequence was that they didn't spend much time on justifying themselves. The best justification of their course was the inculpation of their opponents; in this they were resourceful and indefatigable.

Enough examples of the charges made against the traffic have been given to make further illustration unnecessary. Two special developments in strategy, however, deserve some comment.

The first of these concerns the difficulties encountered in keeping the "dry" parts of the country really dry while there were "wet" areas adjacent to them, whether under the regime of local option or under state-wide prohibition. Local option, it will be remembered, was a concession won by the temperance forces where state-wide prohibition was not politically possible at first. It allowed each community to choose for itself whether or not it should have within its bounds establishments for the dispensing or manufacture, or both, of alcoholic beverages. Often there would be wet communities adjacent to dry ones, which made access to supplies of liquor easy for those in dry territory who wished it. In such circumstances, the line taken by the liquor forces was to say: "You see, such regulations don't work—they ought to be abandoned." The reply of the temperance men was two-

[133] ZH, 73 (1895), 27.
[134] QRS (third series), 40 (1914), 290.

257

fold: for one thing, even when there are leaks in the dike, conditions are better than when there was no dike at all;[135] for another (and this was especially applicable under local option), the thing to do is not to abandon such laws as exist, but to increase the size of the dry units.[136]

The difficulties of enforcement in small dry communities were illustrated by the "Beatty Local Option Bill," proposed in 1888 in the Ohio Legislature. It provided for a "dry zone" two miles wide in the township outside an incorporated town where prohibition had been adopted. The *Volksblatt* of Cincinnati was much disturbed at what might happen if certain small towns on the city's outskirts should go dry, and the "dry belt" should cut into the city itself. The paper defied the legislators in Columbus to do "their worst."

The spirit of liberty [it said] is still alive and powerful in the Germans of Cincinnati; indeed, so powerful that with all their loyalty to reasonable laws every attempt to force prohibition upon them will . . . be laughed to scorn.[137]

Here was obviously one case of many in which the "liberties" of adjacent sections jostled each other, in a way which, in the view of the temperance forces, could best be reconciled by increasing the size of the dry units wherever possible. So state-wide prohibition began to regain some of the ground it lost after the Civil War. By 1907 it was in force in Maine, Kansas, North Dakota, Georgia, and Oklahoma; two years later, four other states could be added to the list: Alabama, Mississippi, North Carolina, and Tennessee.[138]

---

[135] For example, the argument of an editorial in the *Western:* "The logic is clear. If thus inadequately enforced under circumstances the most unfavorable that could be imagined, the ordinance has accomplished good, how much more good it will certainly accomplish when the conditions are improved and the ordinance enforced" (WCA, 15, no. 2 [Jan. 11], 28).

[136] It would be interesting to trace out what influence, if any, increasing ease of travel had on this process of enlarging units. For instance: Trains and cars became so full of riders who came into the city of Boston for drink, that special constables were hired to put them off if manifestly drunk. (WCA, 15 [1888], no. 5 [Feb. 1], p. 8). If "trains and [street] cars" helped make the change from local option to state-wide prohibition necessary, we may likewise bracket the increase of automobile travel with the change from state-wide to nation-wide prohibition. Of course, ease of transportation helped too. The General Conference of the Methodist Episcopal Church, South, in 1906 asked the Federal Government to enact a law to prevent the shipment of intoxicants into dry states (Allen, *op. cit.*, p. 54).

[137] Quoted in WCA, 15 (1888), no. 10 (March 7), p. 5.

[138] *Encyclopaedia Britannica* (11th ed.), 16, 767.

A second phase of the strategy of the reformers amounted to a position where only complete prohibition of the traffic would satisfy them, though it was stated in negative terms. The cry "no license!" began before the Civil War, and had reached formidable proportions by the end of the century. It was raised by the United Agency of the Workers for Temperance in New York in 1856.[139] In 1884, the General Convention of The Methodist Protestant Church resolved: "We are unalterably opposed to any form of license, high or low, as being wrong in principle and pernicious in practice." [140] The Tennessee Conference of the Methodist Episcopal Church, South, in 1887 took its stand on this platform: "No license, however high—our goal is prohibition." The General Conference of the Methodist Episcopal Church held the next year said that the only proper attitude of a Christian toward the traffic is one of relentless hostility. The license laws are its strongest bulwark of defense. "It can never be legalized without sin." [141]

As has already been suggested, the legal prohibition of the traffic as a goal was not new; but there was a new note in the attack on the licensing system. Toward the end of the century, the opinion was frequently expressed that the system of licenses put the government in partnership in an enterprise which was devoted to the debauching of the people; the revenue derived therefrom was "blood money." Furthermore, the system gave the traffic a legal shelter it did not deserve. For these reasons also, prohibition became the only acceptable solution of the problem for increasing numbers of people. Several of the Methodist papers watched with interest the movement in Norway to put the sale of liquor under a government agency, and rejoiced in its defeat.[142]

1. THE PROHIBITION PARTY

The most complete adoption of political methods by the temperance forces was embodied in the Prohibition Party. Formed in 1869, it presented a Presidential candidate in 1872 on the single issue of prohibition. It continued agitation for the cause, but its political

---

[139] NWCA, 4 (1856), p. 36.
[140] Journal of the Proceedings of the General Convention of The Methodist Protestant Church, 1884, p. 39.
[141] Quoted in Olaf R. Miller, Methodism and Temperance, p. 3.
[142] For example, ZH, 73 (1895), 248.

effectiveness was marred by splits over economic issues which it could not avoid discussing.[143] Not all of those who were zealous for the promotion of prohibition were convinced that a third party was the best way to secure the desired end. *Zion's Herald* in Massachusetts, fearing that national unity might be endangered thereby, and preferring to work through the already established parties, said in 1900: "The effort to found a party whose only or main issue is the restriction of the liquor traffic has humiliatingly . . . failed." [144]

In New York in 1888, a "Temperance Symposium" was held, in which ways to advance the cause were discussed from all sides, including the creation of a third political party of those who prefer temperance. A report of the discussions sadly concluded: "Temperance sentiment is hopelessly divided in New York. Unity may come in ways we wot not of, but come it certainly must before what is dear to . . . all its exponents can be achieved." [145]

In 1885 a discussion of the question of the third party in the *Methodist Review* condemned the scheme as chimerical and impracticable, one which would ensure the defeat of the cause, and result only in attracting the "cranks and visionaries . . . the rejected material of the other parties." [146]

Ten years later, John G. Woolley, an ardent prohibitionist, and at the same time a practiced politician, declared that the cause must capture the executive branch of the government, or fail.[147] This was not in itself an unequivocal declaration for a third party, but Woolley himself became the candidate of the Prohibition Party in 1900.

Discouragement at not finding candidates in the great parties who were willing to pledge themselves to prohibition was a factor in the continued activity of the Prohibition Party. Methodist temperance advocates had long advocated voting for prohibition men in either party; but if they were not to be found, what was to be done? In 1884, the *Methodist Protestant* declared:

---

[143] Charles and Mary Beard, *Rise of American Civilization* (2 vols. New York: Macmillan Co., 1928), II, 321. Used by permission. Miller (*op. cit.*, p. 7) reports that in the national election of 1884, it received 150,626 votes.

[144] ZH, 57 (1880), 276; *ibid.*, 78 (1900), 966-67.

[145] WCA, 15 (1888), no. 8 (Feb. 22), p. 3.

[146] BHMM, III, 56, and 1069, no. 50, where the author of the article is identified as John W. Mendenhall.

[147] ZH, 73 (1895), 435.

It must be confessed that the platform attitude of both the old parties on this question, is the strongest apology for a Prohibition Party. . . . A million of votes would get cast for them if we could stand together.[148]

In 1900, the Prohibition Party had a strong advocate in Olaf R. Miller, pastor of the Highlands Methodist Episcopal Church in Holyoke, Massachusetts. In an address printed during that year he reported the New England Conference as insisting that any political party should stand for prohibition to deserve the Christians' vote. But since neither of the old parties fulfilled that requirement, "the prohibition party is the only party worthy of Methodist votes." [149]

The Prohibition Party did not come near success, if we estimate success by the tables of election returns. But doubtless, as is the way with third parties, they influenced political tendencies far beyond anything indicated in such statistics. The greatest power in the final drive toward National Prohibition was exercised by the Anti-saloon League, whose leaders, it has been said, were among the shrewdest politicians of the time. They did not ally themselves with any political party, but attracted the allegiance of enough advocates of temperance to wield what was ultimately a decisive balance of political power. With the emergence of the Anti-saloon League a new note of hope pervaded the utterances of the advocates of the cause. In 1908 nearly every issue of the *Methodist Protestant* contained an editorial on the subject; the general tone conveyed the impression that the fight was entering on its last stages, with the liquor interests everywhere on the defensive. One of them said:

Nearly every state in the Union is profoundly stirred. The people are getting tired of the domination of the saloon and the ruin it is working. The saloon men are almost at their wits' end.[150]

On the eve of World War I, the end of which was to witness the enactment of the Eighteenth Amendment, Henry Beach Carré, of Vanderbilt University, wrote an article called "In Sight of the End of the Liquor Traffic Beneath the Stars and Stripes," in which he

[148] MP, 54 (1884), Sept. 27, p. 4.
[149] Olaf R. Miller, op. cit., p. 14.
[150] MP, 78 (1908), Feb. 19, p. 5.

spoke of the enthusiastic and determined conventions of the Anti-saloon League, the Women's Christian Temperance Union, and the "Committee of One Hundred," which envisaged in the next few years the success of the movement for nation-wide prohibition. Professor Carré's comment was that the movement was "bound to succeed sooner or later, and probably within the next few years." [151]

E. Changes in American Methodism

1. THEOLOGICAL EMPHASES

This is not the place for a thorough discussion of Methodist theology in the nineteenth century. We must confine our attention to two of its aspects which bore most closely on Methodism's social outlook: the preaching of free grace and the insistence on the possibility of Christian perfection.

Methodists continued to insist, throughout the nineteenth century, on the connection between the availability of God's redeeming grace to every man who would accept it, and his moral accountability. This emphasis was congenial to the sturdy activist temper bred by the frontier, and no less so to the self-made men of the succeeding era. Methodist Arminianism did not feel under the necessity of modifying its formulas to bring them into harmony with either revival exhortations or with a steady insistence on strict moral accountability. They persisted in regarding the Calvinists' modifications in the New England Theology as unsuccessful contortions to achieve just such a reconciliation. Nathan Bangs's attack on Samuel Hopkins' "Consistent Calvinism," with its emphasis on "disinterested benevolence," contended that "the doctrine of gracious ability . . . is Methodism's response to the dilemmas of the New England Theology." [152] The emphasis of Bangs and the other Methodist theologians of the nineteenth century—Whedon, Fisk, Dempster, Miley, Ralston, Lee, and the rest—was to maintain that man's freedom to accept or to reject the forgiving grace of God constitutes the true and essential basis of his moral accountability, and so of his strenuous moral activity in the world.

We turn now to the social bearing of the doctrine of Christian per-

---

[151] QRS, (third series), 40 (1914), 292.
[152] L. H. Scott, *Methodist Theology in America*, p. 100.

fection. Early American Methodism's witness to this doctrine was much less prominent than it had been in Wesley's time. There was, it is true, no time when it had not its exponents, but, considering that Wesley had regarded it as the "grand depositum" for the maintenance of which God had raised up the Methodists, they were surprisingly few, and must have felt themselves a scattered minority.

Benjamin Lakin tells in his journal in 1814 how he was led by the observations of "an old Brother" to find the decline of religion partly in preaching and testimony which stopped with justification, "and ... no talk of sanctification. ...." He said, "[I] immediately set about a reform in myself and began to preach and enforce the doctrine of holiness." [153] In 1831, a Methodist Protestant wrote, just after the founding of their church,

> The ministers and members of the Methodist Protestant Church, when they consider how strangely the Lord has made them free from ecclesiastical bondage, may well exclaim, "What hath God wrought?" But there is another freedom, still more highly to be admired and prized,—it is freedom from inward and outward sin.[154]

It was not till about 1840 that these isolated voices could feel themselves a part of what could be called a perfectionist movement. Perfectionism was a vigorous element in the mid-century revivals. It was only to be expected that Methodism should have contributed largely to this movement. The surprising aspect is that a number of non-Methodists adopted perfectionist views, including the greatest leader of the revivals of the time, Presbyterian Charles Grandison Finney.

The Methodist part of the revival was initiated by two sisters, Sarah A. Langford and Phoebe Palmer of New York City. Mrs. Langford in 1835 gathered the women of two Methodist churches there into a "Tuesday Meeting for the Promotion of Holiness." By 1840, several ministers were helping them organize the increasing number of people who were interested.[155] Mrs. Palmer became a leader in the movement, and accepted invitations from many cities to speak. She also carried on correspondence with other leaders, and in social contacts

[153] W. W. Sweet, *Religion on the American Frontier*, IV, 249.
[154] MRMP, 1 (1831), 194.
[155] T. L. Smith, *Revivalism and Social Reform* (Nashville: Abingdon Press, 1957), pp. 105-6. Used by permission.

263

and conversations with interested individuals led them into an acceptance of the doctrine and into an experience the possibility of which Wesley had so strongly maintained.

a) The Social Bearing of the Holiness Movement

The researches of Timothy L. Smith have shown that the fervent revivalism of the mid-century went hand-in-hand with a broad and powerful interest in the regeneration of society as well as the individual. Many of the revival's leaders, though not all of them, took extreme stands on the abolition of slavery, and most of them took a vigorous interest in the temperance cause. Phoebe Palmer's most intimate circle did not declare itself on the slavery question;[156] but Gilbert Haven, a staunch perfectionist, was the most militant abolitionist among the Methodist leaders. They all thought of personal regeneration as the chief means of social reform.[157] In addition to their perfectionism, most of the leaders "held optimistic views of a temporal millennium and of the necessity of social action to achieve it."[158]

Just after the Civil War, Gilbert Haven

urged Methodists to make their lives an offering . . . to speed the achievement of social equality, racial intermarriage, woman's suffrage, temperance reform, and other beauties of the millennium: "Let Christ abolish sin from your souls, of whatever sort, by His indwelling grace. Let your heart become His peaceful realm. . . . Labor by every word and deed to make all other hearts equally perfect. Strive to bring the laws of society into subjection to His control. Root up the gnarled tusks of prejudice. Toil cheerfully, hopefully, faithfully, to bring in the Grand Sabbatic Year, the Jubilee of Heaven![159]

Frances E. Willard, whose broad social interests have already been mentioned, was one of the best examples of the combination of such interest with the search for holiness. While she was a student at the Female College in Evanston, Illinois, she read Phoebe Palmer's works, and professed sanctification under a revival conducted in Evanston by Dr. and Mrs. Palmer.[160]

[156] T. L. Smith, op. cit., p. 223.
[157] Ibid., p. 151.
[158] Ibid., p. 232.
[159] Ibid., p. 235.
[160] Ibid., p. 133.

b) The Free Methodist Church

The formation of a separate Free Methodist Church in the Northeast came about partly as a result of its founders' impatience with the resistance of the Methodist Episcopal Church to their emphasis on holiness, and partly from a complex of social causes which are exceedingly difficult to unravel. In addition to their emphasis on holiness, they espoused a much more radical stand on the slavery question than the Genesee Conference from which they took their departure. The movement was in part a protest against what they considered abuse of disciplinary authority, as is shown by their adoption of lay representation in their new constitution. They also protested against what they felt was a conspiracy to keep the advocates of holiness from getting better appointments. Since they felt that this collusion was exercised through the sinister medium of secret societies, they embodied in their new organization the antisecret society provision which had cropped up before in the same region at the formation of the Wesleyan Methodist Church.

It is quite possible that this schism was a manifestation in part of a growing cleavage between city and country churches in the Genesee Conference.[161] Certainly Bishop Simpson, who read the leaders out of that conference in 1859, acted as a disciplinarian, for he was himself an ardent professor of the doctrine of Christian perfection. After the Civil War, abolition having disappeared from the list of questions at issue, a number of Free Methodists, both ministerial and lay, returned to the Methodist Episcopal Church, without apparent uneasiness lest their emphasis on holiness would render them suspect.

c) The fading of social interest

The interest in social questions which, as we have seen, characterized the revivals of mid-century, both perfectionist and otherwise, faded toward the end of the century, or rather, departed from their ranks, and took up its abode with those whose readiness to embrace newer modes of thought, both scientific and social, provided a more congenial atmosphere. Neither revivalism nor perfectionism died; but concentrating more and more on an intensely personal gospel of sal-

[161] T. L. Smith, op. cit., pp. 132-33.

265

vation and perfection, they tended more and more to leave social concerns to others.

Let us consider the social outlook of Dwight L. Moody, the most eminent representative of the revivalism at the end of the century. He made, it is true, a real effort to get the poor of the cities to his revival meetings; but there was little in his sermons to attract them, and his hearers were mostly from the middle class; many of his sponsors, indeed, were wealthy businessmen. Even in the matter of temperance reform, Moody shied away from other procedures than personal conversion; he opposed Prohibition; he even broke with Frances Willard over signing a temperance pledge, saying "Only conversion could save a man from drink." [162] "Hard times" were the result of sin and iniquity—"the money that is drunk up! The money that is spent for tobacco!" [163] He did hope the Moody Bible Institute would "raise up men and women who will lay their lives alongside of the laboring class and the poor," but his answer to the question, "What should be done with and for the working man?" was, "Save their souls." [164]

The Holiness Movement, which never really died out after the middle of the century, attained a new impulse by the 1880's. In 1867 the National Association for the Promotion of Holiness was organized in New York City.[165] The association spread rapidly and soon became national in scope as well as in name. It instituted camp meetings for the special promotion of holiness; before long it had presses busy turning out pamphlets and periodicals devoted to the same end. The association was interdenominational, but most of its members were Methodists. The church authorities, while not repudiating the doctrine, objected to the exclusive emphasis of the holiness groups on the doctrine, and to their pretensions to a monopoly of the teaching and the experience. "Come-outer" tendencies developed pari passu with opposition in the churches.

Though the separatist tendencies were resisted, they ultimately prevailed. During the last six years of the century, no fewer than ten

[162] William G. McLoughlin, Jr., Modern Revivalism (New York: The Ronald Press Co., 1959), pp. 232-33.
[163] Ibid., pp. 254-55.
[164] Ibid., pp. 272-73.
[165] John L. Peters, Christian Perfection and American Methodism (Nashville: Abingdon Press, 1956), p. 134.

separate bodies of predominantly Methodist background were founded, with entire sanctification as their cardinal doctrine. The First Church of the Nazarene, founded in 1895, was to furnish the name and the nucleus around which, in 1907 and 1908, a number of such formed the Church of the Nazarene.[166]

The Holiness Camp Meeting Associations were predominantly composed of folk of agrarian outlook, and from the lower strata of social and economic life. Geographically speaking, it has been noted that they flourished chiefly in the South and Midwest. The holiness movement generally, toward the end of the century, concentrated on personal salvation to the exclusion of interest in social problems.[167]

At the beginning of its career in America, Methodism had proclaimed a double objective: to reform the nation and to spread scriptural holiness. Till the crusading fervors of the fight against slavery had subsided, the perfectionists kept the complementary halves pretty well in balance. But afterwards, they beat a retreat from the responsibility for the state of society as a whole, which Methodism at its best has steadily acknowledged.

2. LAY REPRESENTATION AND LENGTHENED PASTORATES

In two organizational changes, namely, the admission of lay representation to the conferences, and the removal of the time limit from their pastorates, the Methodist churches reflected transformations in the social conditions about them. The former change had, of course, been embodied in the Methodist Protestant Church from the beginning; in the Episcopal Methodist Churches, it came as a result of their growing need for lay help in managing the increasingly complex business affairs. The lengthening time limit on pastorates and its final removal reflect the recognition of the needs of the new urban communities.

The Methodist Episcopal Church, South, voted, in their first General Conference after the war, (1866), to grant lay representation henceforth. They were prepared by the dislocation of their organization to make far-reaching changes to speed recovery. Bishop McTyeire conveyed the message of what they had done to the Methodist

---

[166] *Ibid.*, pp. 148-49.
[167] See *ibid.*, especially p. 144: "In a Methodism conditioned from its earliest days to an awareness of social need, . . . the message of the holiness advocates sounded strangely, and irritatingly irrelevant."

Protestants, who appreciated the courtesy with which the message was conveyed, and congratulated the Southern Episcopal Methodist Church on having taken so long a step forward. That strenuous anti-Episcopal Methodist, Edward Drinkhouse, professed not to be convinced that clerical control over the delegation had been abolished. Nevertheless, in the General Conference of 1870, laymen were present in equal numbers with the ministerial delegates.[168]

The Methodist Episcopal Church was slower to act on this important matter. Agitation for lay representation was begun as early as 1852 by a convention of Methodist laymen meeting in Philadelphia. The General Conferences of 1852 and 1856 returned the same answer to their pleas: it is inexpedient. By 1860, the bishops said in their address that they could see laymen being safely introduced into General Conference—provided that they were kept in a separate house or assembly, and that the church clearly voiced its desire to have it so. In 1862, the subject was presented to the annual conferences, but lost. In 1868, the General Conference voted to submit it once more to the annual conferences; this time it got the required majority.

Accordingly in 1872 laymen sat for the first time in a Conference of the Methodist Episcopal Church. However, there were only two laymen present from each conference, and agitation for equal representation was not long in beginning. It has been noticed more than once that the admission of laymen to the General Conference coincided with the uncovering of some serious frauds in connection with the management of the Publishing House. Into that unsavory affair we have no need to enter here; we will only notice that the Publishing House was entirely managed by ministers under appointment from the General Conference. The probability is that the desire to get competent businessmen on the committee influenced the vote in this instance.[169] It was not until the General Conference of 1900 that laymen attained equal representation.

In 1888 several women were elected to the delegations of the General Conference of the Northern church; there was considerable debate over whether they were included in the term "laymen" as

---

[168] MP, 32 (1865-66), May 19, p. 2; and Edward Drinkhouse, *History of Methodist Reform*, II, 469.

[169] SMAH, pp. 323-24.

defined by the General Conference of 1872. That definition read: "Laymen are all members of the Methodist Episcopal Church who are not members of an Annual Conference." Most of the editorials on the subject recognized that if the law were kept in spirit and in letter, the women would be seated; but others pleaded long-standing custom. The broader interpretation did not prevail until 1900, when women were allowed for the first time to sit as delegates in the same General Conference in which the laity first had equal representation with the ministers.

The itinerancy is still a part of the Methodist system, in the sense that a minister is a member of a conference, and is under orders to serve anywhere within the conference's limits where he may be sent by the appointing powers. The itinerancy is not the same as the limit on the time a minister might serve in any one place, which was so rigorously observed up until 1900 in the Northern church, and in 1918 in the the Southern. But, just as it is obvious that the time limit was made a rule in 1804 to keep the itinerancy in force, it is likewise evident that it could not be modified or done away without seriously altering the operation, if not the principle, of itinerancy.

We have already spoken of the usefulness of the itinerancy in keeping up with the frontier. It enabled the bishops to cover the widest territory with the fewest men; it necessitated very salutary steps in the employment of laymen to supplement the wide-ranging preachers' point of view; it distributed the burdens of work in the most demanding places as nearly evenly as possible; and, from the people's point of view, it enabled them to hear new sermons, even though their preacher at any one time might not be well enough educated to compose new ones year after year. Changing conditions lessened its usefulness. The frontier dwindled, then disappeared; ministers were better educated and by so much the better qualified to serve longer in one place; and, with the growing complexity of our culture, more specialized kinds of ministry were required, or at least more pastoral oversight. The "preacher" was perforce becoming the "minister," and the "pastor."

There was no written prescription regarding the time limit in Methodism's earliest days in this country. The restriction lay in Asbury's determination to keep the preachers from settling down in the cities and living like gentlemen. But in 1804 the General Con-

269

ference laid it down that the bishop "shall not allow any [ordinary active preacher] to remain in the same station more than two years successively." [170] The limit remained at two years till 1864, when it was changed to three. There it stayed (save for a brief period after 1888, when it was five years) till 1900, when it was removed altogether. In the Southern church, it was changed to four years in 1866; in 1918 the bishop was authorized to make longer appointments where it is necessary.

The close connection between urbanization and the removal of the time limit was indicated in an article by H. K. Carroll in which he said: "Is there necessity for a modification of the itinerancy?" We might answer the question by asking another: "Is it necessary for us to succeed in the cities?" [171]

Agitation for a change in the time limit began at least as early as the General Conference of 1856. The chief reasons advanced for it were that "it would drive the preachers to reading and study [and], . . . that two years was too short a time to become acquainted with his flock, so as to become a profitable pastor." Peter Cartwright, who gives us this report, replied that in such circumstances there would "be but little pastoral duty performed, and but little spirituality in these forced sermons." [172]

In 1887, an editorial in the *Western Christian Advocate* deplored the fact that the number of Methodist ministers who had had volumes of sermons published during their lifetime could be counted on the fingers of one hand. It went on to say: "The itinerant system is the death of literary effort. . . . It is time we . . . do our share." [173] Just before the General Conference of 1888, when the matter of the time element was again under discussion, there was a long article in the *Methodist Review* by O. H. Warren, in which he declared that there was a difference between the itinerant system, which should be kept, and the time limit, which should be abandoned. He concluded:

Great as the utility of the itinerancy continues to be, there is now none in the time-limit itself . . . the sooner the Church shall demand its repeal,

[170] JGC, I, 56.
[171] Frederick A. Norwood, "The Americanization of the Wesleyan Itinerant" (unpublished ms. of an address delivered at Nashville, Tenn., July, 1959), p. 19.
[172] Charles L. Wallis, ed., *Autobiography of Peter Cartwright*, pp. 326-27.
[173] WCA, 54 (1887), 296.

the sooner will she be able to utilize to the best advantage the forces at her command.[174]

3. DISCIPLINE, EVANGELISM, AND RELIGIOUS EDUCATION

In our brief survey of the changes which took place in the life of the Methodist Churches, it is well to consider the realms of discipline, evangelism, and religious education in connection with each other, for the changes which took place in them were correlative. As, in the task of Christianization, emphasis on discipline declined, and methods of evangelism changed, reliance on Christian education increased. We have already mentioned the decline in the use of the discipline of excommunication in the churches. Doubtless it was partly cause and partly result of the disappearance of the sharp line between the Church and "the world." So far as excommunication is concerned, we must depend rather on the absence of data—the argument from silence—than on any documentary evidence. Records of church trials and expulsions simply become less and less numerous, and finally fade out altogether.

There are other indications of the decline of discipline in the church. Expulsion from membership depends on the meaning attached to membership and, in a consistent view, is correlative with the terms of entrance upon membership. A good deal of light is shed on these matters by the popular half-facetious saying that whereas once it had been hard to get into The Methodist Church, and very easy to get out, now it was the other way round: indeed dying didn't always suffice to remove one's name from the membership rolls.

Dr. Norwood has pointed out that though a probationary period was required before full membership in the Methodist churches through most of the nineteenth century (it has since disappeared altogether), it was a very different state of things from the eighteenth century when members never got off probation! [175] Changes of the sort we are considering here may be described as the changes which overtake a "sect" on its way to becoming a "church," using the words in Troeltsch's sense. Of course, Methodism never attained, never even envisaged, the attainment of a state of "churchliness" which would

[174] MR (1888), p. 244.
[175] F. A. Norwood, *Church Membership in the Methodist Tradition* (Nashville: Methodist Publishing House, 1958), p. 41 *et passim*.

save its people by the process of infusing grace objectively conceived by means of the sacraments; but it did move toward the church end of the spectrum, in that it became a cross section of the world being led on the way to salvation by the path of Christian nature rather than by way of catastrophic and instantaneous conversion and rigorous discipline.

A striking incongruity in the changes which Methodism went through in the last half of the nineteenth century is that during this very period, while sectarian discipline was declining in its rigor, the sectarian standards of conduct were pitched higher and more querulously insisted on. It seems as though the Methodist churches, uneasy over the decline in discipline, tried to hide that failure even from themselves by heightened exhortations on amusements.

Revivalism played less of a part in the general life of the church as time went on.[176] In 1858 there occurred a great revival which seemed to "go of itself," and was led largely by lay people. But after the war revivalism fell more and more into the hands of the "professionals," which is not necessarily a term of reproach, for the great revivalist leaders, Dwight L. Moody and his like, were men of consummate sincerity and, under God, mighty in soul-winning. But some of the lesser figures were undeniably tainted with professionalism in the bad sense; and sensationalism crept in as professionalism's dubious ally. At the best, the "campaigns" of such men presupposed an amount of promotion which the earlier, more spontaneous revivals like that of 1858 had not needed. Again, it must be emphasized, there is a difference between revivalism and evangelism; and The Methodist Church has not abandoned the latter, although the former method has declined in usefulness and favor.

Horace Bushnell's *Christian Nurture*, published in 1847, was one

---

[176] A good illustration of growing doubt about the adequacy of the traditional revivalism will be found in the Bishops' Address to the General Conference of the Methodist Episcopal Church, South, as reported in RCA, 25 (1890), May 22, first page. In 1876 an elaborate editorial called "The Revival We Need" appeared in Zion's Herald recognizing the inadequacy of emotional revivalism unaccompanied by ethical "stiffening." "Truly it is a startling fact that this country, which has had more frequent and extensive 'religious revivals' than any other, should now be the most profoundly corrupt, financially at least, of all the Christian nations. . . . The revival we need is one which will address itself directly to the prevalent demoralization . . . not a revival merely of the religion which luxuriates in the devout fervors of the camp prayer meeting . . . which sings sweet hymns and applauds sweet sermons and goes straightway off, seeking to pander to self and sin (quoted in NWCA, 24 [1876], p. 4).

of the great "watershed" books in American religious thought. Bushnell was a Congregationalist, born in the Calvinist tradition, and his proclamation that a child born into a Christian family need never know a time when he was not a Christian marked a recognizable breaking point in the hold of the doctrine of original sin. Methodists, too, though they had retained the baptism of infants in the Church, believed in the doctrine of original sin, and acted as though, until the crisis of conversion overtook the grown or half-grown person, he was not fully a Christian. Yet all along, unreconciled contradictions had prevailed on the subject. Stephen Olin, President of several Methodist colleges, in both North and South, said he had believed on the matter as Bushnell did for twenty years.[177] The growing reliance of Methodists on Christian training for children and young people was early reflected in the declaration of the Northern church's *Discipline* of 1856:

We hold that all children, by virtue of the unconditional benefits of the atonement, are members of the Kingdom of God, and, therefore, graciously entitled to baptism; . . .
We regard all children who have been baptized as placed in visible covenant relation to God, and under the special care and supervision of the church.[178]

But it was not until the twentieth century that the *Discipline* acknowledged that baptized children were to be regarded as preparatory members in the church.

The Methodist Protestants arrived at this position much earlier. In 1880 the Committee on the Relation of Children to the Church reported to their General Conference in words which combined both positions: "The infant children of our members, upon receiving baptism, shall be enrolled as probationary members of our Church, and shall be taught and watched over as lambs of the flock, with a view to their confessing Christ publicly, as soon as their knowledge and experience shall enable them to do so." [179]

[177] Leland H. Scott, *Methodist Theology in America in the Nineteenth Century*, p. 162. See also, BHMM, III, 93-94.
[178] Quoted in BHMM, III, 95.
[179] *Journal of the Proceedings of the General Conference of The Methodist Protestant Church*, 1880, p. 56.

In the early days of the Sunday school movement, the conversion theory of making Christians prevailed in many of its workers' minds. In 1867 J. M. Gregory declared in the *Sunday School Teacher* that the first aim of the Sunday school should be the conversion of the pupils. The steps to this end should be:

1st, to bring the pupil to a knowledge and sense of his need as a fallen being with a sinful soul—a guilty transgressor of a divine law and of a father's commandment; and 2nd, to develop in his understanding and impress upon his heart the character and work of Christ—the suffering, saving love of Jesus; the complete ability and willingness of this Saviour to redeem, purify, and bless him.[180]

The passage of time has weakened this emphasis and strengthened instead a reliance on the developing sense of the love of God as ministered through the nurturing Christian community. Regardless of how the theology has been expressed, or whether the method has been by revivals or "Decision Day," the church membership was recruited more and more from the membership of the Sunday school and the Epworth League, and correspondingly less from revivals or evangelistic preaching campaigns.

a) *Sunday Schools*

The beginnings of Sunday-school organization appeared in 1791 with the formation of a "First Day or Sunday School Society" in Philadelphia. Formed largely on Quaker initiative, it was nevertheless undenominational in character, and developed into the American Sunday School Union in 1824. So successfully did it fill a crying need[181] that the denominations began forming their own Unions; the Methodists' dates from 1827. The latter was required at first by the church to diffuse its energies by distributing Bibles and Tracts in addition to its work with Sunday schools.[182] The Methodist Protestants hoped in 1831 that a false denominational pride would not pre-

---

[180] Quoted in BHMM, III, 93, n.
[181] "It is easy in the light of our modern educational science to criticize the poor endeavors of early religious education, but no history of the wonderful development of the Mississippi valley would be adequate which failed to recognize the social significance of the little Sunday Schools that went far ahead of the organized Church into the pioneer communities. . . . Many schools . . . were obliged to give much of their time to the simplest lessons in reading and spelling." (*Encyclopaedia of Religion and Ethics*, [James Hastings, ed., 13 vols., New York: Charles Scribner's Sons, 1917-27], 12:112b.)
[182] SHMEC, IV, 465.

vent them from joining in the support and work of the American Society.[183] The first Sunday school in Nashville was organized by the Methodists in 1820. Soon after its beginning, a sign was found hanging on the door which read: "No desecration of the holy Sabbath, by teaching on the Sabbath in this church." [184]

We cannot here go into the voluminous story of the development of Sunday-school "methods." The first lesson helps emanating from the Union relied largely on the question-and-answer method made familiar by generations of catechizing. Many churchmen were reluctant to see the passing of that time-honored method. In 1890 the Bishops' Address to the General Conference of the Southern church reported that the International Lessons were used by most of their Sunday schools, but urged the advantages of catechetical instruction.[185]

The Sunday School Union of the Northern Church was rescued from its doldrums by John H. Vincent, who continued the old policy of depending heavily on the printed word, but introduced new ideas into the material. He made a beginning at uniform lessons, which may fairly be said to have been the forerunner of the International Uniform Lessons. He advocated the latter so successfully that it prevailed long after more closely graded lessons might profitably have been adopted.[186] During the second half of the century the number of Methodist Sunday schools increased from 5,005 to 30,259, and the number of pupils from 268,775 to 2,585,178.[187]

b) The Epworth League

Between 1864 and 1890 a number of young peoples' leagues were formed in the Methodist Churches. Of these, four were more vigorous than the rest; one of these four, founded by the Lowreys, was devoted especially to the cultivation of holiness. The others were for the pur-

---

[183] MRMP, 1 (1831), 218. The Northern church was determined to maintain its own Union, however, in spite of the work of the American Union. In 1864 it complained in the *Advocates* of the way in which the agents of the A. S. S. U. thrust themselves into Methodist pulpits, and stated the official position on the relations of the two Unions: there was no official connection; Methodists were urged to support the Methodist Union; "when an agent claims greater cheapness for the books of the A. S. S. U., he claims what he cannot sustain by fact" (NWCA, 12 [1864], 36).

[184] Cullen T. Carter, *op. cit.*, pp. 69-70.

[185] RCA, 25 (1890), May 22, extra leaf.

[186] BHMM, III, 100.

[187] BHMM, III, 101.

pose of developing (to use the words of one of them) "symmetrical intellectual and spiritual culture." The disadvantages of having a number of such societies in the church was sufficiently apparent by 1890 to bring about their amalgamation in the Epworth League, which was officially recognized by the General Conference of the Northern church in 1892.[188] The Southern church had already, in its General Conference of 1890, established "Young Peoples' Leagues," which soon after became the Epworth Leagues of the Methodist Episcopal Church, South.[189] The Methodist Protestant Church again followed the interdenominational channel more readily than its two bigger sisters. About the same time as others they adopted the model constitution of the United Society of Christian Endeavor, and established the Young People's Societies of Christian Endeavor of the Methodist Protestant Church.[190]

The organization of the Epworth League provided for four departments: Spiritual Work, World Evangelism, Mercy and Help, and Literary and Social Work. The League's great contribution, over and above the Sunday schools' as we would view it today, was that it gave the young people a channel through which they could do as well as learn something. Yet Zion's Herald was not long in voicing a complaint over that very aspect of the League: "It is feared that our Epworth Leagues are being given so much to do that soul-saving is becoming to them a lost spiritual art." [191]

One of the good things the Epworth League did was to begin bringing together young Methodists from the Northern and Southern churches. A joint convention was held in Chattanooga in 1895. There was a good deal of discussion in the Northern papers afterward about the treatment accorded the Negro delegates. The picture which emerged was not very clear: some asserting that the Negroes were kept to a section by themselves, others that they weren't, or if they were, it was a "central" section. The story seems to be that the arrangements included a special section for the seating of colored delegates, but the attendance was so large that in the subsequent confusion the color line could not be drawn, and white and black delegates were

[188] BHMM, III, 103 ff.
[189] C. T. Carter, op. cit., p. 247.
[190] Journal of the General Conference of The Methodist Protestant Church, 1892, p. 65.
[191] ZH, 74 (1896), 296.

mixed indiscriminately through the hall. A pastor in Bangor, Maine, deplored the segregation, but said the best thing for the Northerners to do, being guests, was to ignore it.[192]

4. MIDDLE-CLASS METHODISM
LOSES TOUCH WITH WORKING PEOPLE

The rise of Methodism to middle-class status was partly a matter of wealth, but also a matter of cultural outlook. Already by 1850, according to the U. S. census, the Methodist churches formed the wealthiest denominational family in the nation, reckoned by worth of church property.[193] Through the latter half of the century, the educational level rose as Methodist young people patronized the institutions of higher learning provided by the conferences and others. These factors worked themselves out in changing patterns of church life: worship became soberer and more formalized; disciplinary procedures lost their rigor; revivalism declined in favor, while other ways of evangelism and especially religious education came to focus in the churches' attention; the itinerancy declined before greater emphasis on pastoral functions which called for greater continuity of residence; and finally, the Methodist churches become less appealing to the common people.

The rise of the bulk of the Methodists to the middle ranges of the economic and cultural scale was not in itself deplorable; but the accompanying development of a "middle-class mind" was. The newfound comfort of the Methodists betrayed them into relinquishing those sympathies for the common man which had been one of their glories in the time when they were themselves "common men."

It is too early, in our period, to speak of the "flight from the city," or "the suburbanization" of Methodism, in any significant sense. Indeed even at the end of the century, the center of gravity in Methodism was still in the towns and the country. But in the sense that Methodists developed a disdain for and resentment against the alien hordes who crowded into the slums of the growing cities, they put up a psychological barrier to effective work among them which was but the precursor of the geographical gap of later times.

There were other barriers, of course—notably the fact that most of

[192] ZH, 73 (1895), 436.
[193] BHMM, III, 49.

277

the immigrants were Roman Catholic when they came; and it is partly due to this fact, no doubt, that the Roman Church made a much stronger effort at staying with the workmen of the cities, and had much greater success in retaining their sympathy and support. Indeed there is some evidence that the church worked at the problem from the other end as well, and deliberately tried to keep the immigrants in the cities, where they would be within reach. Thus she compounded the social problem for the sake of continuing her spiritual ministrations. There were, it is true, several colonization societies for settling Catholic immigrants on the land; but they were not very successful, and their activities were vigorously opposed by at least one Archbishop.[194]

Nevertheless, while we may doubt the social wisdom of some of the Roman Church's methods, we cannot but grant that she was more successful in identifying herself with the urban proletariat than was Protestantism, which, for the greater part, has been content to follow the middle classes.[195] Protestant attacks on the problem, impressive in the aggregate, were made; but they were quite incommensurate with the magnitude of the task, and only partly successful.[196]

The widening gap between the Methodists and the working people was noted with anxiety by the bishops in their address to the Northern church in 1888:

Are [the masses] . . . drifting away from us? Have we lost our love for them, or the aggressive spirit which carries the Gospel to their homes and hearts? Nothing is more alarming . . . than the alienation of the laboring people from the evangelical churches. . . . If we have given too much attention to the rich, or cherished too much regard for social position, or have in any wise neglected the poor, we have departed from the spirit of our calling.[197]

The succeeding chapter will be for the most part a commentary on the issues raised in these last few pages.

[194] John Tracy Ellis, *American Catholicism* (Chicago: University of Chicago Press, 1956), p. 86.
[195] Francis X. Curran, S. J., *Major Trends in American Church History* (New York: The American Press, 1946), p. 142.
[196] This is the conclusion of Aaron Ignatius Abell in his study, *The Urban Impact on American Protestantism* (Cambridge, Mass.: Harvard University Press, 1943), p. 255.
[197] BHMM, III, 62-63.

CHAPTER SEVEN

The Social Gospel in Methodism

A. Changes in American Society

IF WE LOOK AT THE MATERIAL BASES OF THE SWIFT AND bewildering changes which took place in the life of the American people after the Civil War, we can distinguish two which underlay all the rest: the transfer of what seemed at the time unlimited natural resources from the public domain to private hands for exploitation; and the availability of new sources of power together with the elaboration of machines to apply it to the satisfaction of human wants.

Enacted in the midst of the Civil War, the Homestead Act gave free farms to all adult citizens and even to aliens who had filed declaratory papers, if they were willing to stake out their claims and take up residence. This in itself was admirable; but Congress also was free with its gifts to those in positions of influence and to corporations whose purpose was to exploit them for their own profit. Land speculators who were shrewd enough to pitch on tracts whose value would be vastly increased by subsequent changes got a good deal of it. The railroads, the building of which was a prime factor in *post bellum* expansion, got immense domains not only on both sides of their rights of way but in detached portions of the land through which they passed. Immensely valuable deposits of mineral wealth passed into the hands of enterprisers determined to make the most of them while the golden opportunity lasted.

The last arable land was occupied around 1890; with it passed the frontier which had so long influenced in the most pervasive ways the life of the Republic, even in those portions which it had long since passed over in its westward course. Agriculture underwent great changes as a consequence. It was no longer possible to run away from a run-out farm and find a better one farther west, merely for the trouble of moving family and goods. That meant a change from an outer to an inner frontier: exploration of better ways of farming whose thrust would be intensive, rather than extensive. The farmers were subject to the changes taking place in other sections of society as well. The self-sufficiency of the frontier family was no longer the goal of effort; the successful farmer was one who developed a specialized crop to be sold on the market for cash. The tendency toward mechanization and large-scale operation began (more slowly, but just as surely) to operate in producing fruits of the soil as well as in manufacturing and transportation. That meant a need for ever greater investment of capital, and that in turn disqualified many marginal farmers, and reduced them to the status of renters or propertyless workers for others. The villain about to foreclose the mortgage on the family farm appeared so often in the fiction of the time because foreclosures were frequent in real life.

The voracious appetite of the growing population for goods stimulated American inventive energies to prodigies of accomplishment. The crude water-run machinery of factories beside New England streams gave way to complicated machines run by powerful steam engines, the power for which was produced at first by coal and later by oil. The railroads were enormously expensive to build, even with the munificent gifts of a paternal government. The scramble to obtain rights-of-way which might prove profitable in the near or even not-so-near future led to overexpansion and cut-throat competition. After a period of such struggle, which descended to actual violence in more than one case, the railroad kings discovered the advantage of combination. Competition for top positions in the new combinations persisted, but the centralization went irresistibly on. It went on likewise in the other heavy industries: in steel it produced the United States Steel Corporation in 1901; dominance of the oil industry was gathered into the Standard Oil Company under John D. Rockefeller. The end of the century was the age of the "trusts."

As the shifts and struggles of the great corporations required quick availability of large financial resources, the masters of finance acquired powerful positions in the business world. The concentration of financial power in Wall Street in New York City made it a symbol

for mysterious powers whose caprices ordinary men could not fathom
—only dread. So the kings of finance—men like Jay Cooke and J.
Pierpont Morgan—took their places beside the captains of industry
like Rockefeller, Carnegie, and Armour, and the rulers of railroad em-
pires like Hill and Harriman.

It has been pointed out [1] that all of these men (save the somewhat
skeptical Carnegie) were members, most of them active and loyal
ones, of the Protestant churches. Jay Cooke was a teacher in a Sunday
school at great personal sacrifice, was liberal in his gifts to many different denominations, and was all through his life a faithful member
of the Protestant Episcopal Church. Rockefeller's loyalty to the
Baptists was no less strong, and his benefactions, though more cir-
cumspect, were no less munificent. Even Carnegie seemed to feel some
sort of responsibility for the way he disbursed his money: his gifts of
libraries and organs were widespread, as well as his endowments of
organizations for peace—these last made, ironically enough, out of
money partly acquired in making the weapons demanded by modern
warfare. All of these men recognized the demands of Christian stewardship so far as concerned their use of money once made; but they
did not let a Christian code of ethics dominate their money-making
activities, which were often characterized by a lawlessness and ruth-
lessness limited only by the needs of the competitive situation in
which they found themselves.

In 1860 around a billion dollars was invested in manufacturing. In
less than fifty years this had increased to twelve billion dollars. The
successful concerns were fabulously successful; but the casualties in
business failures were high. Society was the victim, rather than the
master, of the enormous forces thus let loose; head-long periods of
"boom" were followed by periods of no less violent "bust" in which
financial panic was followed by a period of stagnation in business and
slow recovery.

The working force for these enterprises expanded with commensurate rapidity. In 1860 it consisted of a million and a half workmen; in
less than fifty years, it had mounted to five and a half million. Many of
these workmen came from abroad, lured hither by the highly em-
broidered tales of our prosperity assiduously circulated by the steam-

[1] Charles and Mary Beard, *Rise of American Civilization*, II, 173-74.

ship companies; or they were brought over on a contract basis by concerns whose need for cheap labor was insatiable.[2] Speaking different tongues, for the most part with little education or none at all, even in their mother tongue, this swiftly increasing mass of folk, most of whom landed with only a few personal possessions to call their own, had no cohesion, no leaders, and almost no champions in the bewildering land where they hoped to make their fortunes.

The movement to form trades and labor unions was the inevitable result of the workman's attempt to meet their employers on the more nearly even terms of combined action. It can hardly be said to have attained the proportions of a movement till the formation of the Knights of Labor in 1869, though the National Trades' Union had lived through a short life in the 1930's. The Knights of Labor made a valiant effort to include in its membership workmen of all degrees of skill and all races and nationalities; but the task of holding together such varied elements with diverging interests was too great. After the formation of the American Federation of Labor in 1881, the influence of the Knights of Labor gradually receded before that of the new organization, and ceased altogether before the end of the century. The American Federation of Labor was for the most part composed of the more highly skilled laborers, and devoted itself primarily to their interests. At the end of the century, unskilled laborers still lacked an organization inclusive enough and strong enough to defend them.

Strikes had become more frequent and more violent toward the end of the century. Some of them were comparatively blind, impulsive blows launched with the fury of desperation.[3] Others, like the

---

[2] In 1850, there were 2,240,535 people of foreign birth in the United States. In 1860, this number had increased to 4,131,866. Most of them were from Germany, England, and Ireland (Ernest Ludlow Bogart, *Economic History of the American People* [New York: Longmans, Green and Co., 1930], pp. 421-22). After 1880, the character of the incoming hosts began to shift, the greater proportion of them coming from the countries of Southern and Eastern Europe. Two peak years of immigration were 1882, when 789,000 arrived, and 1907 when there were over a million and a quarter (*Ibid.*, pp. 602, 604). The new arrivals numbered more than a million in each of half a dozen years after 1900.

[3] A good example of such an unpremeditated strike was the railroad strike of 1877. The railroads had been cutting wages ever since the panic of 1873; a final cut of ten per cent caused some employees of the Baltimore and Ohio to stop work. "Apparently without prearrangement and without any active direction from the officials of the Brotherhood [of Locomotive Engineers] the strike spread rapidly all over the East." (Beard, *op. cit.*, p. 229.)

series launched by the Knights of Labor in 1886 were evidences of the growing power of the unions, even though these all failed in such a way as to contribute to the downfall of the Knights. The repeated sequence was depression, wage-cutting, strikes. The great strikes toward the end of the century were accompanied by fearful violence: the Haymarket Riots of 1886, the Homestead Steel Strike of 1892, and the Pullman Strike of two years later, for example. As yet the unions were no match for the companies, who could and did command the aid of armed police, public and private; repression was thorough and ruthless.

The concomitant of industrialization and immigration was the rapid growth of cities.[4] As they mushroomed, slum sections became concentrated pools of people, all poverty-stricken, mostly foreign-born with their numerous children. The American proletariat was coming into being. The harmful effects of their overcrowded and unsanitary living conditions posed problems so complex as to defy even accurate appraisal, let alone adequate solution.

B. The Social Gospel in American Protestantism

The social gospel is to be understood as American Protestantism's way of responding more adequately than it had yet done to the problems created by the changes toward an urban and industrial society.[5] In spite of the zeal for reform manifested in strength up through the period of the Civil War, we cannot but admit that Protestantism's disposition to exercise influence over society, and its ability to do so, declined during the century. In addition to the swift social changes near the end of the century, other factors in the situation conspired to produce this result.

[4] In 1840 there were forty-four cities with a population of eight thousand or more; in 1860, the number had grown to 141. During this period the city population grew five times as fast as that of the country as a whole (Bogart, *Economic History*, p. 424). In 1860, "not more than one-sixth of the people lived in towns of eight thousand and upwards; by the end of the century one third of the people were in centers of that class." (Beard, *Rise of American Civilization*, II, 206.)

[5] C. H. Hopkins, author of the standard history of the movement defines it thus: "The social gospel . . . may be regarded as American Protestantism's response to the challenge of modern industrial society" (*The Rise of the Social Gospel in American Protestantism, 1865-1915* [New Haven: Yale University Press, 1940], p. 318). Dr. Hopkins also quotes a formula from Shailer Mathews: The social gospel is "the application of the teaching of Jesus and the total message of the Christian salvation to society, the economic life, and social institutions, . . . as well as to individuals" (*ibid.*, p. 3).

There can be no doubt that the separation of church and state adopted by our Constitutional Fathers was a vast improvement over the prevalent state-church system. Although that system had proved bankrupt as a way whereby the church might exert its influence over society, yet it had stood, since Constantine's time, as an expression, however imperfect, of the conviction that the Christian ideal was one which concerned society as a whole. When the American Republic, for the first time in Christian history, dissolved the alliance, it created a gap which had to be filled in other ways.

The expansive revivalism of the nineteenth century filled it admirably for a time. When, toward the end of the century, the force of the revival movement was spent, the social gospel came on the scene. Its exponents explicitly proclaimed what had been only implicit in revivalism: organized Christianity had a duty not only to individuals, but also to society as a whole, to its institutions, to its laws, and to its public morals. In its turn, it sought to fill the function which had at least been symbolized by the close connection of the state with the church. It is significant that the first prophets of the social gospel emerged from the churches with a state-church tradition—that is, the Congregationalists, the Episcopalians, and the Unitarians.[6]

Most of the adherents of the social gospel welcomed and emphasized tendencies in doctrine which had been held at arm's length by their predecessors. These included an optimistic view of human nature consonant with the new shift from the preaching of repentance and a cataclysmic conversion to the emphasis on "Christian nurture," and with the high hopes they held for the transformation not only of individual men but of society as a whole. They were hospitable to the new critical approach to the Bible. They accepted the evolutionary hypothesis as a description of the way God was working out his plan in the world. With some—not all of the social gospel men—the evolutionary hypothesis was combined with a doctrine of the divine immanence in such a way as to issue in the view that the evolutionary process was a kind of automatic escalator which would in time (and perhaps less time than one might think) lift men to Utopian heights.

But if some of them were betrayed into a kind of cosmic compla-

---

[6] Hopkins, *Rise of the Social Gospel*, p. 318. Of course not all the American Churches with such a background made such a contribution. The Rev. J. H. W. Stuckenberg's brilliant *Christian Sociology* (1880) was almost the only noteworthy contribution of the Lutherans to the literature of the social gospel (Hopkins, *ibid.*, p. 111).

cency which we have since learned to think was unwarranted, they were not betrayed into complacency with the situation in which they found themselves. They fulfilled their function as critics of what they saw wrong with it.[7]

They may have used the language of the evolutionist and the social scientist but the word they had for their generation was a word from God, and they fulfilled the function of the prophets in rebuking unrighteousness in high places.

The theology of Walter Rauschenbusch, who came to be recognized as the representative leader of the whole movement, was much more fully in the evangelical tradition. It has been said of him that "he continued to speak the language of the prophets and St. Paul." [8] He accepted the critical approach to the scriptures and the evolutionary theory, but he shared the Pauline view of the sinfulness of man and the necessity of regeneration. "Both the consciousness of sin and the message of salvation must be enlarged and intensified, but they should not be rejected." [9] The framework of his thought was a thoroughgoing evangelicalism, and he phrased the conception of the kingdom of God, around which he built his social gospel, primarily in scriptural terms, drawn especially from the teaching of Jesus.

One other phase of the intellectual hospitality of the leaders of the social gospel was their willingness to use the data of the social sciences as a contribution to the understanding of the magnitude and nature of the problems which confronted them, and even as giving hints as to methods to be taken for their solution. The enemies of social justice were using concepts taken from economics—should not the friends of the workingman do the same? For instance, the doctrine that labor was no more than a commodity was combined with the "law of supply and demand" to support the contention that employers had no responsibility to pay their workmen any more than they must—for the market price of labor must fluctuate according to the demand. On the other hand, the social gospel men steadily proclaimed the duty of conserving the human values inseparable from

[7] In Josiah Strong's book, Our Country, was an incongruous mixture of both social criticism and "culture-Protestantism." See p. 311.

[8] H. R. Niebuhr, The Kingdom of God in America (Chicago and New York: Willett Clark & Company, 1937), p. 194.

[9] Winthrop S. Hudson, The Great Tradition of the American Churches (New York: Harper & Brothers, 1953), p. 233.

285

the wage-paying process. They went further, and appealed to the established connection between poverty and the complex operation of the market. Thus they countered the moralistic idea, too prevalent in evangelical circles, that poverty was simply the result of defects of character, such as laziness and dissolute spending.

In sum, the men of the social outlook were persuaded that the road between social righteousness and individual righteousness was a two-way street. An individual cannot be completely redeemed in an unredeemed society, any more than a society can be redeemed without a leaven of redeemed individuals in its midst. This truth was already implicit in the activities on behalf of social reform among the mid-century sons of the revival, though explicitly they maintained that the way to redeem society was to redeem individuals. Their successors emphasized the complementary truth that the redemption of society and its institutions was essential to the redemption of individuals, especially of those who had been victimized by it.

The most pressing problems within the purview of the social gospel movement were those raised by the industrialization of our society. There was, of course, the legacy of problems left from the era of Reconstruction: problems of civil rights and desegregation. To these was now added, in the eyes of those accustomed to see things largely from an economic point of view, the marginal employability of great numbers of Negroes. So viewed, their disabilities seemed but a more intense instance of the needs of the mass of white workers pitted against the owners of industry in a warfare which frequently broke out into overt violence. How could the slum dwellers' lot be mitigated, how could they be persuaded that the church's Christ had died for them? The prohibition of the liquor traffic was not neglected—quite the contrary; but the traffic was now regarded as a result, as well as a cause, of the miseries of the poor. How could society's treatment of the criminal be improved in such a way as to secure not merely the protection of society by his punishment, but even more his reclamation and restoration to the ranks of useful citizens?

All these and other questions occupied the horizon as the social gospel developed within the prevalent framework of a nationally organized society. However—and this was noticeable especially after the First World War—as the concept of a society international in scope and unity came into focus, the movement occupied itself likewise with questions of international comity, international law, arbitration, and replacing belligerent ways by peaceful ways of settling international disputes.

After this general account of the ideas borne aloft by the movement, we cannot pause further for more than a mention of some of its typical prophets. It is generally agreed that the "father of the social gospel" was Washington Gladden, a Congregationalist minister, who in 1876 published a series of lectures he had given Sunday evenings in his church under the title *Working People and Their Employers*.[10] He was to live until 1915. The movement owed him much for his continuous and strenuous insistence that ·economic questions were also moral questions, and that the pulpit should have something to say about them.

The greatest protagonist of the movement during the 1880's was Richard T. Ely, of Johns Hopkins University, a layman, who in 1889 published a book called *The Social Aspect of Christianity*.[11] During the final decade of the century, the most brilliant representative of the movement was another Congregationalist minister, George D. Herron. His base of operations was the Chair of Applied Christianity at Grinnell College in Iowa. In 1890, he published *The Message of Jesus to Men of Wealth*, in which the idea of stewardship was stressed. This idea ran like a thread throughout Herron's teaching, and was later made a plea for sacrificial living which ultimately would lead to a Christian socialism as an ideal, if not as a political program.[12]

Up until 1890, the new movement had been engaged in much earnest discussion, but had not done much in the way of organized activity. As C. H. Hopkins, the author of the standard history of the social gospel, says, it "had entered the national forum, but not as yet the national arena." [13]

Thereafter a number of organizations appeared, for shorter or longer periods, to exert influence in the whole field of social Christianity or to promote certain facets of it. Such, for instance, was the Open and Institutional Church League, founded in 1894, whose name indicates its purpose; it is said to be the first of the organizations which finally

[10] C. H. Hopkins, *op. cit.*, p. 24 ff.
[11] *Ibid.*, p. 68.
[12] *Ibid.*, pp. 185, 190-91.
[13] *Ibid.*, p. 117.

emerged as the Federal Council of Churches. A very active association of Episcopalians, called the Church Association for the Advancement of the Interests of Labor (C.A.I.L.), was formed in 1887 under the leadership of Henry Codman Potter of Grace Church in New York City. He had been preaching sermons on social themes in his pulpit, and after he became bishop, he continued his interest in them. He was probably the first churchman to repudiate sharply, in the interest of Christian values, the doctrine that labor was merely a commodity. C.A.I.L. was active till 1926. During its forty years of activity it held many discussion groups and disseminated much literature on social themes; it supported committees on tenements and sweatshops, and was responsible for the first observance of Labor Sunday in America.

On the whole, the most influential of these organizations was the "Brotherhood of the Kingdom," founded in 1892, largely by Baptists. The Brotherhood was a rather informal group, given to study of the principles which should animate the social gospel as found in scripture and Christian history. It held summer meetings in which the members communicated their enthusiasm and their researches to each other. Out of the fraternity thus nourished came a great dynamic for the prosecution of the cause. Its fundamental purpose was declared to be the propagation of the idea of the kingdom of God in word and deed. The subjects which came up for discussion were not all theoretical, however. Papers were read on socialism, the ethics of business, the techniques of social work, and so forth.

The spokesman from among this group whose writings gained him the widest influence, and even today may be taken as the best expression of the ideas and aspirations of the movement in its early maturity, was Walter Rauschenbusch. After a period of sacrificial and compassionate service in a church in the slums of New York City, he became a Professor at Rochester Theological School. He published his epoch-making books in the decade between 1907 and 1917. They were entitled: *Christianity and the Social Crisis, Christianizing the Social Order, The Social Principles of Jesus,* and, most comprehensive of all, *A Theology for the Social Gospel.* Nor should we forget the memorable *Prayers of the Social Awakening,* composed by himself, and instinct alike with social passion and Christian fervor.[14]

[14] *Ibid.,* p. 131 ff.

Socialism in any form had not gained many adherents, even among the workers in the United States, by or during the 1880's. Samuel Gompers, after leanings toward socialist doctrine in his earlier days, later consistently opposed it as a basis for the activities of American Federation of Labor. Nevertheless criticism of capitalist economy had spread widely enough to attract considerable attention. Fearful observers, remembering the railroad strike of 1877, dreaded the effect it might have on future outbreaks. Some of the leaders of the social gospel movement, notably Washington Gladden and A. J. F. Behrends, were more sympathetic. Indeed, the development of the social gospel may be regarded as in some sense the Protestant Church's response to the challenge of socialist criticism. None of the social gospel leaders took a really socialistic position until the 1890's; they were always few. But most took a greater or lesser part of socialism's criticism seriously, and cast about for alternatives compatible with Christian teaching.

The pioneer in the always small Christian socialist movement was the Protestant Episcopal clergyman, W. D. P. Bliss, who in 1889 founded the Society of Christian Socialists. He was convinced that the competitive economy developed by capitalism was incompatible with the Christian teaching on the Fatherhood of God and the brotherhood of man. Natural resources and capital, he held, were God's gift to mankind as a whole and should be used for the good of all. Bliss established the "Mission of the Carpenter" in Boston, and began a kind of social settlement in connection with it. He was a tireless worker, an indefatigable writer and speaker in the propagation of his ideas. He was the center of a group of zealous intellectuals who advocated attack on the problem of poverty from a number of angles; but their Christian socialism remained a spirit without crystallizing in a sharply defined program.[15]

C. The Social Gospel in Methodism

Methodism adopted the social gospel heartily when she did adopt it, but considerable resistance had first to be overcome. These barriers lay in her social and economic standing, in the distribution of her membership, and in her teaching tradition. We have already discussed the phenomenon of Methodism's rise to the middle class and the conse-

---

[15] Hopkins, op. cit., Chap. X, gives an account of Christian socialism, especially as advocated by Bliss and his society.

quent loss of sympathy with the laborers. Though the Methodists had been developing the middle-class mind, they were still predominantly to be found in small towns and the country. Only a small proportion of them had personal contact with the problems of the city, and were acquainted with the apparatus necessary to understand and prescribe for urban problems. They were overtaken unawares by the manifold complexities involved. And finally, the highly individualistic attitude which had become traditional in Methodist thinking in both religious and economic realms interposed to delay Methodist sympathy for and understanding of the plight of the urban poor. The Methodists of America, as well as those of England, had clung to the individualism prominent in Wesley's teaching longer and harder than to his message of social concern.

An article by David H. Wheeler in *Zion's Herald* in 1895 is so revelatory of the thinking of the majority of Methodists on this point that it deserves extensive quotation.

In common with other evangelical bodies, Methodism has only a New Testament economic creed. . . . All the allusions . . . in the New Testament recognize private property. . . . Most of us agree that the laws of ownership and contract are Christian, while abuses of these laws are emphatically unchristian. . . . Methodists are not socialists . . . in the scientific sense of that term. . . . The existing social order is the work mainly of Christian men. . . . Our eyes are open to the vast growth of wealth, to the dangers arising from [its concentration in a] few hands; but very few of us believe that the individual freedom condensed into the law of contract is a serious menace to the . . . less fortunate. . . . [It has been said that] "Labor does not get its just share." Some Methodists believe this is a true indictment, others do not. . . . Methodism has borne an honorable part in . . . [the] great uplift of the rewards of industrial ability. . . . If there has come a change [in her attitude from the time when Methodism was the church of the poor], it is because Methodism has made Methodists rich. . . . They have grown rich by ability, economy, and abstinence from expensive vices. Our people pay nothing toward the . . . drink bill of the nation. . . . The other vices cost . . . as much. . . . If these . . . millions were annually saved, the saving would abolish more poverty than any socialistic scheme. . . .

But we still . . . cheerfully go about abolishing . . . poverty in the old way—by character and by charity. . . . We are almost necessarily individualistic in our economic spirit: charity for the needy, character for all. A

290

socialistic scheme [would abolish] the difference between the results of good and bad character.

After going on to intimate that most of the poor workmen are Roman Catholics, and it is a problem for that church to solve, the author goes on to say, "any 'great duty' which Methodism owes to the economic struggles of the day can best be performed by plain gospel preaching, by teaching the simple Wesleyan economics . . . and by a sound conservatism in political feeling and action." [16]

Perhaps by way of reaction from the close involvement of the church with the violent political conflicts of the *post bellum* period, there was a good deal of feeling among Methodists that the best contribution they could make to the cure of public ills was by transforming the hearts of men. The corruption in government, for instance, can never be cleared up till such a transformation is wrought.[17] At the end of the century, the bishops were still holding out against taking sides in economic quarrels:

The solution of particular economic problems is not within [the church's] province. [It] has no authoritative message concerning trusts or labor unions, lockouts or strikes, capital or wages, tariffs and taxation, currency and colonies. . . . Character and not outward condition is the supreme sphere of the church. . . . [Its] largest contributions . . . are Christian men and not social theories. . . . The church must avoid partisanship toward classes. . . . Selfishness is the universal sin.[18]

On the other hand, individual Methodists, lay and ministerial alike, had already begun to express their conviction that the Christian message, and hence the Church's responsibility, included questions of broader social interest. John G. Woolley, a Methodist layman actively engaged in politics, said in 1895: "I have no question that monopoly, suffrage, franchise, money, labor, and so forth . . . are becoming moral and religious questions." [19] In 1900 Henry Clay Hall contributed an article to the *Methodist Protestant*, in which, after asserting that

[16] ZH, 73 (1895), 562.
[17] ZH, 53 (1876), 249.
[18] The Bishops' Address to the General Conference of the Methodist Episcopal Church, as reported in Zion's Herald, 78 (1900), 587-88.
[19] ZH, 73 (1895), 435.

economic inequalities were not decreed by divine law, but were the creation and the responsibility of society, he went on to say: "To study this problem and to master the many intricate questions connected with it and to arrive at its solution is . . . the work of Christianity."[20]

A Methodist lay preacher was an influential member of the earliest known organization in America for the proclamation of the social gospel, the Christian Labor Union of Boston, founded in 1872 and dedicated to improving the relations between labor and capital. The lay preacher was Edward H. Rogers, a ship carpenter by trade. He was for a time a member of the State Legislature and took a considerable part in its commission on the eight-hour day in 1865. Rogers told a Methodist convention that modern civilization stood in direct hostility to the great ideas of Christianity, and that the church should see to it that wealth was managed for the common good of the people.[21] The first labor church in this country was founded in Lynn, Massachusetts, by Herbert N. Casson, who had been a Methodist minister, but had withdrawn from the church because of impatience with its ineffectiveness in reaching the working class. His message was that the church must repent and be converted; it should take responsibility for developing the moral nature of the labor movement, and proclaim the co-operative commonwealth as the ideal of society. The labor church flourished during the last six years of the century, but declined when Casson left Lynn in 1900.[22]

D. Methodism and Specific Social Questions

As we turn to a consideration of the attitude of Methodism on more specific social questions, we discover that comment on them appears in the press before the General Conference pays much attention to them. It is difficult to find any orderly pattern in these comments; no special "Methodist" point of view emerges. The *Advocates* often reflect sectional differences; sometimes an advanced point of view taken by one editor may be repudiated by a later one in the same paper.

A striking instance of this is found in the attitude of *Zion's Herald*

[20] MP, 70 (1900), Feb. 28.
[21] C. H. Hopkins, *The Rise of the Social Gospel*, pp. 42-43, 48.
[22] C. H. Hopkins, *op. cit.*, pp. 86-87.

toward the treatment of criminals. In the first decade of its existence, that is in the 1820's, it was protesting against the infliction of the death penalty because it was neither needed as a deterrent, nor consistent with Christ's teaching against the exaction of an eye for an eye. But in 1888, the same paper was protesting against the proposal to introduce the electric chair for executions, doubting that its adoption would prove so deterrent as the current one; "it would also lack the elements of odium and terror." [23] This shift in position probably reflects Massachusetts' early pre-eminence in penology, and its subsequent loss of ground to other states.

In spite of these discrepancies, however, a general tendency is observable in Methodist papers to comment more widely on social questions as the century grows older, and to treat them as though they were proper subjects for judgment from the religious point of view.

1. CRIME AND THE TREATMENT OF CRIMINALS

Toward the middle of the century the *Methodist Quarterly Review* carried a long and learned article supporting the use of the death penalty; and in 1898 the *Christian Advocate* reported that the abolition of the death penalty in Colorado had been followed by an increase of murders, and that a popular move to restore it was on foot. "No legislative action is more absurd," it said, "than that which attempts to punish a murderer by simply guaranteeing him his board and clothing and life in an equable temperature," with a good prospect, especially if he has political influence, of ultimate release.[24]

At the very end of our period, the *Western Christian Advocate* is protesting against the morbid elaboration of violent crime in newspaper stories, and observing that such stories incite others to the same kind of violence.[25] A few weeks later, the same paper was protesting against "such a sentimental view of crime as makes it like an attack of measles, or chicken-pox." The criminal must be made to feel some real suffering for his crime; along with every effort for his reformation, the condemnation of society and of God for his lawbreaking and his guilt must be impressed upon him.[26]

[23] ZH, 2 (1824), 52; 4 (1826), 14; and *ibid.*, 66 (1888), 28.
[24] *Christian Advocate* (New York), 73 (1898), no. 44, (Nov. 3).
[25] WCA, 69 (1903), 4.
[26] *Ibid.*, Feb. 18.

2. ECONOMIC LIFE

a) Poverty

Toward the end of the century a number of articles appeared calling the attention of the Methodists to the existence of increasing poverty. This in itself is testimony to the rising prosperity of the Methodists as a whole. The burden of many of them is that most Methodists have no idea of the extent of poverty and misery which exists all around them.

O ye comfortably housed and well-fed Christians! There are woes in this world that you little dream of. If the hungry and shivering ones complain, do not curse them. If you were in their case, would you be silent? [27]

In the *Western Christian Advocate* is an article called "Prisoners of Poverty," in which is described the plight of women who do "shop work" in the garment industry, making "jeans pants," at a dollar for a dozen pairs, or, at best, for fifteen cents a pair. The writer gives an estimate that there were twenty-five thousand women and children working for wages in Cincinnati.[28] Yet two months later, the same paper carried an article by a minister who repudiated the statements of Henry George and other leaders that monopoly was the cause of poverty, in favor of the theory that the laborers were poor because they spent too much for drink.[29]

[27] WCA, 15 (1888), no. 3 (Jan. 18).

[28] *Loc. cit.*

[29] WCA, 15 (1888): no. 10 (March 7). Near the end of the century *Zion's Herald* said: "Followers of the Lord Jesus Christ do not realize as they ought the misery, suffering and injustice of the world in which they live. . . . Thousands of their brothers and sisters are huddled in haunts of misery and shame . . . fathers are driven to the devil by the merciless Moloch of poverty. . . . The dawning of the new epoch of social service in the spirit of Jesus Christ means the dawning of the new epoch of social redemption for millions of downcast and downtrodden men and women" (ZH, 73 [1895], 72). In 1903 a Methodist editor had to repudiate a charge of complacency made by a Unitarian minister: "Does Unitarianism itself speak out more boldly against social pretensions and popular evils than Methodism? Where are the Methodists who are using up all their spare time in gazing at the cornered coal, while poor folks are shivering or dying of cold? . . . Really, Brother Jones, we are compelled to ask for a bill of particulars" (WCA, 69 [1903], Jan. 21, p. 1). In 1901 the editor of the *California Christian Advocate* felt impelled to repudiate the charge that a breach was widening between Methodism and labor. This he did with enough heat to raise suspicion that he half-feared it was true (cited from the *California Christian Advocate* for Sept. 12, 1901, pp. 3, 4, by S. Raynor Smith, Jr. in "The Attitudes and Practises of the Methodist Church in California with Reference to Certain Significant Social Crises, 1847 through 1949" [unpublished Ph.D. dissertation, University of Southern California, 1955]), p. 151.

b) Unemployment

The question of unemployment does not take up much space in Methodist periodicals during the time under consideration. Great numbers of workmen were thrown out of work by the recurrent periods of business depression; but it seems to have been assumed for the most part that these periods were unavoidable and temporary, and before long there would be work for all again. Indeed, the *Methodist Protestant* refused to acknowledge that the unemployment of 1908 was necessary at all. "There is plenty of labor for every man who is willing to work," it said, and commended the Salvation Army as the only institution which was attacking the problem in a useful way by trying to transport workmen from the cities where there was a surplus of laborers to the farms where the farmers had not been able to get enough help.

> In our judgment the problem of labor will not be solved by labor unions, by legislative enactments, nor political gerry-mandering. . . . If a healthy redistribution could be effected with an equitable compensation agreed upon . . . the problem would be solved, and it will never be solved in any other way.[30]

c) The Labor Problem

For the first decades of the social gospel movement, the labor problem occupied the center of attention, indeed with the subsidiary questions of unionization, socialism, and strikes, it filled most of the horizon as well.

Frances Willard insisted that capital and labor were like two hands, neither of which can accomplish anything without the other.[31] An editorial in the *Western Christian Advocate* meant much the same thing when it said (without much surface justification), "Wealth and labor are mutual friends. We have often urged mutual concession as the only mode of solving this . . . problem."[32] Repelled by the violence of the struggle between labor and capital, rather than understanding what was at stake, Methodists often proposed the remedy of piety. "Nothing can right the wrongs of rich and poor alike but the spirit of Christ in the hearts of men," said the California Con-

[30] MP, 78 (1908), May 6, p. 3.
[31] Reported in ZH, 73 (1895), 84.
[32] WCA, 54 (1887), 241.

ference.[33] Bishop Vincent in the Episcopal Address of 1892 urged Methodists to consider prayerfully the question of personal rights and liberties on the one hand, and on the other to be watchful to conserve the rights of the common people. In other words, he warned against both monopolies and labor organizations.[34]

If one follows the utterances of two of the Northern *Advocates* on the question through the later decades of the nineteenth century, one finds that in general those of the *Western Christian Advocate* are more sympathetic with the struggles of the workingman than those of *Zion's Herald*. The latter sometimes suspended judgment or balanced it, sometimes declared flatly against the workman when disputes reached the stage of strike.

Considering the coal miners' strike in Pennsylvania in 1888, *Zion's Herald* refused to give judgment on its justifiability till the facts were all in; but violence on the part of the strikers can never be justified, it said.[35] In 1895 the same paper reflects on the figures given by the Labor Commissioner on the losses due to strikes, and concludes that the workmen themselves must see in them proof that a strike is "one of the clumsiest and most doubtful methods for . . . trying to improve . . . [their] condition." [36] The same year it says of a strike, "It ought never to have occured," and blames the men for violating their agreement, assuming that the employers would have granted their just demands.[37] The *Methodist Protestant* at the very end of the century professes no sympathy with "corporations . . . employing labor, who regard their employees as mere . . . machines." But it likes still less the prospect of an eight-hour day. "The employer works sixteen hours a day, . . . and [the Lord] has no time for idleness, amusement, and debauchery." [38]

Two editorials in one number of the *Western Christian Advocate* both manifest sympathy for the long hours imposed, in one case, on shop girls in New York City, in the other case, on coal handlers.

[33] S. Raynor Smith, op. cit., p. 154. A similar statement in ethical terms may be found in the *Western Christian Advocate:* "When all employees and all employers have a disposition to do exactly right, strikes will end" (55 [1888], no. 11 [March 14], p. 1).
[34] S. Raynor Smith, op. cit., p. 149.
[35] ZH, 66 (1888), Jan. 25, p. 28.
[36] Ibid., 73 (1895), 693. The editorial was headed "Strikes and Lockouts," but no comment whatever was made on lockouts.
[37] Ibid., 73 (1895), 129.
[38] MP, 70 (1900), June 13, p. 1.

In the latter case, it suggests that the strikers would further their own cause faster if they would choose a better class of men to represent and lead them. [39] The same year, the *Western* described sympathetically the hardships inflicted by the Hazelbrook Coal Company on their workers. Since they owned the houses, the Company could evict the men without mercy when a strike began; they owned the stores, and compelled the miners to trade only in them. The editorial said there ought to be a revolt against such brutality. Even the poor have rights which God commands all men to respect.[40] Of a strike on the Santa Fé Railroad the next year, it said: "Such strikes cause great inconvenience to travelers, but in the end they will lead to a better understanding . . . and thus will confer positive benefits at last." The fact that the strike had been accompanied by no violence was approved as commending the cause of the strikers to the public.[41]

Comment in the Southern *Advocates* was much less frequently trained on the industrial situation, because it was not nearly so tense as in the North. The North Georgia Conference in 1902 resolved to favor legislation to restrict the "labor of young children in factories, both as to age as to number of hours per diem." [42] The *Wesleyan Christian Advocate* admonished the cotton weavers of Lancashire to submit to a reduction of wages rather than depend on charity.[43]

The *Richmond Christian Advocate* complained of Northern interference on "poor white" mill operatives who were working longer hours for the same wages earned by Northern workers. It defended the practice by saying they do it because of competition, and that the workers are much better off than they were before they came to work in the mills.[44]

A long article in the Southern church's *Quarterly Review* faced the problems posed by the coming of textile mills to the South, and the migration of rural folk to the towns for work.

These questions must be answered by the capitalist if business continues successful. They must be answered by the state if her society is to be safe.

[39] WCA, 54 (1887), 98.
[40] *Ibid.*, 54 (1887), 337.
[41] WCA, 15 (1888), no. 12 (March 21), p. 1.
[42] MNGC, 1902, p. 41.
[43] WCAS, July 6, 1878.
[44] RCA, 33 (1898), April 21, p. 1.

They must be answered by the church if she is to prove true to the purpose of her existence. And they must be answered now.

The author makes the bold statement that the superintendent of the Southern cotton mill is pretty close to being an absolute monarch, and that the church can command the situation if she can get control of the superintendent. He makes an elaborate proposal for combining study for half the time with half-time work, and for the inclusion of a church and provisions for the physical and cultural welfare of the workers in the mill community. These "will be easy propositions when you have superintendents trained by the institution." [45]

d) *Big Business*

The Methodist press is more noteworthy for what it does not say about big business than for what it does. Protests against the misappropriation of public resources in the "Great Barbecue," reproofs of the ruthless methods by which industrialists wiped out or absorbed one another, while grinding workingmen between their wheels in the process, are few or nonexistent. During the time of the railroads' most predatory operations, the chief ground of complaints against them was that they ran trains on Sunday—and these were interspersed with thanks from the preachers for transportation at reduced rates to and from conferences.

Wall Street, on whose mysterious manipulations so many small investors and savers depended, was sometimes the target of criticism.[46] The immorality of bank managers who know failure is imminent, but give no warning, was reproved.[47] Dealing in futures and on margins was an object of protest.[48] In the *Quarterly Review* of the Southern church, Professor Dyer admits that some form of dealing in futures is essential to modern business, but the kind in which no commodities change hands amounts to little more than a bet as to where the price will be at a certain time, and is more nearly akin to gambling than to legitimate business.

Professor Dyer also condemns the temporary monopoly of a commodity called a "corner." It is reprehensible because it combines

[45] QRS (third series), 35 (1909), p. 67 ff.
[46] For example, in ZH, 49 (1872), 583.
[47] WCAS, for July 13, 1878.
[48] *Ibid.*, Jan. 21, 1882.

with certain elements of gambling an unjustifiable intention to profit by an artificially induced scarcity.[49] One comment by Dr. Wheeler of Meadville, Pa., traces the existence of dishonest companies to the speculative thirst in the people themselves, who keep hoping to get something for nothing.[50] Toward the end of the century increasing attention is given to the dangers, as reflected chiefly in rising prices, of the "trusts"; also to the more scandalous operations of stock market manipulators. This was noticeable in 1900, and reflected (perhaps partly inspired) the popular fear which culminated in Theodore Roosevelt's "trust-busting" campaign.

3. THE CITY'S CRY

The General Conference (North) of 1848 urged the ministers not to concentrate on work in the cities. But during the next quadrennium the call of the city became too great to be ignored, and the General Conference of 1852 urged that "the myriads of immigrants who are constantly crowding to our country be not neglected." [51] The attack on the spiritual destitution of the cities has taken three forms chiefly: city missions, in which the chief form of activity was evangelization; institutional churches, which combined evangelization with social service, and the social settlement movement, which because of its nature could not carry on a set program of worship, much less of evangelization.

The first kind is the oldest: an example is the Boston City Missionary Society (interdenominational), founded in 1817. Its object was "not to give physical relief, but to preach the glorious Gospel of Jesus Christ." [52] The institutional church was a device which, without giving up the program of evangelization, sought to minister also to the physical, social, cultural, and intellectual needs of the populations in city areas. The first institutional church in Methodism grew up under the ministry of J. W. Magruder in Cincinnati. He said that downtown churches could "succeed only by being an institution of all-round salvation . . . with educational, musical, and industrial work doing their part . . . along with the sermon." By 1895 Magruder's

---

[49] QRS (3rd series), 35 (1909), 719 ff.
[50] WCA, 62 (1895), 186.
[51] Frederick A. Norwood, "The Americanization of the Wesleyan Itinerant" (unpublished ms.), p. 15.
[52] ZH, 73 (1895), 192.

Wesley Chapel included a kindergarten, a day nursery, a legal aid society, a building association, and a visitation society.[53] The idea is capable of indefinite variations which were tried out in other Methodist Churches, such as Calvary and Washington Square Churches in New York City. Some missions of the spiritual sort successfully absorbed the functions demanded by the new program. One of these was the mission of Henry Morgan, which later became the Morgan Memorial of Boston with its Church of All Nations, its industrial plants which give "not charity but a chance" to the destitute, and other features which have spread to a number of cities in the "Goodwill Industries." The Institutional Church movement was promoted by the General Conference of 1892, which authorized the combination of effort made possible by the City Evangelization Union. The movement flourished for a while under this stimulus, but most of the missions have since yielded up their more secular ministries to secular agencies.[54] The Social Settlement movement, as it has flourished in this country, and especially in England, has been manned by religious people for the most part, but its primary purpose is one which cuts across denominational lines, and so has been content to dispense with religious services. The Methodist Church has not participated deeply in such projects.

In 1895 *Zion's Herald* was mourning the loss of the downtown churches Boston Methodism had given up. After speaking of the influx of foreigners, the article said: "Now when the church is awaking to the duty of ministering to these strangers, we look longingly but in vain for the sanctuaries we have deserted.[55]

a) *Immigration*

The immigrant population represented an intensification of the problems presenting themselves to Protestants during the latter part of the nineteenth century. The immigrants were, for the most part, Roman Catholics with no inhibitions against the use of alcoholic beverages or enjoying themselves on Sunday, and their increasing numbers here represented a threat of disturbing proportions to the Protestant ethos. As a consequence, Methodist papers, along with the rest of the Protestant press, paid a good deal of attention to the

[53] BHMM, III, 67.
[54] *Ibid.*, p. 68.
[55] ZH, 73 (1895), pp. 98-99.

300

matter. A good deal of it was by way of "viewing with alarm." Protestants did their best by establishing foreign language missions, and by trying to protect the new arrivals from the exploitation of the liquor business; but their efforts were quite inadequate to the task. The Protestant forces of the country asked for restrictions on immigration long before they were accorded; it is significant that the quota system was not imposed on immigration in any fashion till the need of the expanding industries for labor was thoroughly satisfied.[56] In this, as in so many other cases, the insight of the religious folk became actuality when the considerations they advanced were re-enforced by factors of more "practical" import. It must be said, too, that the labor unions had been seeking the same end for some time, so that the restrictive enactments were as much their victory, as the churches', if not more so.

The Methodists were not unaware of the economic aspects of the situation, and did not hesitate to cite them. For instance, Zion's Herald argued in 1896 that immigration (especially by "the vast throngs of ignorant and brutalized peasantry from . . . eastern and southern Europe") *should* now be restricted to protect the American rate of wages, and it *could* be because the railroads were built, the canals dug, and the public land occupied.[57] That paper's discussion of the subject goes back at least to 1880.[58]

The Chinese constituted a special case, one of more concern for the West than for the East. They were the first to feel the resentment of the California miners when the "digging" became crowded. Work among the Chinese was not undertaken immediately; but the first Chinese minister was ordained in Los Angeles in 1868. The next year the California Conference declared: "Any attempt to repel Chinese immigration by means of intimidation and discriminatory action is . . . anti-Christian." In 1870 the same conference established a Chinese Mission Institute.[59]

---

[56] This was in 1921. Of course not all the idealistic considerations were on one side. Restrictive laws meant the abandonment of the concepts of "asylum" and "melting pot," long-cherished elements in America's way of thinking about itself.

[57] ZH, 74 (1896), 357.

[58] *Ibid.*, 57 (1880), 188. This article stressed the "vital importance that our home missionary institutions . . . should be vigorously prosecuted; and the right of suffrage should be sacredly guarded . . . from ignorance and superstition."

[59] S. Raynor Smith, Jr., *op. cit.*, pp. 76-79, 137-41.

In spite of protests, the first of the Chinese Exclusion Acts was passed in 1882 in a highly insulting and discriminatory form. The free arrival of laborers from the Spanish-speaking Southwest was not stopped; there was more behind the exclusion of the Chinese than the protection of the native-born workmen. The Mexican-born workman who "arrived" could—and frequently did—also "depart." Also he did not manifest the disposition, so prominent in the Chinese, to acquire property and on the basis of that and unremitting toil to attract an eager market.

A broadly Christian and humane expression of interest in the Chinese in this country was contributed by a missionary in China, H. H. Lowry, who urged his fellow Americans to stop deploring the "indigestibility" of the Chinese and ask rather what we owe him.

Had we any responsibility in bringing him here with all his vices [e. g., must we share with Great Britain the responsibility for forcing the opium habit on him]? Do we owe him anything for building our railroads, developing our mines, and redeeming valuable farm lands from the swamps and covering them with golden harvests? And, on higher grounds, are we not under special obligations to give him the Gospel which has crowned our own land with such inestimable blessings? [60]

4. RACE PROBLEMS

a) *The Civil Rights of the Negro*

The enfranchisement of the Negro, imposed during the Reconstruction period, dwindled away to almost nothing before steady Southern opposition. The opposition went through two phases: the first was exerted through extra-legal means by the Ku Klux Klan, employing terrorism and violence.[61] This began before the Recon-

[60] WCA, 54 (1887), 307.

[61] Farish says (op. cit., p. 226 and n.), "Although as late as 1876 the *Methodist Review* of the Northern Connection charged that their condemnation [of the personal violence wrought by the Klan against Negroes] was 'so mixed with apologies, and with curses against the Government and the North, that to any Northerner and to any Ku Klux' it would be apparent that the Southern journals 'held the outrages to be about right,' the [Southern] *Advocates* became increasingly energetic in their denunciation of all deeds of violence against the blacks." Farish quotes Summers ("the dogmatic editor of the Nashville *Advocate*") as saying, "we are . . . indignant when the insinuation is made that the Methodist Episcopal Church, South, was the protégé of the Ku Klux conspirators. We assume not a single Southern Methodist ever belonged to the Klan, whatever it might be."

struction period ended, and lasted beyond it until the arrival of the so-called "bourbons" at political power enabled the Southern states to give legal form and permanence to the process of disfranchisement. The process was complete early in the twentieth century in most of the Southern states.[62] It took various forms in various states, grandfather clauses, tricky registration laws, and so on. If the earlier methods were violent, the later ones were patently fraudulent. The grandfather clauses, the poll tax laws, and other legislation were enacted with the deliberate purpose of accomplishing indirectly what could not be done directly, the Constitution's provisions being what they were. Ostensibly designed to keep illiterate persons from the polls, they were so administered as to be a matter of color: illiterate Negroes were kept from voting, but illiterate whites were not. Though, as we have seen, the Southern Methodist press denounced the violence of the earlier methods, and continued to do so through the "lynching period" at the turn of the century, it allowed the process of codifying the disfranchisement into law go unchallenged. The violence was deplorable; but to turn the law, which should be the instrument of securing equity to all men, into an instrument for depriving a large proportion of them of their civil rights, was equally so.[63]

Disappointment at the fading of their dream of creating equal

---

The last is a pretty large assumption—one the present writer would not dare to make of his small Methodist congregation in Pennsylvania in 1926, let alone the whole Southern Methodist Church in the 1870's. Nevertheless, Farish has made his case for the Advocates' denunciation of violence against Negroes both in the 'seventies, and toward the end of the century, when lynchings increased in number. The point to be made here, however, is that, though extra-legal violence was vigorously denounced, the process of codifying the Negroes' disabilities, civil and social, into "Black Codes," "Grandfather Clauses," and "Jim Crow Laws" evoked little, if any, protest in the Southern Methodist press.

[62] Agitation which had begun much earlier in Mississippi culminated in the late 'eighties in a revision of the state constitution which imposed conditions for the franchise which no Negro could fulfill. South Carolina followed in the 'nineties. In 1898 Louisiana, following another device, embodied the "grandfather clause" in its electoral law, which required adding to the permanent voting list the names of all voters whose fathers and grandfathers were qualified to vote in the State in 1867—a year when no Negroes could vote. By 1910 the Negroes had been disfranchised also in North Carolina, Alabama, Virginia, Georgia, and Oklahoma (J. H. Franklin, *From Slavery to Freedom*, pp. 335-36).

[63] Gerald W. Johnson, "a distinguished journalist and man of letters, a Southerner by birth and residence," in a recent article insists on the original disingenuousness of the legislation in question, and also on its deleterious effects on subsequent Southern political and cultural life ("To Live and Die in Dixie," *Atlantic Monthly*, 206 [1960], No. 1 [July], 29-34).

opportunity for the Negroes enfeebled protest in the North, but did not silence it. "We have given the freedmen the ballot, [but] it is becoming more and more apparent that our beautiful . . . theory of equality is finding very poor exemplification in actual life." So wrote the editor of *The Presbyterian* as copied in *Zion's Herald* in 1896.[64] "The friends of the Negro have been badly rattled of late because of his slow progress," the *Herald* wrote on its own account not long after.[65] Nevertheless, protests at Southern policy continued. So did Methodist help, administered by the Freedmen's Aid and Southern Education Society, which kept up its work all through our period. The efforts of the Supreme Court to buttress the Negroes' rights by rulings on their right to sit on juries in 1880, elections in which intimidation was employed to keep them from the polls, and South Carolina's attempt to circumvent the Fifteenth Amendment by their constitutional article on suffrage in 1895 evoked critical comment.[66] Protest in Southern Methodist papers apparently was not made. One of the prices the South paid for its policy of racial unity and white supremacy was the stifling of dissent, which had been made so reprehensible, by public pressure, that even Christian opinion, one of the functions of which is to criticize the society in which it operates, was silenced.

b) *Social Segregation*

In private social gatherings, there never was much question of the mingling of the two races in the South. In political meetings, there was not much likelihood that the Negroes, who were excluded from a voice at the polls, would willingly forgather. We have already seen how the color line was drawn in religious and educational institutions.[67] In public places and conveyances segregation, at first only loosely observed as a matter of preference and custom, became rigidly codified in "Jim Crow" laws toward the end of the century. It began in the deep South, but in Virginia and the Carolinas little public segregation existed till after 1900.[68] This process seems to have evoked some comment in Northern Methodist papers, but rather mild and

---

[64] ZH, 74 (1896), 537.
[65] ZH, 78 (1900), 645.
[66] ZH, 57 (1880, 84; 73 (1895), 641; WCA, 15 (1888), Jan. 11, p. 1 and Jan. 18, p. 1.
[67] Pp. 203 ff.
[68] Hodding Carter, op. cit., p. 477.

sparse it was. *The Southwestern Christian Advocate*, published in New Orleans by the Northern church, tells an interesting story of an early "riders' strike" in Atlanta.

[Segregation] was tried on the line which leads to our Clark University till the company saw that the school and community were profiting more by their exercise in walking than the company was; then it said come on, we were just joking.[69]

Typical of the comments which appeared in the Northern Methodist press late in the nineteenth century is the folowing:

The colored people of Georgia have appealed to the railroad commission to prevent unjust discrimination against them on Georgia railroads. The commission ought to redress their grievances and we believe it will do it. It is time to end that wrong in Georgia and through the whole South.[70]

There are indications that the Methodist papers realized that all was not as it should be between the races in the North, and were concerned about it. *Zion's Herald* carried an unsigned article on "The Negro in Boston," which spoke of the difficulties Negroes were having in finding living quarters outside certain well-defined districts; birds of a feather were being *compelled* to flock together. Even those capable of taking on skilled work or with training for the professions had little scope for the exercise of their gifts. Boston opens her schools, but closes her shops.

We fail to see any difference in the nature of the feelings against the Negro north or south of Mason and Dixon's Line. It is a mere matter of the way they are expressed.[71]

Southern Methodist opinion on the race question can be glimpsed from several articles in their *Quarterly Review*. The first, quite early

---

[69] SWCAN, 32 (1897), Feb. 4, 1.

[70] WCA, 15 (1888), no. 12 (March 21), 1.

[71] ZH, 74 (1896), 454. The *Methodist Protestant* describes the determined fight made by the parents of white children in New York City when an attempt was made by the school board to force a colored teacher on them. "It all shows that the races cannot be mixed anywhere without trouble, and that Northern people are just like Southern people when the matter is forced upon them" (MP, 70 [1900], Jan. 10, p. 2).

in the century, consists of a book review by Mrs. John D. Hammond in which she describes the new democracy of the South as "not a democracy of outward institutions, but a democracy of the heart, where each man knows, and rejoices to know that he is his brother's keeper." She defends the seeming smallness of the amounts spent for education by the Southern states by pointing out that a far greater proportion of their total revenue goes for that purpose than in the wealthier states of the North. As to the Negroes' political status, she admits that no democracy can permanently maintain a dependent class. The distinction made between the ignorant white voter and the ignorant Negro is justified by the success with which it met an actual situation. "The real effect of these amendments is, and will be increasingly, to give the qualified Negro a voice at the polls." At present the dilemma of the South is that she must maintain a democracy in the presence of a class which is "incapable of self-government." She pleads for patience and respect instead of blame from the lookers-on.[72]

In 1914, somewhat beyond the end of our period, but useful nevertheless for our purpose here, the Southern *Review* published an address made at Nashville on "Fifty Years of Freedom," by Booker T. Washington, and an article by Walter Rauschenbusch called "The Belated Races and the Social Problem." Washington said:

If I have to solve the problem of living by the side of any white man, I prefer to take my chances . . . by the side of a *Southern white man*. There is . . . something in the atmosphere of the South which makes the black man and the white man understand each other.

In a polite, kindly way we should constantly remind the officers in the cities where we live that our people . . . are not treated with justice in the matter of lighting, streets, or in the conveniences of sewerage and drainage.

We should remind the white man . . . that, if he expects us to live a clean, orderly life, we should have better facilities for the education of our children. In one county of the South, each white child had spent upon him for his education last year about twenty-one dollars, while each Negro child in the same county had spent upon him for his education about ninety-eight cents.

We should too, with equal politeness, remind those in charge of the railroads of the South that in few cases do our people receive justice or are

[72] QRS (third series), 31 (1905), 28 ff.

treated with common humanity when they travel upon the railroads.[73]

Rauschenbusch said:

We of the North have come to realize that the problem of the black man was dealt with fifty years ago in anger . . . and therefore solved very poorly. We realize that we cannot solve it for the South. But no solution by Southern men can be permanent which does not satisfy the Christian conscience of the whole nation. . . . The Christian way out is to take our belated black brother by the hand and urge him along a road of steady and intelligent labor, of property rights, of family fidelity, of . . . pride . . . in his race's achievements; and this work can best be done when North and South join hands . . . not ostracizing, but aiding and honoring everyone who puts his life alongside that of the Negro in the spirit of Him who never broke the bruised reed . . . but through [the poor] worked miracles.[74]

The editor of the *Review* preferred Washington's approach. He said:

The sterling article of Booker T. Washington will help relieve suspicions and pessimism of good men of other sections of the country who, like Professor Rauschenbusch, do not know as much about the race problem in the South as Booker Washington does, and as the Negroes and white people of the South do.[75]

c) *Methodist Work for Negroes*

The Northern Methodists continued to promote and defend their work in the South, while the Southern church continued to nourish resentment against their presence there, and to feel that even the work among the Negroes was not being done the right way. A speaker at the Northern General Conference of 1896 reminded his hearers that "the Colored Conferences" constituted one-twelfth of the entire membership of the church.[76] The New York *Advocate* reported in 1898 a constant growth, not only in the numbers, but in the intelligence, morals, and Christian culture of the Negro membership in the South.[77] *The Southwestern Christian Advocate* rejoiced that

[73] QRS (third series), 40 (1914), 297-98.
[74] Ibid., pp. 258-59.
[75] Ibid., p. 259, n.
[76] ZH, 74 (1896), 329.
[77] The Christian Advocate (New York), 73 (1898), no. 21 (May 26).

after prolonged urging in its columns a Negro Epworth League Secretary had been appointed for work among the Colored Conferences in the South.[78]

Bishop Foss cited the opinion of "a distinguished Southerner" to the effect that Northern teaching was leading the Southern Negro to "inevitable destruction." He needs "sensible, kindly instruction from those of us who know his place, and will see that he does not get out of it." Bishop Foss protested that the Negro would find his place if doors were opened to him. It was not the educated, but the uneducated Negro, who menaced our society.[79] The Bishop goes on then to plead for continued support of the Freedmen's Aid and Southern Educational Society. "The Southern Church," said Zion's Herald, "ought to be grateful for what we have done, instead of hindering our work." [80]

The Southern Methodists, however, retorted that they stood aloof because they had been regarded as unfit to help. They described the formation of the Colored Methodist Episcopal Church as an attempt to save a remnant of those who had not yet been lured away by the proselyting "of other denominations." "We labored," they said, "and others entered into our labors." [81]

The Southern church, in the meantime, took its educational responsibility very seriously. Conference organs and the conferences themselves frequently presented the claims of their "literary institutions," including Paine College for Negroes. Missions to Negroes were continued, though not vigorously. In 1886, the North Georgia Conference appointed a missionary to Negroes, "the first, and only appointment, as yet, in pursuance of the action of the last General Conference." [82]

The magnitude of the problem created by the contiguity of the two races in close quarters in the South is sharply outlined by the

[78] SWCAN, 32 (1897), Feb. 25, p. 13.
[79] ZH, 74 (1896), 27.
[80] Ibid., 74 (1896), 258.
[81] Article by Foss, editor of the Nashville Christian Advocate in ZH, 74 (1896), 258. It was a sign of growing tolerance of the views in the other half of the United States that Northern papers were beginning to print articles by men of the Southern church such as this one, and that the Southern Methodist Review could print articles by Northerners like Rauschenbusch (above, p. 1059). This in spite of the fact that the articles were often, indeed usually, frankly critical.
[82] WCAS, Dec. 22, 1886.

persistence of colonization schemes, or of less ambitious plans to expel numbers of them to other states. *The Western Christian Advocate* protested against a plan ascribed to "some citizens of the South" to ship colored people to South America.[83] In 1900 *Zion's Herald* likewise protested against a deportation scheme. In times when work was slack, the economic competition of the Negro increased the aversion in which he was held, and sometimes brought down violence, more or less organized, on his head.[84]

The Southern Methodists discouraged all such schemes. H. D. Farish says:

> Perhaps the chief influence exerted by the Methodist Episcopal Church, South, on the race problem was the outcome of the efforts exerted by its leaders to convince the Southern people of the possibility of a satisfactory adjustment between the two races.[85]

A critic might be inclined to raise the question, "A solution satisfactory *to whom?*" But Farish's point is clear: the Methodists of the South insisted that driving the Negroes out of a community by intimidation or more highly concerted plans of deportation or colonization was no solution at all. *The Nashville Christian Advocate* said:

> It is not schemes of colonization, but efforts at Christianization we should encourage. Religion will remove passion and violence from white ruffians who would oppress a feeble people, and it will cleanse Negro agitators of those dangerous forms of ambition and insolence which impel some of them to seek the establishment of Negro governments that they may rule over them.[86]

In 1890, the same paper was still insisting on this theme, occasionally with expressions of impatience that the North would not let them settle it their own way.

> We will settle our troubles, and we will do it without forcing the colored people to emigrate, or asking the government to assist in colonizing them

---

[83] WCA, 15 (1888), no. 5 (Feb. 1), p. 1.
[84] SWCAN, 32 (1897), Jan. 21, p. 1: "Denounced for worthlessness, persecuted for his diligence." ZH, 73 (1895), 177, has a story of Negroes fired on by white unionists in New Orleans, after refusing to be driven away from work by white men who said there wasn't enough work for both white and black workers.
[85] H. D. Farish, *op. cit.*, p. 229.
[86] *Nashville Christian Advocate*, Oct. 10, 1879, quoted in H. D. Farish, *op. cit.*, p. 231.

in Africa. It is true that we are 'hopelessly Southern', as a certain writer recently put it, but we have manhood and statesmanship and religion. We can solve our problems honorably to all.[87]

Add to this the honorable protest repeatedly lodged by the Southern *Advocates* against the lynchings which increased ominously at the turn of the century, and the best part of the story of the work of Southern Methodism for the free Negroes is told. Farish himself was constrained to admit that the Southern Methodist church showed "little inclination to revise its former notions with regard to the relations of the races in Church and in Society." [88] The subsequent story of the race problem as dealt with by Methodists is so intimately bound up with the union of its three branches, that it lies beyond the scope of this volume, and must be dealt with in Volume II of this series.

5. War and Peace

The social gospel did not include serious consideration of the question of war till after the First World War. Antiwar sentiment had existed in a thin stream in the United States from colonial days. It took its rise in Pennsylvania, where the Quakers and the nonresistant German sects exemplified as well as preached it. It can hardly be said to have run an uninterrupted course throughout the century; and its course during that time was quite as much fed by the humanitarian and optimistic currents set on their way by the Enlightenment as by the Christian tradition.

Benjamin Franklin was an early supporter of peace societies. After the War of 1812 two Unitarians, Noah Worcester and William Ellery Channing, began a movement to banish war from the world. Opposition to the War with Mexico broadened into opposition to all war by the transcendentalist Emerson, and put his neighbor Henry Thoreau into the Concord jail for refusing to pay his war tax. We have already mentioned the nonresistance doctrines of William Lloyd Garrison. The Civil War, devastating as it was, does not appear to have produced any revulsion against war as such in the hearts of either victors or vanquished. As that war faded into the past, the

[87] *Nashville Christian Advocate*, Feb. 22, quoted in H. D. Farish, *op. cit.*, p. 231, n.
[88] H. D. Farish, *op. cit.*, p. 232.

nation slipped, not without some opposition it is true, but on the whole, almost imperceptibly into the imperialism which has been the breeder of so many wars, even though, perhaps even because, it is often found consorting with a high ideal.

A notable early exponent of the social gospel itself was not exempt from adopting an ideology which had been used for less lofty purposes than he intended, and would be so used again. Josiah Strong, a Congregationalist minister, and for thirty years a dynamic leader of the social gospel movement, sprang into national prominence with the publication in 1885 of a book called *Our Country*. In a trenchant analysis of social conditions in our own nation he exposed the dangers which threatened it in the concentration of great wealth in the hands of a few, the growing gap between the rich and the poor, the corrupting influence of mammonism on the ballot box, and other such dislocations of equity.[89] In one chapter of his book, however (which seems at this distance to consist but ill with the rest), he turned to a glorification of Anglo-Saxon American qualities, institutions, and religion, making their superiority a warrant for carrying them into the remote quarters of the globe.

This race of unequalled energy, with all the majesty of numbers and wealth behind it—the representative, let us hope, of the largest liberty, . . . the highest civilization—having developed peculiarly aggressive traits calculated to impress its institutions upon mankind, will spread itself over the earth.

Before this "superior race," the inferior races were only precursors, destined to give way, voices crying in the wilderness, "Prepare ye the way of the Lord!" [90]

Imperialism was a large, though of course not the only issue in the election of 1900, and the nation put its seal of approval on it by electing William McKinley over William Jennings Bryan. McKinley it was who, not long before, had said to a gathering of his Methodist brethren, in explanation of his decision to hold on to the territory captured from Spain:

[89] C. H. Hopkins, op. cit., p. 100.
[90] Quoted from Merle Curti, *The Growth of American Thought* (New York: Harper & Brothers, 1943), p. 671.

I walked the floor of the White House night after night, and I am not ashamed to tell you, gentlemen, that I went down on my knees and prayed to Almighty God for light and guidance more than one night. And one night late it came to me. . . . There was nothing left for us to do but to take them all, and to educate the Filipinos, and uplift and civilize and Christianize them, and by God's grace do the very best we could by them as our fellow-men for whom Christ also died.[91]

Turning to a consideration of peace sentiment among Methodists, we should recall first that there were a few conscientious objectors among them during the Revolutionary War.[92] Thereafter, only one notice of conscientious objection has come to light, and, as will be seen in a moment, that instance happened in circumstances which make it difficult to conclude that it was a matter of broad Christian principle. Notices of interest in the removal of the scourge of war from among the evils with which humanity was beset, however, do occur from time to time in the Methodist press.

Zion's Herald adverted to it twice during its first year. The keynote of its protest was: "War is a great crime. It is not so much a violation as a repeal of the laws of morality and of God. The precepts of the Bible are directly opposed to the maxims of war."[93]

Articles depicting the horrors of war in graphic terms and enlarging on the waste of material goods and human energies involved occur from time to time, but the topic was not a frequent one.[94] In 1835 the *Western Christan Advocate*, after mentioning that there are several peace societies in the East, called for the creation of one west of the mountains. The abolition of war, it said, cannot be accomplished by a miracle, hence the need for societies. "The fundamental principle of society is that *all* war is inconsistent with the spirit of the Gospel."[95]

There was some increase in comment on the subject after the Civil War. The *Richmond Christian Advocate* made enquiry among min-

[91] Quoted from C. and M. Beard, *op. cit.*, II, 375-76.
[92] See above, pp. 90 ff.
[93] ZH, I (1823), 136.
[94] MM, 8 (1825), 29 ff. ZH, 3 (1825), 9. *Ibid.*, 6 (1828), 4 (This is a report of a forerunner of the machine gun, run by steam or compressed air; "the horrible idea and proposal have been excused by saying, that to prove the possibility of such havoc, must have the effect of putting an end to war altogether"). *Ibid.*, 15 (1844), no. 36 (Sept. 4). NWCA, 24 (1876), Feb. 23.
[95] WCA, 1 (1835), 203.

isters after a Quaker had reported a revulsion against war in the Southern mind, and found that, though most ministers said war was wrong, yet national self-defense is necessary, and the innocent must be protected.[96]

The *Quarterly Review* of the Northern church published an article headed "Christianity and the War Power," just at the war's end. The author concluded: "There is nothing in the true scriptural notion of nonresistance which can interfere with the right of a government to wage and conduct war." In the General Conference of 1864, one of the members, presumably intoxicated with the wine of victory, launched into a summons to extend God's work behind the Army still further south, into Mexico:

There are, sir, three B's in the divine government, which follow each other in marked succession—ball, bayonet, and Bible . . . the martial sons of Columbia, with the 200,000 veteran colored troops, will vindicate the rights of a sister republic and drive the frog-eating Frenchmen from the soil of Mexico. . . . Let us . . . [strike] the manacles from the limbs of our fellow men . . . and thus recompense them for the wrongs we have inflicted upon them. But to keep them ever dependent upon us will be but to dwarf their nature, [and] defeat the efforts of Christian philanthropy.

The *Advocate* which reported this outburst apparently did not take it very seriously, for it headed its notice, "Military Apocalypticism in the General Conference." [97]

The ninth General Conference of the Methodist Protestant Church in 1864, attended by delegates from the states of Maryland, North Carolina, Virginia, and Alabama, inserted in its *Discipline* the following decision: "The bearing of arms in military service by ministers of the Methodist Protestant Church is inconsistent with their professional calling, and the nature and intent of their ordination vows." [98] This statement alleges ministerial standing rather than gospel principles as the ground of their action; and is, in view of the time and composition of the body which made it, open to the suspicion that objection to serving in the Federal Army *at that time* had something to do with it.

[96] RCA (new series), 1 (1867), no. 2, first page.
[97] NWCA, 12 (1864), 154.
[98] D. J. Drinkhouse, *op. cit.*, II, 467-68.

Toward the end of the century, the tone of *Zion's Herald* had changed. In 1895 it justified war as one example of the force that lies at the basis of all government. It was by war that the national life had been saved, and slavery removed. "Everything is sanctified by sacrifice and suffering, and without the shedding of blood, there is no remission of national sins or advance in liberal institutions." [99] During the same year, however, it urged that, while all sympathy should be accorded the rebels against Spain in Cuba, the nation ought to keep its neutrality, and suppress any movement secretly to supply them with war material.[100] The next year it was supporting arbitration between Great Britian and the United States.[101]

The *Southwestern Christian Advocate* of the Northern church was a good deal more belligerent. It was glad that the proposed arbitration with Britain affected only two nations and no more. "We are sorry to confess it," they said, "but we find it impossible to settle in our mind that a war with some foreign nation would not be helpful to the United States. . . . Our flag is not respected . . . as it should be. . . . These [Northern and Southern] sections of our nation . . . we fear will never be united till they are called to stand together against some common foe. Then, too, what the Negro needs . . . in this country is to be let alone. . . . What would be more absorbing than two or three years of good hard fighting by land or sea." [102]

In 1898, while the fever for war with Spain over Cuba was mounting, *The Christian Advocate* opposed our entering on hostilities; but once war was declared, supported it,[103] while deprecating its effects on movements for political and social reform.[104]

Among the Southern papers, the *Richmond Christian Advocate* showed considerable skepticism in the the face of the bellicose propaganda, and said: "The weight of evidence favors a spontaneous combustion in the powder stores [of the Maine]." [105] After the declaration of war it declared its policy as follows: "The President has uttered the word. There is war. Let us maul well the Spaniard, but

[99] ZH, 73 (1895), 328.
[100] *Ibid.*, p. 209.
[101] *Ibid.*, 74 (1896), 540.
[102] SWCAN, 32 (1897), April 1, p. 1.
[103] *The Christian Advocate* (New York), 73 (1898), no. 17 (April 28).
[104] *Ibid.*, no. 23, June 9.
[105] RCA (new series), 33 (1898), Feb. 24, p. 3.

never forget to settle with the Congress that coerced the country into war." [106] And still later: "Cruel . . . has been the path of Spain on the American continent . . . [but] where are the red men of our own country? Are [we] pure enough to lay the lash on guilty Spain?" [107] The *Wesleyan Christian Advocate* also counseled patience in the face of the blowing up of the "Maine," and, when war came, faced it with regret, believing it might have been averted if Spain had had "a better type of Christianity, and hence a better form of civilization." [108]

Early in the twentieth century the *Western Christian Advocate* printed an article by the still-active pioneer of the social gospel, Washington Gladden. He wrote at some length of the destructiveness of newly improved weapons, and concluded:

Possibly there may be yet one more great war, to place before the eyes of the world . . . the facts we have been considering; but that . . . will not be, if everything [possible] is done . . . to . . . create the public sentiment . . . to find some less monstrous method. . . .

The arbitrament of reason is far more likely to secure justice than the arbitrament of force.[109]

E. The Methodist Social Creed

A good way to measure the rise of the tide of social interest in the Methodist Episcopal Church at this period is to note the levels indicated by the bishops' addresses at the successive General Conferences. New themes made their appearance beside old ones in 1896. The Episcopal Address of that year mentioned the familiar topics of popular amusements, the use of intoxicants, and divorce. In addition, however, it took notice of the increasing pressure of the need to evangelize the city, which downtown churches had already begun to desert. The bishops urged that downtown churches be combined if need be and adapt themselves to new programs, but to remain and save the people there. The tension between Great Britain and the United States over the Venezuela border question was taken account of (though without specific mention of this particular issue) and the great principle of arbitration recommended. Arbitration, more-

[106] *Ibid.*, April 28, p. 9.
[107] *Ibid.*, May 12, p. 8.
[108] WCAS, Feb. 23, and March 27, 1898.
[109] WCA, 69 (1903), Jan. 7, p. 9.

over, was recommended as a way of settling disputes not only between nations, but between capital and labor within the nation.

Several principles on the use of property and the rights of labor were enunciated: Every man has a right to acquire property by the legitimate means of activity, foresight, invention, and inheritance. No man has a right to use his possessions to oppress his fellow men. Every man has a right to profit by his own labor. Every free man has a right to refuse to work for another, but no man has a right to prevent another from working when and for whom he will. The concluding statement is a reiteration of the principle, historic in Methodism, of stewardship: every man is accountable to God for the use of his time, labor, and wealth.[110]

In 1900 the chief themes beside the traditional ones touched upon in the bishops' address are the growth of class violence, the denial of civil rights to Negroes, and the growing power of "a foreign hierarchy." [111]

For an indication of the social thinking in the Southern church at the turn of the century we turn to an editorial in its *Quarterly Review*. J. M. Hawley there surveys the trends in both the church and society which cause concern, or, on the other hand, give reason for rejoicing.[112] The writer finds reason to deplore the following: 1. The gross infidelity of a century ago has given place to a scientific skepticism. 2. The rapid growth of intemperance during the past quarter-century. 3. The rapid increase of divorces, an evidence of moral deterioration. 4. The increase of crime and mob violence menaces society. 5. The antagonism between capital and labor leads to violence and bloodshed. 6. A growing contempt for law and social order among certain classes. 7. The Sabbath has lost its religious significance. 8. The appalling growth of the non-church-going spirit among the male population.

Over against these may be set some grounds for encouragement: 1. The growth in numbers and vigor of the Protestant denominations. 2. The growth of a fraternal spirit which makes for co-operation for them, though "the call for union is scarcely audible." 3. The growth of liberality and latitude for individual statement of old truths. 4. In-

[110] As reported in ZH, 74 (1896), 293 ff.
[111] ZH, 78 (1900), 588.
[112] QRS (third series), 26 (1900), 315 ff.

creased attention by the churches to social life. "Sociability is recognized as the handmaid of religion," and libraries, lyceum courses, literary clubs, and the Epworth League are playing their part in church life. 4. The introduction of a large aesthetic element into the church services. "So closely related is the aesthetic to the moral nature of man that to minister to the latter it is often necessary to awaken the former." 5. The conviction is increasing that religion is organized philanthropy.

A religion that impels its professors to seek to save themselves out of the world, while doing nothing to save the world, is an utter caricature of that taught by Christ . . . by means of asylums, hospitals, and infirmaries they will seek to reach all classes.

Deaconesses, city missionaries, visiting committees, and institutional churches will be utilized on a larger scale.

Questions touching the social, industrial, and moral improvement of the masses will receive ample attention, . . . and practical means will be employed to effect needed reforms.

6. The strongest evidence of vitality in the church is their educational and mission work, much of which will be devoted to the foreign populations in the cities.

A developed form of the view that the church had a legitimate mission in the social field was expressed in the *Quarterly Review* of the Methodist Episcopal Church, South, somewhat beyond the end of our period; but it may be cited here as a culminating instance of the development which was taking place in the thought of Southern Methodism.

The church and the social movement must be wedded, not divorced. There is need on the one hand for a quickened social conscience in the church and on the other for the Christianization of the social movement. Let the church be brought closer to the real problems of humanity, that humanity with its cry for social justice may see in the church its friend and champion, and that the tremendous moral dynamics within the church may be released for lifting those burdens that are grinding men and women and little children to despair.[113]

[113] QRS (third series), 40 (1914), 118. There are four other articles in this number which bear with greater or less directness on the need of socializing the gospel, and also

At the General Conference of 1908, the social gospel was officially adopted by the Methodist Episcopal Church and made to feel at home in the ecclesiastical edifice. One of the phases of the official welcome was the approval of an infant voluntary society for the furthering of social thought and action in the church. Its name was the Methodist Federation for Social Service.

The Federation was formed as a result of the enthusiastic co-operation of five men, all of them in close touch with the city and its problems. Two of them, Frank Mason North and Herbert (later Bishop) Welch were New Yorkers; two, Elbert R. Zaring, Assistant Editor of the *Western Christian Advocate*, published at Cincinnati, and Worth M. Tippy, pastor of the Epworth Memorial Church in Cleveland, were Ohioans; and one, Harry F. Ward, was a Chicagoan, being pastor of the Union Avenue Methodist Church in the stock-yards district of that city.

Frank Mason North is now most widely known as the author of the hymn which begins "Where cross the crowded ways of life," so vividly expressive of concern for the city, whence the Christ of the mountainside was being banished by greed and indifference. It beseeches Him to tread the city's streets again." North was among the earliest of the Methodist ministers to express an interest in the social gospel. In 1891 he wrote for *Zion's Herald* a series of four articles on the relations of Socialism and Christainity. The thesis of these articles is that the objective of Socialism is Christian, but that its materialistic and atheistic trends are alien to it. He shows considerable familiarity with social thought, both socialist and Christian, not only in this country, but abroad.

Socialism must be Christianized, said North, who identified himself with American Christian Socialism. His interest in the city comes out

---

an enthusiastic review of Rauschenbusch's *Christianizing the Social Order*. The review includes the test of the Social Creed of the Churches as adopted by the Federal Council of Churches and reports: "*Nearly every great denominational convention* since that time has felt the obligation to make a serious pronouncement on the social question." (*Ibid.*, p. 150.) This review is concluded by its author, Alexander Gross, of Nashville, in a later number of the *Review*. He says, "Those who hold to the view that the message of Jesus was primarily to the individual . . . are inclined to be afraid of the new social interpretation . . . of Christianity. But really, when it is clearly understood, there need be no clash between the two views" (*ibid.*, p. 390).

when he says: "The city will test the Church, and decide its competence." [114]

North's interest in the city grew out of a long connection with the American metropolis. He had been born (1850) in New York City, and entered on his first pastorate on Manhattan Island. Much of his active life was spent in administrative connection with church organizations for ministering to the needs of urban dwellers. In 1892 he became executive secretary of the New York City Missionary and Extension Society. By 1900, this society had listed forty-five projects on which two and a half million dollars had been spent. He helped to found the Open and Institutional Church League in 1894, and became its third president.[115] For twenty years he edited a periodical called *The Christan City*, which was influential chiefly in Methodism.[116] It was North who, in 1908, presented to the Federal Council of Churches the first report of its committee on the church and modern industry. In this report was embodied the Methodist Social Creed, which was, with a few changes, adopted as the "Social Creed of the Churches." [117] Because of his connection with the Methodist Federation, and the Federation Council's Committee, Worth Tippy said of him: "More than any other person, he shaped the social policies of the Protestant churches of this country between 1892 and 1912. Rauschenbusch was the prophet, North the leader." [118]

Worth M. Tippy remained in the pastorate, but had contributed to the social gospel movement at the turn of the century by his interest in J. Stitt Wilson's fervid "Social Crusade," an evangelistic movement with a strong emphasis on "brotherhood and social justice," which was carried on by street-corner preaching in many cities. The movement also published a small paper called *The Social Crusader*. Tippy wrote for this paper an account of "The Terre Haute Campaign in 1899." [119] He was persuaded that new methods must be found if the gospel was to be made effective in the condtions brought

[114] ZH, 69 (1891), Jan. 14, 21, 28 and Feb. 4.
[115] Milton J. Huber, "A History of the Methodist Federation for Social Action" (unpublished doctoral dissertation, Boston University, 1949), pp. 40-47; also Hopkins, *op. cit.*, pp. 172 and 250.
[116] Hopkins, *op. cit.*, p. 250.
[117] *Ibid.*, pp. 306-7, and Huber, *op. cit.*, pp. 354-55.
[118] Quoted in Huber, *ibid.*, p. 43.
[119] Hopkins, *op. cit.*, p. 199, and n. 49.

about by the industrial revolution. He wrote of "the socialized church":

Its basis of doctrine may be changed in no particular, but there is added to its purpose to reach with the gospel the individual, a profound concern that the gospel shall be applied to the associated life of men. . . . [Feed the hungry, yes, but also] let us have laws that will wipe out the slums . . . check the greed of landlords, and . . . force the sweater to let his victims out of his mephitic den.[120]

Tippy insisted that the new approach meant not the secularization of the church, but the sanctification of life.[121]

Herbert Welch's first pastorates were in New York City. A subsequent pastorate in Middletown, Connecticut, did not weaken his allegiance to the social gospel, nor did his election to the presidency of Ohio Wesleyan University in 1905. In 1896 he had been a member of a committee of the New York East Conference which had memorialized the General Conference of that year, expressing interest in labor organization, combinations of capital, business ethics, plutocracy in the church, and similar problems.[122] Two years after Welch's presidency at Ohio Wesleyan had begun, the Merrick Lecture Series had for its theme the social applications of Christianity. Jane Addams lectured on "The Conscience of Women and Social Amelioration," Graham Taylor on "Industry and Religion," and United States Commissioner of Labor Charles P. Neill on "Some Aspects of the Labor Movement." In the Merrick Lectures of 1911, Walter Rauschenbusch gave material which went into his book *Christianizing the Social Order.*[123] Welch was the first president of the Methodist Federation for Social Service during its formative years from 1907 to 1912.

It was fitting that he should have been the Federation's first President, for he had a large part in bringing together the interested and active men who formed its nucleus. It was he who connected Frank

[120] Worth M. Tippy (ed.), *The Socialized Church, Addresses before the First National Conference of the Social Workers of Methodism* (New York: Eaton & Mains; Cincinnati: Jennings & Graham, 1909), pp. 244, 252-53. (In Tippy's own address under the same title.)

[121] *Ibid.*, p. 264.

[122] Huber, *op. cit.*, pp. 57-58.

[123] Henry Clyde Hubbart, *Ohio Wesleyan's First Hundred Years* (Delaware, Ohio: Ohio Wesleyan University, 1943), pp. 112-13.

Mason North of New York with the men in Ohio and Illinois. Tippy of Cleveland was in England studying the Wesleyan Union for Social Service. When he returned to this country, Welch and North met with him in Cleveland.[124] The decline in the effectiveness and popularity of the Open and Institutional Church League, to which North had given so much of his time and effort, indicated the insufficiency of its method and program. Charity was not enough. Tippy had discovered that the English Union had been operating Central Halls, which were centers of both evangelism and social service; and they had assumed the task of socializing the thinking of the Wesleyan Churches. The last two of these objectives bulked large in the early conception of the task of the Methodist Federation for Social Service.

The meeting at which the Federation was organized was held in Washington, D. C. in December of 1907. It was attended by ministers, especially those connected with city missionary work, and laymen from diverse business and professional fields. A considerable range of social outlook was represented. The purpose was declared to form "a society to stimulate . . . study of social questions by the church, side by side with practical social service, and to bring the church into touch with neglected social groups." [125] The temper of the gathering may be described as that of "social liberals who accepted social order in principle, but proposed its modification in some details . . . through social legislation." Its task was to be education and agitation.[126] The social service it advocated at the beginning differed from both social reform and socialism. It was wider than the former, and in contrast with the latter was motivated by the spirit of Christian love.[127] Its program the first year was based on a close connection with the local Methodist churches, and on bringing them into close cooperation with the social service agencies in their respective communities.

The General Conference of the Northern Methodist church in 1908 demonstrated how great a hold the needs of the city and the industrial problem had laid on Methodist leaders. The Conference ordered the organization of a National City Evangelization Union to co-ordinate

[124] Huber, op. cit., pp. 60-61.
[125] Hopkins, op. cit., p. 289; Huber, op. cit., p. 62-63.
[126] Huber, op. cit., pp. 64-65, 67.
[127] Ibid., p. 71.

the work of local unions, and to help them with both their property and their program.[128] It was recommended that their program include the transformation of downtown churches into new centers with modern methods of service, missions to the foreign population, the maintenance of kindergartens and industrial schools, social and settlement work, the support of rescue missions, and similar enterprises.[129]

Nearly a third of the episcopal address at the General Conference of 1908 was devoted to social themes,[130] and it was received with considerable enthusiasm by the conference. There was a section on the liquor traffic. The section on child labor urged upon legislatures the passage of "such laws as will, in securing freedom to children from exhausting toil, contribute to the vitality, the growth . . . and the moral sense of all youthful employees."

The section on international peace noted with gratification the great advance made during the quadrennium toward a peaceful settlement of international disputes by Christian methods. Tribute was paid to President Roosevelt and Mr. Carnegie, the mention of whose names evoked applause. Regret was expressed that questions of national honor were still withheld from the jurisdiction of the Hague tribunal, which might greatly delay the day of abiding peace.

The section on workingmen gave a good deal of attention to the terrible hazards to which workmen were exposed, especially in the mines and on the railroads. "So far as greed makes such things possible, the Master whom we serve demands from us the protest of His church, and for the sufferers the tenderest sympathy."

The section on immigration acknowledged the dangers to American civilization of unrestricted entry of the immense populations of China and Japan. Nevertheless, it claimed

for the immigrants from Eastern Asia who are already here, and for those who lawfully come, the most just and equitable treatment. Especially do we insist upon protection for them from the mob spirit, so often inspired and led by those who are themselves new arrivals upon our shores.

The section on labor unions insisted that The Methodist Church was not opposed to the aspirations of the working classes.

---

[128] *Doctrines and Discipline of The Methodist Episcopal Church*, 1908, 262-63.
[129] *Journal of the General Conference of The Methodist Episcopal Church* (New York: Eaton and Mains; Cincinnati: Jennings and Graham, 1908), pp. 615-617.
[130] *Ibid.*, p. 121 ff.; the section of the address dealing with social themes begins on p. 130.

We hold the right of those working men who desire to do so to form labor unions for the advancement of their interests, as we hold the right of individual laborers who prefer to do so, to keep control of their own labor. . . . The church and the trade union should seek each other's help for the uplift of mankind. . . . By so much as a capitalist is selfish, miserly, exacting, oppressive, the Church has business with him. She cannot throw him off and away until the last day of his dessicated and shrunken life brings him before God.[131]

The General Conference was not slow to follow the lead thus unequivocally announced in the bishops' address. Its epoch-making action came in the adoption of a report of the committee on the state of the church to whom the memorials on the obligations of the church on the social question had been entrusted. The report of this committee said:

We recognize the gravity of the social situation and the responsibility of the Church collectively, and of its members severally, for bringing about better conditions, through the practical application of the ethics of the New Testament.

The report recapitulated the concerns indicated in the Episcopal Address, and contained what became, on its adoption, the famous "Methodist Social Creed." [132]

This latter was the work of Harry F. Ward, as the Minutes of the activities at the seat of the conference show:

Harry F. Ward of the Executive Committee gave particular attention to the matter, both in the composition and through conferences with the leaders of the General Conference Committee.[133]

The creed was introduced by an eminently fitting statement that the church itself, insofar as she was an employer, should exemplify the principles it set forth. The text of the creed follows:

The Methodist Episcopal Church stands—
For equal rights and complete justice for all men in all stations of life.

---

[131] This summary is extracted from the report of the Bishops' Address given in NWCA, 56 (1908), 613 ff.
[132] *Journal of the General Conference* (1908), p. 546 ff.
[133] Huber, *op. cit.*, p. 355. This corrects the erroneous statement by Hopkins, who says (*Rise of the Social Gospel*, pp. 310-11) that North was chiefly responsible. Huber cites also a letter of Bishop Welch, and a conversation with Ward himself in support of Ward's authorship (*loc. cit.*).

For the principle of conciliation and arbitration in industrial dissensions.

For the protection of the worker from dangerous machinery, occupational diseases, injuries, and mortality.

For the abolition of child labor.

For such regulation of the conditions of labor for women as shall safeguard the physical and moral health of the community.

For the suppression of the "sweating system."

For the gradual and reasonable reduction of the hours of labor to the lowest practical point, with work for all; and for that degree of leisure for all which is the condition of the highest human life.

For a release from employment one day in seven.

For a living wage in every industry.

For the highest wage that each industry can afford, and for the most equitable division of the products of industry that can ultimately be devised.

For the recognition of the Golden Rule and the mind of Christ as the supreme law of society and the sure remedy for all social ills.

The report then took note of the organization of the Federation for Social Service, stated its objectives, and gave it hearty approval. The report concluded:

And now we summon our great Church to continue and increase its works of social service. We summon all our ministry, . . . to patient study of these problems, and to fearless but judicious preaching of the teachings of Jesus in their significance for the moral interest of modern society . . . upon every member rests a solemn duty to devote himself with his possessions, his citizenship, and his influence to the glory of God in the service of the present age. And thus by their works, as by their prayers, let all "the people called Methodists" seek that kingdom in which God's will shall be done on earth as it is in heaven.[134]

With the adoption of the report of the committee on the state of the church, the Methodist Social Creed was given at least semiofficial standing, and the Methodist Federation for Social Service entered on its task of carrying to the church as a whole the meaning of what the general conference had done.

[134] *The Doctrines and Discipline of the Methodist Episcopal Church,* 1908 (New York: Eaton and Mains; Cincinnati: Jennings and Graham), p. 479 ff. Used by permission of The Methodist Publishing House.

Methodism had not furnished up to this time any of the major prophets of the social gospel. But it was not behindhand in having thus given quasi-official status to a statement of its social principles, and to a voluntary organization to permeate the thinking of the church with its message. Though the Presbyterian Board of Home Missions had, as early as 1903, called Charles Stelzle to be its special missionary to workingmen, conservatives had him ousted ten years later. In 1901 the General Convention of The Protestant Episcopal Church, influenced by the agitation of C.A.I.L., took preliminary action which resulted in the formation of a standing commission on the relations of capital and labor. By 1910 it had a full-time secretary. At the same time the National Council of Congregational Churches erected an Industrial Committee. In 1908, the American Unitarian Association erected a Department of Social and Public Service. The Northern Baptist Convention, which gave attention to social questions in 1908, had an official and fully organized commission to deal with them by 1912.[135]

The Methodist Episcopal Church, at its General Conference of 1912, gave still more express approval to the Federation for Social Service, and Harry F. Ward was called to be its executive secretary. Calling its statement of social principles a "creed" was perhaps a mistake, for it was destined, in the nature of the case, to undergo modifications under the changing conditions and widening social views of its exponents in the years ahead. But it was no small thing to have adopted a set of principles by which the social thinking of its membership would be stimulated. The story of the subsequent activities of the Federation for Social Service, and the changing and enlarging scope of Methodist social thought and action belong in Volume II of this series.

---

[135] Hopkins, op. cit., p. 280 ff.

Conclusion

John Wesley believed that the gospel had a social element. This conviction he not only taught, but lived. His saying, "The Gospel of Christ knows no religion but social, no holiness but social holiness," meant considerably less than the social gospel adopted by some of his twentieth-century followers; but the subsequent developments have been in the legitimate line.

Wesley's declared purpose was "to reform the nation . . . and to spread scriptural holiness over the land." Admittedly his primary objective was to preach the gospel of repentance and salvation to individuals. But his precept and example alike give convincing demonstration that he was interested not only in the heavenly Kingdom for which he would prepare men's souls, but also in the society in which their minds and bodies lived on earth.

His legacy of social thought and activity to his followers was a variegated one. On the one hand, he was a staunch Tory supporter of the stiff political and social stratifications of English society of his day; on the other hand, he manifested a passionate interest in the plight of the poor. He not only urged and practiced the traditional methods of relieving their necessities, but he also devised institutional experiments of social import. His preaching required men not only to repent and believe the gospel, but also to work hard and save money. He gave the poor courage to believe in themselves, made them exemplars of industry and frugality, and raised them in the economic scale. It was partly cause and partly effect of this rise when subsequent generations of Methodists clung tenaciously to the conservative side of Wesley's teaching, but gradually forgot his inculcation of compassionate help for the poor. They remembered when he said, "Earn all you can, and save all you can," but their practice of the injunction "give all you can" was less consistent.

Nevertheless some of Wesley's sons (they were found more often in fringe groups like the Primitive Methodists than in the Wesleyan Conference) played an active part in the trade unions' movement to better the workingmen's lot. They were all loyal supporters of Wilberforce's crusade to abolish slavery. The same Evangelical spirit which animated the Methodists' compassion likewise stirred Evangelicals in the Church of England to fruitful action which their position in the governing classes made possible. The first factories and collieries acts were their doing.

When American Methodists had shaken off their Royalist predilections, they entered with vigor into the life of the new nation. Originally from the humbler ranks of the society, before the Civil War they had become a fairly representative cross section of the population. This fact and their wide geographic distribution qualified their social outlook.

The greatest problem they faced in the course of the nineteenth century was slavery. On slavery, the Methodists spoke with two voices, and ultimately the two voices became two churches. That the Methodists were the first to divide over the slavery question is testimony to the fact that there was in the ranks an irreducible minimum of conscience on the question which finally assumed paramount importance. It also indicates that the Methodist Church was unable to avert the "inevitable conflict," and may even have hastened it. Certainly when abolition finally came, it came on the crest of a mighty, but very secular wave. When that wave subsided it left behind it the wrack of racial tensions, which still litter the land.

The other problems Methodism faced during the nineteenth century were connected with the frontier during the earlier years and with the urban-industrial development toward the end. On the whole, Methodism was better equipped to serve the needs of the frontier than of the city. The Methodist spirit and the Methodist organization which had been developed in England were even more valuable in the new environment.

Methodism had been born in a revival, and the United States was a country where revivals were to flourish all through the first century of its existence. It preached a message which appealed to the common

327

man, and it used common men to preach it. Its disciplined and flexible itinerancy, with a large place for the use of laymen, was to prove even more valuable in the new country's wide-open land and swiftly moving frontier. As Methodism had proved effective in forming the rude proletariat of the English towns into orderly, self-respecting groups, so in America it helped to subdue the unruly backwoodsmen to the responsibilities of life in ordered communities.

During the nineteenth century, Methodism maintained the fight against the liquor traffic with some degree of success; she retarded public capitulation to the demand for an "open Sunday." She inaugurated foreign-language missions, established institutional churches, and continued to build colleges and universities for her young people.

After the Civil War, Methodists were well on their way to becoming a middle-class, "respectable," and fairly well-educated people. They "outgrew" the strict disciplinary practices of the earlier, more strenuous days. At the same time, as though in compensation, they pitched still higher their exhortations against minor evidences of worldliness in the church. Revival methods lost their power. The holiness movement, no longer at home in the church, withdrew from it. The "big three" Methodist churches lost interest in "spreading Scriptural holiness," and their efforts at "reforming the continent" fell behind the swiftly changing needs of the situation at the end of the century. The Methodist churches, like other middle-class Protestant denominations, were suspected by the working people of being "run" by the employers, and so lost their worker constituency, and lost, too, a sense of compassion for their plight. A still largely rural and small-town constituency was not closely touched by the miseries of city slums, and a comfortable middle-class existence insulated them from the poverty of the new proletariat.

Consequently, the adoption of the Social Creed in 1908 came with the rush generated by a sudden awareness that lost time needed to be regained. It came when the General Conference of the Northern Church recognized the truth which the pioneering few had for some time been proclaiming, recognized what the deeper social issues were, and that in the Methodist heritage they were an inescapable part of her concern. The Methodism which had been born in the cities of England was rediscovering the cities of America, and acknowledging their claims. At the same time, the little advance guard organized themselves into the Methodist Federation for Social Service, and, armed with the approval of the General Conference, girded themselves for the task of inciting the church anew to meet the challenge of the social problem.

Bibliography

Abbey, Charles J. and Overton, John H. *The English Church in the Eighteenth Century.* Revised Edition. London: Longmans, Green and Company, 1896.

Abell, Aaron Ignatius. *The Urban Impact on American Protestantism, 1865-1900.* Cambridge, Massachusetts: Harvard University Press, 1943.

Allen, Joseph Land. *The Methodist Board of Temperance as an Instrument of Church Policy.* Ph.D. dissertation, Yale University, 1957. Microcard Theological Studies, Vol. 25.

Asbury, Francis. *The Journal and Letters of Francis Asbury.* Edited by Elmer T. Clark, J. Manning Potts, and Jacob S. Payton. 3 vols. London: The Epworth Press; Nashville: Abingdon Press, 1958.

Barclay, Wade Crawford. *History of Methodist Missions.* 3 vols. published. New York: The Board of Missions and Church Extension of The Methodist Church, 1949-1958.

Barnes, Gilbert Hobbs. *The Antislavery Impulse 1830-1844.* New York: D. Appleton-Century Company, 1933.

Bascom, Henry Bidleman. *Methodism and Slavery.* Frankfort, Kentucky: Hodges, Todd and Pruett, printers, 1845.

Bassett, Ancel H. *A Concise History of the Methodist Protestant Church.* Pittsburgh: Press of Charles A. Scott, 1877.

Beard, Charles A. and Mary R. *The Rise of American Civilization.* 2 vols. New York: Macmillan Company, 1928.

Bebb, E. D. *Nonconformity and Social and Economic Life, 1660-1800.* London: The Epworth Press, 1935.

Bogart, Ernest Ludlow. *Economic History of the American People.* New York: Longmans, Green and Company, 1930.

Bready, J. Wesley. *England: Before and After Wesley.* New York: Harper & Brothers, 1938.

Brookes, Iveson L. *A defense of Southern Slavery against the attacks of Henry Clay and Alexander Campbell.* Hamburg, South Carolina: printed by Robinson and Carlisle, 1851.

————. *Defence of the South against the Reproaches . . . of the North.* Hamburg, South Carolina: printed at the Republican Office, 1850.

Brown, Forrest Raymond. "The Development of the Social Creed of the Methodist Church." Unpublished dissertation, Boston University Graduate School, 1942.

Buckley, J. M. *A History of Methodists in the United States.* (American Church History Series, vol. V). 4th. edition. New York: Charles Scribner's Sons, 1900.

Carter, Cullen T. *History of the Tennessee Conference; and a Brief Summary of the General Conferences of The Methodist Church.* Nashville: printed at the Parthenon Press. Copyright by the author, 1948.

Carter, Hodding. *The Angry Scar: The Story of Reconstruction.* Garden City, New York: Doubleday and Company, 1959.

Channing, Edward. *A History of the United States.* 6 vols. New York: The Macmillan Company, 1919-1925.

Clark, Robert D. *The Life of Matthew Simpson.* New York: The Macmillan Company, 1956.

Cole, Charles C. *The Social Ideas of Northern Evangelists.* New York: Columbia University Press, 1954.

Cole, G. D. H. *A Short History of the British Working-Class Movement 1789-1947.* Revised Edition. London: George Allen and Unwin, 1948.

Coomer, Duncan, *English Dissent under the Early Hanoverians.* London: The Epworth Press, 1946.

Culver, Dwight W. *Negro Segregation in the Methodist Church.* New Haven: Yale University Press, 1953.

The Doctrines and Discipline of The Methodist Episcopal Church.

The Doctrines and Discipline of the Methodist Episcopal Church, South.

Douglass, Paul F. *The Story of German Methodism: The Biography of an Immigrant Soul.* New York: The Methodist Book Concern, 1939.

Drinkhouse, Edward J. *History of Methodist Reform.* 2 vols. Baltimore and Pittsburgh: Board of Publication of the Methodist Protestant Church, 1899.

Duvall, Sylvanus Milne. *The Methodist Episcopal Church and Education up to 1869.* New York: Teachers' College, Columbia University, 1928.

Edwards, Maldwyn. *After Wesley: A Study of the Social and Political Influence of Methodism in the Middle Period (1791-1849).* London: The Epworth Press, 1935.

————. *John Wesley and the Eighteenth Century. A Study of His Social and Political Influence.* New York: The Abingdon Press, 1933.

————. *Methodism and England. A Study of Methodism in Its Social and Political Aspects During the Period 1850-1932.* London: The Epworth Press, 1943.

Elliott-Binns, L. E. *The Early Evangelicals: A Religious and Social Study.* Greenwich, Connecticut: The Seabury Press, 1953.

Farish, Hunter Dickinson. *The Circuit Rider Dismounts; A Social History of*

Southern Methodism 1865-1900. Richmond, Virginia: The Dietz Press, 1938.

Franklin, John Hope. *From Slavery to Freedom. A History of the American Negro.* New York: Alfred A. Knopf, 1948.

Hall, T. C. *The Social Meaning of Modern Religious Movements in England.* New York: Charles Scribner's Sons, 1900.

Haven, Gilbert, *National Sermons: Sermons, Speeches, and Letters on Slavery and Its War.* Boston: Lee and Shepherd, 1869.

Hogue, Wilson T. *History of the Free Methodist Church of North America.* Chicago: The Free Methodist Publishing House, 1915.

Hopkins, Charles Howard. *The Rise of the Social Gospel in American Protestantism, 1865-1915.* New Haven: Yale University Press, 1940.

Huber, Milton J. "A History of the Methodist Federation for Social Action." Unpublished Ph.D. dissertation, Boston University, 1949.

Hudson, Winthrop S. *The Great Tradition in the American Churches.* New York: Harper and Brothers, 1953.

Jenkins, William S. *Pro-Slavery Thought in the Old South.* Chapel Hill: University of North Carolina Press, 1935.

Johnson, Charles A. *The Frontier Camp Meeting: Religion's Harvest Time.* Dallas, Texas: Southern Methodist University Press, 1955.

Jones, John Bayley. "The Approach of Baltimore Methodism to Social Problems." Unpublished S.T.M. thesis, Wesley Theological Seminary, Westminster, Maryland, 1942.

Journals of the General Conference of the Methodist Episcopal Church. 1796-1844.

Journal of the General Conference of the Methodist Episcopal Church. New York: Eaton and Mains; Cincinnati: Jennings and Graham, 1908.

Journals of the General Conference of the Methodist Protestant Church.

Korngold, Ralph. *Two Friends of Man. The Story of William Lloyd Garrison and Wendell Phillips.* Boston: Little, Brown and Company, 1950.

Luccock, Halford E. and Hutchinson, Paul. *The Story of Methodism.* Nashville: Abingdon Press, 1926.

MacArthur, Kathleen Walker. *The Economic Ethics of John Wesley.* New York: The Abingdon Press, 1936.

McFerrin, J. B., et. al. (ed.). *History of the Organization of the Methodist Episcopal Church, South, with the Journal of its First General Conference.* Nashville: The Methodist Publishing House, Methodist Episcopal Church, South, 1925.

McLoughlin, William G., Jr. *Modern Revivalism, Charles Grandison Finney to Billy Graham.* New York: The Ronald Press Company, 1959.

Matlack, Rev. Lucius C. *The Antislavery Struggle and Triumph in The Methodist Episcopal Church.* New York: Phillips and Hunt, 1881.

Miller, Olaf R. *Methodism and Temperance.* (An address delivered Oct. 26,

1900, and subsequently printed. Mr. Miller was pastor of the Highlands Methodist Episcopal Church, Holyoke, Massachusetts.)

Minutes of the Annual Conference of the Methodist Episcopal Church, for the Years 1773-1828. New York: Mason and Lane, 1840.

Minutes of Florida Conference, 1886, 1906, 1918, 1938, 1940, 1948.

Minutes of Holston Conference, 1886, 1902, 1914, 1926, 1938, 1939, 1940, 1948.

Minutes of Louisiana Conference, 1902, 1906, 1910, 1914, 1918, 1922, 1926, 1930, 1934, 1938, 1939, 1940, 1944, 1948, 1952.

Minutes of North Carolina Conference, 1874, 1878, 1882, 1890, 1898, 1902, 1906, 1910, 1914, 1918, 1922, 1926, 1930, 1934, 1938, 1939, 1940, 1944, 1948, 1952.

Minutes of North Georgia Conference, 1878, 1882, 1886, 1890, 1894, 1898, 1902, 1906, 1910, 1914, 1918, 1922, 1926, 1930, 1934, 1938, 1939, 1940, 1944, 1948, 1952.

Mudge, James. *History of the New England Conference of the Methodist Episcopal Church.* Boston: Published by the Conference, 1910.

Nail, Olin W. *The First Hundred Years of the Southwest Texas Conference of the Methodist Church.* San Antonio, Texas: Published by the Conference, 1958.

Niebuhr, H. Richard. *Christ and Culture.* New York: Harper & Brothers, 1951.

————. *The Social Sources of Denominationalism.* New York: Henry Holt and Company, 1929.

North, Eric McCoy. *Early Methodist Philanthropy.* New York: The Methodist Book Concern, 1914.

Norwood, Frederick A. "The Americanization of the Wesleyan Itinerant." Unpublished manuscript of an address given at Nashville, Tennessee, July, 1959.

————. *Church Membership in the Methodist Tradition.* Nashville: The Methodist Publishing House, 1958.

Nutter, Charles (ed.). *Reprints of the first five editions of the Discipline of the Methodist Episcopal Church.*

Overton, J. H. and Relton, Frederick. *The English Church from the Accession of George I to the End of the Eighteenth Century.* (Vol. VII of *A History of the English Church,* edited by W. R. Stephens and William Hunt), London: Macmillan and Company, 1906.

Peters, John Leland. *Christian Perfection and American Methodism.* Nashville: Abingdon Press, 1956.

Prentice, George. *The Life of Gilbert Haven.* New York: Phillips and Hunt, 1883.

Schlesinger, Arthur Meier. *The Rise of the City 1878-1898* (*A History of American Life,* Vol. X). New York: The Macmillan Company, 1933.

Scott, Leland H. *Methodist Theology in America in the Nineteenth Century.* (Ph.D. thesis, Yale University, 1954). Microcard Theological Studies, Vol. 20.

Simpson, Matthew (ed.). *Cyclopedia of Methodism*. Philadelphia: Louis H. Everts, 1880.

Simon, John S. *John Wesley the Master Builder*. London: The Epworth Press, 1927.

————. *John Wesley and the Methodist Societies*. Second Edition. London: The Epworth Press, 1937.

Smith, S. Raynor, Jr. "The Attitudes and Practises of the Methodist Church with Reference to Certain Significant Social Crises, 1847 through 1949." Microfilmed Ph.D. dissertation, University of Southern California, 1955.

Smith, Timothy L. *Revivalism and Social Reform in Mid-Nineteenth-Century America*. Nashville: Abingdon Press, 1957.

Stevens, Abel. *History of the Methodist Episcopal Church in the United States of America*. 4 vols. New York: Carlton and Porter, 1864.

Swaney, Charles Baumer. *Episcopal Methodism and Slavery, with Sidelights on Ecclesiastical Politics*. Boston: Richard G. Badger, 1926.

Sweet, William Warren. *Methodism in American History*, revised. Nashville: Abingdon Press, 1954.

————. *Religion in the Development of American Culture*. New York: Charles Scribner's Sons, 1952.

————. *Religion on the American Frontier*. Vol. IV, *The Methodists*. Chicago: University of Chicago Press, 1946.

————. *Revivalism in America. Its Origin, Growth, and Decline*. New York: Charles Scribner's Sons, 1944.

Sykes, Norman. *Church and State in England in the Eighteenth Century*. Cambridge: The University Press, 1934.

Taylor, E. R. *Methodism and Politics, 1791-1851*. Cambridge: The University Press, 1935.

Thrift, Minton. *Memoir of the Rev. Jesse Lee, with Extracts from His Journals*. New York: Bangs and Mason, 1823.

Tippy, Worth M. (ed.). *The Socialized Church, Addresses before the First National Conference of the Social Workers of Methodism*. New York: Eaton and Mains; Cincinnati: Jennings and Graham, 1909.

Trevelyan, G. M. *English Social History. A Survey of Six Centuries, Chaucer to Queen Victoria*. London: Longmans, Green and Company, 1942.

Troeltsch, Ernst. *The Social Teaching of the Christian Churches*. 2 vols., Tr. by Olive Wyon. New York: The Macmillan Company, 1931.

Tyerman, Luke. *The Life and Times of the Rev. John Wesley, M.A.* 3 vols. New York: Harper & Brothers, 1872.

Wallis, Charles L. (ed.). *Autobiography of Peter Cartwright*. Nashville: Abingdon Press, 1956.

Warner, Wellman J. *The Wesleyan Movement in the Industrial Revolution*. London, etc.: Longmans, Green and Company, 1930.

Wearmouth, Robert F. *Methodism and the Common People of the Eighteenth Century*. London: The Epworth Press, 1945.

————. *Methodism and the Working-Class Movements of England, 1800-*

1850. London: The Epworth Press, 1937.

————. *The Social and Political Influence of Methodism in the Twentieth Century*. London: The Epworth Press, 1957.

————. *Some Working-Class Movements of the Nineteenth Century*. London: The Epworth Press, 1948.

Wesley, John. *The Journal of the Rev. John Wesley, A. M.* Edited by Nehemiah Curnock. 8 vols. New York: Eaton and Mains, n.d.

————. *The Letters of the Rev. John Wesley, A.M.* Edited by John Telford. 8 vols. London: The Epworth Press, 1931.

————. *The Works of the Rev. John Wesley, A.M.* Edited by John Emory. Reprint of 1831 Edition. New York, Lane and Scott, 1850.

————. *The Works of the Rev. John Wesley, A.M.* Edited by Thomas Jackson. 14 vols. London: John Mason, 1856.

General Index

337

Index of Persons and Places